How to pass

New CLAIT 2006

Using Microsoft® Office 2003

Jackie Sherman

PEARSON

Prentice
Hall

Harlow, England • London • New York • Boston • San Francisco • Toronto • Sydney • Singapore • Hong Kong
Tokyo • Seoul • Taipei • New Delhi • Cape Town • Madrid • Mexico City • Amsterdam • Munich • Paris • Milan

Pearson Education Limited
Edinburgh Gate
Harlow
Essex CM20 2JE
England

and Associated Companies throughout the world

Visit us on the World Wide Web at:
www.pearsoned.co.uk

First published 2007

ISBN (13): 978-0-13-236935-0
ISBN (10): 0-13-236935-4

British Library Cataloguing-in-Publication Data
A catalogue record for this book is available from the British Library

Library of Congress Cataloging-in-Publication Data
A catalog record for this book is available from the Library of Congress

10 9 8 7 6 5 4 3 2 1
10 09 08 07 06

Typeset in 10/12.5pt Stone Serif by 30
Printed and bound by Ashford Colour Press Ltd., Gosport

The publisher's policy is to use paper manufactured from sustainable forests.

contents

Introduction   viii

unit 1   File management and e-document production   1

What is word processing?   3
Working safely   4
Starting up a computer   5
Using log-in procedures   5
The desktop   6
Files   8
Folders   9
Working with files   12
Searching   14
Opening Word   16
Starting a new document   16
Entering text   16
Inserting new text   18
Closing a document   19
Overtyping   20
Deleting text   20
Undoing mistakes   20
Creating new paragraphs   20
Saving a document   21
Printing a document   24
Opening a saved document   25
Taking a screen print   25
Selecting text   26
Formatting text   26
Alignment   29
Spelling and grammar checker   30
Proofreading   31
Setting margins   32
Line spacing   32
Print preview   33
Page orientation   35
Moving text to a new position   35
Edit and replace   37
Tables   39
Headers and footers   41
Bullets and numbering   42
Indents   43
Word count   43
Using Help   45
Exiting the application   46
Shutting down procedures   46
Self-assessment checklist   51
Summary of critical errors   52

unit 2   Creating spreadsheets and graphs   53

What are spreadsheets?   55
Opening Excel   56

Entering and amending text 57
Entering numbers 58
Creating a new file 58
Saving a spreadsheet 58
Closing a spreadsheet 59
Formatting text 60
Formatting numbers 60
Widening columns 61
Cell alignment 62
Opening a saved spreadsheet 63
Printing a spreadsheet 64
Formulae 67
Functions 68
Copying (replicating) formulae 70
Inserting columns/rows 71
Deleting columns/rows 72
Printing formulae 73
Headers and footers 73
Charts 75
Opening a data file 77
Creating a chart 77
Closing a chart 81
Opening an existing chart 82
Selected charts 82
Formatting a chart 82
Printing charts 85
Comparative charts 86
Print preview 86
Scaling charts 89
Exiting Excel 90
Self-assessment checklist 93
Summary of critical errors 94

unit 3   **Database manipulation** 95

What is a database? 96
Opening Access 97
Creating a database file 97
Opening a table 98
Starting a new file 102
Closing a file 102
Opening a database 103
Entering records 103
Widening columns 104
Amending records 105
Printing a table 105
Deleting records 107
Finding and replacing 107
Sorting records 109
Queries 111
Adding personal details 117
Reports 117
Exiting the application 122
Self-assessment checklist 125
Summary of critical errors 126

unit 4   **Producing an e-publication**   127

What is desktop publishing?   128
Opening Publisher   129
Starting point   129
Page orientation   130
Margins   131
Saving a publication   132
Saving a file as a different version   132
Opening an existing publication   132
Viewing a publication   132
Adding text   133
Closing a publication   134
Formatting text   135
Alignment   136
Indents and spacing   137
Printing a publication   138
Inserting a text file   138
Borders   142
Spelling   142
Drawing objects   143
Pictures   145
Headers and footers   150
Exiting the application   150
Self-assessment checklist   154
Summary of critical errors   155

unit 5   **Creating an e-presentation**   157

What are presentations?   158
Opening PowerPoint   159
New presentation   160
Views   160
Working with text   160
Closing a presentation   161
Exiting PowerPoint   162
Formatting text   162
Deleting text   163
Text alignment   163
Saving a presentation   163
Promoting and demoting text   165
Inserting and deleting lines of text   166
Bullets   166
Opening a presentation saved earlier   167
Images   168
New slides   171
Changing slide order   173
Spelling   173
Drawn shapes   174
Page orientation   175
Slide Master   175
Edit and replace   176
Headers and footers   177
Printing   178
Backgrounds   181
Self-assessment checklist   186
Summary of critical errors   186

unit 6   **e-image creation**   187

What is computer art?   188
Selecting appropriate software   189
Using Microsoft Word   189
AutoShapes   189
Closing artwork   191
Working with AutoShapes   192
Saving artwork   196
Setting the size of artwork   196
Picture files   198
Importing an image   198
Flipping or rotating an image   199
Moving an image   199
Cropping an image   202
Resizing an image   202
Text   203
Printing in colour or black and white   207
Using Paint Shop Pro   210
Launching the program   210
Toolbars   210
Measurement units   211
New file and artwork size   211
Selecting   212
Pictures   213
Saving a file   216
Working with colours   218
Vector objects   219
Printing   224
Digital camera images   224
Self-assessment checklist   226
Summary of critical errors   227

unit 7   **Web page creation**   229

What is web page authoring?   230
Selecting the appropriate software   231
Opening the software   231
Views   231
Entering text   232
Formatting text   232
Saving web pages   233
Opening web pages   235
Closing web pages   235
Links   235
Applying a background colour   239
Printing a web page   240
Viewing web pages in a browser   242
Testing links   243
Inserting a text file   244
Importing and positioning images   245
Exiting the application   247
Self-assessment checklist   251
Summary of critical errors   251

unit 8   Online communication   253

What is online communication?   254
Opening Outlook   255
Reading e-mails   257
Creating messages   258
Printing e-mails   263
Attaching files to e-mails   264
Saving a draft e-mail   267
Contacts (addresses)   267
Help   269
Exiting Outlook   270
The World Wide Web   270
Opening a browser   271
Searching web pages   274
Printing web pages   276
Bookmarking web pages   277
Saving from the Web   279
Reading pages offline   281
Netiquette   281
Viruses   281
Self-assessment checklist   287
Summary of critical errors   287

Glossary   289
Index   293

Acknowledgements

We are grateful to the following for permission to reproduce copyright material:

Unit 7/243 screenshot from The Royal Society for the Protection of Birds website: www.rspb.org.uk. Reproduced by permission; Unit 8/274 screenshots from The British Museum website: www.thebritishmuseum.ac.uk and www.thebritishmuseum.ac.uk/visit/index.html © Trustees of the British Museum, reproduced by permission; Unit 8/271 and 272 screenshots from the homepage of Pearson Education website: www.pearsoned.co.uk Reproduced with permission; Unit 8/274 screenshot from The Royal Society for the Protection of Birds website: www.rspb.org.uk/birds/guide/r/robin/index.asp Illustration ROBIN by Mike Langman, www.mikelangman.co.uk reproduced by permission; Unit 8/277 screenshots from the Worthing College website: www.worthing.ac.uk/courses/electronic.htm Reproduced by permission of Worthing College; Unit 8/280 screenshot from The Met Office website: www.metoffice.gov.uk/weather/europe/uk/warnings.html © Crown copyright 2006, published by The Met Office; Unit 8/286 screenshot from "The Bathroom Design Guide" Thanking Masco Corporation (www.masco.com) for its contribution.

In some instances we have been unable to trace the owners of copyright material and we would appreciate any information that would enable us to do so.

The aim of this book is to help you pass the assignments and gain the OCR Level 1 computing qualification known as New CLAIT 2006.

In order to do this, the book provides eight vital elements.

1. *An overview of the qualification* and what you must know in order to complete each unit.

2. *Clear guidance on how to carry out all the activities* – from opening the appropriate software package to changing the look of a graph, from adding a new slide to a presentation to inserting the correct picture into your publication.

3. *Exercises* that offer you the chance to practise your skills.

4. *An opportunity to work through entire assignments.* These are set out in the same manner as the final assessment, but they also provide model answers. You can compare these to your own work and see where you might have lost marks.

5. *Help in avoiding mistakes.* Some errors, known as *critical errors*, lead to instant failure. Within each unit, critical errors are highlighted in the text and summarized at the end. All other errors are known as 'accuracy errors' or 'data entry errors' and you are allowed four of these per unit. Errors may occur because you misspell a word, or fail to follow an instruction correctly. Some errors are more common than others, and this book highlights the mistakes made frequently by other learners studying for New CLAIT.

6. *A final self-assessment checklist* for each unit that will allow you to review your own skills and ensure that there are no gaps in your knowledge or capabilities.

7. *Guidance based on the most widely used software* – Microsoft Office 2003.

8. *A comprehensive glossary* so that all the technical terms and computer jargon mentioned in the book – or met during your studies – are clearly understood.

The qualification

New CLAIT 2006 is offered by the OCR examining board and accepted by the majority of British employers as an indication that holders have reached a good level of computer competency.

To achieve a Certificate you need to pass three units, and a Diploma requires a pass in five units. Most units are based on a single software application. There is a wide choice, but everyone has to pass *Unit 1 – File management and e-document production*.

The other units can be chosen from the following:

- *Unit 2 – Creating spreadsheets and graphs*
- *Unit 3 – Database manipulation*
- *Unit 4 – Producing an e-publication*
- *Unit 5 – Creating an e-presentation*

- *Unit 6 – e-image creation*
- *Unit 7 – Web page creation*
- *Unit 8 – Online communication.*

The choice of units will depend on various factors.

- If you are studying in an educational establishment, then you may find that some colleges or community centres do not have access to the Internet or web page creation packages.
- Some tutors may have more experience with particular software applications than others, or they may feel that some units are more appropriate for certain vocational courses.
- You may have a specific interest in learning how to use some of the applications.
- Equally, you may have no use for some skills – for example, using computer art tools or working with databases – and so these units would not be relevant to you.

Assessment takes the form of an OCR-set practical assignment that is expected to take no more than $2\frac{1}{2}$ hours. All the units are centre-assessed and externally moderated by OCR. In many institutions, you may be able to take some assessments online.

For paper-based assignments, marking requires evidence in the form of printouts. Missing printouts will always result in a fail, so it is very important to check these before they are handed in at the end of an assessment.

No specific software package is required, but most educational establishments will offer access to Microsoft Office and Internet Explorer.

If you pass Unit 1 together with two other units, you will receive an OCR Level 1 Certificate for IT Users (New CLAIT). With Unit 1 plus four other units you will receive an OCR Level 1 Diploma for IT Users (New CLAIT).

In the future, having achieved New CLAIT 2006, you may feel confident enough to tackle the Level 2 qualification – CLAIT Plus 2006.

Using the CD-ROM

In order to complete the assessments, you must be able to access and open files that have been provided. To give you practice in doing this, all the files and images that you will need for the exercises are included on the accompanying disk which you should place in your CD-ROM drive (usually labelled D:).

The original files on the CD are read-only so that they cannot be changed by mistake. This means they cannot be saved or amended in the normal way. Instead, you will need to make copies.

You could do this by opening each one and selecting **File/Save As**, but it is quicker to use Windows Explorer – and this is the only method available for Access database files. Open **My Computer** and then the drive containing the disk (unless it opens automatically), select all the files using **Edit/Select All** and then copy them across onto your own computer (see Unit 1 for how to do this). You may like to create a new folder to hold the files so that you can locate them easily when you are working.

If you find that any of the files you copied are still read-only, right-click the file name, select **Properties** and take off the tick in the *Attributes* box displayed on the *General* tab before clicking **OK**.

Take off tick in box

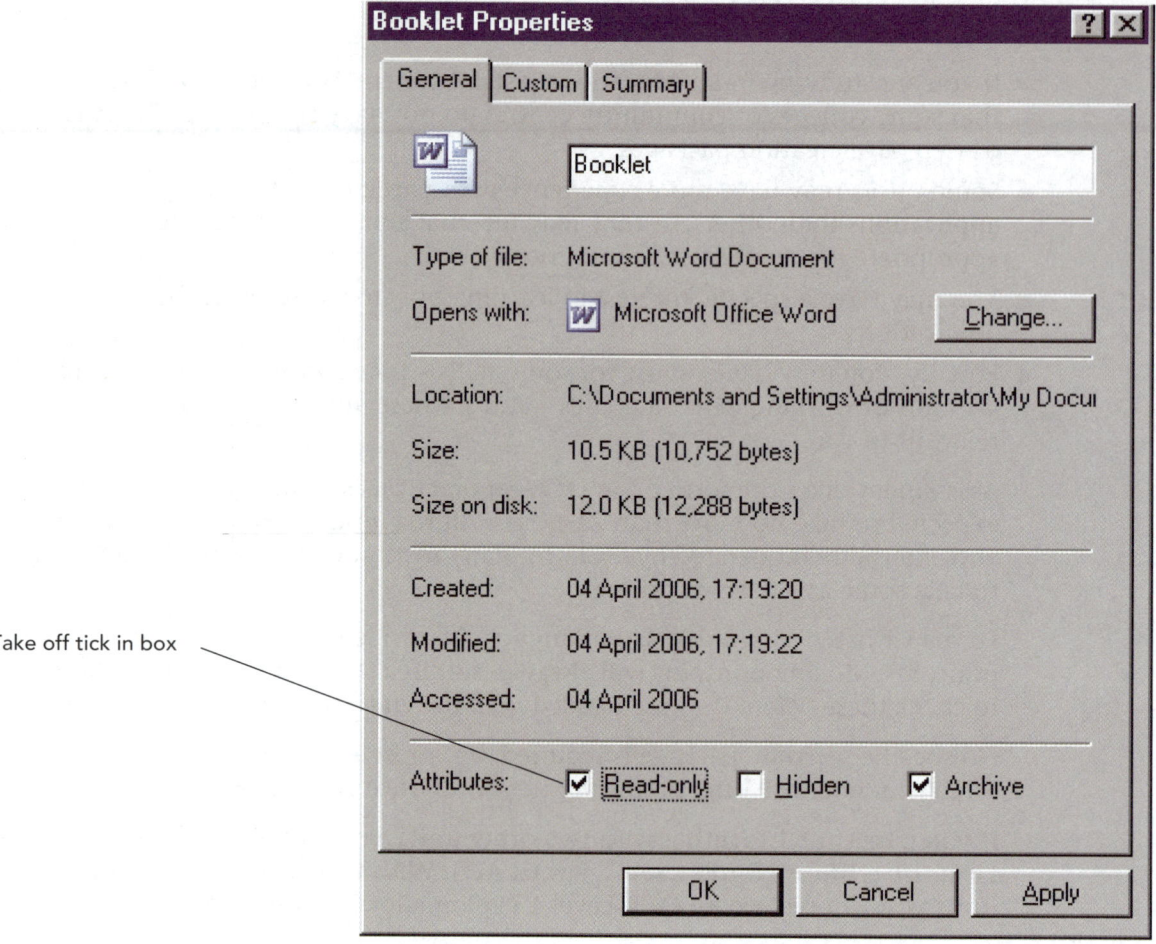

If you right-click a whole folder and select **Properties**, you can take off the *Read-only* attribute for all the subfolders and files it contains at the same time.

For some units, you should also be able to insert text files or images directly from the CD into your work.

File management and e-document production

- What is word processing? 3
- Working safely 4
- Starting up a computer 5
- Using log-in procedures 5
  Username 5
  Password 5
- The desktop 6
  Clicking the mouse 7
  Launching programs 7
- Files 8
  File names and extensions 8
  Storing files in folders 8
  Opening files 9
- Folders 9
  Creating and naming folders 9
  Renaming a file or folder 11
  Deleting a file or folder 12
- Working with files 12
  Moving a file 12
  Copying a file 14
- Searching 14
- Opening Word 16
- Starting a new document 16
- Entering text 16
  New lines 17
  Awkward symbols 17
  Word wrap 18

- Inserting new text 18
- Closing a document 19
- Overtyping 20
- Deleting text 20
- Undoing mistakes 20
- Creating new paragraphs 20
  Joining up paragraphs 21
- Saving a document 21
  Saving 21
  Updating a document 22
  Saving a new version of a
  document 23
- Printing a document 24
- Opening a saved document 25
- Taking a screen print 25
- Selecting text 26
- Formatting text 26
- Alignment 29
- Spelling and grammar checker 30
- Proofreading 31
- Setting margins 32
- Line spacing 32
- Print preview 33
- Page orientation 35

Moving text to a new position   35
    Drag and drop   36
    Cut and paste   36
Edit and replace   37
Tables   39
    Displaying all data   40
    Borders   40
Headers and footers   41
Bullets and numbering   42
Indents   43
Word count   43
Using Help   45
Exiting the application   46
Shutting down procedures   46
Self-assessment checklist   51
Summary of critical errors   52

This is the only mandatory unit – you must pass this unit to gain the qualification. It has been designed to develop your skills in carrying out some of the basic computer operations including logging into a computer, managing files and producing word processed documents.

What is word processing?

Applications such as Microsoft Word allow you to create professional-looking documents including letters, reports, memos, articles and invitations. You can enter, amend or move text to different parts of the document, and emphasize words and paragraphs by applying different formats. Unlike simple text editors, modern word processing applications allow you to see how your documents will look when they are printed by using the concept of WYSIWYG – what you see is what you get.

You will be asked to carry out the following tasks:

- Log on using a username and/or password
- Locate and rename files and folders
- Create subfolders
- Copy and move files
- Delete files and folders
- Take screen prints
- Create new documents
- Enter text
- Format text
- Align text
- Set margins
- Set page orientation
- Set line spacing
- Use a spellchecker
- Save a document into a specified folder
- Print a document
- Insert headers and footers
- Close and reopen documents
- Create new paragraphs
- Delete specified text
- Move text
- Create tables
- Add or remove borders
- Use bullets/numbering
- Indent text
- Replace specific words
- Save a document as a new version
- Carry out a word count
- Exit the application

- Log on to a computer
- Manage files and folders
- Take screen prints
- Select and use appropriate software to word process documents
- Create new documents
- Enter text using word wrap
- Insert and delete text
- Save a document
- Save a new version of a document
- Print a document
- Proofread and spellcheck a document
- Select and format text
- Change text alignment
- Set margins and page orientation
- Amend line spacing
- Create new paragraphs
- Insert headers and footers
- Move selected text to a new position
- Replace specified text
- Create tables
- Add or remove borders
- Create bulleted or numbered lists
- Indent text
- Carry out a word count
- Close a document
- Exit the application

Working safely

Although you will not be assessed on this topic, it is important for anyone spending time at a computer to think about health and safety. Here are a few checks you should make before starting a computer session.

- Do everything you can to reduce glare, such as drawing blinds and tilting or moving the screen (monitor).
- Sit at a comfortable height with your lower back and feet supported and with space to move your legs. Keep your eyes roughly level with the top of the monitor.
- Avoid over-reaching or twisting by keeping all necessary documents or notes close at hand.
- Take regular breaks away from the computer to stretch yourself, as well as to rest your eyes.
- Stop work if you get a headache or fuzzy vision.
- Do not grip the mouse too tightly or use the keyboard in an uncomfortable position – if possible use a wrist rest.
- Work in a well-ventilated room.

Starting up a computer

Pressing on the power button will start up a computer. If the computer was shut down correctly during the previous session, you will soon see your opening screen or, if access is restricted, a *log-in* box.

If the computer was shut down by someone simply turning off the power, you may need to wait as the system runs a program such as Scandisk to check for errors.

Using log-in procedures

If you have registered on a website you will have come across these procedures, which help keep information secure. Most people sharing computers on a network will also need to log in so that they have access to their personal work area and computer settings.

Logging in involves typing in two separate entities – a user or account name (also referred to as your user ID) and a password. It is this *combination* that verifies whether or not you are given access, just in case an unauthorized person knows one or other of these entries.

Username

A system administrator will often assign usernames to employees or learners so that they conform across the organization. These names, therefore, are not private. Commonly, the username will contain some form of your own name with perhaps extra text or codes to identify your department or course of study.

On the Internet, usernames may be used for the main part of an e-mail address as well as logging in to the system. They can be typed in upper or lower case. Typical examples are *jsherm17* or *shermanj.*

Password

The password should be kept private and is normally decided by you. When you type it into the box, you see only a string of asterisks (*) so that no one working nearby can read and make use of it. It is normally suggested that the password is six or more characters long and starts with a letter, but you can use a combination of upper or lower case letters, numbers and some allowed symbols.

As so many people find remembering passwords difficult, they often rely on easy-to-guess words such as the names of their children or pets or their birthday, and so it is recommended that you change your password frequently and try to be inventive.

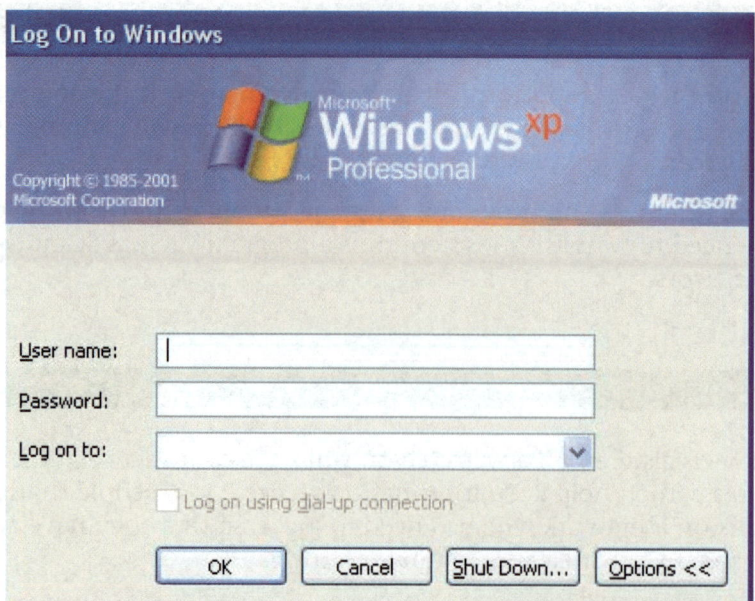

The desktop

After logging in successfully, the opening screen will appear. This is referred to as the *Desktop* as it displays small pictures (*icons*) of items commonly found in an office – e.g. a waste paper basket (the *Recycle Bin*) and a computer (*My Computer*) as well as shortcuts to various programs such as Word or PowerPoint.

If an icon is not labelled, rest the mouse pointer over it and a definition (a *screen tip*) should appear.

Screen tip

Icon

All icons open into *windows*, and there can be several open at the same time. Any open windows, apart from the active (current) one, will appear as labelled buttons on the grey *Taskbar*, visible along the bottom of the screen. Click any button to make it the active window. Close a window completely by clicking the button marked **X** in the top right-hand corner.

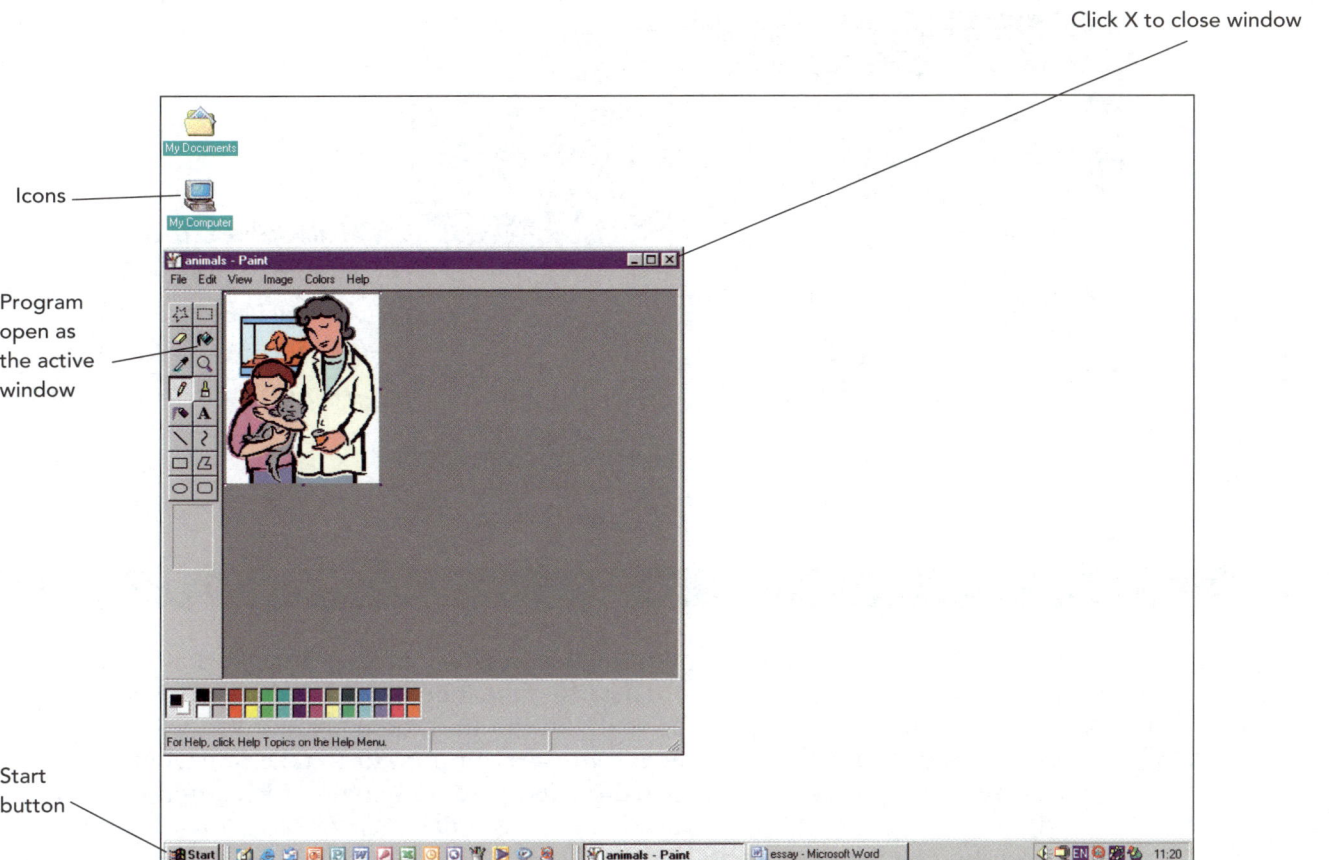

Click X to close window

Icons

Program
open as
the active
window

animals - Paint

File Edit View Image Colors Help

For Help, click Help Topics on the Help Menu.

Start
button

Start   animals - Paint   essay - Microsoft Word   EN   11:20

Open program   Inactive program   Taskbar

Clicking the mouse

Open any icon in one of three ways.

- *Double-click* – position the pointer over the icon and click the left mouse button very fast, twice.
- *Single-click* – click once to select it – the colour will change – and then press the **Enter** key on the keyboard.
- *Right-click* – whenever you click the right mouse button, you are offered a short menu of options from which to choose. After right-clicking an icon, one option is **Open**. Clicking this with the left mouse button would confirm your selection.

Launching programs

If there is a shortcut icon on the desktop, double-click this to open the application. Programs launched from the *Taskbar* require only one click.

Alternatively, find the program in the *Start menu*. Click the button labelled **Start** in the bottom left-hand corner of the screen on the *Taskbar* to open the menu and then slide the pointer up to **Programs** (or **All Programs** in Windows XP). A new menu will open automatically. Position the pointer over the program name, or open a second menu if necessary (it will show by an arrow that it contains further options), and then click once to launch the program.

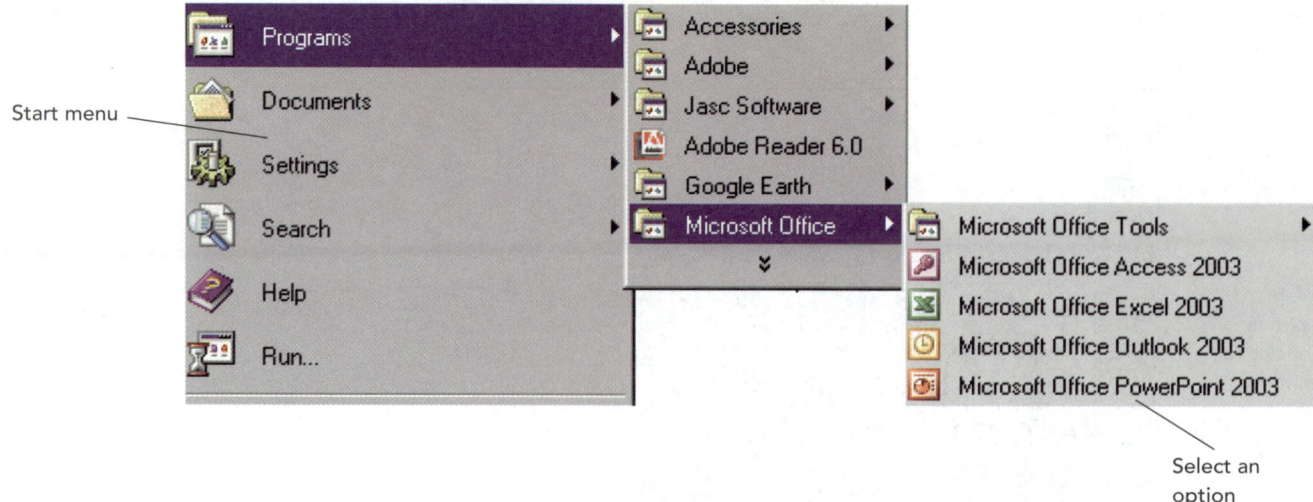

Start menu

Select an option

Files

When working with any program, the documents, charts or images that you create are all known as *files*. These files must be named and saved somewhere on your computer so that you can find them again if you want to print copies or make any changes. It is very important to take care when naming files, so that they can be easily identified. Otherwise, the computer will simply name them generically – e.g. *Document1*, *Book2* or *Untitled* – depending on which program you are using.

File names and extensions

Within each program, the files that are created have a common name and are usually saved by default as a particular file *type*. This is shown by the file *extension*, i.e. the last few letters after the file name.

For example, when using Microsoft Word for word processing, files are known as *documents* and are normally saved as *.doc* files. In Microsoft Excel, files are referred to as workbooks and saved as *.xls* files.

It is also possible, within a program, to save files as different file types. Using Word, you could save your document as plain text *.txt*, rich text *.rtf*, as a template *.dot* or as a web page *.htm*.

Storing files in folders

There are various locations on a computer for storing files. This can be on a disk, or within a named area on the disk known as a *folder*. You can even subdivide folders into separate subfolders if you want to group related files together.

- If you have access to a floppy disk drive, commonly the A: drive, you can store a small number of files on the floppy disk and take them with you to other machines.

- You could possibly save work on a CD (CD-R or CD-RW) in the E: drive.
- Normally, part of the hard disk in the C: drive is set aside for saving work, a folder is provided labelled *My Documents*.
- You may be asked to save work to a disk on a network that has a drive letter such as S: or F:

Each time you create a file, you should decide on the appropriate location and name for the file before it is saved.

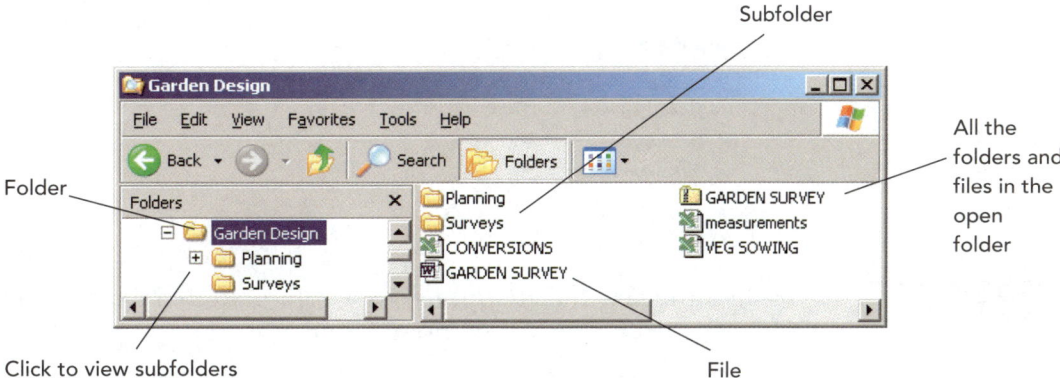

Subfolder

All the folders and files in the open folder

Folder

Click to view subfolders

File

Opening files

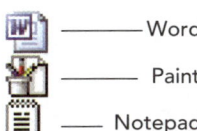

—— Word

—— Paint

— Notepad

To view all the files on your computer, open the **My Computer** icon on the desktop. Open **3½" Floppy A:** to see files on a floppy disk, the **D: drive** to see files on a CD, or **My Documents**, or the appropriate drive, to see files elsewhere. You may need to click the **+** sign next to a drive or folder to display subfolders.

Any file can be opened by double-clicking it in the window. It will open in the program with which it is associated automatically (the 'default'). In most cases, this is the appropriate program. An icon for that program will be visible next to the file name.

Folders

Areas on a disk set aside for storing files are known as folders. You can create separate subfolders inside folders if you want to group related files together and build up a hierarchy of folders. Folders appear as yellow boxes with a small tab.

Creating and naming folders

There are several ways that you can create new folders in which to store your files.

- Using the *File and Folder Tasks* pane – open the parent folder (e.g. *My Documents*) on the desktop. Click **Make a new folder** in the *File and Folder Tasks* pane visible on the left of the window. This will add a new folder inside the folder that is currently open.

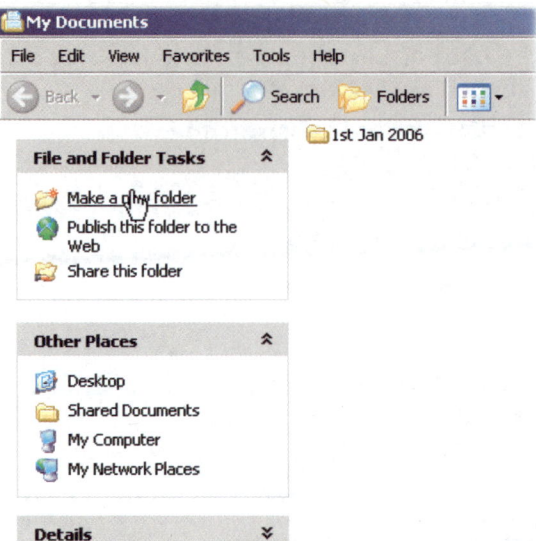

When the new folder appears, type your preferred name over the highlighted text and then press **Enter**.

■ Using the *menu* – select **File/New** and click the **Folder** option.

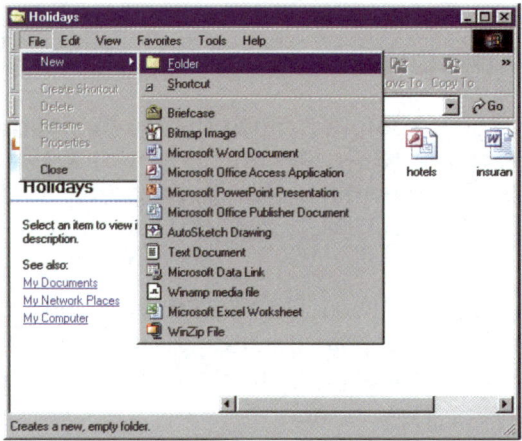

■ Using the *Folders* list – an alternative method is to click the **Folders** button on the toolbar. This will reveal a pane showing all the folders in your computer. Click any folder in the left pane to reveal its contents in the right. Where there is a **+** next to a folder, it means that it contains further folders and you can click the symbol to reveal them. It will then display a **–** sign which you can click to close up the folder's structure again.

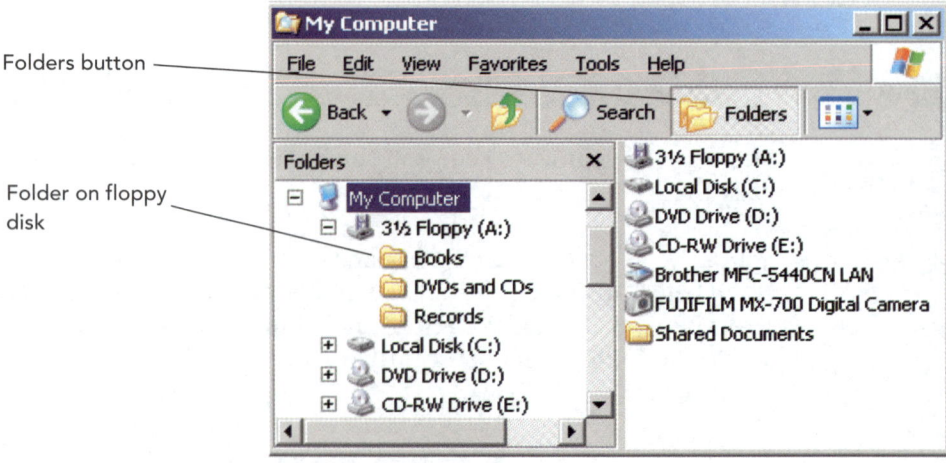

Folders button

Folder on floppy disk

To create a new folder, click the parent folder to select it in the left pane and then go to **File/New/Folder** before typing a new name.

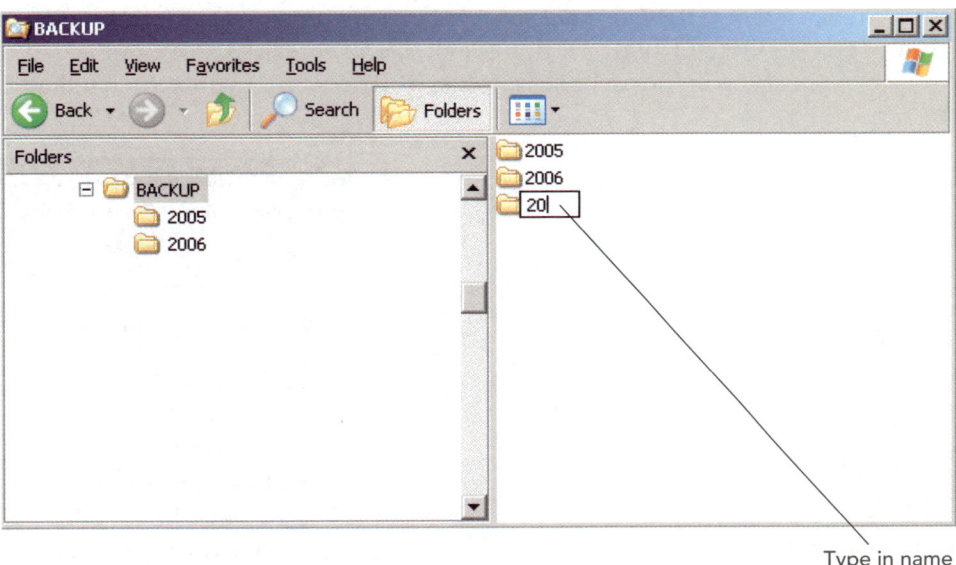

Type in name

Renaming a file or folder

If you want to change the name of any folder or file on the desktop, right-click and select **Rename** from the menu that will appear. You can then amend the entry in the folder name box.

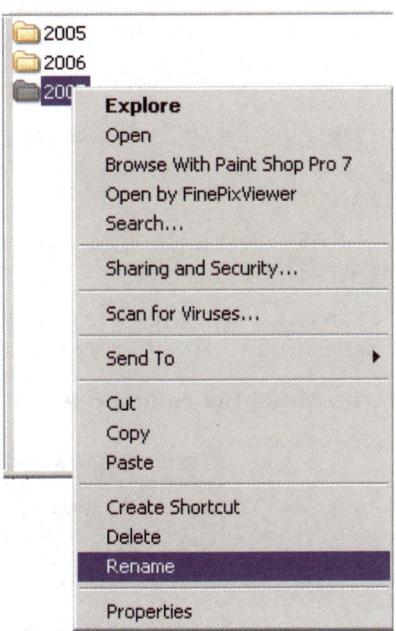

Deleting a file or folder

Select the target file or folder and then press the **Delete** key, click **Delete this file** in the *File and Folder Tasks* pane or click the **Delete** option on the menu offered when you right-click. Don't forget to move out any files you want to keep before deleting a folder as its contents will be deleted at the same time.

FAILURE TO DELETE THE SPECIFIED FILE OR FOLDER IS A CRITICAL ERROR.

Delete selected file

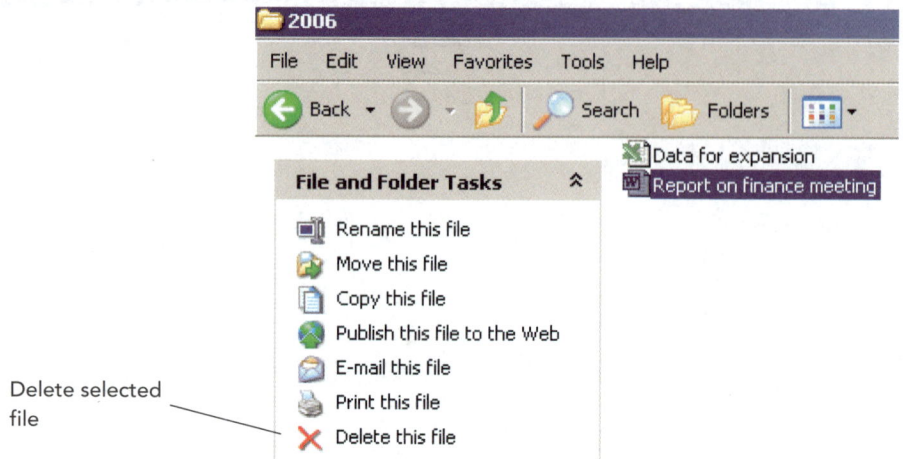

Working with files

Moving a file

Once you have created some folders, you may want to move in files saved elsewhere or move files from one folder to another. Once again, there are three methods you can choose.

- Using the *File and Folder Tasks* pane – open the parent folder to reveal the files you want to move. Select one by clicking it or select more than one as follows:
- adjacent files – click the first, hold down **Shift** and click the last in the range. All will be selected.
- non-adjacent files – click the first and then hold **Ctrl** as you click further files individually. All will stay selected.

Click the **Move the selected items** option in the *File and Folder Tasks* pane.

Click move option

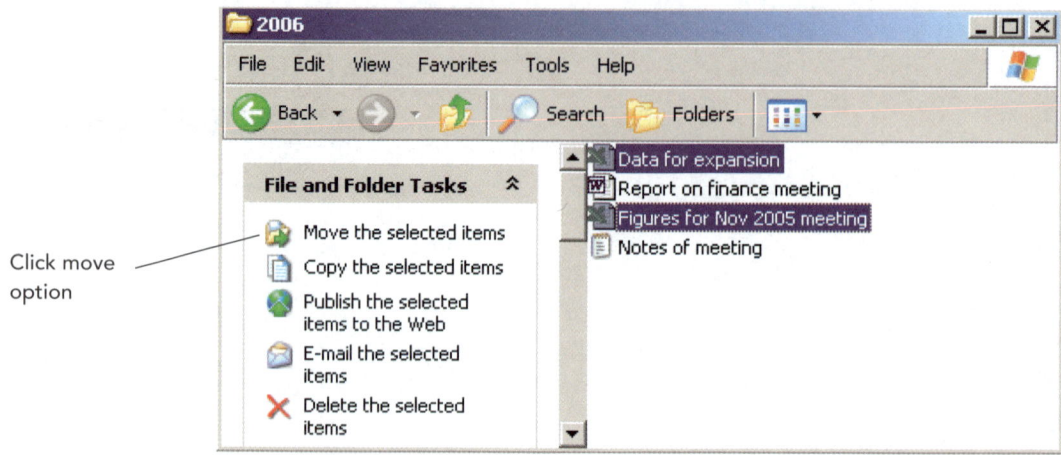

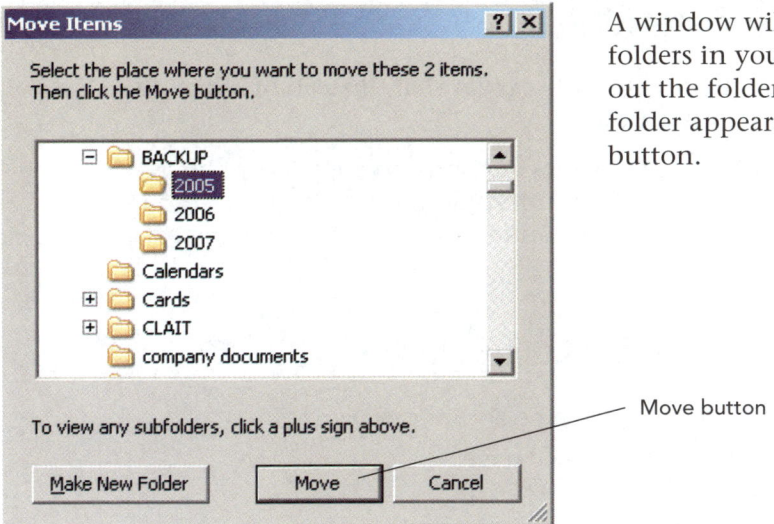

A window will open displaying all the top level folders in your computer. Click the **+** sign to open out the folders structure until the destination folder appears. Select it and then click the **Move** button.

Move button

■ Using *Cut and Paste* – right-click any selected file, or open the **Edit** menu, and select **Cut**. The files will become faded. Now use the **Up arrow** or double-click any visible folders until the target folder is open on screen. Right-click in the window, or open the **Edit** menu and select **Paste** and the files will appear.

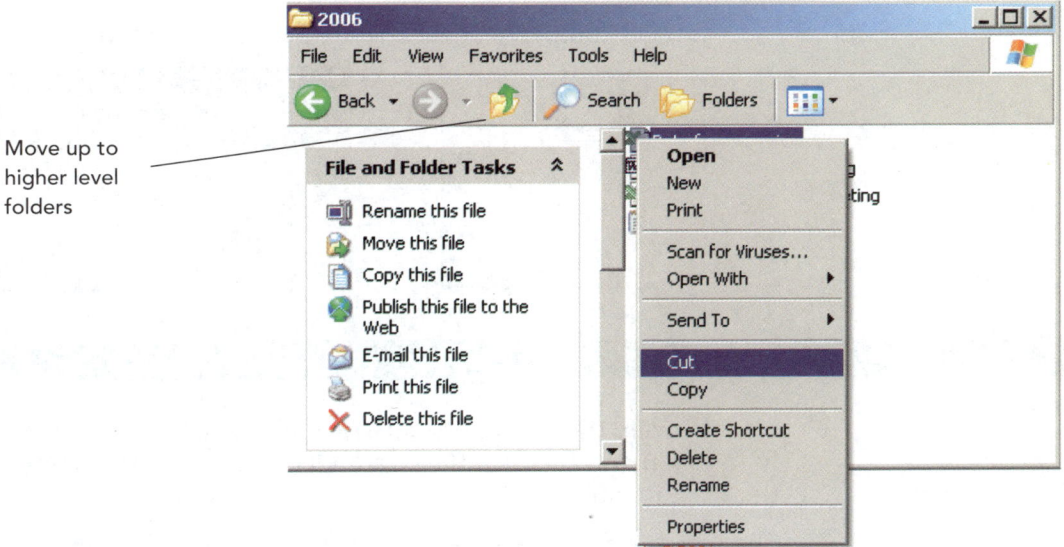

Move up to higher level folders

■ Using the *Folders* list – click the parent folder to reveal the files you want to move. Select one or more files and then click and hold to drag them across into the left-hand pane. They will all move together. When the target folder turns blue, let go and the files will drop into place.

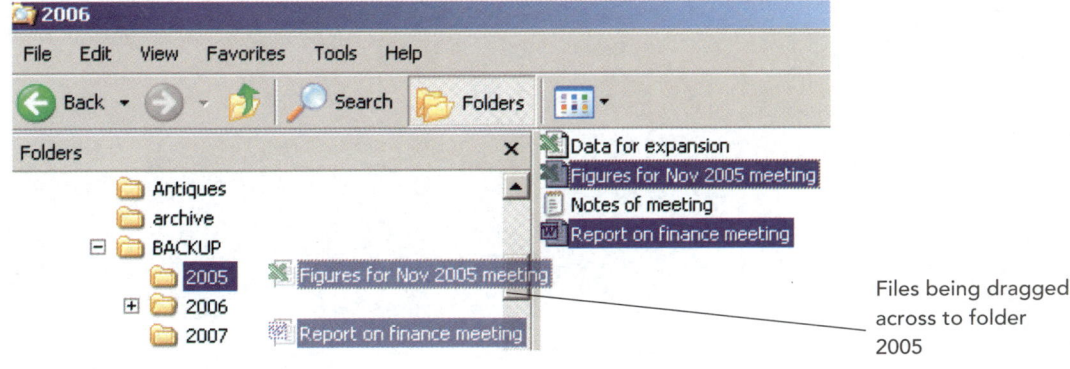

Files being dragged across to folder 2005

Copying a file

The process is identical to moving a file except that, instead of selecting **Cut** from the menu, you select **Copy**.

When using the *Folders* list, drag any files you want to copy using the right mouse button. When the target folder turns blue and you let go the mouse button, you can select the **Copy Here** option from the menu that appears.

✓ Exercise 1

1. Log on to your computer using your username and/or password.
2. Open *My Documents* or go to your area on a drive.
3. Create a new folder and name it `Visits`.
4. Create a second folder and name it `Countries`.
5. Rename the *Countries* folder and call it `Places`.
6. Create a new subfolder inside *Places* and name it `Italy`.
7. Delete the folder *Visits*.
8. Open the folder *Europe* (from the CD) and locate the file *Rome*.
9. Copy this file into the *Italy* subfolder.

Step 6   Step 9

 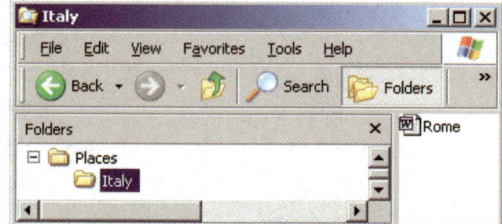

Searching

However carefully you name and save files and folders, it is quite common to mislay them. Locate a file or a folder by clicking the **Search** option on the **Start** menu.

The *Search Results* box will open on screen. Click the type of search you want to carry out – you can look for all files and folders, or for a specific type of file.

Enter as much of the file or folder name as you know and select the lowest
level of drive or folder in which the file should be found. If necessary, click
Browse to locate a particular folder on your computer, and add other
criteria to help you such as keywords or the date on which the file was
created.

File or folder name —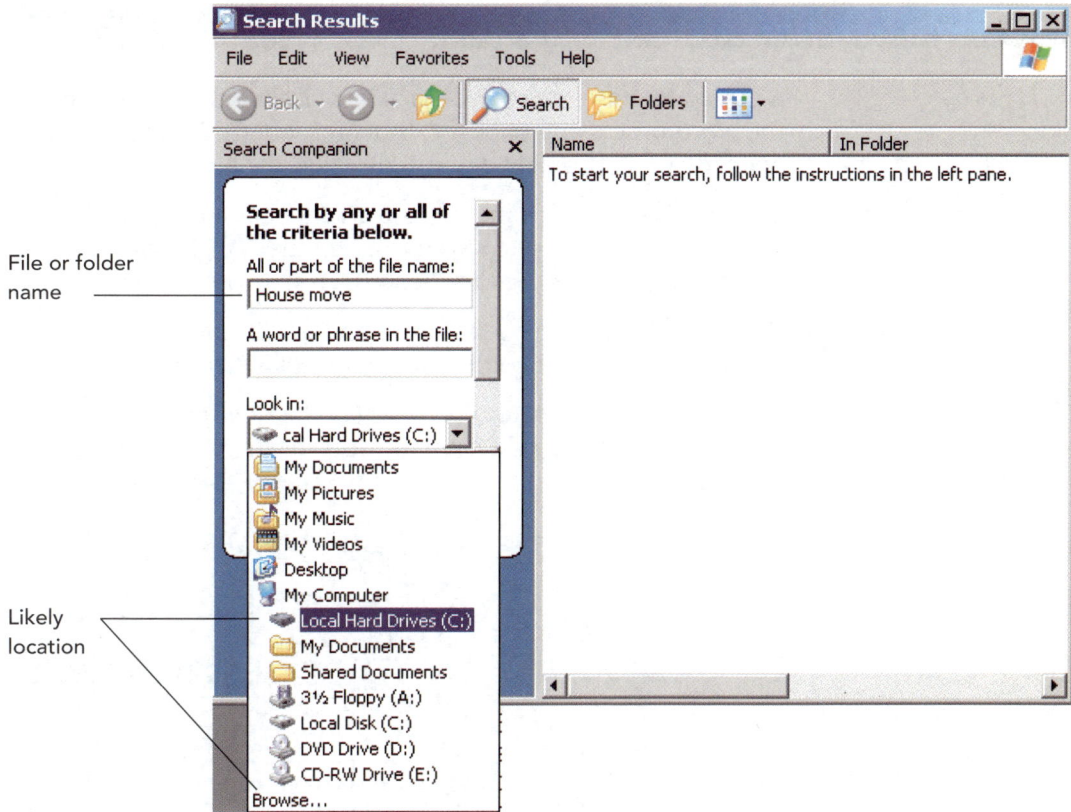

Likely location —

After clicking the **Search** button, all files or folders with similar names will
appear in the window. You can double-click a file to open it fully on screen.

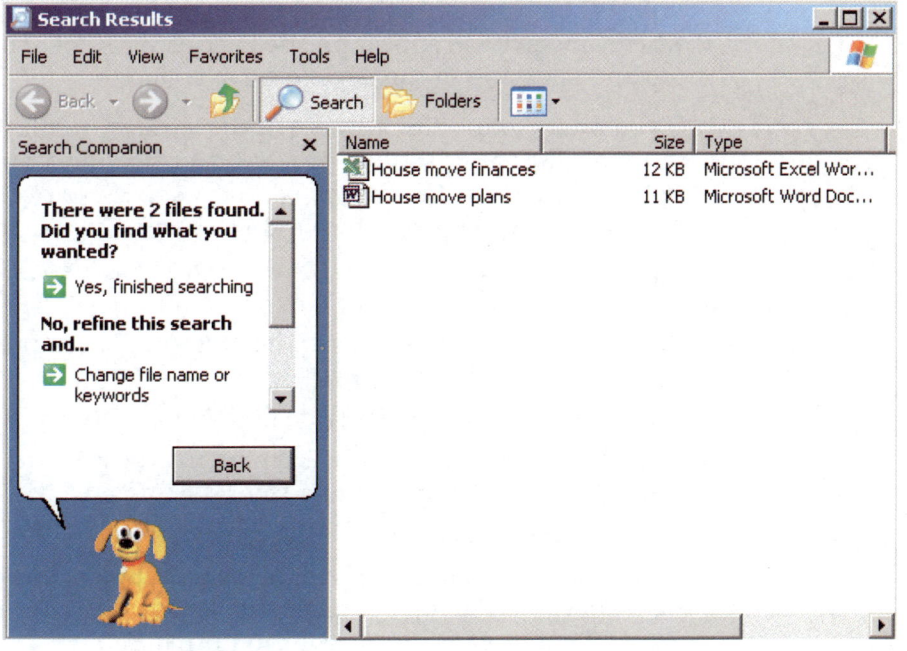

Opening Word

If you have an icon for the application on the desktop, double-click this to launch Word **W**, or open the program from the **Start/All Programs** menu.

Starting a new document

A blank document entitled *Document 1* always appears when you first open the word processing package, but subsequent documents will need to be opened. To start a new document, click the **New** button on the toolbar.

In Word 2003 an extra pane, the *Task* pane, will open that provides shortcuts to menus and saved documents. To give yourself more room you can close it by clicking the **Close** button at the top of the pane.

To create a new document based on a ready-made design, such as a fax cover or memo, you could select a template from the **File/New** menu.

If a toolbar button is not visible, click the down-facing arrow at the end of the toolbar and then click any button to add it to your toolbar. You may need to find a button by clicking the **Add or Remove Buttons** option.

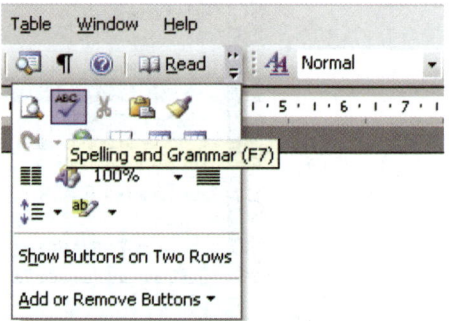

Entering text

You will need to familiarize yourself with the keyboard before starting this unit. When a document opens, a flashing black bar – the *cursor* – shows where any text will appear on the page as you type. This is set in from the top and left edges of the page to leave a margin.

If you prefer to increase the size of the window to fill the screen, maximize it by clicking the central control button (showing a **square**) in the top right-hand corner. The button will now show two overlapping squares. Clicking this will restore the window down to its original size.

To enter text:

- Press any key to type a lower case letter, number or punctuation symbol showing at the bottom of the key.
- Press the **spacebar** to create a space between letters.
- Hold down the **Shift** key when typing to type a capital letter or punctuation symbol showing at the top of a key.
- Press the **Enter** key to move on to a new line.
- To type a line of capitals, press the **Caps Lock** key on – you should see a light appear in the top corner of the keyboard to confirm that this option is active. Turn it off again to revert to normal typing.

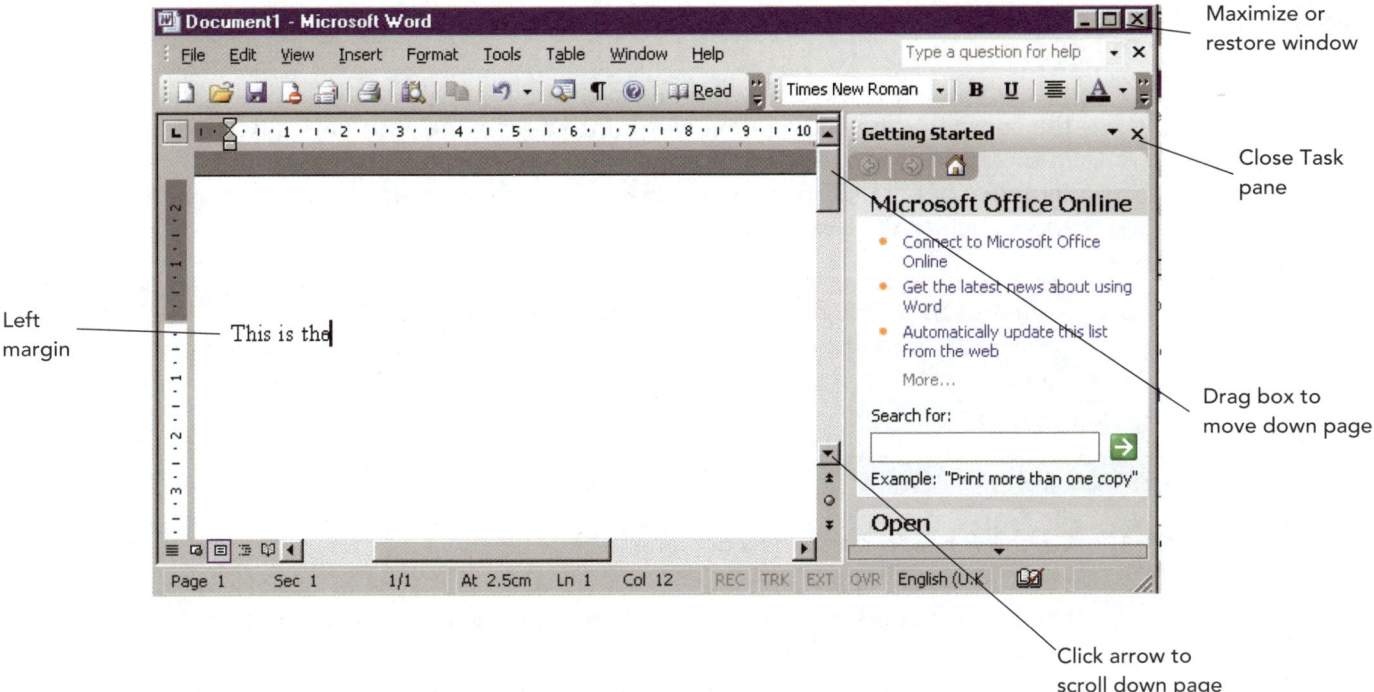

Left margin — (points to the left edge of the document area)

Maximize or restore window

Close Task pane

Drag box to move down page

Click arrow to scroll down page

New lines

To move down the page and begin on a new line, press **Enter**. Make sure the cursor is at the end of the line or any typing to the right of the cursor will be taken down as well. If this happens, close the gap by pressing the **Backspace** key.

Awkward symbols

- Underscore _ (found with the hyphen -) requires **Shift**.
- Apostrophe **'** (found under the **@**) does not require **Shift**.
- Hyphen or subtract **-** does not require **Shift**.
- Comma **,** does not require **Shift**.
- Quote marks **" "** (found above '2') require **Shift**. The computer will normally 'angle' these correctly round your text.

Common mistake

Too many spaces after a comma or at the end of sentences. There should be no more than two spaces after any punctuation.

Common mistake

Incorrect spacing in hyphenated words – there should be no space between letters and hyphens. For example, snap-shot is correct; snap -shot, snap- shot and snap - shot are all incorrect.

Common mistake

Holding Ctrl and not Shift for upper case – this may open a new document (Ctrl + N), or save your work (Ctrl + S).

Word wrap

When you reach the end of a line, continue typing and you will find that the computer moves the next word onto a new line automatically. This is known as word wrap. Do not press **Enter** unless you want to start a sentence or paragraph on a new line, or you need to insert one or more line spaces before the next piece of text.

> **Common mistake**
>
> Pressing Enter at the end of every line, so that paragraph formatting does not apply correctly later.

Exercise 2

1. Open Word and start a new document.

2. Type the letters of the alphabet in their correct order. Type **a – m** in lower case and **N – Z** in upper case, with a space between each letter – e.g. **k l m N O P** etc.

3. After typing **Z**, press **Enter** to move down to a new line and type the numbers from **1** to **9** and then **10, 11** and **12**.

4. On the next line, work across the keyboard and type all the lower case symbols you can find, noting their position:

   `-=#[ ];'\,./`

5. On a new line, hold down **Shift** as you type the following symbols:

   `!"£$%^&*( )_+~{ } :@|< >?`

6. Now type the following mix of upper and lower case letters and symbols:

   `!CoHeN-%&£;?`

7. Finally, type the following on a new line, adding spaces where shown:

   `Zvw_soPy =#: 780 (/, @)`

8. At the end of the text, leave two or three lines and then type your name and today's date.

Inserting new text

It is common to change your mind when word processing, or to discover you have left something out. To add new text between words or sentences, you need to place the cursor in position. New text will then push the original text to the right.

There are several ways to position the cursor:

- Click in place with the mouse.

> The day was ve|hot and it had started

Inserting new text

- Click the mouse at the end of the text and press **Enter** to type new text below the last line.
- Move across your page in the appropriate direction using one of the **arrow** (cursor) keys.
- Press the **Home** key to move to the start of a line.
- Press **End** to move to the end of the line.
- Hold **Ctrl** as you press **Home**/**End** to move to the start/end of all the text.
- Once you have typed enough text to fill the screen, find the insertion point by moving up or down the page using the **Page Up** or **Page Down** keys. You can also click the arrows in the scrollbar or drag the grey box in the scrollbar up or down.

Closing a document

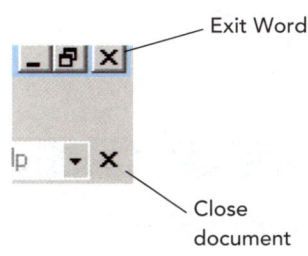

Exit Word

Close document

To close an open document, click the lower **Close** button visible in the top, right-hand corner of the screen. (The top **Close** button will close Word and you will exit the application.) An alternative method is to open the **File** menu and click **Close**.

If your work has not yet been saved, you can decide whether to save it or not.

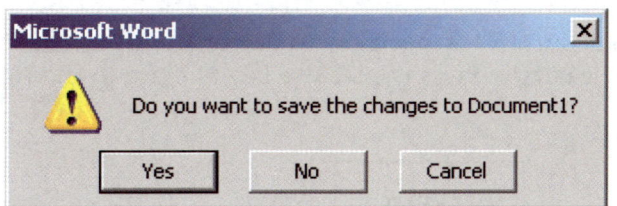

✓ Exercise 3

1. Start a new document.
2. Type the following heading: `FOREIGN COUNTRIES`
3. Leave a blank line and then type this paragraph: `More people spend their holidays abroad than ever before. Now that the Channel Tunnel has opened, they can drive to France in a few hours and no longer have to wait at airports or fight sea-sickness on a ferry crossing.`
4. Leave a few lines and then type your name and the date.
5. Now add the following words after *their holidays:* `and even weekends and the odd lunch break`
6. Change the heading to read: `HOLIDAYING IN FOREIGN COUNTRIES`
7. Close the document without saving.

Answer

```
HOLIDAYING IN FOREIGN COUNTRIES

More people spend their holidays and even weekends
and the odd lunch break abroad than ever before. Now
that the Channel Tunnel has opened, they can drive to
France in a few hours and no longer have to wait at
airports or fight sea-sickness on a ferry crossing.



My name and date
```

Overtyping

Sometimes, new text being inserted replaces the original text rather than moving it to the right. This is the result of pressing the **Insert** key on the keyboard by mistake and moving into *overtyping*. Revert back to normal by pressing the **Insert** key again.

Deleting text

Press the **Backspace** key to delete an unwanted space or letter to the left of the cursor. Press the **Delete** key to erase to the right.

FAILURE TO DELETE THE SPECIFIED TEXT OR DELETING THE WRONG TEXT IS A CRITICAL ERROR.

Undoing mistakes

If you make an error, such as deleting text by mistake, click the **Undo** button one or more times, or select the **Undo** option from the **Edit** menu. Do this as soon as you can before carrying out any other tasks, as this will step back through your actions sequentially.

Creating new paragraphs

Each paragraph should be separated from the paragraph above by a clear line space – sometimes referred to as a paragraph break. To create a new paragraph, position the cursor at the end of the text or in front of the first word that will start the new paragraph and press the **Enter** key twice – once to move it onto a new line and again to leave a blank line space.

Joining up paragraphs

If the cursor is flashing at the end of a line, press the **Delete** key to join this line to the beginning of the following paragraph.

If the cursor is flashing at the beginning of a line, press the **Backspace** key to join this line to the paragraph above.

> **Common mistake**
>
> Creating a new paragraph, because a short sentence in the middle of a paragraph finishes before the end of the line. As the next sentence begins on the following line it is *not* the start of a new paragraph.

Saving a document

You can save your work at any time by clicking the **Save** button or by opening the **File** menu and selecting **Save**. This opens the *Save As* window (a dialogue box) and you have two decisions to make:

- where to save the file – e.g. onto a $3\frac{1}{2}''$ floppy disk, in *My Documents* or in a folder that has been created
- what name to give the file so that it is easy to locate in future.

Saving

A location for your file will appear in the *Save in*: box at the top of the window. If this is not the correct folder, click the **down arrow** in the box, the **up arrow** toolbar button or one of the options in the *Places* bar to select an alternative location to store your file.

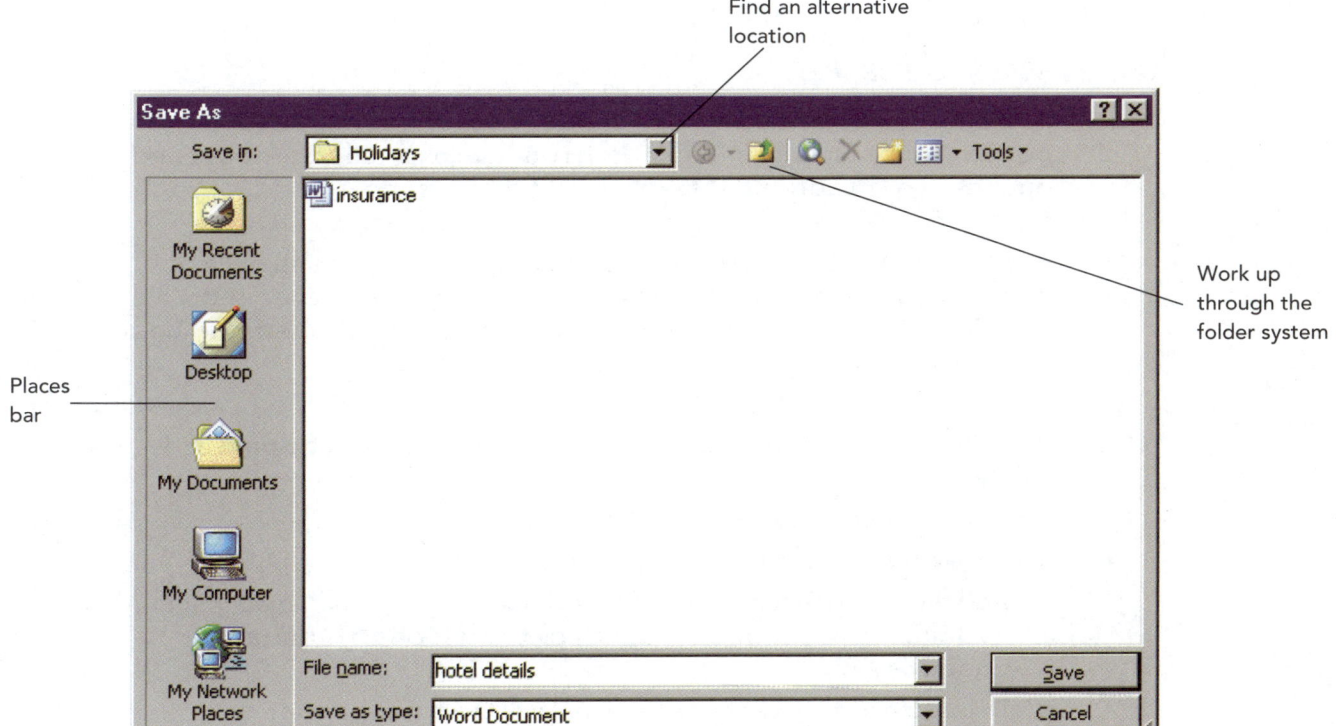

Find an alternative location

Work up through the folder system

Places bar

You can accept or amend the name that automatically appears in the *File name* box. Replace the name by typing when the entry is blue, or make changes by clicking into the **File name**: box and then using your keyboard as normal to delete or add text.

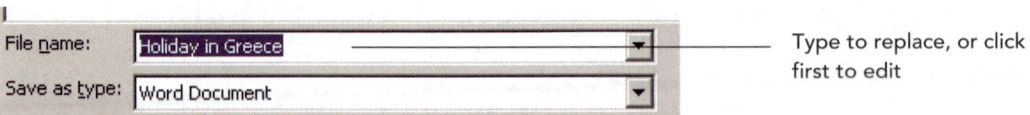

File name: Holiday in Greece   Type to replace, or click first to edit

Save as type: Word Document

When you are ready to save, press the **Enter** key or click the **Save** button. Back in your document, you will see that the title of the document has changed to display the new name.

> **Common mistake**
>
> Saving incorrectly – e.g. giving your work the wrong file name. This will be obvious when you add the name to your document later.

> **Common mistake**
>
> Not taking care when saving and forgetting where the file is stored.

Updating a document

As you add or delete text, your document will change. Update your work regularly by clicking the **Save** toolbar button again. This will not open the *Save As* dialogue box or require you to make any changes to the file name or location, but will simply overwrite the original document.

Exercise 4

1. Start a new document and enter the following text. Use capitals where these are shown.

    SURFACE FEEDERS

    All the fish found just under the surface have a perfectly straight back, which allows their upturned mouths to reach right up to the surface. Foods which float for some time are ideal for these fish.

    A common surface feeder is the glass catfish. This fish is a native of India and is very active and lively. It can reach a size of about 5 cm and is best kept in shoals.

2. Read through and check for errors. If you find any, use the **backspace** and **delete** keys to make corrections.

3. Save the document as `Surface Feeders`.

4. Now make these changes:
    - Add the following text, including the brackets, after … *upturned mouths*:
      `(ideal for scooping up floating foods, usually insects)`
    - Delete the name *glass catfish* and replace it with `zebra danio`.
    - Create a new second paragraph beginning: *Foods which float …*

5. Add your name and today's date on a new line at the end of the text. Update the document to save the changes.

6. Close the document.

Answer

```
SURFACE FEEDERS

All the fish found just under the surface have a
perfectly straight back, which allows their upturned
mouths (ideal for scooping up floating foods, usually
insects) to reach right up to the surface.

Foods which float for some time are ideal for these
fish.

A common surface feeder is the zebra danio. This fish
is a native of India and is very active and lively.
It can reach a size of about 5 cm and is best kept in
shoals.


My name and date
```

Saving a new version of a document

To keep an original document intact and save a second version, open the **File** menu and select the **Save As** option. This will open the dialogue box and you can now change the location and/or the file name for your work before clicking **Save**.

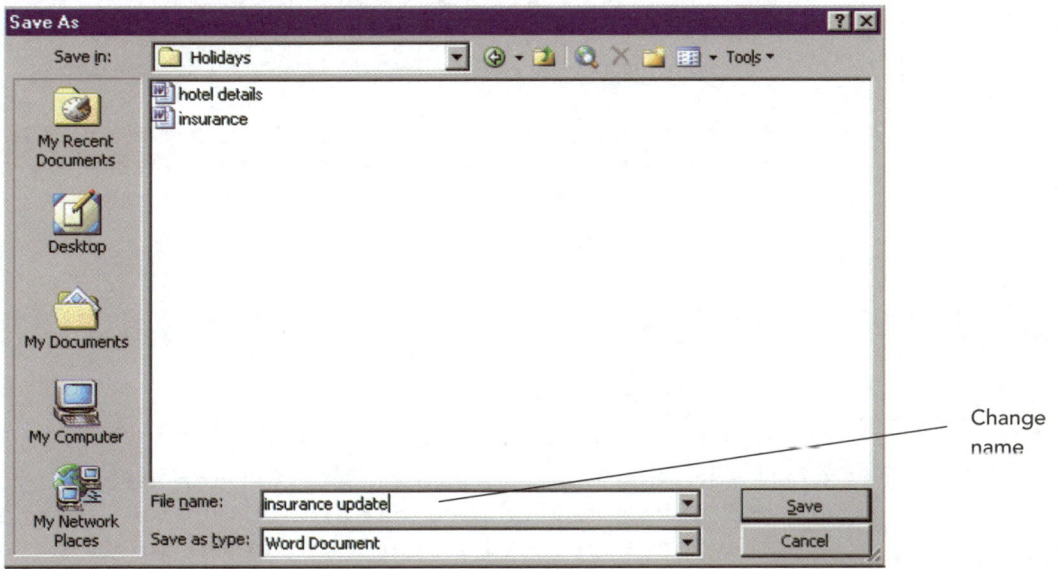

Change name

Common mistake

Saving, and so updating, the first document with later changes. Save As should be carried out early to retain the original intact, in case you spot a mistake before handing in a printout.

Printing a document

For a single copy of the current document, click the **Print** toolbar button 🖨.

If you want to print particular pages or make several copies, you need to go to **File/Print** and select from the various options in the dialogue box before clicking **OK**.

Set which printer to be used

Set pages to be printed

Set number of copies

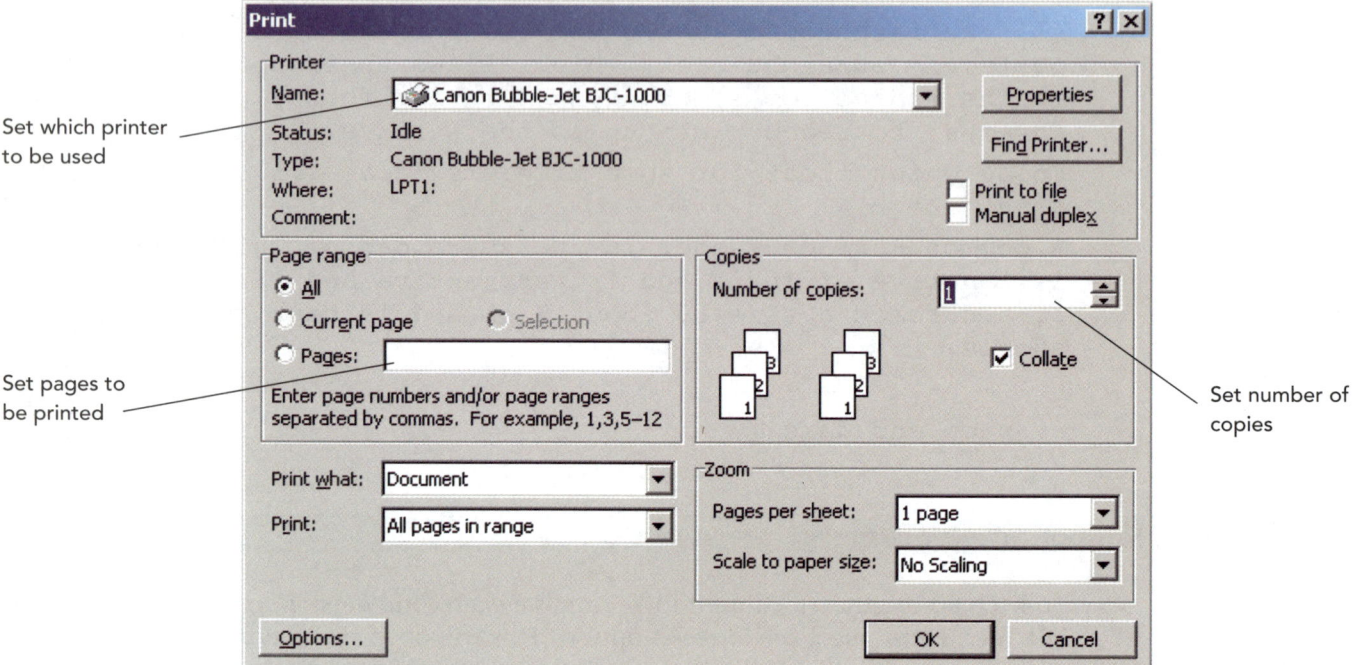

Common mistake

Omitting to carry out a print instruction at the appropriate time. Lack of evidence of any amendments that should have been made will then be penalized.

Common mistake

Not checking that all the required evidence is visible on printouts or handing in the wrong printouts.

✓ Exercise 5

1. Start a new document.

2. Type the heading: GOING TO COLLEGE

3. Now type the following paragraph: At the age of 16, young boys and girls may have a difficult choice. Whether to stay on at school, start a job or go to a further education college.

4. Save the document as College.

5. Now make the following changes:

    ■ *COLLEGE* should be UNIVERSITY

    ■ *16* should be 18

6. Delete the words: *stay on at school* and replace them with: go to university.

7. Save the amended document with the file name `University`.

8. Print one copy.

9. Close the document.

```
GOING TO UNIVERSITY

At the age of 18, young boys and girls may have a
difficult choice. Whether to go to university, start
a job or go to a further education college.
```

Opening a saved document

Click the **Open** toolbar button 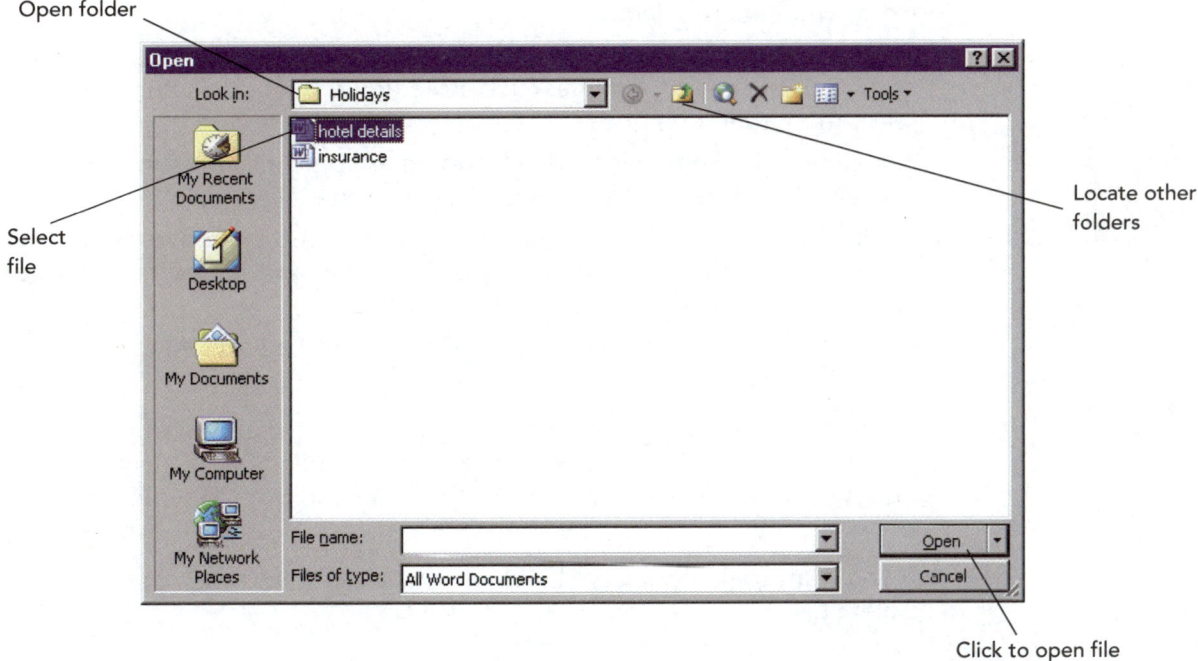 or go to **File**/**Open**.

If the file is not visible in the window, find it in one of the following ways:

- Click and open a yellow folder that may hold the file.
- Click the **up arrow** to work up through the folder pathways on your computer.
- Click the **down arrow** in the *Look in:* box to select an alternative location.

When you can see the file, click to select it and then click **Open**.

Open folder

Select file

Locate other folders

Click to open file

Taking a screen print

Sometimes you may want to print a picture of objects on screen, such as files in folders or icons on the desktop, rather than an actual document. You can do this by taking a screen print and pasting this image into a document.

1. With the image on screen, press the key labelled **Print Screen** (or **Prt Scr**) on your keyboard. This places the image in the computer's memory.
2. Open a new document.
3. Select **Edit/Paste** or right-click and select **Paste**.
4. When the image appears, treat the document as any other word processed document and carry on working, saving or printing as normal.

Selecting text

Before you can make changes to text already typed, the letters, words or sentences must be *selected* (often referred to as highlighting). They will show as white characters on a black background.

Welcome to the ▮October▮ meeting

There are many ways to select text:

- Double-click in the middle of one word with the mouse.
- Triple-click to select a complete paragraph.
- Click at the start of the text and when the pointer shows as a vertical bar hold down the mouse button and drag it across the words. Let go and the words will remain selected.
- Move the mouse pointer into the left margin. When it shows a right facing arrow, click to select one line; click, hold down the button and drag to select more than one line.
- Hold down the **Shift** key on the keyboard as you click an **arrow** key in the relevant direction to select a letter/line at a time.
- Click at the start of a section. Let go the mouse button, move to the end of the section via the **scrollbar** and hold down the **Shift** key as you click again. The complete section should become selected.
- Use **Edit/Select All** (or hold down **Ctrl** and type the letter **A**) to select the complete text.

To cancel a selection, click the mouse once on the main part of the screen. However, do not press a key on the keyboard when text is selected otherwise that text will be deleted – this is a good time to remember the **Undo** button!

If you want to delete a large block of text, select it and then press the **Delete** key.

Formatting text

After selecting the chosen words in one of the above ways, or before you start typing, you can make various changes to the appearance of your work. For example, you can emphasize headings or particular sections, choose a different style of character (font) from that automatically selected by default and increase or decrease the size of any text or figures. (See Unit 4 for details of different font types.)

- Click one of the toolbar shortcuts: **B** = **bold**, **I** = *italics* or **U** = underline. When *on*, these toolbar buttons show a lighter colour. Click the button again to turn *off* the formatting.

Welcome to the **October** meeting

- Use one of the shortcuts on the toolbar for different font types or sizes – click the **down-facing arrow** in the boxes to display alternatives.

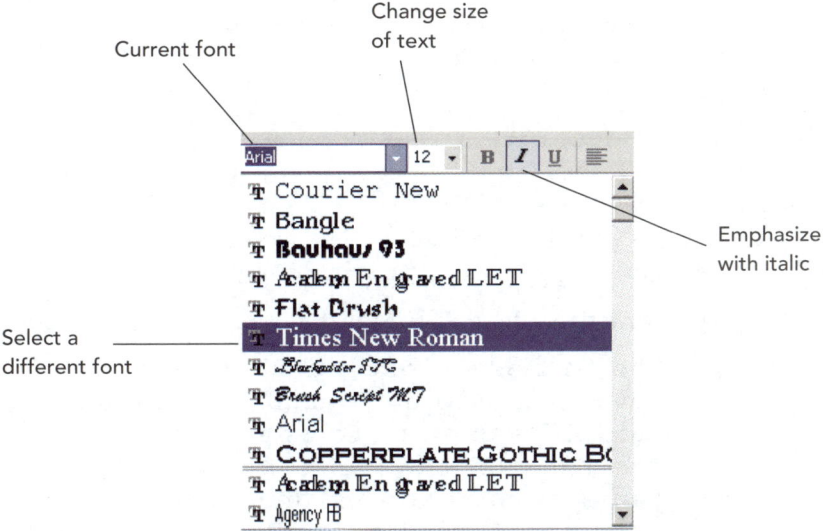

Change size of text

Current font

Emphasize with italic

Select a different font

- To preview changes or choose other options, open the **Format** menu, select **Font** and use the relevant drop-down menus or checkboxes before clicking **OK**.

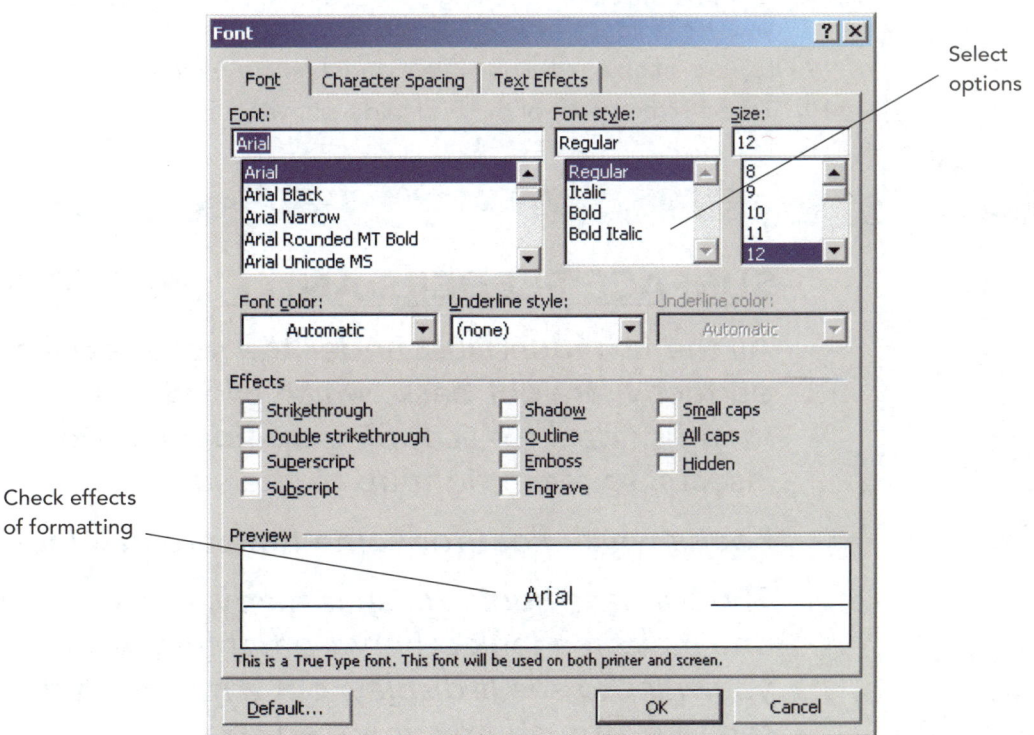

Select options

Check effects of formatting

✓ Exercise 6

1. Create a folder named `Fish` on your computer.
2. Reopen *Surface Feeders* – the file you created in Exercise 4.
3. Print one copy of the document.
4. Now insert the following text as a new third paragraph:

   `The Siamese fighting fish is hardy, but you can only have one male in a tank otherwise fighting will break out. If you want to see it display, put a mirror on the side of the tank. Aquarium-cultivated strains usually have bodies and fins of one colour, apart from the Cambodia fighter that has a cream body and coloured fins.`

5. Amend the heading to read `SURFACE FEEDERS AND FIGHTING FISH`
6. Select the heading and make it bold and underlined, font size 16.
7. Select the main text and apply a different font, size 14 italic.
8. Save the document as a new version with the name `Fighting Fish` into your *Fish* folder.
9. Print one copy of the document and then close the file.
10. Take a screen print of the *Fish* folder showing the file inside.

Answer

SURFACE FEEDERS AND FIGHTING FISH

All the fish found just under the surface have a perfectly straight back, which allows their upturned mouths (ideal for scooping up floating foods, usually insects) to reach right up to the surface.

Foods which float for some time are ideal for these fish.

The Siamese fighting fish is hardy, but you can only have one male in a tank otherwise fighting will break out. If you want to see it display, put a mirror on the side of the tank. Aquarium-cultivated strains usually have bodies and fins of one colour, apart from the Cambodia fighter that has a cream body and coloured fins.

A common surface feeder is the zebra danio. This fish is a native of India and is very active and lively. It can reach a size of about 5 cm and is best kept in shoals.

My name and date

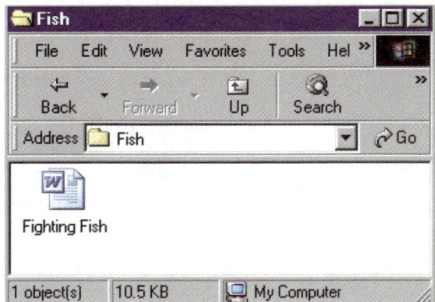

Alignment

Instead of every sentence beginning on the left of the document, you may want items centred on the page or situated on the right. *Alignment* is the term used to describe the way text lines up on the page. To make changes, select a line, paragraph or block of text and then click the correct alignment button on the toolbar:

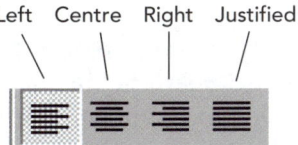

Left (normal – text lines up on the left margin)

Centre (text spreads around a central point)

Right (text lines up with the right margin)

Justify (text is spread across the page by adding extra spaces to 'neaten' the right margin). Sometimes this alignment will be described as fully justified.

Note: OCR assignments in the past used to describe left-aligned text as an unjustified right margin and a justified left margin.

Alignments work on complete lines, so you cannot have two separately aligned texts on the same line. To change from, for example, centre to left alignment, press **Enter** first to move onto a new line.

To add and align a new entry, such as the date at the top of a document, click in front of the first word and press **Enter** to move the whole text down a few lines. Then click in the space you have made and apply the appropriate alignment.

Common mistake

Pressing **Enter** at the end of each line (to match the assignment sentences line by line) instead of using word wrap. Text realignment will now apply inconsistently as the lines of text separated by pressing the **Enter** key are interpreted as separate paragraphs.

You may notice red or green wavy lines appearing beneath words after you type your text. Red means the word is not in the computer's dictionary and *may* be spelt incorrectly. A green line means that the text *may* be breaking a common rule of grammar, such as too many spaces after a comma or between words.

■ To correct one word, click the right mouse button on a wavy line to display a short menu of options. You can select a suggested alternative word, or set the machine to ignore the word in future. Take care if you decide to click **Add** as this will add the word to the dictionary. You may add a misspelt word by mistake and it will not be picked up in the future.

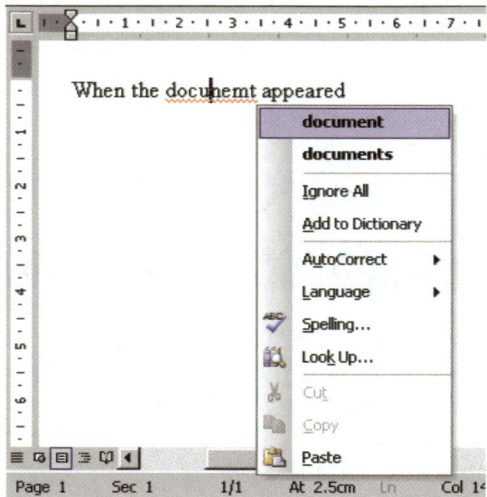

■ To check through the whole document, click the **Spelling and Grammar** button to open the dialogue box and start the process. For each word highlighted, you can click the **Ignore Once** or **Ignore All** buttons, select an alternative offered in the window, or click in the box and manually alter the word. Click a **Change** option to amend the word in your document.

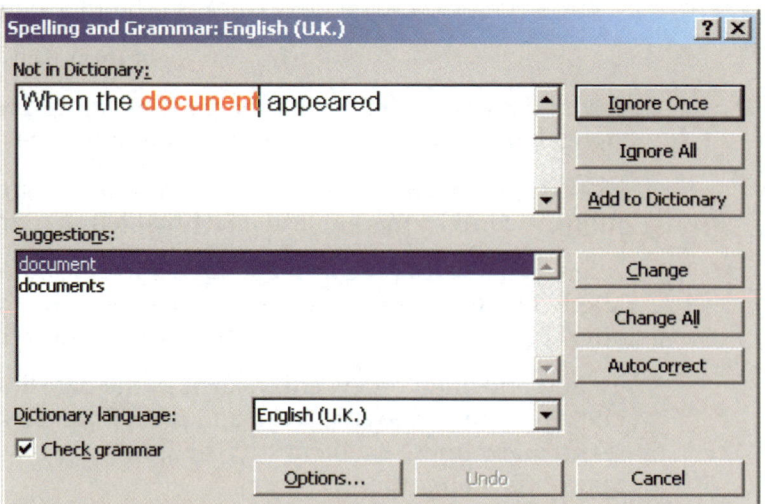

Common mistake

Accepting a suggested grammar correction that changes the sentence structure or text. For New CLAIT, your text must match the assignment *exactly*.

Proofreading

Before printing a document, you must check for any errors that will not be highlighted by the spelling or grammar checker. Letters can be transposed so that words take on a new meaning – e.g. *raw* for *war* – or the wrong word or tense can be used – e.g. *had* instead of *has*, or *it's* instead of *its*.

✓ Exercise 7

1. Start a new document and enter the following text. Type the words as shown, even if they do not make grammatical sense, and retain spelling mistakes to the words *deaths*, *pump* and *arteries*.

   ```
   Heart Disease
   Heart disease causes at quarter of all dealths in
   Britain. It has the biggest killer of middle-aged men
   in the developed world.

   You need a healthy heart to pummp blood around your
   body, and hear muscle needs food and oxygen for it to
   keep contracting. These are carried in the coronary
   artereis. If the arteries get blocked, then it can
   cause hearth disease. The risks increases if you
   smoking, become overweight or take no exercise.
   ```

2. Save as **Heart Disease** and print one copy.
3. Use the spelling and grammar checker to correct any obvious mistakes.
4. Now proofread for sense, and correct any other errors – you should find at least four.
5. Format the first paragraph to Courier, font size 10.
6. Format the second paragraph to Times New Roman font size 12, italic.
7. Format the title to font size 16, bold.
8. Centre the heading and fully justify the main text.
9. Save the file as a new version with the name **Heart Disease Corrected** and print one copy.
10. Close the file.

Answer

Heart Disease

```
Heart disease causes a quarter of all deaths in Britain.   It is the
biggest killer of middle-aged men in the developed world.
```

You need a healthy heart to pump blood around your body, and heart muscle needs food and oxygen for it to keep contracting. These are carried in the coronary arteries. If the arteries get blocked, then it can cause heart disease. The risk increases if you smoke, become overweight or take no exercise.

Setting margins

The default settings for page margins in Word documents are usually 2.54 cm for top and bottom margins and 3.17 cm for left and right margins. However, some documents may look more attractive if the margins are wider; at other times, the margins will need to be narrower to allow more text to be displayed on the page.

To amend any of the margins, go to **File/Page Setup** and click the **Margins** tab. Set any of the margins to an exact measure by clicking the **arrows** in the boxes or (for one-hundredths of a centimetre) manually typing over the figures.

Alter measure in box

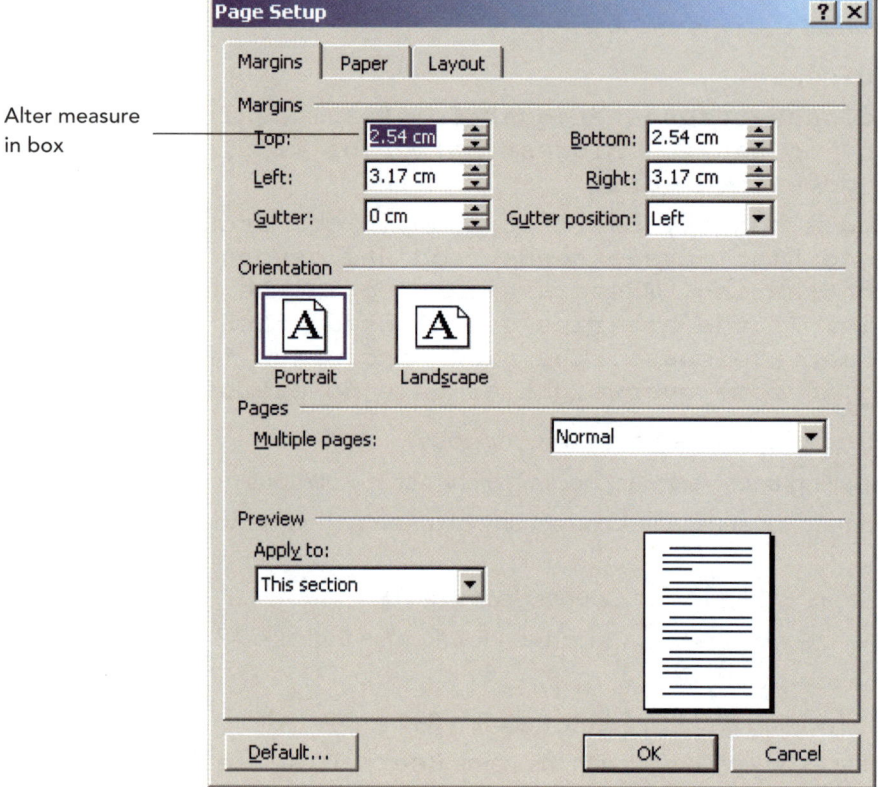

Line spacing

Text normally appears on the next line as you type using word wrap. This is known as *single line spacing*. In many situations, for example when submitting articles to a newspaper or journal, or essays that will be marked, it is better to add more space for written comments by double-spacing the work – that means adding a blank line between every line of text.

To increase the space between lines, select the paragraphs or click in a single paragraph/line. Then use a shortcut, toolbar button or the **Format** menu. Common shortcuts are:

■ double line spacing – hold **Ctrl** and press the number **2** key

- $1\frac{1}{2}$ (1.5) line spacing – **Ctrl + 5**
- single line spacing – **Ctrl + 1**.

To use the menu, select **Format/Paragraph**, click the **Indents and Spacing** tab and select as appropriate from the *Line spacing* drop-down menu.

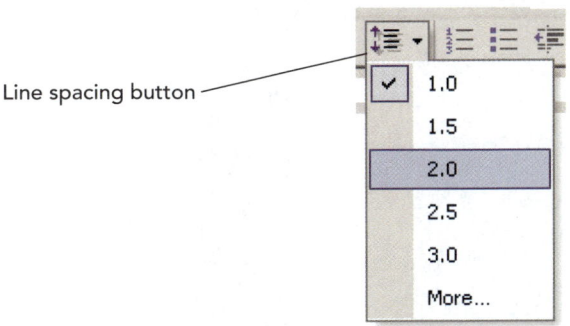

Line spacing button

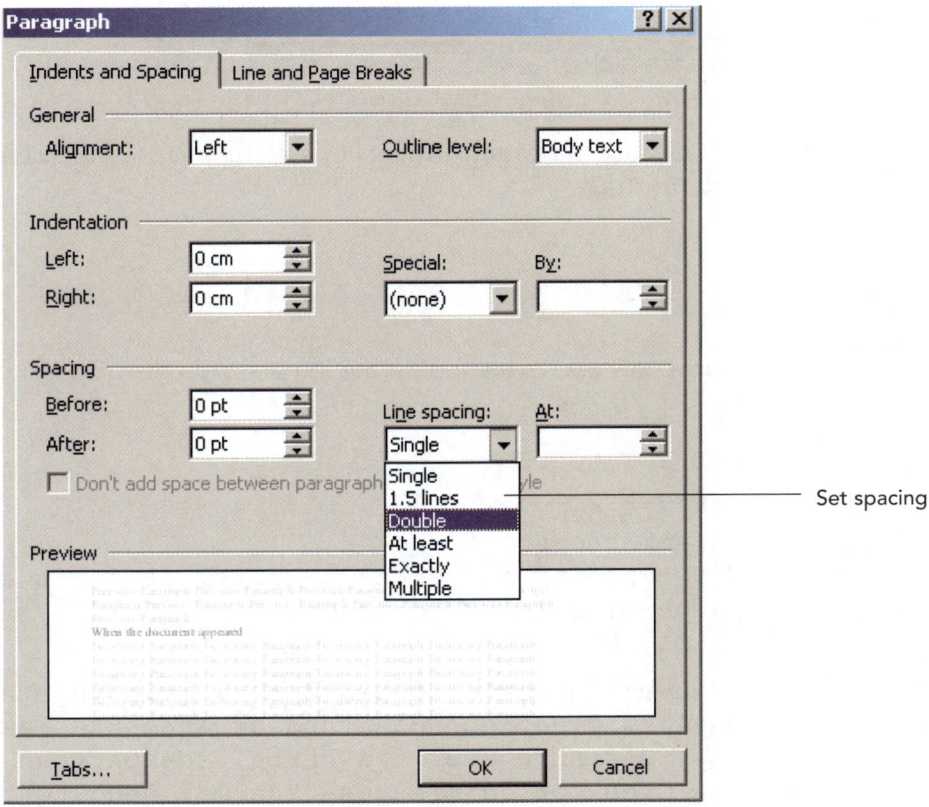

Set spacing

Print preview

Having made changes to margins, text alignment or line spacing, it is a good idea to see what the finished document looks like before printing a copy. Do this by clicking the **Print Preview** button or selecting this option from the **File** menu.

Close this view by clicking the button labelled **Close** on the toolbar

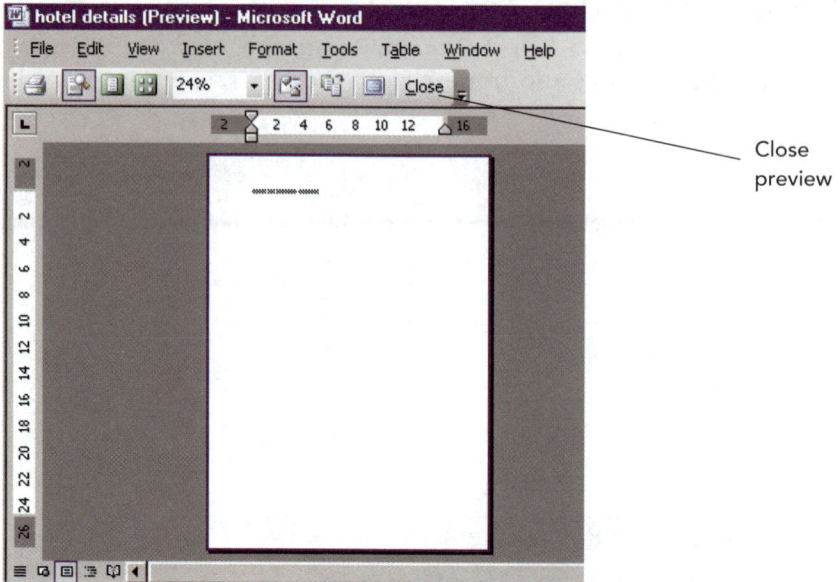

Close preview

(not the document *Close* button in the top right-hand corner).

If necessary, make adjustments to any of your measurements before saving and printing.

Exercise 8

1. Start a new document and set the left and right margins to 3 cm.

2. Type the following text:

   ONE POT WONDER
   (Serves 2 — 3)
   4 lamb chops
   700 g peeled and diced carrots, potatoes and swedes
   pinch of dried oregano
   15 ml tomato puree

   Preheat the oven to gas mark 7. Tip vegetables into a shallow ovenproof dish and arrange the lamb chops on top. Sprinkle over the herbs, season then roast in the oven for 15 minutes. You may need to add extra water if the liquid appears to be drying up.

   Mix the tomato puree with a cupful of hot water and pour over the chops and vegetables. Continue cooking for another 20 minutes.

3. Proofread and save as **One Pot Wonder**.

4. Print one copy.

5. Increase the right-hand margin by 1.5 cm.

6. Select the title and subtitle, centre them and format to bold.

7. On a line *above* the title, enter today's date, right aligned.

8. Format the ingredients to italic.

9. Double space all the instructions, and apply a different font.

10. Check your document in Print Preview.

11. Update the file to save these changes and print a second copy before closing.

date

ONE POT WONDER

(Serves 2–3)

4 lamb chops
700 g peeled and diced carrots, potatoes and swedes
pinch of dried oregano
15 ml tomato puree

Preheat the oven to gas mark 7. Tip vegetables into a shallow ovenproof dish and

arrange the lamb chops on top. Sprinkle over the herbs, season then roast in the oven for

15 minutes. You may need to add extra water if the liquid appears to be drying up.

Mix the tomato puree with a cupful of hot water and pour over the chops and

vegetables. Continue cooking for another 20 minutes.

Page orientation

To change from the default orientation, which is portrait or upright A4, open the **File** menu and select **Page Setup**. On the *Margins* tab, click the **Landscape** button. Your page will now print with the longer sides top and bottom.

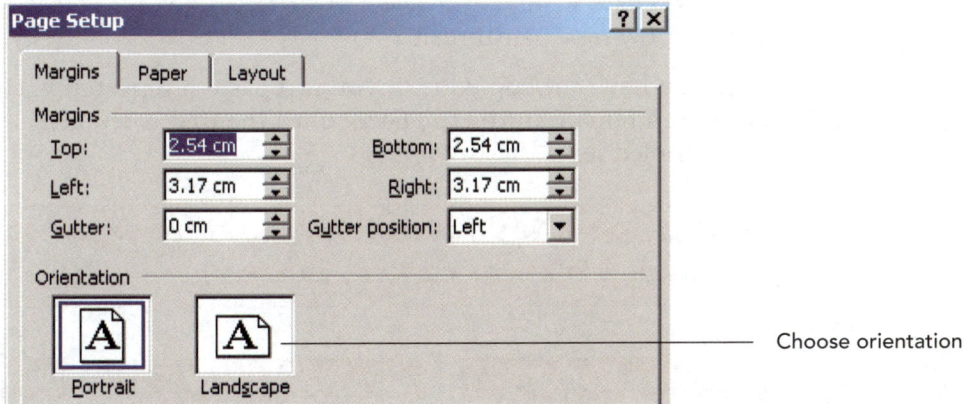

Choose orientation

Moving text to a new position

Having discovered that a block of text is in the wrong place, it is fairly straightforward to use the mouse or keyboard to move it, thus saving you the trouble of typing it all over again. You can also copy text if you want to repeat it somewhere else.

Drag and drop

- To move text a short distance, select the word(s) you want to move and release the mouse. Move the mouse pointer over the selected block until it becomes a pointing arrow facing to the left, then hold down the left button and drag the text to its new location. Let go the mouse and the text will drop into place. (You will see a small box attached to the arrow as you drag, and a vertical line will show its new position.)

Large sizes and shapes were

- If you hold the **Ctrl** key as you drag, you can copy instead of move the text. A + sign will be visible next to the arrow.

Cut and paste

If you want to move text some distance, carry out the move in four steps.

1. Select the text to be moved.

2. Click the **Scissors** icon ✂ (or select **Edit /Cut**). The text will disappear and will have been placed in part of the computer's memory – the *Clipboard*.

   (To copy text and leave the original in place, click the **Copy** icon 📋 or select **Edit/Copy** instead of *Edit/Cut*.)

3. Click the mouse in the new position for the text, placing a flashing cursor bar on the screen. If necessary, use the **Enter** key to help position the cursor correctly.

4. Click the **Paste** icon 📋 (or select **Edit/Paste**). (Note: This is NOT the button showing a paintbrush.)

   Once you have cut/copied text, you can paste it repeatedly. Up to 24 blocks of text can remain in the *Clipboard* until the first is replaced by a 25th block of cut/copied text.

> **FAILURE TO SHOW EVIDENCE OF MOVING THE SPECIFIED TEXT OR MOVING THE WRONG TEXT IS A CRITICAL ERROR.**

Common mistake	**Common mistake**	**Common mistake**
Copying instead of moving so the result is two entries of the same text.	After moving, not amending spacing between blocks of text.	Moving the text to the wrong position – e.g. the *start* of paragraph 3 rather than the *end* of paragraph 3.

Exercise 9

1. Create a folder named `Cooking`.

2. Reopen *One Pot Wonder* from Exercise 8.

3. Move *15 ml tomato puree* so that it becomes the second item in the list of ingredients, after *4 lamb chops*.

4. Delete the phrase *for 15 minutes*.

5. Insert a line break and start a second paragraph with the sentence beginning *Sprinkle over the herbs …*

6. Move the sentence beginning *Mix the tomato puree …* so that it becomes the last sentence in the first paragraph.

7. Left align the date.

8. Change to landscape orientation.

9. Amend the first paragraph line spacing so that it is 1.5 spacing.

10. Save this file as a new version with the name `Recipe amended` in the *Cooking* folder.

11. Print one copy of the file.

12. Close the file.

Answer

date

ONE POT WONDER
(Serves 2 – 3)

4 lamb chops
15 ml tomato puree
700 g peeled and diced carrots, potatoes and swedes
pinch of dried oregano

Preheat the oven to gas mark 7. Tip vegetables into a shallow ovenproof dish and arrange the lamb chops on top. Mix the tomato puree with a cupful of hot water and pour over the chops and vegetables.

Sprinkle over the herbs, season then roast in the oven. You may need to add extra water if the liquid appears to be drying up.

Continue cooking for another 20 minutes.

Edit and replace

Word offers a number of features that make it easier to amend long documents. One of these is the option to replace a repeated entry with another word or phrase. This is particularly useful if you find you have spelt a name wrongly throughout your work, or you want to replace every instance of an abbreviation with the full version of the term.

To replace a repeated word with an alternative, open the **Edit** menu and click **Replace**, or click **Find** and then select the **Replace** tab.

In the *Find and Replace* box, type the original word in the *Find what:* box and the replacement word in the *Replace with:* box. Click **More** to select more detailed options such as searching for words that match upper or lower case letters exactly, or changing the direction of the search.

Original text New text

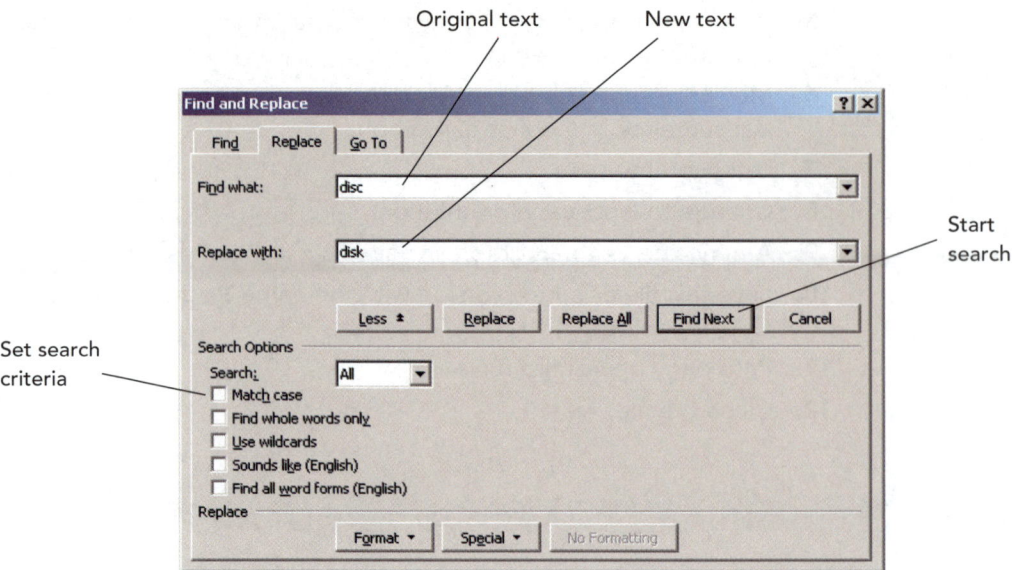

Set search criteria

Start search

If you are sure you want to replace every occurrence of the original word, clicking **Replace All** will do just that throughout the document. To check one by one, click **Find Next** to locate the first entry and then click **Replace** after confirming that it is the correct word. (Mistakes happen when the replacement is *part* of another word and you don't tick *Find whole words only*.)

Keep clicking **Replace**, or skip a word by clicking **Find Next**.

Common mistake	Common mistake
Clicking Replace All when there is an error in the replacement word.	Not using the Edit/Replace menu so that, when replacing manually, one or more words are missed or amended incorrectly.

✓ Exercise 10

1. Start a new document and enter the following text.

   `Spring Colour`

   `Colour in the spring garden comes in waves, as carpets of bulbs — mostly crocus and narcissi — roll like breakers across lawns and up to the tide edge of the border.`

   `You can start the colour wave ahead of time in winter and make it last even longer by using the new range of winter-flowering roses developed over the past couple of years. In borders and woodlands the lengthy flowering times of some roses even overlap that of spring's earliest harbinger, the snowdrop.`

   `The newest roses come in strong, clear shades and range from the millennium colours of purple-black and silvery grey through to citrus yellow and ice-cream white.`

2. Proofread and correct any errors before saving as `Winter flowers`.

3. Print one copy.

4. Increase the left margin of the page by 1.5 cm and double space the first paragraph.

5. Format the heading to font size 16, centred and underlined.

6. Format the main text to Arial, font size 14, italic fully justified.

7. Replace every mention of *roses* with *hellebores*. (3 times)

8. Add your name at the end of the text and format to bold, size 11 in Times New Roman.

9. Move the sentence in paragraph 2 beginning: *In borders and woodlands ...* so that it becomes the last sentence of the final paragraph.

10. Save and close the file.

Answer

<u>Spring Colour</u>

Colour in the spring garden comes in waves, as carpets of bulbs – mostly crocus and narcissi – roll like breakers across lawns and up to the tide edge of the border.

You can start the colour wave ahead of time in winter and make it last even longer by using the new range of winter-flowering hellebores developed over the past couple of years.

The newest hellebores come in strong, clear shades and range from the millennium colours of purple-black and silvery grey through to citrus yellow and ice-cream white. In borders and woodlands the lengthy flowering times of some hellebores even overlaps that of spring's earliest harbinger, the snowdrop.

My name

Tables

You can create tables in Word that will allow you to set out your data in neat columns and rows. These can be displayed with or without visible borders or gridlines.

To add a table, click in place on the page and then click the **Insert Table** button on the toolbar. Click and drag across the squares (cells) to set how many columns and rows you want for your table. When you let go the mouse, the table will appear.

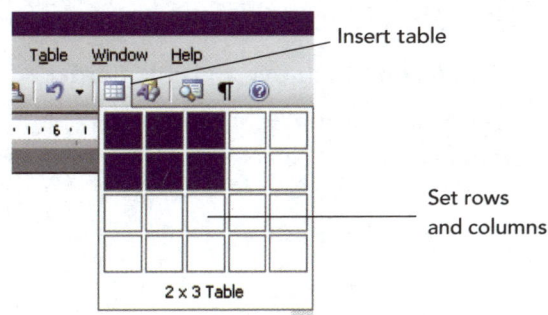

Insert table

Set rows and columns

2 x 3 Table

An alternative is to open the **Table** menu and select **Insert**/**Table**. Type in the number of columns and rows and click **OK**.

You can now start entering your data, moving from cell to cell by clicking with the mouse or pressing the **Tab** key (the key to the left of **Q** showing two arrows). For any cell entry, or entire column or row, select it with the mouse and format as normal. To select the whole table, click the small square showing four arrows in the top left-hand corner of the table.

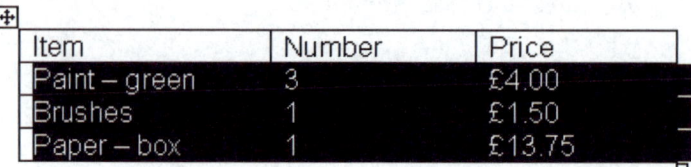

Displaying all data

To widen any column, for example if entries are too long to be displayed in full on one line, position the pointer over a right-hand column boundary. When the pointer shows a two-way arrow, gently click and drag the border to the right with the mouse. It will show as a dotted line. Either click within the table or select the grey column edge in the ruler area under the toolbars at the top of the screen.

Drag column boundary

Borders

To border a table or block of text, select your entry and then choose an option such as **Box** or **Shadow** from the **Format**/**Borders and Shading** menu. Choose different styles or widths of border, or apply a coloured border by selecting from the palette. If you want to restrict the border to any part of the selection, click the appropriate button in the *Preview* window.

Click **None** to remove a visible border.

To fill any selected table cells with colour or shades of grey, click the **Shading** tab and select from the colours available.

Remove all borders

Shade table cells

Limit where border appears

Headers and footers

To add entries at the top or bottom of each page of a document without affecting the main layout, enter them as a header or footer.

1. Open the **View** menu and select **Header and Footer** to display the *Header* box. Type an entry where the cursor is flashing and move across the box with the **Tab** key or mouse for other entries.

2. To insert an automatic page number or date, click the appropriate toolbar button. There are various options you can add from the *Insert AutoText* box, including the file name on its own or the file name and folder pathway.

3. Switch to the footer for entries at the bottom of the page, or click the **Close** button to return to your document. You can also double-click the document text or header/footer entry to return to that view.

Common mistake

Confusing the header with the footer and vice versa.

Common mistake

Displaying the wrong file name because the file was saved incorrectly.

Common mistake

Not checking the date format and displaying an American-style date, e.g. 3/21/06 instead of 21/3/06.

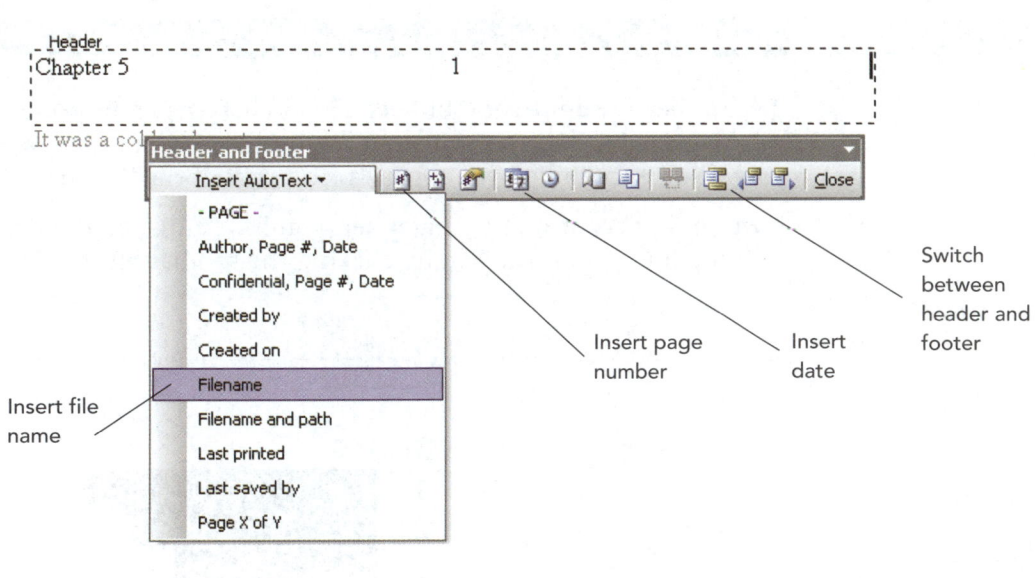

Insert file name

Insert page number

Insert date

Switch between header and footer

1. Start a new document and save as `Visits`.
2. Type the heading: `Programme of Visits` and format to Arial font size 14.
3. Leave a clear line space and then create a table with two columns and four rows.
4. Enter the following data:

MONTH	VISITS
April	Eden project
June	Rose gardens
August	Brighton

5. Centre the heading and data in the right-hand column only.
6. Format the column headings to bold.
7. Add a page footer that contains the page number and file name.
8. Print a copy of the document, making sure the table borders are visible on the printout.
9. Save and close the file.

✓ Answer

Programme of Visits

MONTH	VISITS
April	Eden project
June	Rose gardens
August	Brighton

Visits   1

Bullets and numbering

To number a list or to add bullets, either click the appropriate button first or select the list and then click on the button. Every time you press **Enter**, a new number or bullet will appear at the start of the list entry.

Turn off bullets or numbering when you have finished the list, or for a selected line within the list, by clicking the toolbar button off.

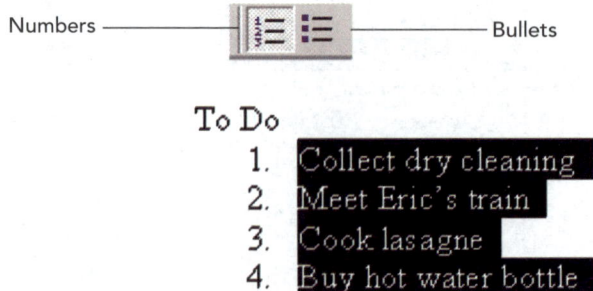

Numbers ——— [icons] ——— Bullets

To Do
1. Collect dry cleaning
2. Meet Eric's train
3. Cook lasagne
4. Buy hot water bottle

Indents

To move a block of text in from one of the margins, you can set an *indent*. Select a paragraph or number of paragraphs and then click the **Increase Indent** button on the toolbar to move the text in from the left margin by 0.5" (1.27 cm). Keep clicking the button to move it in steps of this amount, or click the **Decrease Indent** button to reverse the indentation.

Decrease indent ——————  —————— Increase indent

For an exact indent, or to indent text from the right-hand margin, open the **Format** menu, select **Paragraph** and change measurements in the *Left* or *Right indentation* boxes. *Special*: indents are also available, including indenting just the first line of a paragraph (*First line* indent) or all lines except the first (*Hanging*).

Change measure

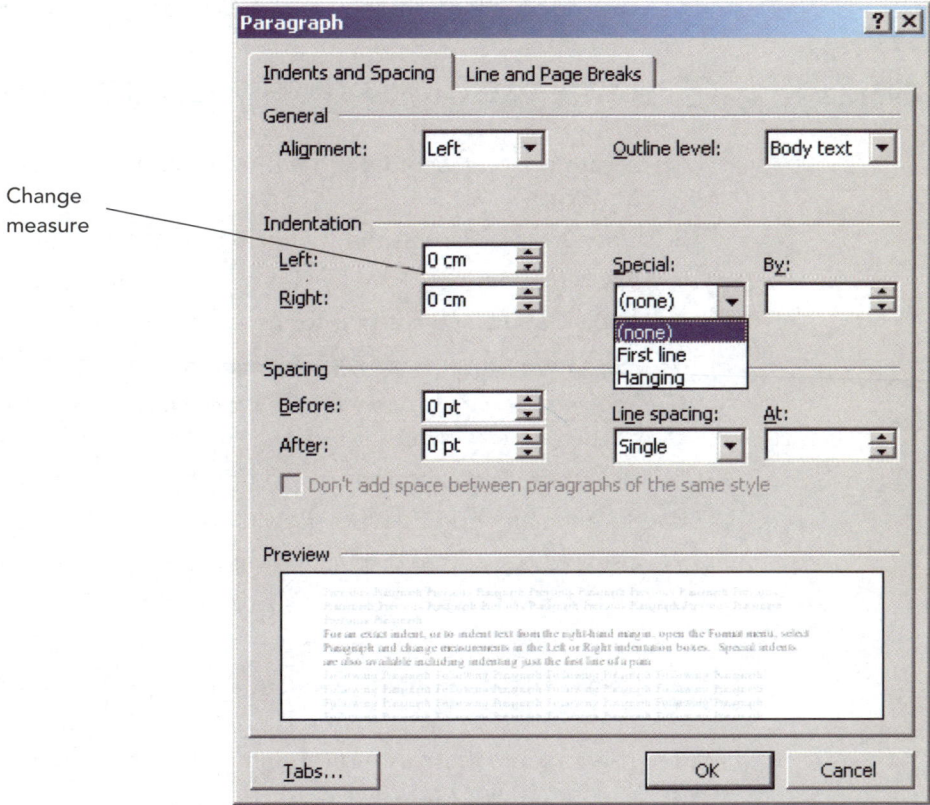

Word count

To count the number of words in a document or selected block of text, open the **Tools** menu and click the **Word Count** option. It will show the number of words as well as the number of pages, paragraphs, characters and lines.

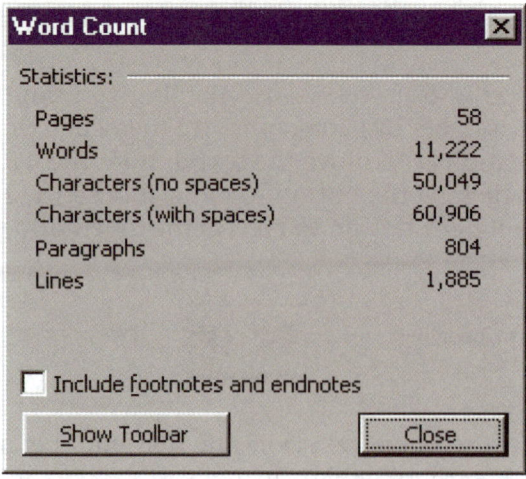

Common mistake

Rechecking the word count before printing, and amending the total figure by mistake. You will be adding in the actual figure you typed as an extra 'word'.

Exercise 12

1. Locate the *Maths* folder (from the CD) and create a subfolder inside it named `At Home`.

2. Open the file *Parents* that is inside the *Maths* folder.

3. Apply numbering to the five list items beginning *You …*

4. Apply double line spacing to the list items only.

5. Indent the sentence beginning: *Helping your child …* from the left margin.

6. Replace the word *child* with the word *children* wherever it occurs in the document (six times).

7. Delete the final *s* from the word *becomes* in list item four.

8. Save the amended document with the name `Helping` in the folder *At Home*.

9. Insert a header that displays the file name and page number.

10. Format the title to bold, font size 14 and centre it on the page.

11. Fully justify the last paragraph.

12. Create a new paragraph and leave a clear line space after the words *children's skills*.

13. Insert a table that has three columns and three rows.

14. Enter the following data:

Age range	In the home	Outside
4 — 8	Sorting shoes	Sort washing
7 — 11	Which way up — predicting	Fly aeroplanes

15. Format the column headings to italic.

16. Centre the age ranges: *4-8* and *7–11* but not the column heading *Age range*.

17. Use the word count facility to count the number of words in the document and enter this figure below the table.

18. Update the document to save these changes.

19. Print a copy and then close the file.

✓ **Answer**

How to Help Your Children with Maths

Helping your children with maths can bring a number of lasting benefits:
1. You learn more about your children

2. You find that talking about school and school work becomes more natural

3. You encourage your children to ask questions

4. Your children become more mathematically aware

5. You reinforce a positive attitude to learning

Maths is all around and using examples from your home or when taking part in outside activities can be fun and a very inexpensive way to develop your children's skills.

Age range	In the home	Outside
4 - 8	Sorting shoes	Sort washing
7 - 11	Which way up - predicting	Fly aeroplanes

115

Using Help

If you forget how to carry out a task, you can always make use of the on-screen help that is available from the *Help* menu:

Click **Help/Microsoft Office Word Help** or press the function key **F1** at the top of the keyboard to open the *Task* pane.

Type a topic into the search box and click the **Start searching** Button.

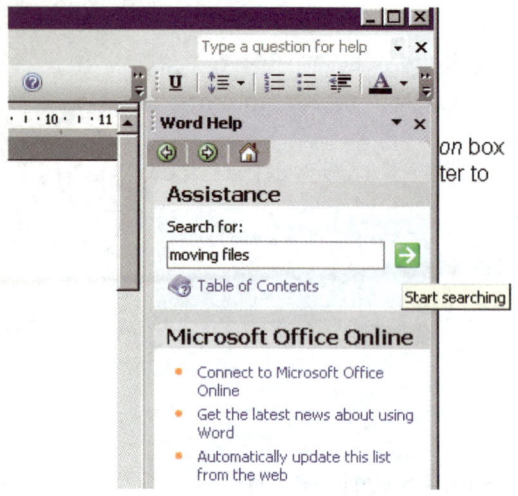

You can also use the *Table of Contents* link to display a menu of main Word topics. For any topic, click the book symbol to display options and click the appropriate heading to see detailed guidance in a new window.

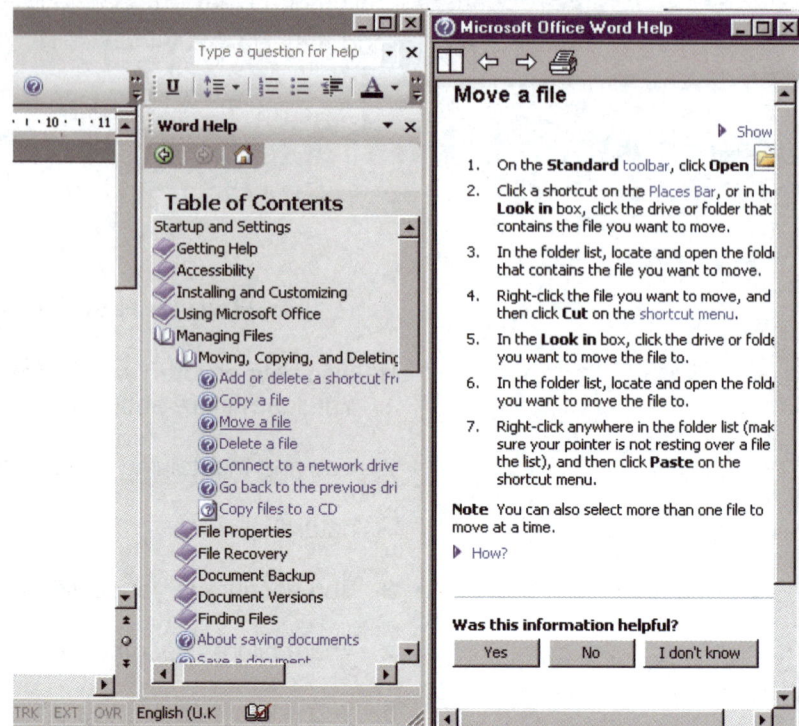

You can also type a phrase or question into the on-screen *Ask a Question* box situated in the top right-hand corner of the document window. Press **Enter** to display links to relevant help options when you have entered a word or question.

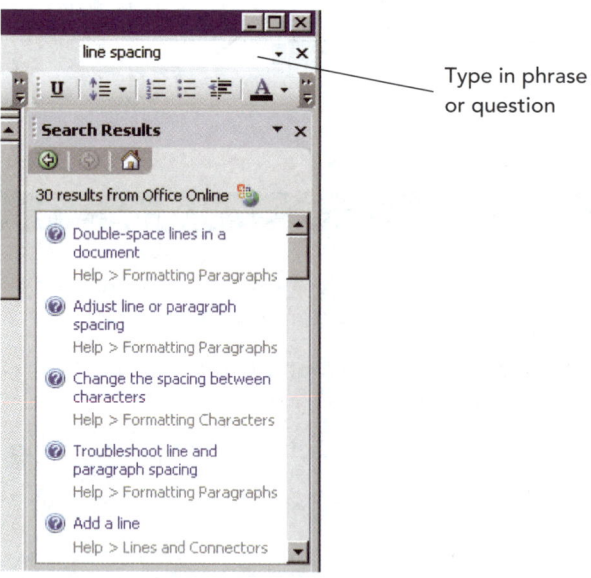

Type in phrase or question

Exiting the application

To exit Word, click the top **Close** button in the top right-hand corner of the screen or go to **File/Exit**.

Shutting down procedures

After any session on the computer, it is important to follow a proper shutdown procedure rather than simply switch off the power. This is to allow the computer time to sort out any temporary files or unsaved work that has been created. Otherwise, next time you switch on you will have to wait for the computer to do this before you can start work.

If you are working in an organization that keeps the machines switched on, you still need to log off so that your private area cannot be accessed by the next user.

Open the **Start** menu and select either **Log off** or **Turn Off Computer**. If shutting down, select **Turn off** in the window. On modern machines, the computer should switch off automatically but in some cases you may be told that it is now safe to turn off the power.

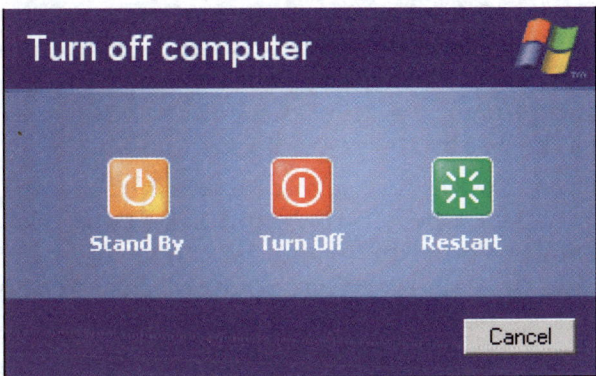

Exercise 13 – A full assignment

Task 1

1. Log in using your username and/or password.
2. Locate and rename the folder *buildings* (from the CD) as `repairs`.
3. In this folder, create a new subfolder called `household`.
4. Copy the text file provided called *plants* to the folder *household.*
5. Move the text file provided called *waste* from the folder *property* into the folder *household.*
6. Delete the folder *property* and its contents.
7. Take a screen print as evidence of the folder called *repairs* and the contents of this folder.
8. Take a screen print of the subfolder called *household* and the contents of this folder.
9. In the footer of the page(s) displaying the screen prints, enter `your name` and the `automatic date`.
10. Save the screen print(s) within your filing structure.
11. Print the file(s) containing the screen prints. Make sure that all the contents of the folder and the subfolder are clearly visible on the print(s).
12. Close any open files.

1. Create a new word processing document.
2. Set the page orientation to *landscape*.
3. Set the top, left and right page margins to 2.8 cm.
4. Set the font to an Eras or Arial font type.
5. Set the font size to 12.
6. Enter the following text in single line spacing.
7. Make sure that the text is fully justified.

SEE-RIGHT-THRU DOUBLE GLAZING

Few people are experts in double glazing, so if you are looking to improve your home with PVC-U windows, doors or a conservatory — and don't fancy entrusting such a major renovation to a possible cowboy — use us. One call to See-Right-Thru and you will be in touch with a nationwide network of approved, fully trained installers who are monitored regularly by a team of inspectors. We use only the best materials, and there is a free 20-year guarantee.

See-Right-Thru conservatories have built an enviable reputation, based upon our high level of commitment in award winning design, manufacture and installation. Our guarantee covers the products themselves, the actual installation and all workmanship involved.

8. Check the file for any errors and carry out a spellcheck.
9. In the header, enter your **name** and **page number**.
10. In the footer, insert an **automatic date** and an **automatic file name**.
11. Save the file using the file name **windows** in the subfolder called *repairs*.
12. Close the file.

Task 3

1. Open your saved file called *windows*.
2. A table needs to be inserted at the end of the document.
3. Insert a paragraph break and a clear line space at the end of the final paragraph immediately after the text ending: *workmanship involved*.
4. Create a table with two columns and four rows.
5. Enter the data below in the table:

Wood	Extra cost
Mahogany	£20 sq.m
Pine	£5 sq.m
Oak	£15 sq.m

6. Make sure all borders will be displayed for the table on the printout.
7. Make sure all data in the table is fully displayed.
8. Format the headings *Wood* and *Extra cost* to be bold.
9. Right align only the heading *Extra cost*.
10. The remaining entries must be left aligned.
11. Save your file keeping the file name *windows*.
12. Print one copy of the file.
13. Close the file called *windows*.

Task 4

1. You will need to make the amendments below in a file that has been provided for you.
2. Open the file called *gardens* that is in your folder called *repairs*.
3. Save the file using the new file name **outdoors** in your folder called *household*.
4. Go to the paragraph that starts: *The ideal is a walled garden*.
5. Insert the following text as a new sentence after *amazing plants*:

   `Many varieties come as dwarf plants that are easier to support, and others have been bred for their hardiness.`

6. Go to the paragraph that starts *Kitchen gardens*.
7. Delete the text: *and saving money*.
8. In the paragraph that starts *Kitchen gardens* move the text: *Kitchen gardens are a great source of joy* to become the first sentence of the first paragraph.
9. Apply a bullet character to the following lines of text:

   Salads
   Root vegetables
   Beans and peas
   Fruit
   Brassicas – cabbage family plants

10. Apply double line spacing to the bulleted text only.
11. Indent the text: *So what are the best plants for new kitchen gardeners to grow?* from the left margin.
12. Replace the word *vegetables* with the word **veg** wherever it occurs (three times in all).
13. In the footer enter: `your name` and an `automatic file name`.
14. Check your text for accuracy.
15. Using the software facilities, carry out a word count on the file.
16. Enter the number of words on your printout at least two lines below the bulleted list. You may use any alignment for this.
17. Save the file keeping the file name *outdoors*.
18. Print one copy of the file *outdoors*.
19. Close all files and folders.

Task 1 Step 7

Task 1 Step 8

Task 3 Step 12

My name   1

SEE-RIGHT-THRU DOUBLE GLAZING

Few people are experts in double glazing, so if you are looking to improve your home with PVC-U windows, doors or a conservatory – and don't fancy entrusting such a major renovation to a possible cowboy – use us. One call to See-Right-Thru and you will be in touch with a nationwide network of approved, fully trained installers who are monitored regularly by a team of inspectors. We use only the best materials, and there is a free 20-year guarantee.

See-Right-Thru conservatories have built an enviable reputation, based upon our high level of commitment in award winning design, manufacture and installation. Our guarantee covers the products themselves, the actual installation and all workmanship involved.

Wood	Extra cost
Mahogany	£20 sq.m
Pine	£5 sq.m
Oak	£15 sq.m

Task 4 Step 18

KITCHEN GARDENS

Kitchen gardens are a great source of joy. Over the last two decades we have become aware of a vast number of new fruits and veg and we are also finding exotic plants in supermarkets. We have therefore become far more ambitious when it comes to growing our own food.

Not only are you out in the fresh air and getting exercise, you are providing healthy food for your family. All these are surely great incentives for anyone worried about their health or purse and not yet convinced about starting to grow fruit and veg.

The ideal is a walled garden. You not only shelter your plants but you have a wonderful support for climbing plants or espalier fruit trees. But even with a small plot or windswept area you can still grow amazing plants. Many varieties come as dwarf plants that are easier to support, and others have been bred for their hardiness. Just find the right plant that will thrive in your environment and on your particular soil.

So what are the best plants for new kitchen gardeners to grow?
- Salads
- Root veg
- Beans and peas
- Fruit
- Brassicas – cabbage family plants

200

Self-assessment checklist

I feel confident that I can now: ✓

Log in using a username and password

Create and name folders and subfolders

Delete files and folders

Move or copy files into folders

Save files into named folders

Rename files and folders

Understand the use of word processing software

Start a new document

Enter text

Delete text

Insert and create new paragraphs

Select and format text

Proofread and use the spell and grammar checker

Set page orientation

Insert headers and footers

Insert and border tables

Create numbered and bulleted lists

Carry out a word count

Set margins

Amend line spacing

Move text to a new position

Use Edit/Replace to amend entries

Save a document

Save a new version of a document

Print a document

Close a document

Exit the application

Summary of critical errors

- Failure to delete specified files or folders
- Failure to move specified text
- Failure to delete specified text
- Failure to replace specified text

unit

2

Creating spreadsheets and graphs

- What are spreadsheets? 55
- Opening Excel 56
  Cells 57
  Cell addresses 57
- Entering and amending text 57
- Entering numbers 58
- Creating a new file 58
- Saving a spreadsheet 58
- Closing a spreadsheet 59
- Formatting text 60
- Formatting numbers 60
  Percent style 61
- Widening columns 61
- Cell alignment 62
- Opening a saved spreadsheet 63
- Printing a spreadsheet 64
  Orientation and margins 65
  Borders and shading 66
  Gridlines and headings 66
- Formulae 67
- Functions 68
  Totals 68
  Averages 68
- Copying (replicating) formulae 70

- Inserting columns/rows 71
- Deleting columns/rows 72
- Printing formulae 73
- Headers and footers 73
- Charts 75
  Chart types 75
  Chart elements 76
- Opening a data file 77
- Creating a chart 77
  Selecting data 77
  Using the Chart Wizard 77
  Using the keyboard 80
  Changing chart type 80
  Adding titles 80
- Closing a chart 81
- Opening an existing chart 82
- Selected charts 82
  Moving a chart 82
  Resizing a chart 82
  Deleting a chart 82
- Formatting a chart 82
  Titles 83
  Legends 85
- Printing charts 85
  Black and white charts 85

■ Comparative charts 86
■ Print preview 86
  Line graphs 86
■ Scaling charts 89
■ Exiting Excel 90
■ Self-assessment checklist 93
■ Summary of critical errors 94

What are spreadsheets?

Spreadsheets are used to display financial or mathematical information clearly and accurately. Applications such as Microsoft Excel allow you to handle vast amounts of numerical data, perform complex calculations automatically and present the results in grid format. They are ideal for anyone who doesn't feel very confident with figures. Once a single calculation has been performed, Excel even offers facilities to copy instructions across the spreadsheet and update values as soon as any of the figures are changed.

Sometimes, data in a spreadsheet can be understood more clearly if presented in chart or graph form. Charting applications such as Microsoft Excel allow you to produce different types of chart including column, bar and pie charts as well as line and scatter graphs based on data in a spreadsheet. The charts can be two or three dimensional, and the elements such as titles, lines and axes can be formatted in different ways.

You will be asked to carry out the following tasks:

- Open a spreadsheet application
- Enter data and create a spreadsheet
- Set page orientation
- Create headers or footers
- Save a spreadsheet
- Insert formulae to add, subtract, multiply or divide figures
- Use functions to total or average cell contents
- Copy (replicate) formulae down columns or along rows
- Insert a new column or row
- Display data in full
- Print a copy of a spreadsheet
- Delete a complete column or row
- Amend cell contents
- Update formulae to reflect changes
- Realign cell contents
- Format numerical data
- Border cells
- Save a new version of a spreadsheet
- Print a spreadsheet showing formulae
- Print a spreadsheet showing gridlines and row and column headings
- Close a spreadsheet
- Open a new workbook
- Select specific data
- Create pie, column or bar charts on a separate sheet
- Create line graphs
- Create comparative charts or graphs
- Add specific chart and axes titles
- Add or remove legends
- Format comparative data so that it is distinguished

- Label pie chart sectors or data points
- Set the scale of a chart or graph
- Insert headers or footers into charts
- Print a copy of a chart or graph
- Save an amended file with a different name
- Close data files
- Exit the application

To pass Unit 2, you must be able to:

- Select and use appropriate software to create a spreadsheet
- Insert and amend text and numerical data
- Set page orientation
- Format and align data
- Widen columns to display entries in full
- Insert and delete columns and rows
- Use formulae and functions to perform calculations
- Replicate (copy) formulae down columns and along rows
- Recalculate results if data is amended
- Save and print spreadsheets
- Show borders, gridlines and row and column headings
- Print a spreadsheet to display the underlying formulae
- Understand the different chart types
- Open a data file
- Create pie charts, column or bar charts and line graphs
- Create charts on a separate sheet
- Base charts on single or comparative sets of data
- Add and format titles, labels and legends
- Deleted unwanted elements such as legends
- Rescale an axis to amend upper and lower limits
- Format chart elements so that comparative data is clearly distinguished
- Add data labels
- Insert headers or footers
- Print charts
- Save charts
- Close files
- Exit the application

Opening Excel

Double-click the **Excel** icon ▨ or open Microsoft Excel from the **Start/All Programs** menu.

Cells

The screen will display a grid of squares known as *cells*. One square will have a black border, and this is known as the *active cell*. To activate another cell do one of the following:

- Click it with the mouse.
- Move to the right by pressing the **Tab** key.
- Move down a column by pressing **Enter**.
- Move in any direction using the **arrow** (cursor) keys.

Cell addresses

Spreadsheets contain information that is organized in *columns* (labelled A–Z, AA, AB ... IU, IV) and *rows* (labelled 1–600+). The address of any cell is given by its column letter and row number – e.g. A1 or B3 – and the address of the active cell will be visible in the *Name box*.

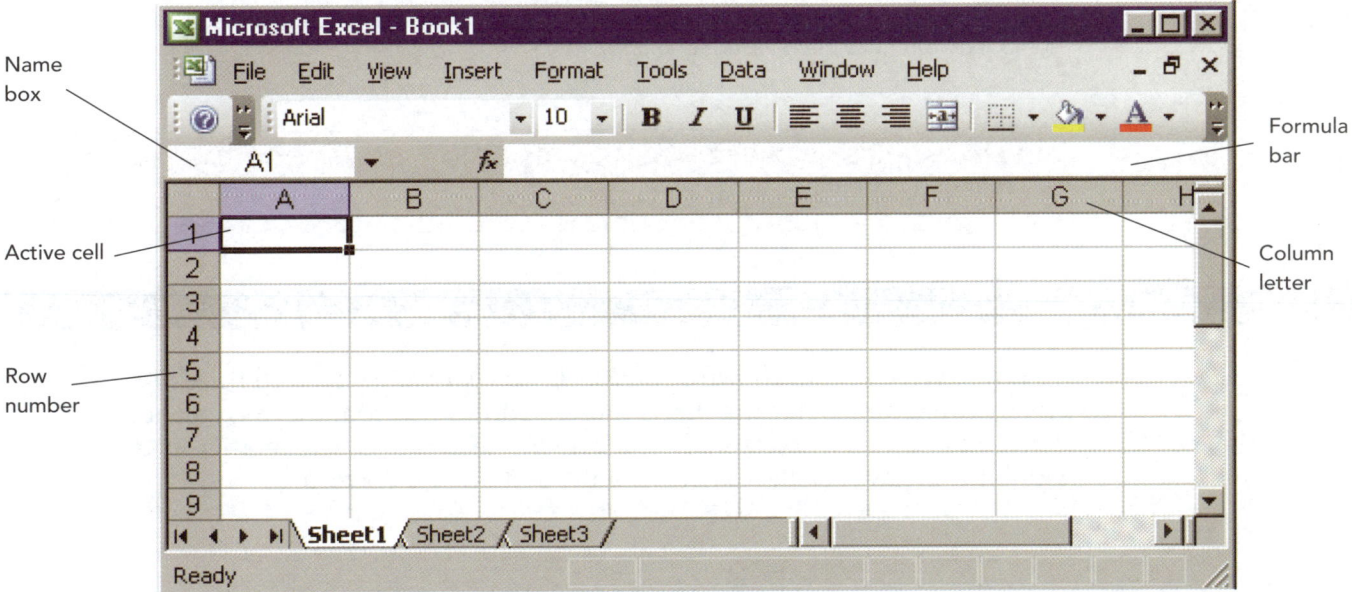

Entering and amending text

When you start typing, entries will appear in the active cell and also in the window above – the *Formula bar*. To amend an entry, either double-click the cell to place the cursor inside that cell, or click in the *Formula bar* and make changes there. Press **Enter** or click the tick to accept the amendments.

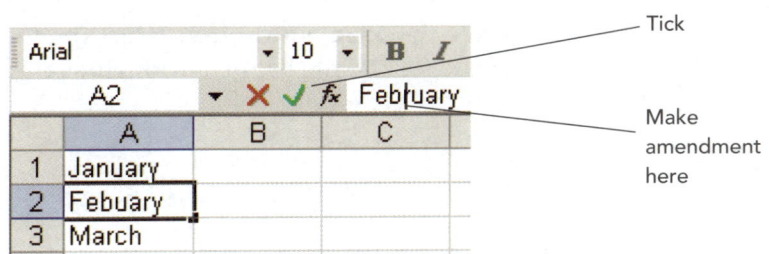

Entering numbers

As you type into a cell, you will see that numerical data are automatically positioned on the right of the cell, whereas text appears on the left.

Calculations are performed within the spreadsheet once the correct instruction – the formula – has been entered. Calculations only work with numerical data, and so, apart from dates, text is not normally included in cells where calculations will be performed.

NO ERRORS ARE ALLOWED WHEN ENTERING OR AMENDING NUMERICAL DATA – ONE MISTAKE IS A CRITICAL ERROR.

Creating a new file

Microsoft Excel files are known as *workbooks*. They usually start with three sheets per file, although extra sheets can be added easily from the *Insert* menu. When creating a new spreadsheet that contains related data, use another sheet within the file by clicking a *Sheet tab* at the bottom of the screen.

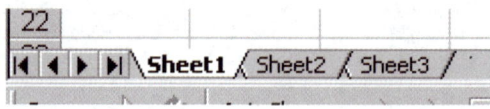

For unrelated data, start a new workbook by clicking the **New** toolbar button 🗋.

Saving a spreadsheet

Click the **Save** button 💾, select the location in the *Save in*: box and type a name for the file before clicking **Save**. All the sheets in a workbook will be saved together.

To update changes as you work, regularly click the **Save** button.

To save a new version of the spreadsheet, go to **File/Save As** and select a new location or rename the file before clicking **Save**.

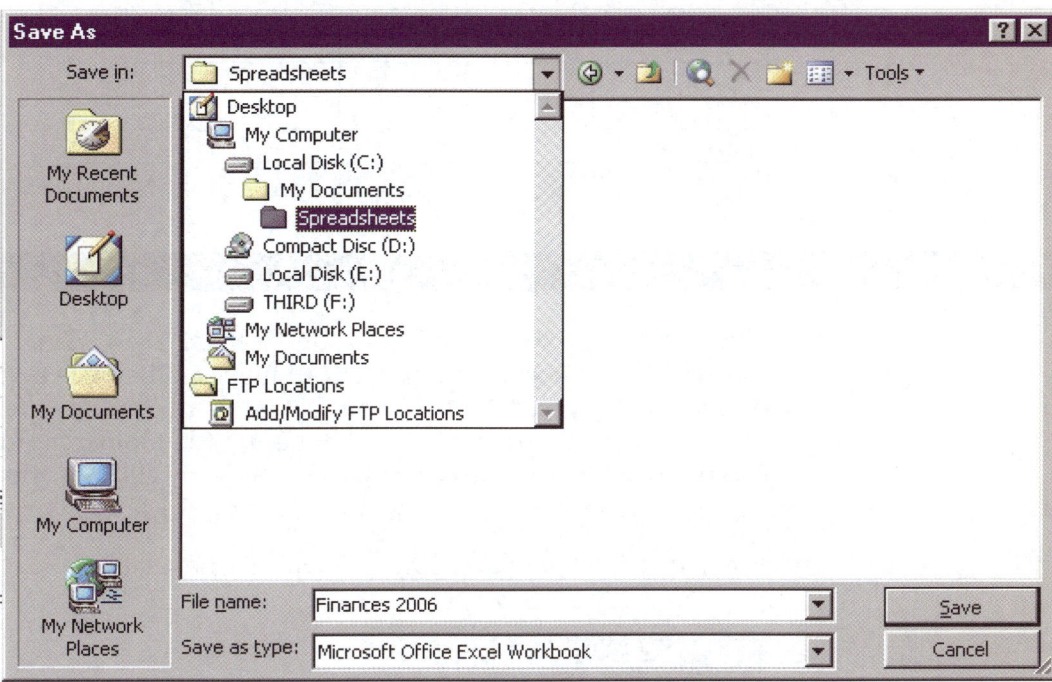

Closing a spreadsheet

Click the lower **Close** button ⊠ in the top right-hand corner of the screen, or go to **File/Close**. If you click the upper **Close** button, you will exit Excel.

Exercise 1

1. Start a new workbook and create the following spreadsheet:
2. Save the file as **Exams**.

EXAMS				
	Science	Maths	English	Book Token
Johnson	22.5	9	44	2
Miller	20	9.5	48.5	5
Smith	14.5	10.3	40	2
Baker	28	6.8	37.8	1.5
Hart	19.3	8	32	1

3. Make the following changes: *Johnson* should be spelt **Jonson**; *Baker* gained **8.5** marks in maths; and *Hart* was absent for English so his score was **0**.
4. Update the file to save the changes.
5. Close *Exams*.

	A	B	C	D	E
1	EXAMS				
2		Science	Maths	English	Book Token
3	Jonson	22.5	9	44	2
4	Miller	20	9.5	48.5	5
5	Smith	14.5	10.3	40	2
6	Baker	28	8.5	37.8	1.5
7	Hart	19.3	8	0	1

Formatting text

Although there is little requirement in New CLAIT to change the look of text entries on your spreadsheet, it can make a difference to the attractiveness or readability of your data if you do apply different formats. Change the look of text in any cell by using the toolbar buttons or the **Format** menu. Click one cell or select a range by clicking and dragging the pointer across the cells when it shows a white cross ✛.

The first cell will remain white, but will still be selected.

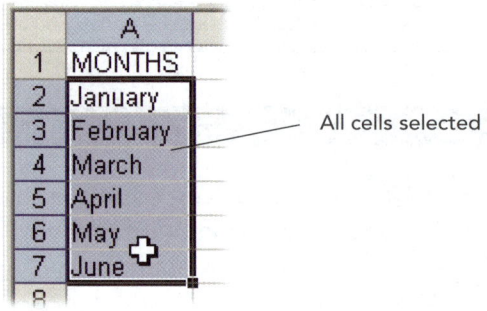

All cells selected

Now use the toolbar shortcuts to change the font type and size and to emphasize with bold, italic or underline. You can apply a wider range of formats by right-clicking or opening the **Format/Cells** menu and selecting **Font**. (Find full details of how to format text in Unit 1.)

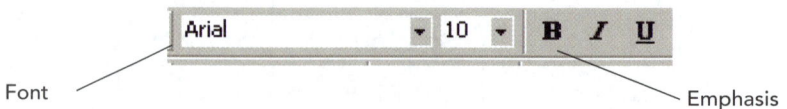

Font — Emphasis

Formatting numbers

To alter the look of numbers but not their underlying value, apply number formats by selecting the cell(s) and going to **Format/Cells/Number**. Before formatting, a general format will have been applied automatically, so click **Number** in the category list if you want to change only the display of decimals. Other options include *Currency* and *Date*.

Numbers showing no decimal places – whole numbers – are referred to as *integers*. You can select a specific number of decimal places to be displayed, the £ sign for currency, comma separators for large numbers and the style of dates and times by choosing the appropriate category and then clicking the relevant checkboxes.

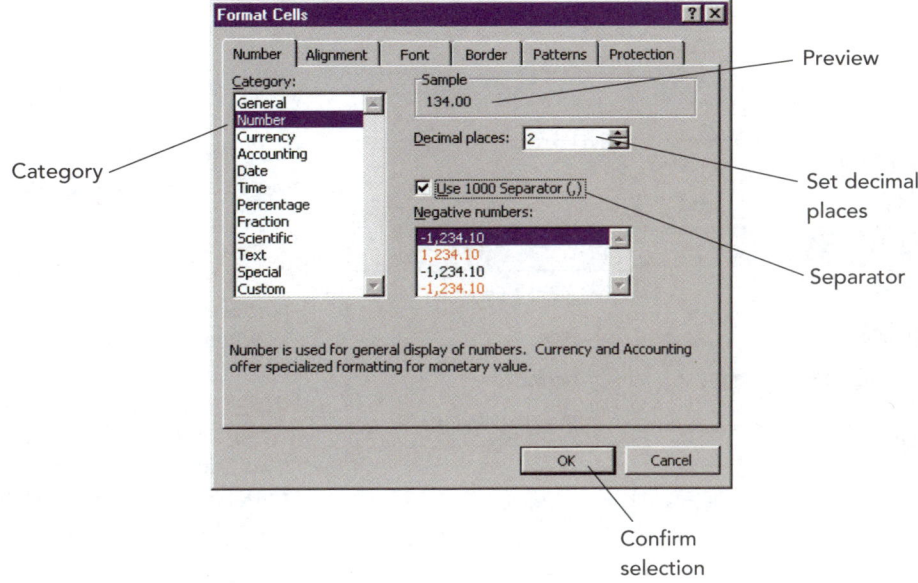

Category

Preview

Set decimal places

Separator

Confirm selection

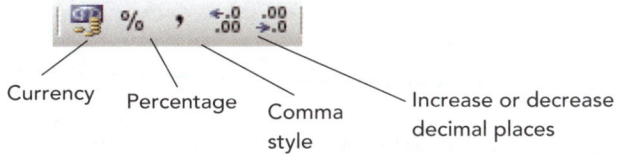

Currency

Percentage

Comma style

Increase or decrease decimal places

Shortcuts to several number formats are also available from the toolbar.

Percent style

Take care with this format. It is used to display decimals as a percentage – the computer multiplies by 100 to give the percentage, so 0.25 will become 25%. If you type 40 and then format to percent style, it will display as 4000%. For whole-number percentages, enter the symbol from the keyboard.

Common mistake

Forgetting to apply a specified format to a range of cells, or applying the wrong format.

Widening columns

To widen a column and display all the entries in full, move the mouse pointer up to the lettered grey area at the top of the column. Position the pointer over the vertical line that separates the column from its right-hand neighbour and the pointer will change to a two-way arrow. Double-click to widen the column to fit the longest entry. Or click and hold down the mouse button, and then drag the boundary of the column to a new width. The exact measure will be displayed.

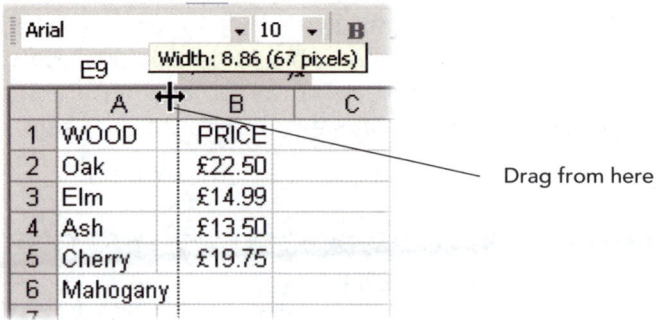

Drag from here

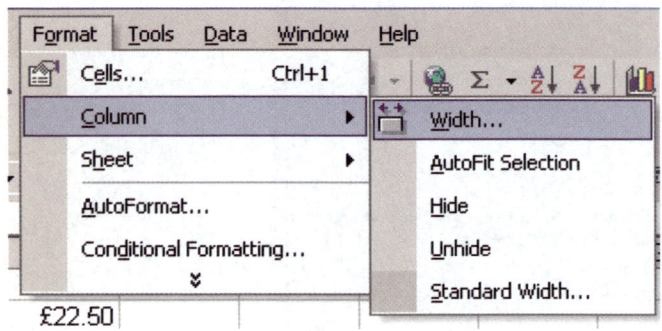

£22.50

For other width options, select a cell and open the **Format/Column** menu.

Common mistake

Not widening columns to ensure that entries such as headings are displayed fully.

Common mistake

If you don't first complete a cell entry (e.g. by pressing Enter or clicking another cell) you will find that the menus are not available to use.

Common mistake

There should be one complete entry per cell. Even if it appears in the assignment that headings are spread over more than one row, enter all the heading text in one cell and widen the column to display it fully.

FAILURE TO DISPLAY ALL NUMERICAL DATA IN FULL IS A CRITICAL ERROR.

Cell alignment

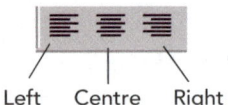

Left   Centre   Right

Text is set by default on the left of the cell – i.e. left aligned – and numbers are set on the right. To change these alignments – e.g. to position headings above columns of figures – select the cell(s) and then use the alignment buttons on the toolbar.

Common mistake

Missing out this instruction and not realigning one or more column headings.

1. Start a new spreadsheet and enter the title: SHOES
2. Now add the following data:

SHOES			
NAME	COLOUR	PRICE	IN STOCK
DAISY	PINK	38.5	10
LADY EMMA	RED	44.75	4
SLINGBACK	GREEN	28	26
SHELL SANDAL	WHITE	26.5	14
FLATTIES	BLACK	19.99	8

3. Widen all the columns to display the data in full.
4. Format the title to italic, Times New Roman font size 18.
5. Format the column headings to bold, font size 14.
6. Right align all column headings except *NAME*.
7. Format the *PRICE* column entries to currency and two decimal places.
8. Centre align all entries in the *COLOUR* column.
9. Make sure all the data are still fully displayed.
10. Save the amended spreadsheet and close the file.

Answer

SHOES			
NAME	**COLOUR**	**PRICE**	**IN STOCK**
DAISY	PINK	£38.50	10
LADY EMMA	RED	£44.75	4
SLINGBACK	GREEN	£28.00	26
SHELL SANDAL	WHITE	£26.50	14
FLATTIES	BLACK	£19.99	8

Opening a saved spreadsheet

To open a file saved previously, click the **Open** toolbar button and ensure that the correct location is showing in the *Look in:* box. When you can see the file listed in the window, select it and then click **Open** or press **Enter**.

Folder the file is
stored in

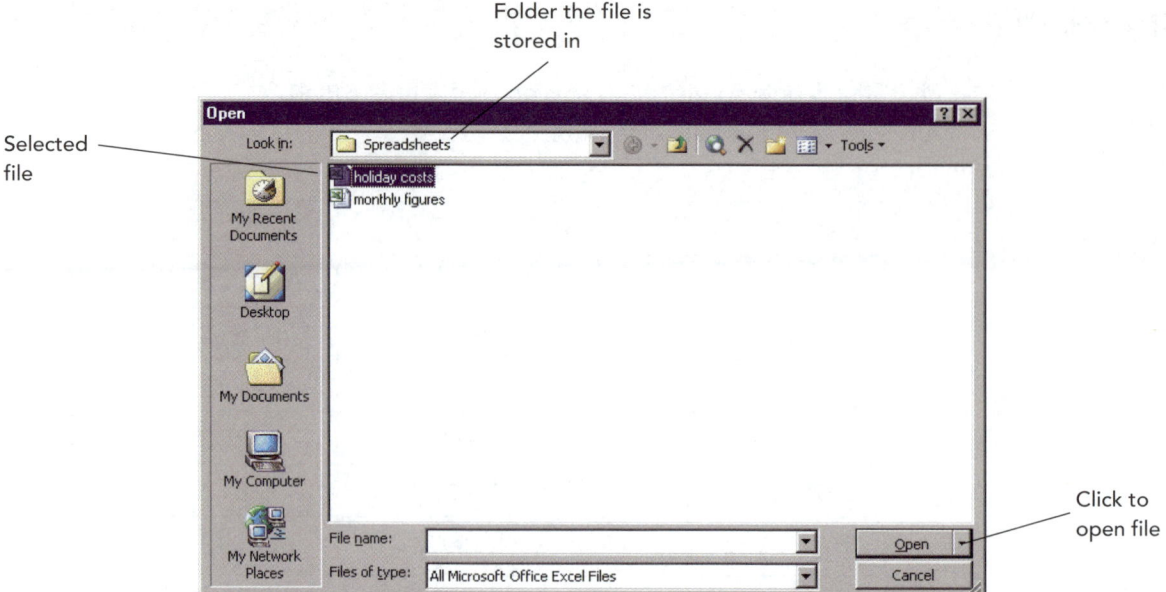

Selected
file

Click to
open file

Printing a spreadsheet

Click the **Print** button 🖨 to print one copy of your work. For other
options, such as printing several copies, select **File/Print** to open the *Print*
dialogue box.

Change any measures in the *Copies* box and select **Entire workbook** if you
want more than one sheet to print at a time. To print selected columns,
highlight them and then click **Selection** in the *Print what* box.

Whenever you print, it is a good idea to click the **Preview** button first, just
to see what the printout will look like. Either print from here or close this
view to return to the spreadsheet.

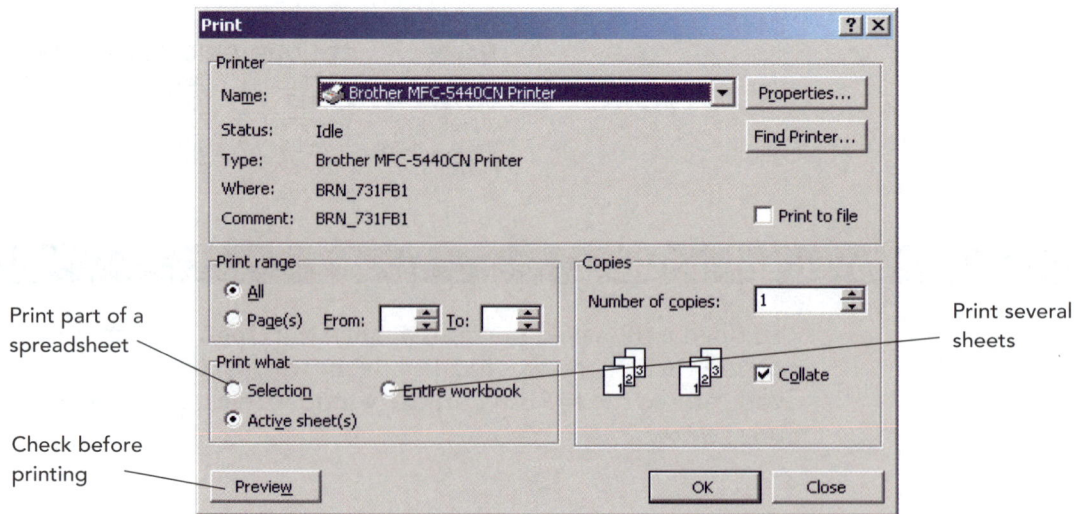

Print part of a
spreadsheet

Print several
sheets

Check before
printing

Common mistake

Not printing at the appropriate time. Printouts should not show any formatting or calculations
that take place at a later stage.

1. Reopen *Exams*, the file you created in Exercise 1.
2. Amend the *Maths* heading to read `Maths for Scientists`
3. Widen this column to display the heading clearly.
4. Select all column headings and right align.
5. Save these changes and print a copy of the spreadsheet.
6. Format the exam results to show one decimal place.
7. Format the prices in the *Book Token* column to currency. Make sure you display the £ sign and two decimal places.
8. Increase the title *Exams* to font size 14, and make it bold.
9. Format all column headings to italic.
10. Save these changes.
11. Print a copy of the amended spreadsheet.
12. Close the file.

Answer

EXAMS

	Science	*Maths for Scientists*	*English*	*Book Token*
Jonson	22.5	9.0	44.0	£2.00
Miller	20.0	9.5	48.5	£5.00
Smith	14.5	10.3	40.0	£2.00
Baker	28.0	8.5	37.8	£1.50
Hart	19.3	8.0	0.0	£1.00

Orientation and margins

Although Excel worksheets are extremely large, you will find that you only print the portion on which you have been working. Even so, many spreadsheets extend across the width of the paper, so you may want to change from portrait (upright A4) to landscape (sideways A4) orientation before printing, and so cut down on the number of pages that will print out. Find this option in **File/Page Setup** on the **Page** tab.

Set margins

Change orientation

Print on single page

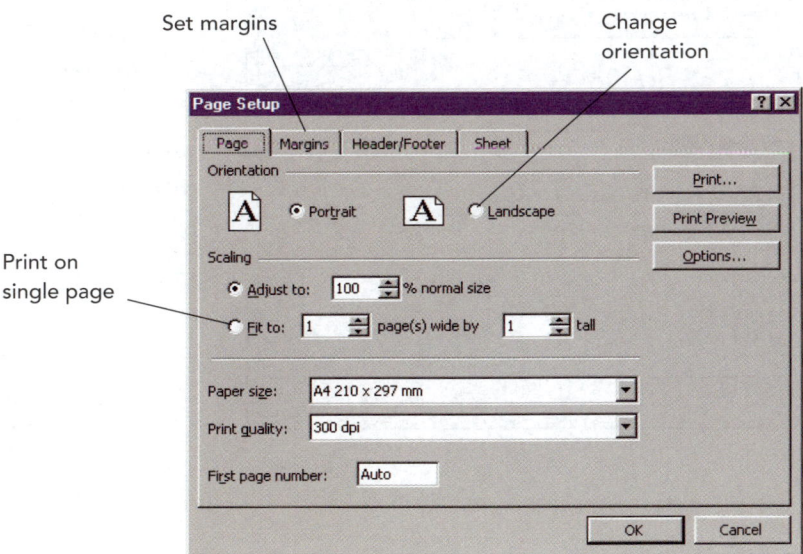

For even larger spreadsheets, click in the **radio button** to fit all the data on one page.

If you want to set exact margins, or centre the spreadsheet data on the page, click the **Margins** tab and set the measurements in the boxes.

Borders and shading

Add a border to a cell or range of selected cells by opening the **Format/Cells** menu and clicking the **Border** tab.

Click the **Outline** option and select a line style before clicking **OK**. Select the **Patterns** tab to add a colour fill to the cell(s).

Add border

Fill cell with colour

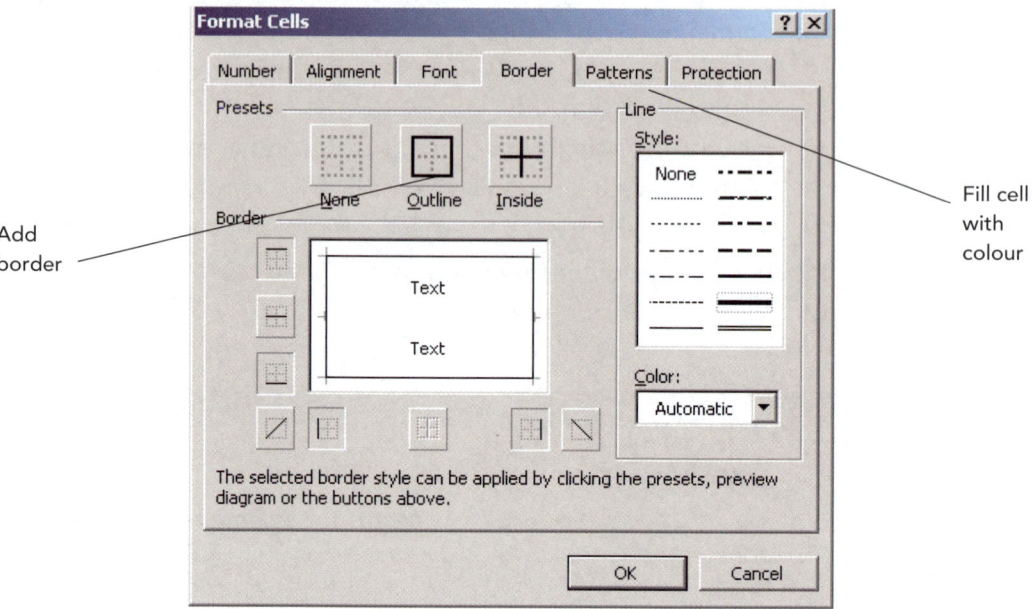

Gridlines and headings

Some computers are set to print out the gridlines with the data, and others are not. Check whether your gridlines will print by clicking the **Print Preview** button on the toolbar , or from the **Page Setup** box. If you want to change your settings, click the **Sheet** tab and select or deselect **Gridlines**.

On the same tab, click in the checkbox to display row and column headings on any printouts.

Gridlines on/off

Check how the spreadsheet will print

Click for headings

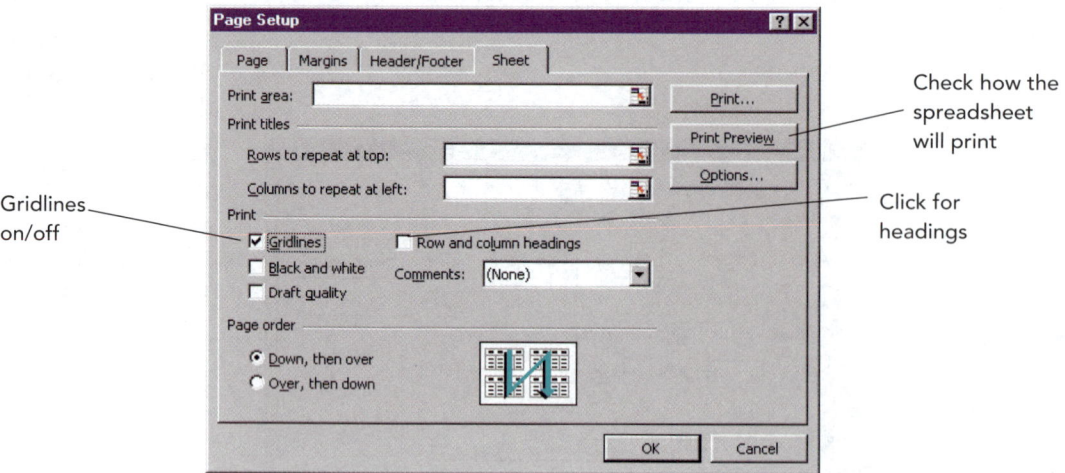

Formulae

Calculations are performed automatically within the spreadsheet once the correct formula has been entered and you have pressed **Enter** or activated another cell.

To perform a calculation:

1. Click the cell in which you want the result to appear.
2. Enter =
3. Enter the correct formula, using one of the following operators

   + add

   — subtract

   * multiply

   / divide.

For example, to multiply 245 by 186, you could click in a cell and then type =245*186.

However, figures on spreadsheets often change – e.g. a price may increase or different numbers of items may be purchased. To allow for this it is better to use the *cell addresses* in your formulae. The calculation will be based on the actual cell contents at all times, so that calculations update automatically whenever the figures change.

The formula therefore should be entered as in the example below, =A1*B1.

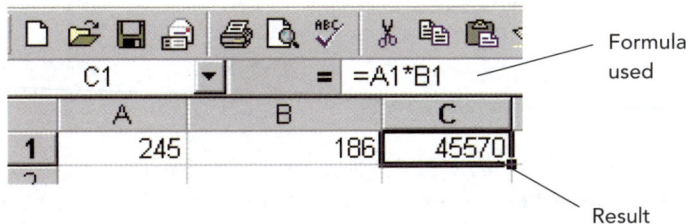

Formula used

Result

You can either type in the cell addresses or enter them into the formulae automatically. Do this by clicking the first cell (in this case, A1) with the mouse after entering =, then typing * and then clicking B1.

To divide 245 by 186, enter =A1/B1

To add the two numbers, enter =A1+B1

To subtract 186 from 245, enter =A1—B1

4. Press **Enter**, click the ✓ in the *Formula Bar* or click another cell. The results of the calculation will be displayed in the cell and the formula will be visible in the *Formula Bar*.

Calculations will produce unformatted results that can display a number of figures after the decimal point. If you see ### appearing after you have performed a calculation, it simply means that the column is too narrow. Widen the column to remove the symbols and display the results in full.

Functions

These are predefined formulae that perform specific calculations. The two you need to be able to use are those that total and average a column or row of cells.

Totals

When data in only two or three cells are to be added, you could enter a simple formula e.g. =A3+A4+A5.

When a larger number of cells is to be added, it is quicker to use the SUM function which totals a range of cells. It can be entered from the keyboard in the form =SUM(*first cell in range:last cell in range*).

For example, to add the five numbers in cells A1 to A5, enter =SUM(A1 : A5).

A6	▾	ƒ*x*	=SUM(A1:A5)	Formula
	A	B	C	D
1	245			
2	440			
3	387			
4	900			
5	128			
6	2100			
7				

Result

Common mistake

Using =SUM(...) for simple calculations as well as totals – e.g. entering =SUM(A1+B1) when the correct formula is =A1+B1.

The word SUM can be typed in upper or lower case, but there should be no spaces between entries, and all punctuation (brackets and colon) must be accurate.

It is often quicker to use the *AutoSum* button Σ . To use this facility, select the range of cells with the mouse and click the **AutoSum** button. The total will appear in the next empty cell. (You could also include the empty cell when selecting the range.)

Averages

The AVERAGE function both totals a range of cells and divides by the number of entries. It is in the form =AVERAGE(*first cell in range: last cell in range*).

▾	ƒ*x*	=AVERAGE(C1:C5)	Formula
B	C	D	
	20		
	18		
	24		
	12		
	19		
	18.6		Result

You can either type in the function or select it from the drop-down list next to the *AutoSum* button. The list also offers other basic functions such as maximum, minimum and count.

AutoSum Activate choice list

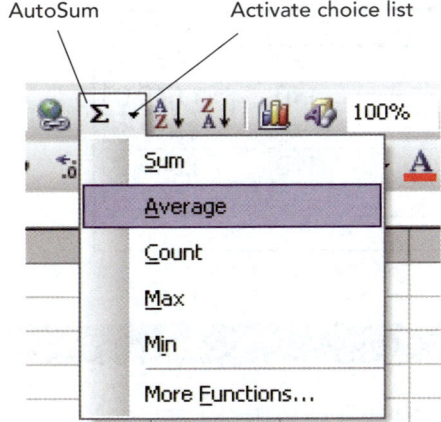

Sum
Average
Count
Max
Min
More Functions…

Exercise 4

1. Start a new *Workbook* and create the following spreadsheet to help you work out the cost of buying carpets.

2. Widen the columns to display all the data clearly and save the file as `Carpets`.

CARPETS		
Type	Cost (per sq.m)	Amount (sq.m)
Berber	8	80
Persian	14	110
Axminster	7.5	45
Tufted	6	140

3. Add a fourth column headed `Final price` and enter a formula to calculate the price of *Berber* carpet (*Cost × Amount*).

4. Enter formulae to calculate the final price for all the other carpets.

5. Update the file to save the changes.

6. Right align all column headings except *Type*.

7. Format all prices to currency displaying the £ symbol and two decimal places.

8. Format all column headings to italic and apply a different font to the title.

9. Add a new row headed **TOTAL** and use the SUM function to work out the total price for all the carpets.

10. Add a further row headed **AVERAGE** and use the AVERAGE function to work out the average *Cost (per sq.m)* of the carpets.

11. Border just the column headings.

12. Check that row and column headings will be printed and that there are gridlines visible.

13. Change to landscape orientation and print one copy.

14. Save a new version of the amended spreadsheet as `Carpets2`.

15. Close the file.

	A	B	C	D
1	CARPETS			
2	Type	Cost (per sq. m)	Amount (sq.m)	Final price
3	Berber	£8.00	80	£640.00
4	Persian	£14.00	110	£1,540.00
5	Axminster	£7.50	45	£337.50
6	Tufted	£6.00	140	£840.00
7	TOTAL			£3,357.50
8	AVERAGE	£8.88		

Copying (replicating) formulae

The most common reason for copying cell entries is to replicate the same formula down a column or across a row. For example, if you have a series of columns that must be totalled, you can total one column and then copy this formula across the row to total all the other columns.

After entering the first formula, move the mouse pointer over the small black square (*Fill handle*) visible in the bottom right-hand corner of the cell. When the pointer changes to a black cross **+** click and drag it down the column or across the row. The contents will now be copied.

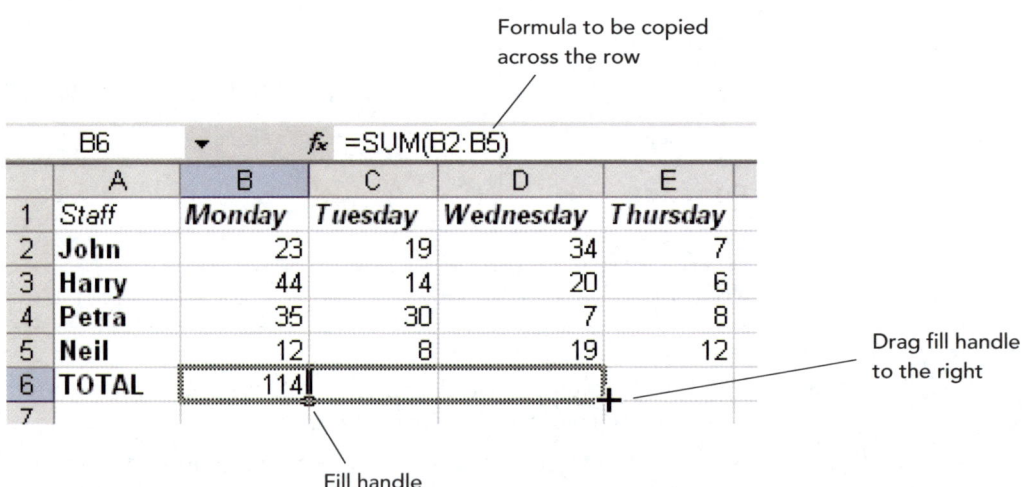

Formula to be copied across the row

Drag fill handle to the right

Fill handle

Copying formulae works because it reflects the *relative* cell positions. Therefore, if the formula of the original cell is =SUM(B2:B5) then the new cells will show the formulae =SUM(C2:C5), =SUM(D2:D5) etc.

If you copy a cell containing text or numerical entries rather than formulae, then these will be copied exactly. However, dates will be recognized and copied as a *series* – e.g. copy *January* across a row to enter all the months, or *Monday* to enter the days of the week.

Common mistake

Entering each formula manually, instead of replicating the source formula. This may mean that formulae are inconsistent.

1. Reopen the file *Shoes* from Exercise 2.

2. Head a new column **VALUE** and format the entry to match the other headings.

3. Enter a formula to calculate the value of *DAISY* shoes – i.e. the price multiplied by the number in stock.

4. Replicate this formula down the *VALUE* column to work out the value of all other shoes.

5. Format the *VALUE* entries to currency with two decimal places.

6. Add a new row heading **TOTAL** and total the entries in the *VALUE* column.

7. Save the file with the new file name **Shoe Value**.

8. Print one copy and then close the file.

Answer

SHOES				
NAME	**COLOUR**	**PRICE**	**IN STOCK**	**VALUE**
DAISY	PINK	£38.50	10	£385.00
LADY EMMA	RED	£44.75	4	£179.00
SLINGBACK	GREEN	£28.00	26	£728.00
SHELL SANDAL	WHITE	£26.50	14	£371.00
FLATTIES	BLACK	£19.99	8	£159.92
TOTAL				£1,822.92

Inserting columns/rows

To add a new column within an existing set of data, click the heading letter of the column to the *right* to highlight the complete column, and then select **Insert/Column**. A new column will slide into place and heading letters will adjust automatically.

To add a new row, click the heading number *below* the position for the new row and then select **Insert/Row**.

New column

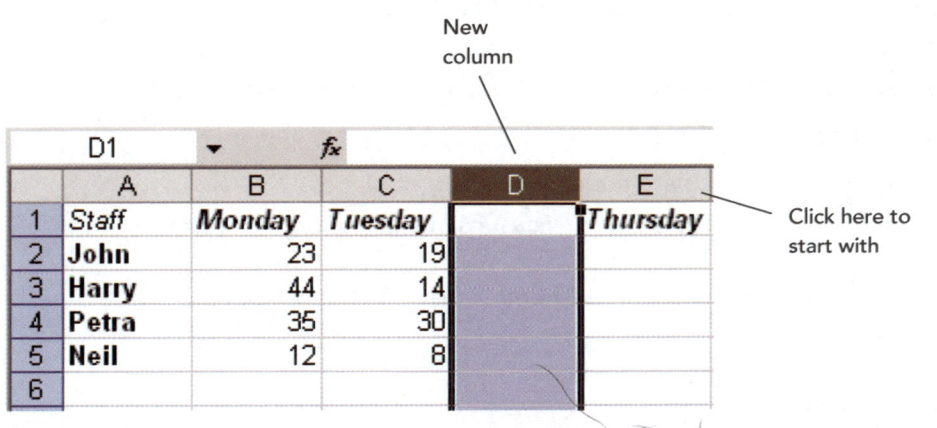

Click here to start with

Common mistake

If totals have been calculated using individual cell addresses (e.g. =B2+C2+D2), the formula will not take into account the new entries. Using the SUM function will update the total to include any new figures in columns or rows added between the first and the last.

NOT INSERTING THE CORRECT COLUMN OR ROW IS A CRITICAL ERROR.

NOT UPDATING FORMULAE AFTER COLUMNS OR ROWS HAVE BEEN INSERTED IS A CRITICAL ERROR.

Deleting columns/rows

If entries in a column or row are selected and you press the **Delete** key, you will remove the *contents* but the empty cells will remain.

You can also temporarily remove contents from view by going to **Format/Column/Hide**.

Delete a complete column or row by clicking the heading letter or number. With the entire column or row selected, open the **Edit** menu and select **Delete**. As with inserting columns and rows, header letters and row numbers will adjust automatically.

> **NOT DELETING THE SPECIFIED COLUMN OR ROW, OR DELETING THE WRONG COLUMN OR ROW, IS A CRITICAL ERROR.**

Exercise 6

1. Create the following spreadsheet and save it as `Cereal`.

CEREAL PRICES	Cornflakes	Toasties	Muesli	Porridge	Grahams
Size of pack (g)	500	750	450	1000	1500
Price per pack	2.5	2.8	2	4.5	3.75
Cost per 100 g					

2. Widen any columns to display the data clearly.
3. The cost of 1 g of cereal is the price of a pack divided by its size, so 100 g of cereal requires the formula (*Price per pack/Size of pack × 100*). Insert a formula to work out the cost of 100 g of *Cornflakes*.
4. Copy this formula across the row to work out the cost of 100 g of all the cereals.
5. Format all prices to currency.
6. Format the cereal names to bold and right aligned.
7. Update the file to save the changes.
8. Now insert a new column to the right of *Muesli* and enter the following details:

   `Oaties` – `1000g` pack costs `£3.50`

9. Copy the formula across to calculate the cost of 100 g of *Oaties*.
10. Delete the column containing the entry for *Toasties*, making sure you leave no empty cells.
11. Save a different version of the final spreadsheet as `Cereal2` and print a copy in landscape orientation.

Answer

CEREAL PRICES	Cornflakes	Muesli	Oaties	Porridge	Grahams
Size of pack (g)	500	450	1000	1000	1500
Price per pack	£2.50	£2.00	£3.50	£4.50	£3.75
Cost per 100 g	£0.50	£0.44	£0.35	£0.45	£0.25

Printing formulae

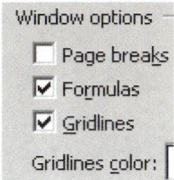

Cells normally display completed calculations. For New CLAIT you need to print out evidence of the formulae that have been used to create your spreadsheet. Display the formulae by holding down **Ctrl** and pressing the ¬ key (to the left of the **1** key). Alternatively, open the **Tools** menu, select **Options** and on the **View** tab click in the **Formulas** box to add a tick.

The spreadsheet can be printed in this mode, but the columns will be much wider to accommodate the formulae. Try to print on one page by changing the *Page Setup* settings.

To return to the normal view, hold down **Ctrl** and press the ¬ key again or remove the tick in the *Formulas* box.

Headers and footers

It is easy to add your name, date and centre number to a cell in a spreadsheet, but the details won't appear on any charts that you print alone, or on separate sheets if your spreadsheet does not fit onto one page.

To print your personal details on a spreadsheet, or add these to the top or bottom of a chart, you must create a *header* or *footer*. This will add text within the margin area, and will print out with the data.

1. Open either **File/Page Setup** or the **View** menu and click the **Header and Footer** option.
2. For entries at the top of the sheet, click the button labelled **Custom Header**.
3. Type your details in the left, centre or right-hand box to add the information in these positions on the sheet. To add the page number or date automatically, click the **Page Number** or **Date** button and the code *&[Page]* or *&[Date]* will appear. Click the **Font** button to format any selected entry.

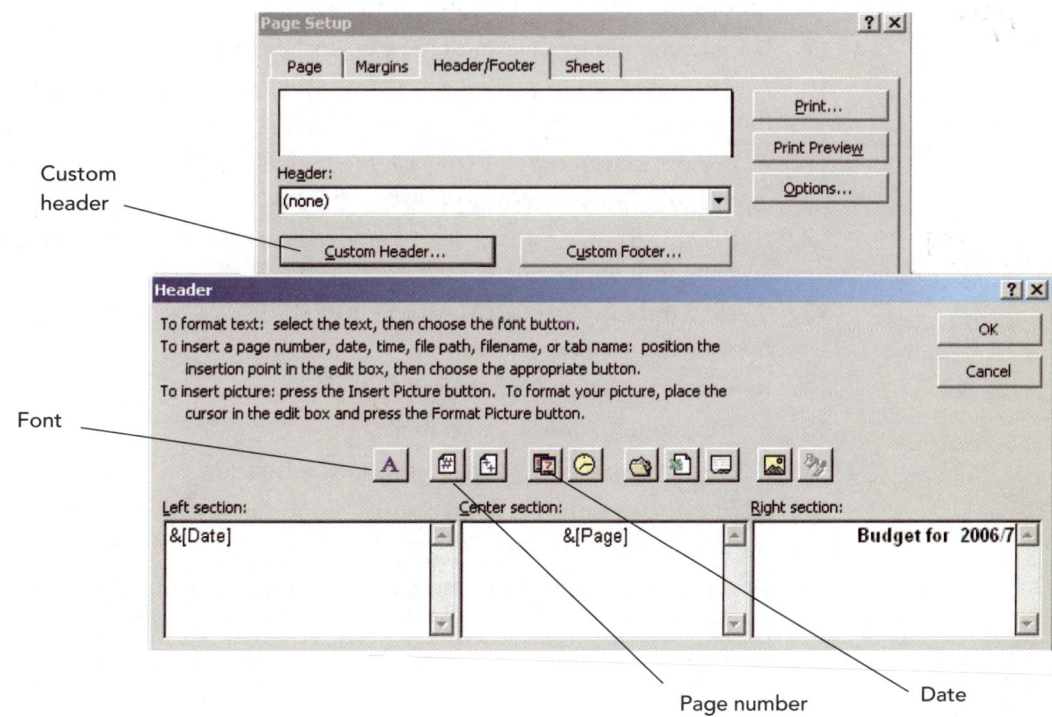

4. When the entries are complete, click **OK** and either click **OK** again to close the *Header and Footer* box or create a custom footer to add entries to the bottom of the sheet.

5. Click **OK** to return to the worksheet or print directly from here.

Exercise 7

1. Create the following spreadsheet and save it as `Writing`.

Writing Costs				
MONTH	PENS	PAPER	DISKS	COFFEE
Jan	2.5	3.7	1.8	0.65
	3.67	9.5	3.5	2.4
	1.8	2.7	4.85	2.5
	5.5	0	2.7	0.9
	2	3.45	1.1	2.45

2. Fill in the months **Feb – May** automatically down the *MONTH* column.

3. Format all prices to currency with two decimal places.

4. Right align all column headings except *MONTH*.

5. Add a new column headed **TOTAL** and use a function to calculate the total expenditure in *January*.

6. Copy the formula down the column to calculate all monthly expenditures.

7. Insert a new column between *PAPER* and *DISKS* headed **TRAVEL**. Enter the following data:

    `Jan £15.34, Feb £22.5, May £12.95`

8. Ensure that the monthly totals now include travel costs.

9. Update the file to save the changes and print one copy.

10. Add two new row headings: **OVERALL TOTAL** and **AVERAGE**. Emphasize these in bold.

11. At the bottom of the *TOTAL* column, calculate the overall expenditure over the five-month period using the SUM function.

12. Under this total, work out the average expenditure per month using the AVERAGE function.

13. Display the *OVERALL TOTAL* and *AVERAGE* figures in integer format (i.e. with no decimal places).

14. Reformat the title in a different font and size.

15. Format column headings to italic.

16. Add your **name** and **page** number as a header.

17. Border the months and make sure the gridlines will not be visible on any printouts.

18. Update the file and print one copy in landscape orientation to display the formulae. Make sure it prints onto one page only.

19. Now print a second copy showing the values and then save and close the file.

Step 18

	A	B	C	D	E	F	G
1	Writing Costs						
2	MONTH	PENS	PAPER	TRAVEL	DISKS	COFFEE	TOTAL
3	Jan	2.5	3.7	15.34	1.8	0.65	=SUM(B3:F3)
4	Feb	3.67	9.5	22.5	3.5	2.4	=SUM(B4:F4)
5	Mar	1.8	2.7		4.85	2.5	=SUM(B5:F5)
6	Apr	5.5	0		2.7	0.9	=SUM(B6:F6)
7	May	2	3.45	12.95	1.1	2.45	=SUM(B7:F7)
8	OVERALL TOTAL						=SUM(G3:G7)
9	AVERAGE						=AVERAGE(G3:G7)
10							

Step 19

Writing Costs

MONTH	PENS	PAPER	TRAVEL	DISKS	COFFEE	TOTAL
Jan	£2.50	£3.70	£15.34	£1.80	£0.65	£23.99
Feb	£3.67	£9.50	£22.50	£3.50	£2.40	£41.57
Mar	£1.80	£2.70		£4.85	£2.50	£11.85
Apr	£5.50	£0.00		£2.70	£0.90	£9.10
May	£2.00	£3.45	£12.95	£1.10	£2.45	£21.95
OVERALL TOTAL						£108
AVERAGE						£22

Charts

Charts and graphs are based on selected data, so you need to have an open spreadsheet on screen. The chart you create can be placed on the same worksheet – where it can be moved and resized – or on its own sheet. If you choose the latter option, the sheet tabs will be labelled *Chart1*, *Chart2* etc. by default, but you can change the names during or after the creation of any chart.

If you are taking data from a single spreadsheet, the data will remain on *Sheet1* and you can return there by clicking the sheet tab.

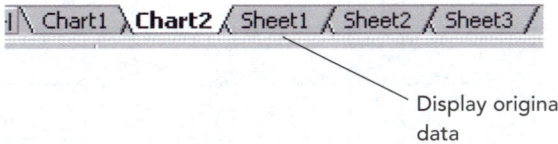

Display original data

Chart types

Excel provides a wide range of two-dimensional (2-D) and three-dimensional (3-D) chart types. If the data are comparative, they can be displayed in normal or stacked format.

For New CLAIT, do *not* select 3-D or stacked examples. However, line graphs with or without markers are equally acceptable.

The three types of chart or graph that you need to be able to recognize and create for New CLAIT are:

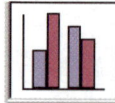 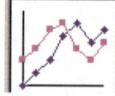 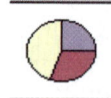

Column chart   Line graph   Pie chart

Although the assignments will refer to bar/column charts and both are acceptable, the instructions may appear to relate only to an Excel column chart. This is because a bar chart displays the *x*-axis category labels vertically, rather than horizontally.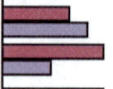

Chart elements

You must be able to identify the different elements of a chart so that you can add or format the correct element when asked to do so. For most chart types these include:

- Chart and axis titles
- Category labels
- Axis values
- Legend (key) showing the data series
- Data series
- Plot area
- Chart area.

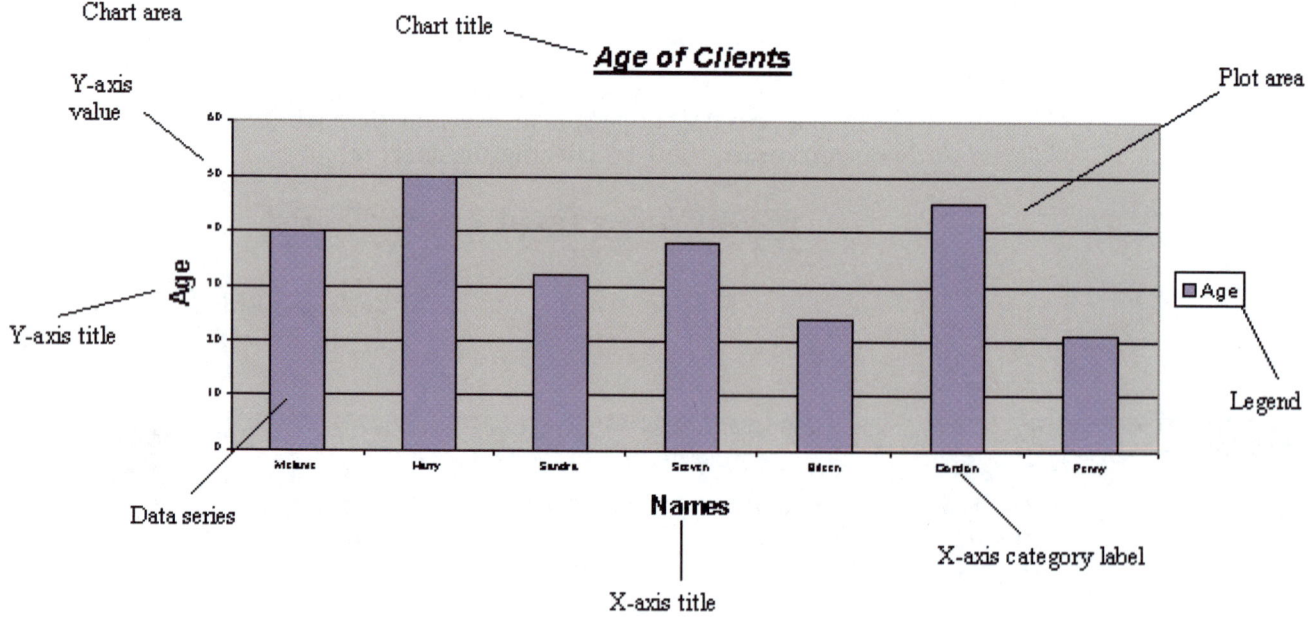

Opening a data file

You will be provided with a data file in the form of a spreadsheet, from which to extract the data required for your charts. Click the **Open** button on the toolbar and browse through the files on your computer. When you locate the named file, select it with one click and either press **Enter** or click the **Open** button.

Creating a chart

Selecting data

Select the data on which your chart will be based by dragging across the columns or rows when the pointer shows a white cross. Make sure you include the column or row headings. Often your selection will be only part of the complete spreadsheet.

Data chosen to base chart on

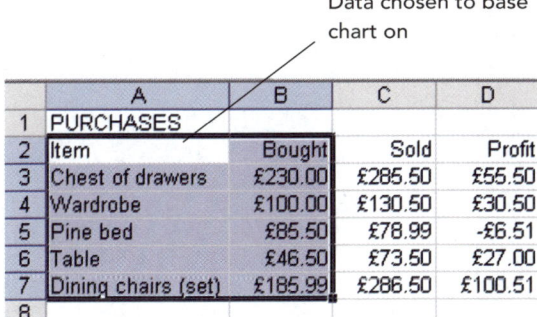

SELECTING AN INCORRECT ROW OR COLUMN OF DATA IS A CRITICAL ERROR.

PRODUCING A CHART OR GRAPH WITH MISSING DATA OR VALUES IS A CRITICAL ERROR.

Using the Chart Wizard

If you click the **Chart Wizard** toolbar button 📊 this will help you to create the chart in four steps.

1. Select the chart type from the list and click and hold down the **Press and Hold to View Sample** button to check that the chart is taking shape correctly. If it is, click **Next** to continue.

Select correct chart type

Preview button

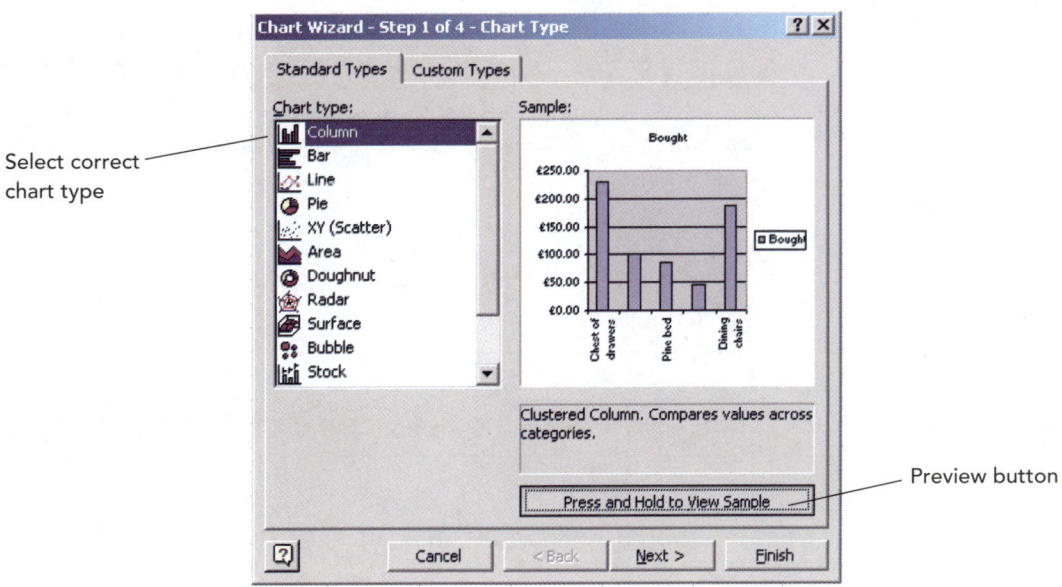

2. Confirm that the right data have been selected and the chart is displaying the data correctly before clicking **Next**.

    If not, you could either cancel the chart and start again or reselect the data. To do this, click the coloured button (referred to in Excel as the *Collapse Dialog* button) in the *Data range:* box to move to the spreadsheet. Use the mouse to select a different range of cells and then click the button again to return to the *Chart Wizard*.

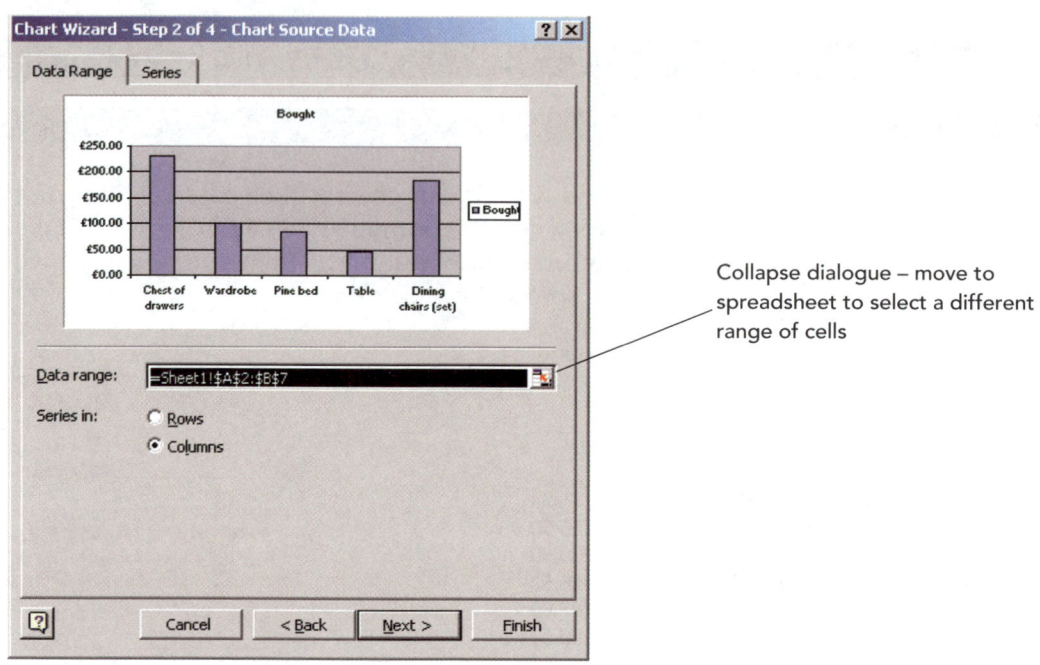

Collapse dialogue – move to spreadsheet to select a different range of cells

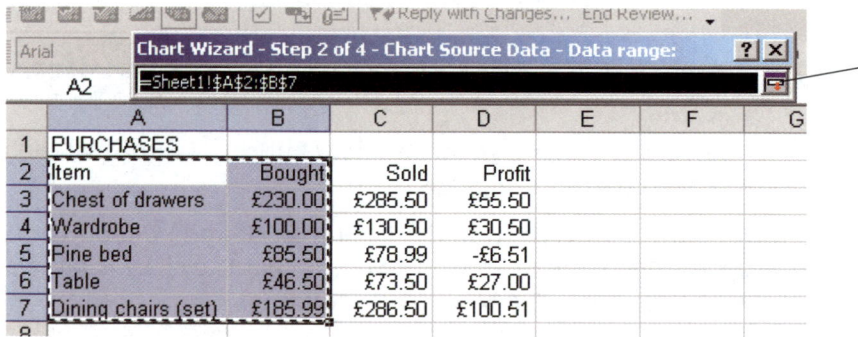

Return to Chart Wizard

FAILURE TO IDENTIFY THE DATA CLEARLY WITH APPROPRIATE LABELS IS A CRITICAL ERROR.

DISPLAYING DATA ON THE INCORRECT AXIS IS A CRITICAL ERROR.

3. On the **Titles** tab, complete the boxes with the chart and axis titles. The titles will appear automatically on the chart.

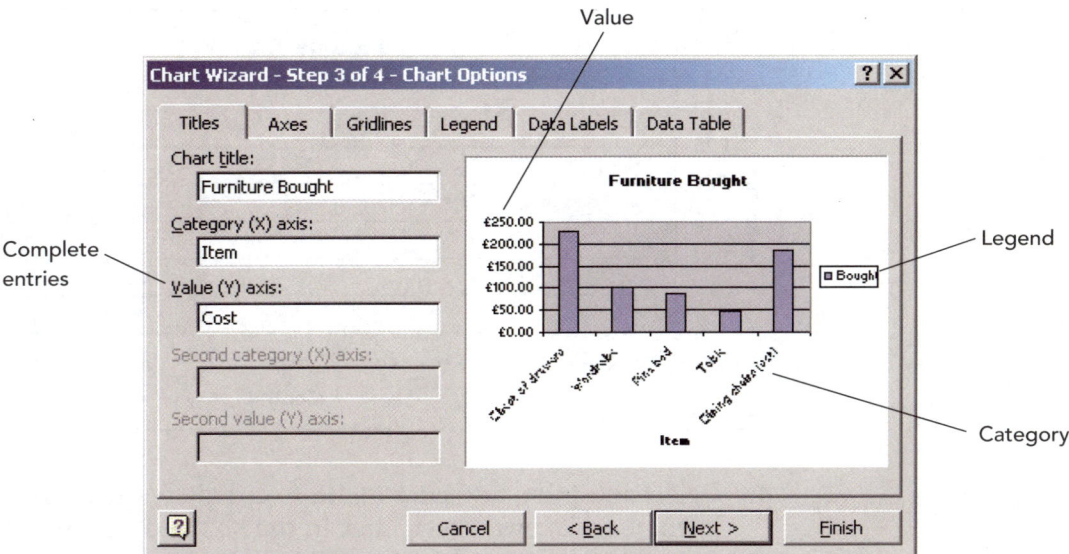

Complete entries

Value

Legend

Category

If you know you do not want a legend displayed, you could click the **Legend** tab and remove the tick in the checkbox, although you can also delete the legend after the chart has been created.

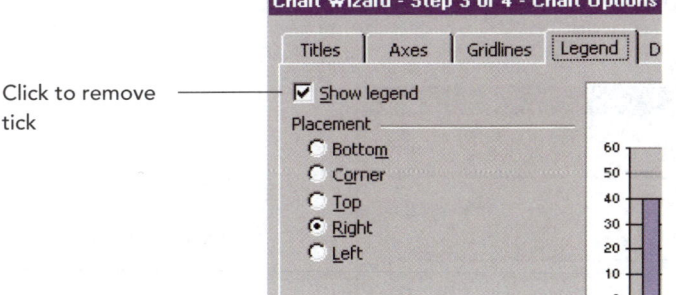

Click to remove tick

Click the **Data Labels** tab if you want to label pie chart sectors with a category name (label), percentage, value or combination of any of these.

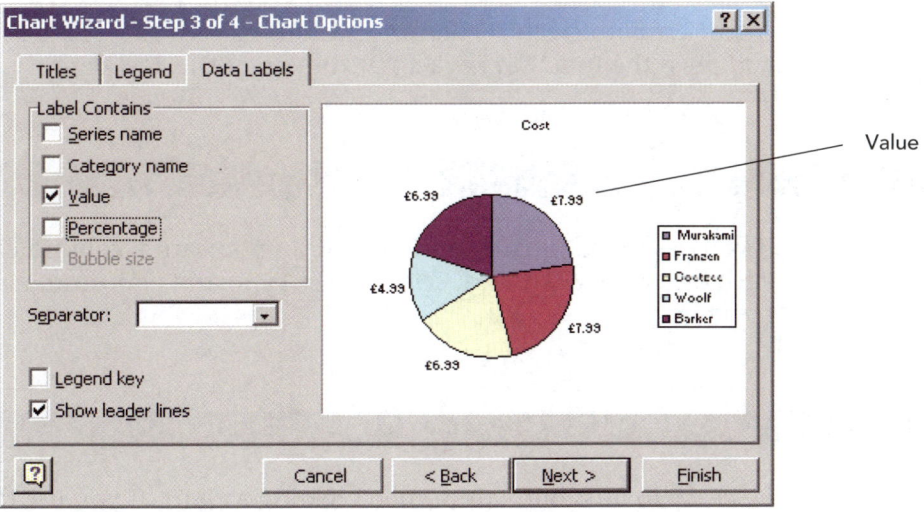

Value

On other charts or graphs, data labels will add values or categories to the data points.

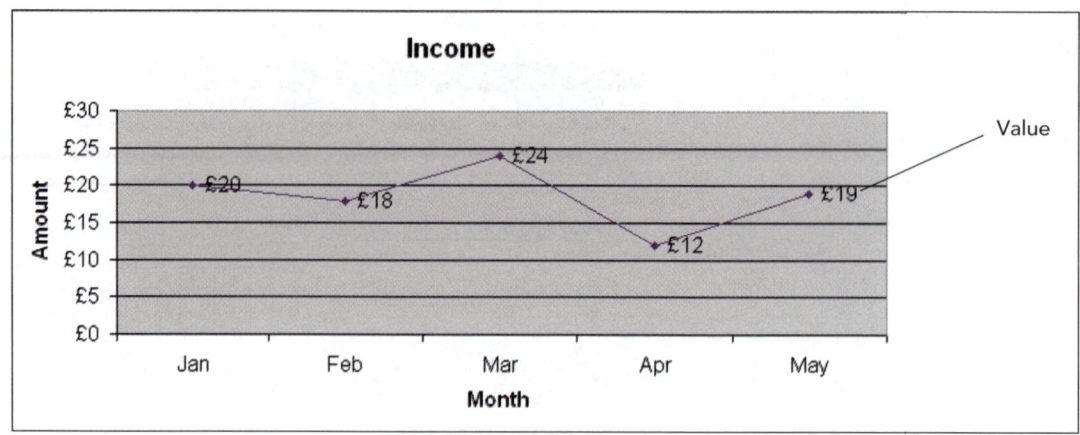

Common mistake

Omitting or selecting the wrong data labels.

4. Select an option and click **Finish** to complete the chart. When placing a chart on its own sheet, click in the box and rename the sheet rather than leave it as *Chart1*. This will help you find it again if switching between data and chart. The default sheet names will be *Chart1, 2, 3* etc. as new charts are created.

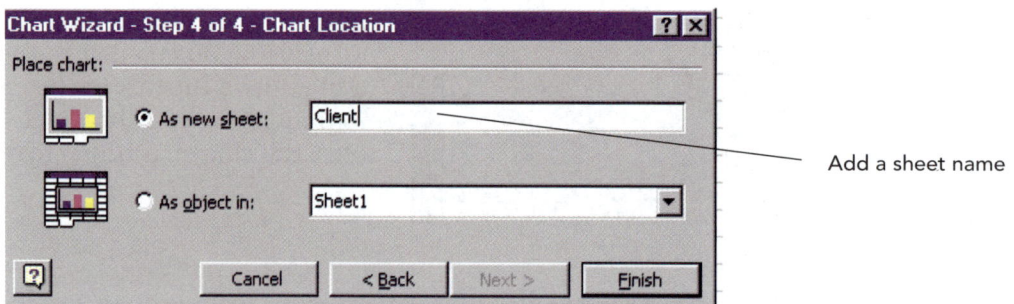

Add a sheet name

Using the keyboard

A quick way to create a column chart on its own sheet is to select the data and press the function key **F11** at the top of the keyboard.

Changing chart type

If you use the keyboard shortcut and do not want a column chart, right-click the white chart area, select **Chart Type** and choose an alternative type of chart.

Adding titles

It is easy to miss out a title when creating a chart. If you use the keyboard shortcut, no axis titles are included. You can add extra titles by right-clicking in the chart area and selecting **Chart Options**.

Closing a chart

Charts are objects within a spreadsheet file and so saving or closing the file will save or close any charts that have been produced. To close the Excel file containing any charts that have been created, click the lower **Close** button or go to **File/Close**.

Exercise 8

1. Open the file *Getting to Work* or create the following spreadsheet.

Getting to Work	
Transport	Numbers
Bus	25
Car	33
Train	7
Walk	18
Cycle	24
TOTAL	107

2. Select the data including the column headings but not the title or total rows and use the *Chart Wizard* to create a column chart.

3. At Step 3 in the *Chart Wizard* process, add a chart title `Getting to Work`; x-axis title `Transport` and y-axis title `Numbers`.

4. Place the chart on a new sheet renamed `Transport`.

5. Save and close the file.

Answer

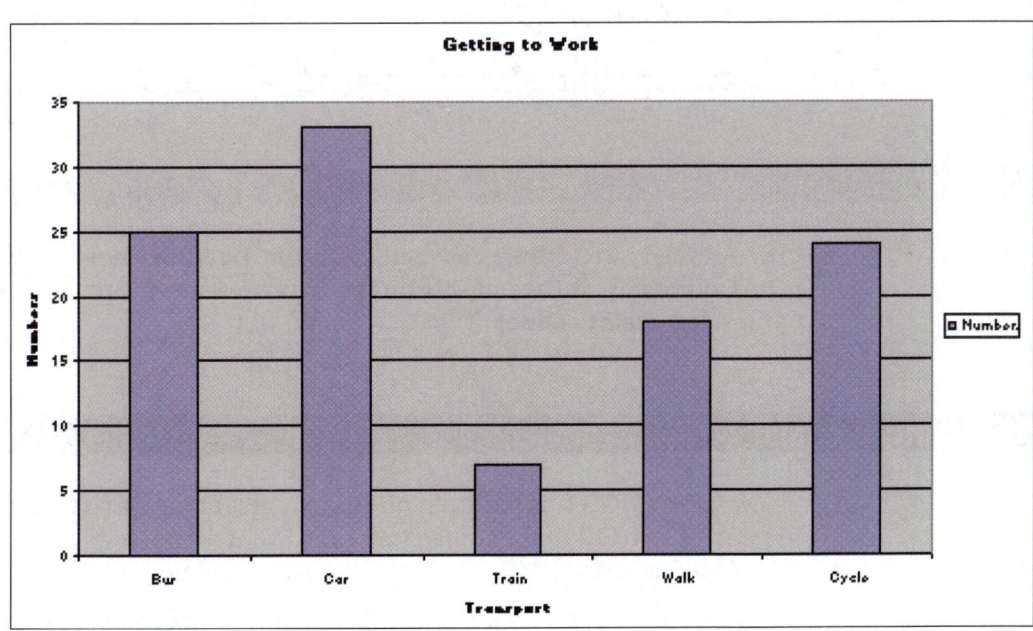

Opening an existing chart

To open a chart, locate and open the Excel file. If the chart has been placed on its own sheet, click the appropriate sheet tab.

Selected charts

Once a chart has been created, there are a number of changes that can be made when it is selected (by clicking) and is showing black boxes (*sizing handles*) around the edge.

Moving a chart

If the chart has been placed alongside the spreadsheet data, you may want to move it so that the data are not hidden. Position the pointer in the white chart area and then click and drag the whole chart to a new position.

Resizing a chart

Charts are often too small to display all the labels clearly. To resize a selected chart, drag a sizing handle outwards with the mouse when the pointer shows a two-way arrow.

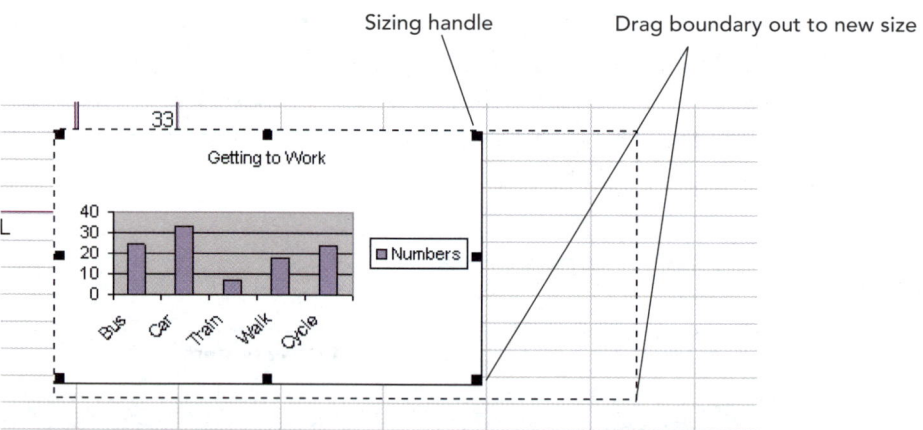

Deleting a chart

If you want to remove a selected chart on the same sheet as the data, press the **Delete** key. If the chart is on its own worksheet, open the **Edit** menu and select **Delete sheet**.

Formatting a chart

New CLAIT does not require you to do a great deal of chart formatting, but you may need to make some changes so that all parts of the chart are displayed clearly.

You can format the appearance of chart elements such as titles, values, legends and lines in one of a number of ways.

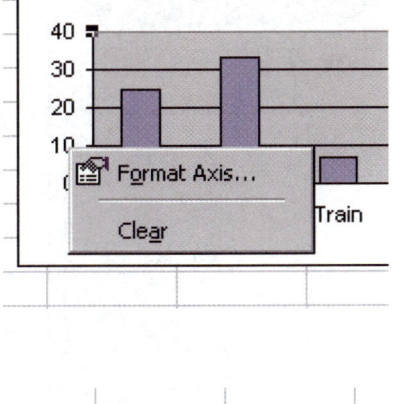

- Double-click or right-click the element and select **Format** ... to open the appropriate dialogue box.

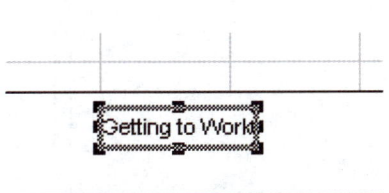

- Click the element and then use the normal formatting toolbar buttons that will become available.

- Click the element and then select options from the **Format** menu.

- Use the *Chart* toolbar which either will have appeared automatically or will be available from **View/Toolbars**. Any selected element will appear in the window and you can click the **Format** button to open the appropriate dialogue box. There are also some other options available on the toolbar.

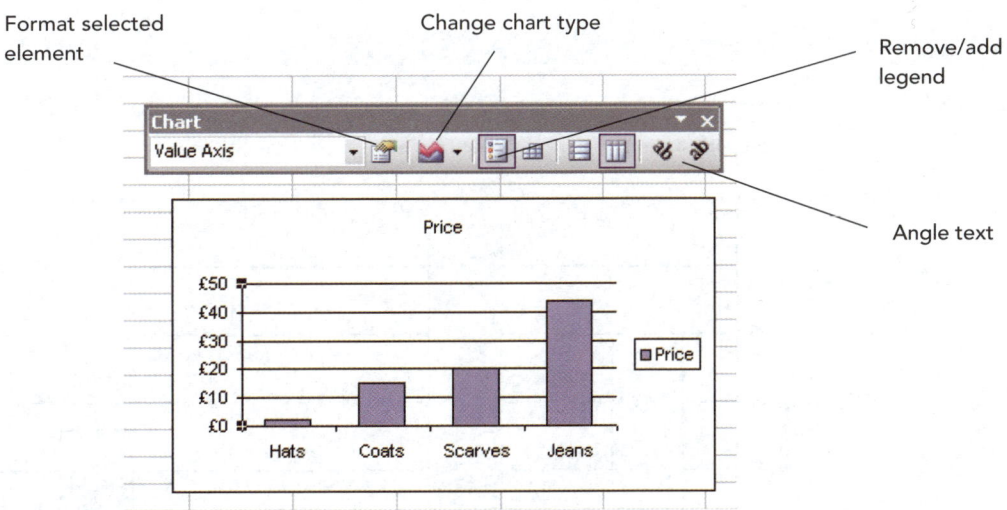

Titles

If the title is in the wrong position, click the box and drag it to another part of the chart area.

Text can be retyped, emphasized in bold or italic, or the font can be increased or decreased in size. You can also realign the text – e.g. from vertical to horizontal if it is too long to view otherwise. Select the **Alignment** tab in the *Format* dialogue box and either drag the red pointer or key in a different number of degrees to change the orientation.

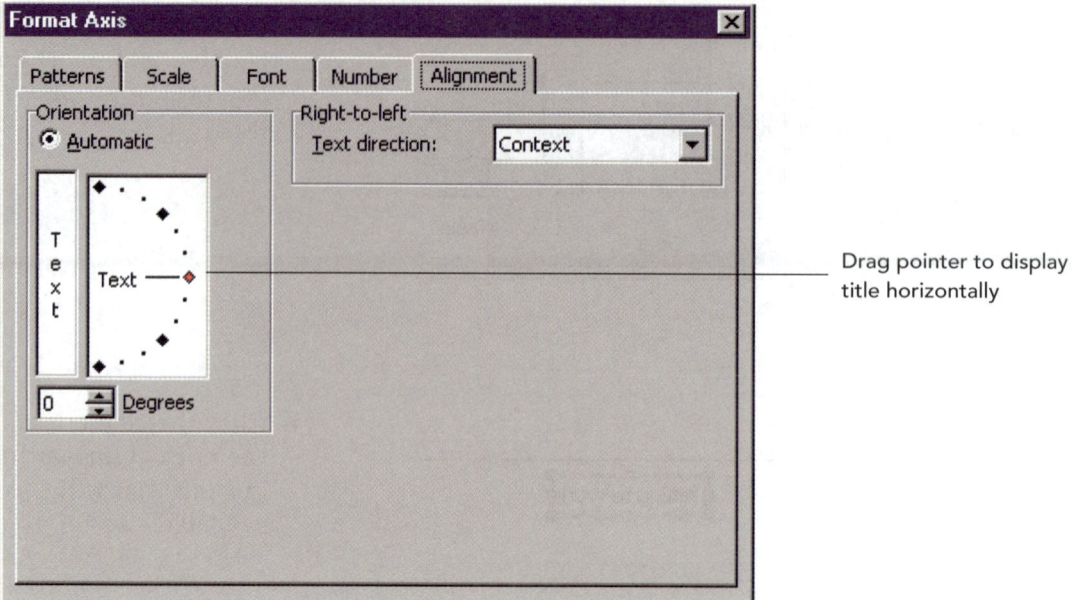

Drag pointer to display title horizontally

Exercise 9

1. Reopen the chart *Getting to Work* from Exercise 8.
2. Format the chart as follows: chart title – font size 14, bold; axis titles – italic font size 12; *y*-axis values and *x*-axis labels font size 10.
3. Move the chart title to the top left-hand corner of the chart area.
4. Realign the *x*-axis labels so that they are vertical instead of horizontal.
5. Amend the chart title to: `Transport to Work`
6. Update the file to save these changes and close the file.

Answer

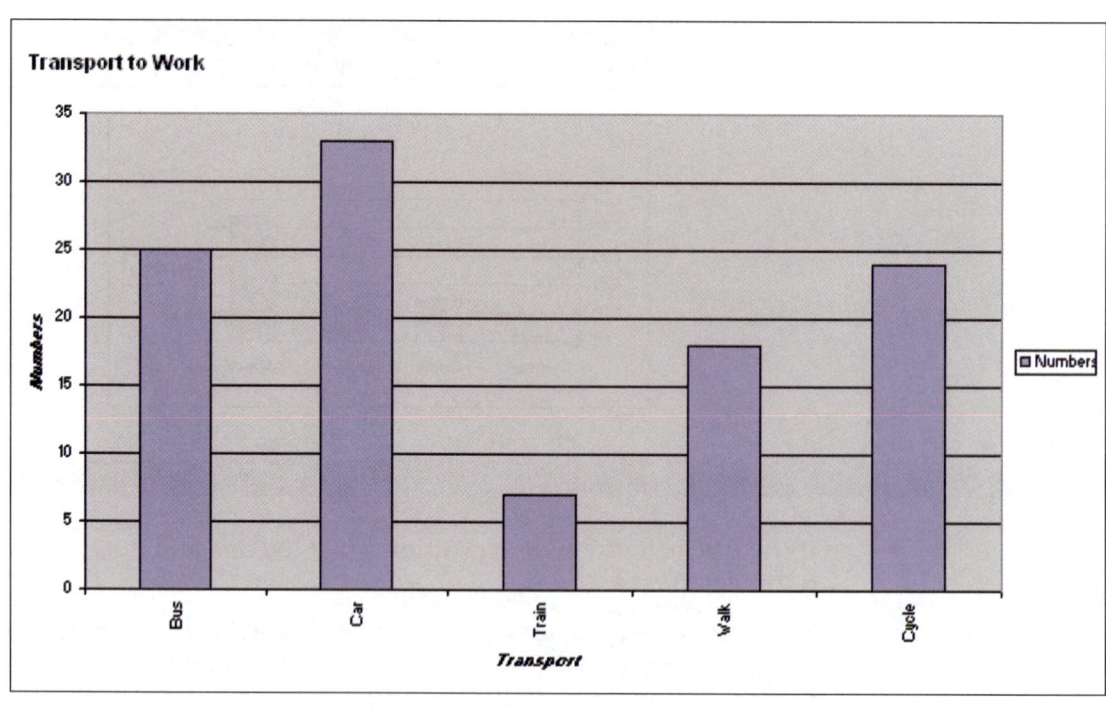

Legends

Click the legend and use the normal formatting toolbar buttons if you want to change the font.

Common mistake

Not deleting the legend when instructed to do so.

To remove a legend click it and press the **Delete** key or click the button off on the *Chart* toolbar. If you delete the legend by mistake, add it again by right-clicking the chart area, selecting **Chart Options** and clicking the checkbox on the *Legend* tab.

Printing charts

For charts on the same sheet as the spreadsheet data, select the chart to print it on its own. Otherwise, both chart and data will print together.

To print a copy of the selected chart or a chart on its own sheet displayed on screen, click the **Print** button.

Black and white charts

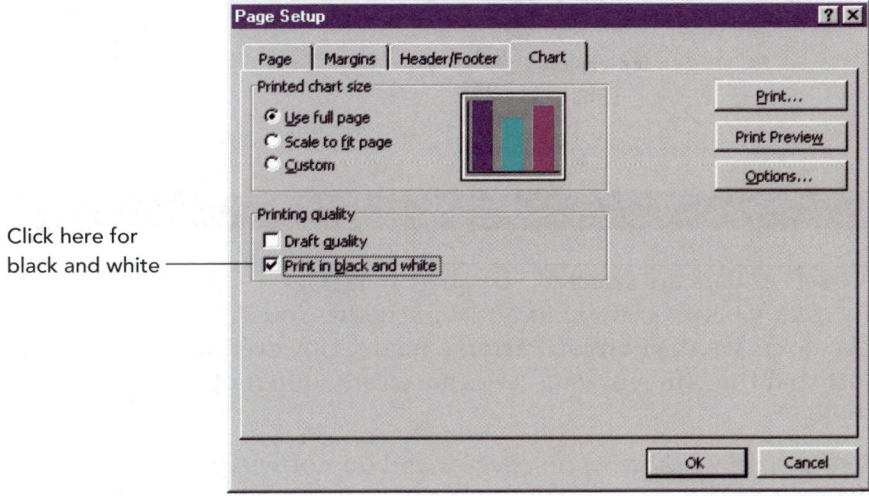

Click here for black and white

In many organizations, you will only have the facility to print your charts in black and white. To ensure that the different sectors of a pie chart are clearly differentiated, open the **File** menu, select **Page Setup** and click the **Chart** tab. Click in the **radio button** for printing in black and white; this will increase the contrast between sectors.

Exercise 10

1. Open *Meal* or create the following spreadsheet.

MEAL	
Food Item	Price (£)
Pizza	5.50
Salad	1.40
Ice-cream	2.25
Gateau	4.75
Coffee	1.00

2. Create a pie chart with the title: `Eating Out`
3. Add data labels showing the food item and percentage of the total cost.

4. Save the chart on the same sheet as the data.

5. Increase the chart size and move it to just below the data.

6. Delete the legend.

7. Format the title text to Arial, font size 14, bold.

8. Format the data labels to Times New Roman, bold, font size 11.

9. Save these changes and print a copy of the chart alone.

10. Close the file.

Answer

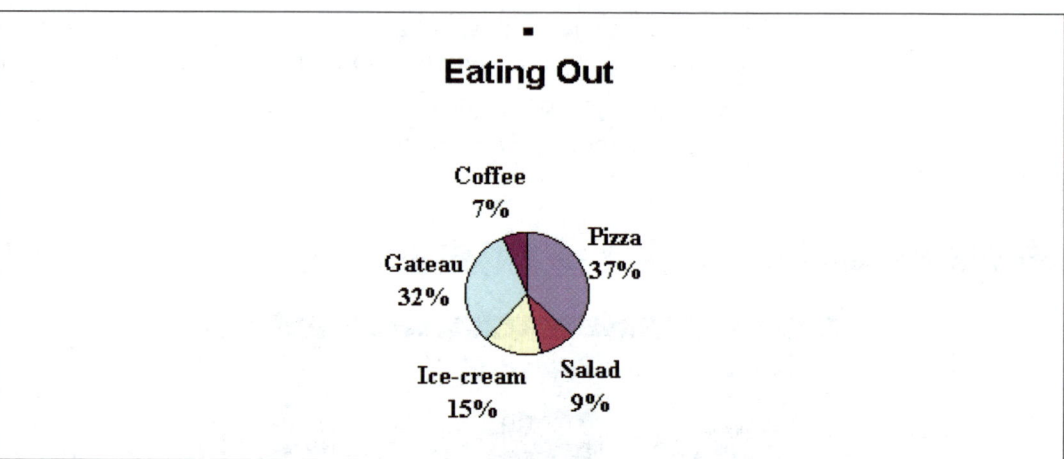

Comparative charts

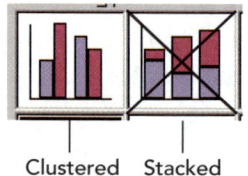

Clustered   Stacked

When two or more sets of data are selected, the chart normally distinguishes fairly clearly between them in terms of colour. You can also change individual colours via the **Format/Patterns** menu. However, it is important to ensure that the different data series are clearly differentiated when they print out.

Note: for column charts, select *clustered* not *stacked* and do not select stacked line graphs.

> **CREATING A STACKED COMPARATIVE CHART OR GRAPH IS A CRITICAL ERROR.**

Print preview

To see what a chart will look like when it's printed, click the **Print Preview** toolbar button ▧ or go to **File/Print Preview**. If necessary, click the **Setup** button and follow the guidance provided earlier to set the printer to print in black and white, as the different data series may be reformatted.

Return to the chart by clicking the **Close** button.

Line graphs

Lines may be too similar to be distinguished easily in a comparative line graph. It is therefore a good idea to thicken or select a different style for one line, and add or amend markers.

When the chart appears, right-click a line and select **Format Data Series**.

Select alternative line styles and weights, and add or amend markers for one of the lines.

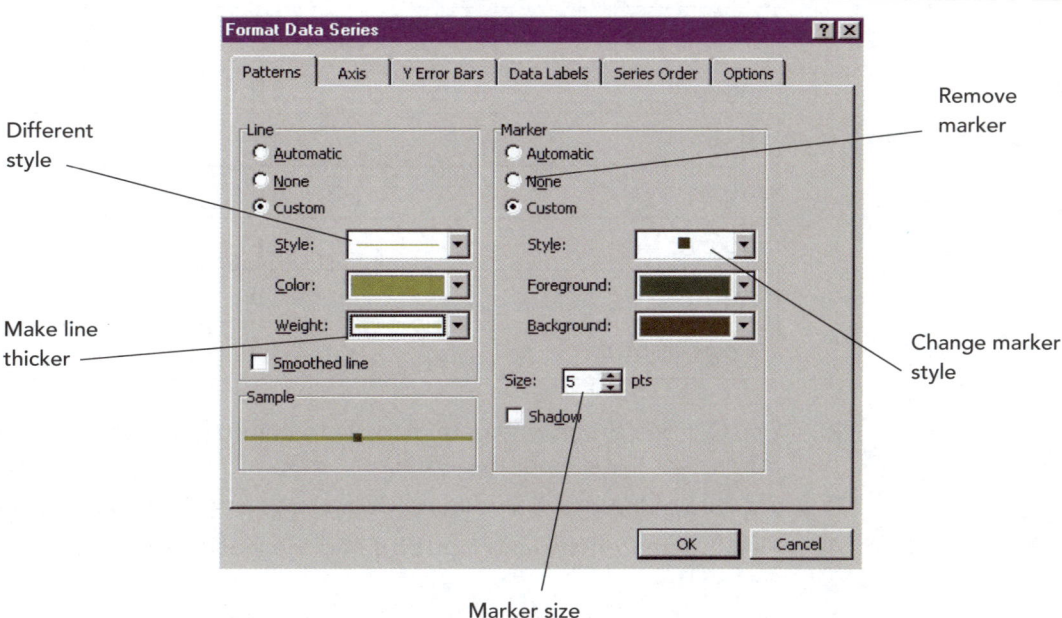

Different style

Make line thicker

Remove marker

Change marker style

Marker size

Print

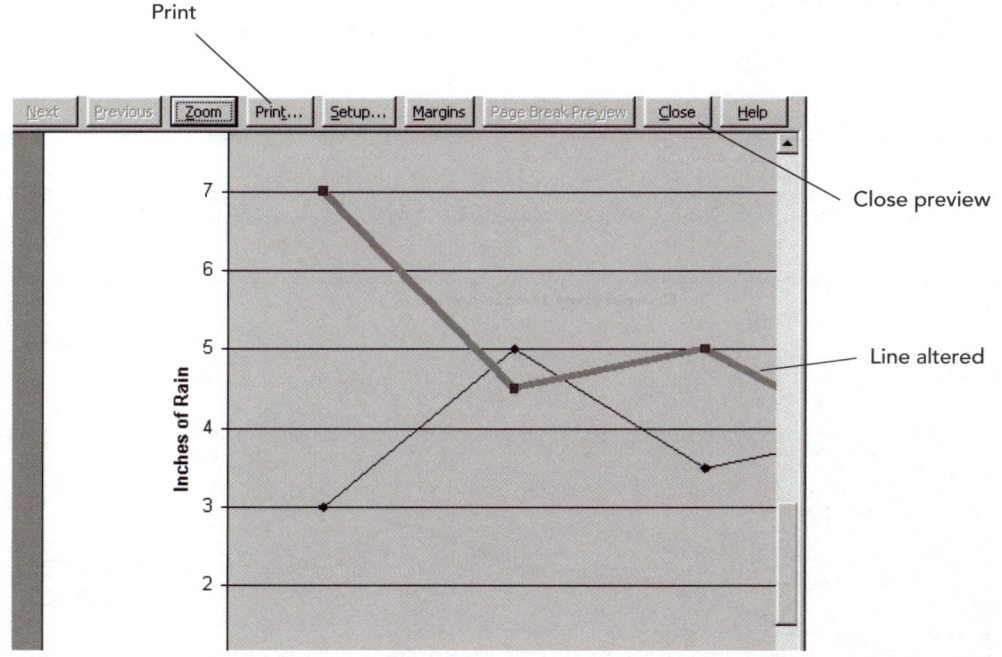

Close preview

Line altered

FAILURE TO IDENTIFY COMPARATIVE DATA CLEARLY IS A CRITICAL ERROR.

1. Open the file *Temperatures* (*Celsius*) or create and save the following spreadsheet.

	ABERDEEN	SOUTHAMPTON
April	10	14
May	12	17
June	15	20
July	16	22
August	19	24
September	15	19

2. Create a line graph with data markers to compare the temperatures in both towns over the six-month period.
3. The title of the graph should be `Comparative temperatures`.
4. Title the horizontal *x*-axis `Months` and the *y*-axis `Temp in degrees Celsius`.
5. Save the graph on its own sheet renamed `Temp`.
6. Make sure the legend is visible.
7. To ensure that the data for the towns are clearly differentiated, make the Aberdeen line much thicker, and amend the style of marker to large and triangular.
8. Print a copy of the chart and update the file to save the changes.

Answer

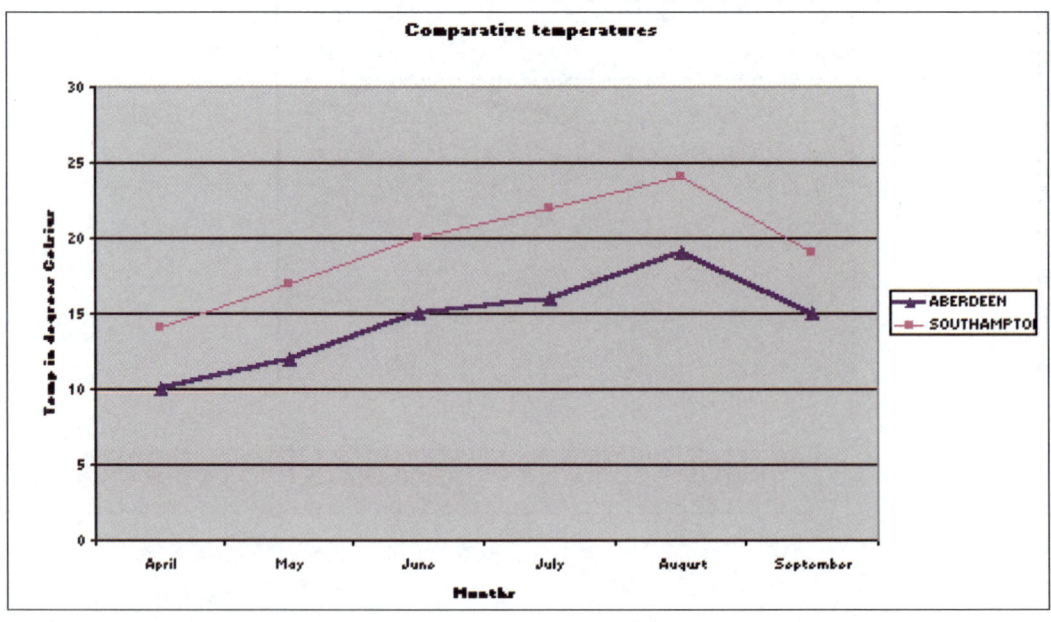

Scaling charts

The range of values on the *y*-axis will be set automatically when you use the *Chart Wizard*. If you would like a different range of values, you must change them manually.

Right-click or double-click the **y-axis**. In the *Format* dialogue box, click the **Scale** tab.

Amend the maximum and minimum values and, if necessary, alter the major units before clicking **OK**.

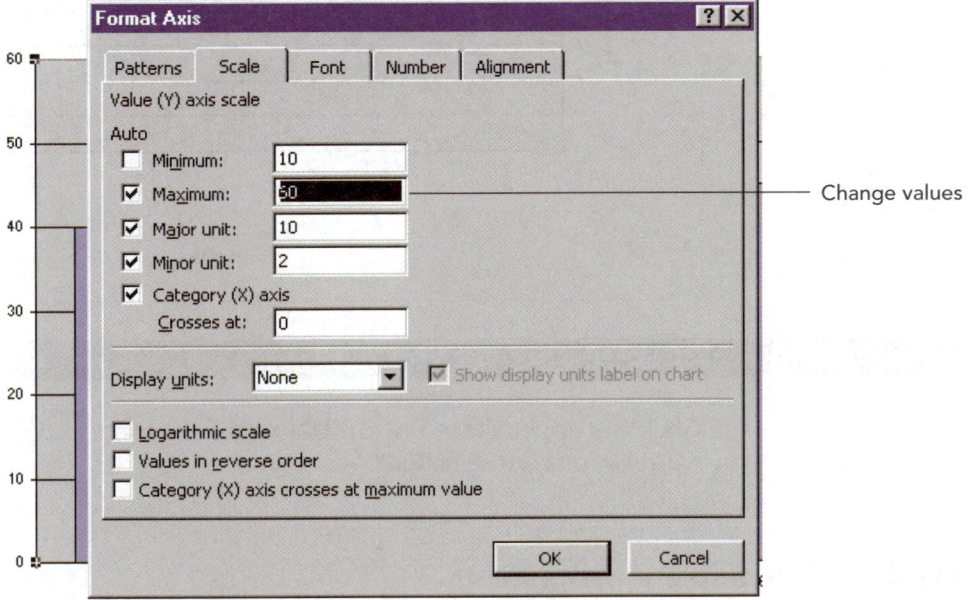

Change values

Exercise 12

1. Open the graph *Comparative temperatures*.

2. Amend the *y*-axis scale so that the minimum is 5 degrees and the maximum is 25 degrees.

3. Format the *x*-axis labels and *y*-axis values to italic, font size 11 and increase the size of the chart title to font size 14, bold.

4. Realign the *x*-axis labels so that they are vertical.

5. Colour the *Southampton* data series line green and remove the *Aberdeen* markers.

6. Save these changes and close the file.

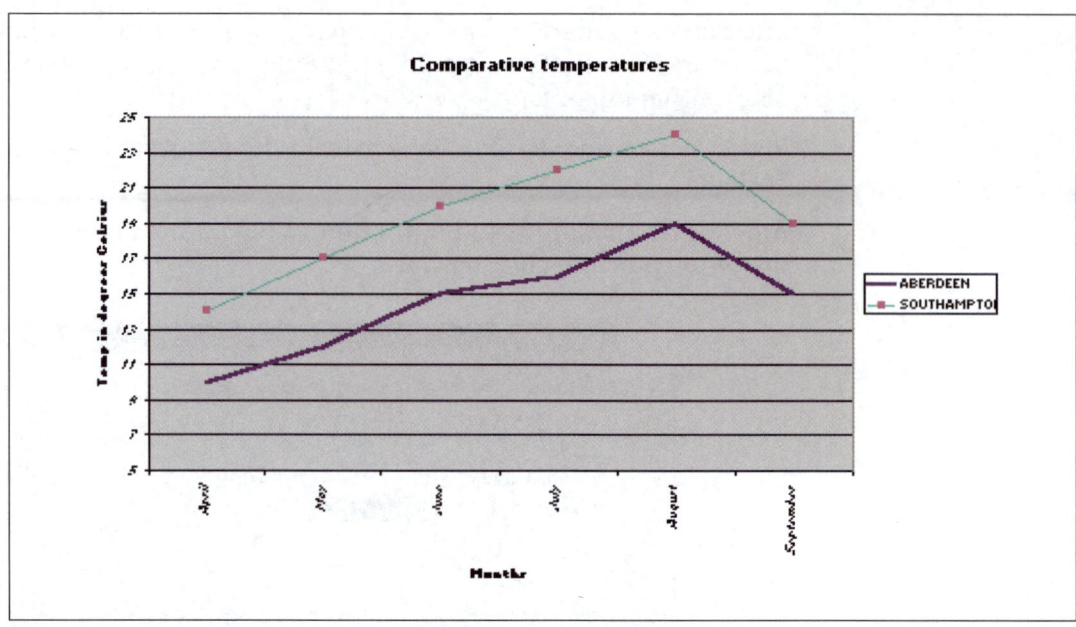

Exiting Excel

Click the upper **Close** button ⊠ visible in the top right-hand corner of the window, or go to **File/Exit**.

Exercise 13 – complete assignment

Task 1

1. Create a new spreadsheet showing sales of Christmas crackers.
2. Set the page orientation to landscape.
3. Enter the following data, leaving the *TOTAL SALES* column blank.

VARIETY	OCTOBER	NOVEMBER	DECEMBER	PRICE OF BOX	TOTAL SALES
SUPREME	16	22	36	25	
DELUX	28	40	45	33.99	
PREMIUM	17	26	50	28.5	
STANDARD	9	18	25	16.5	
KIDS	26	34	47	11.99	
FAMILY	29	45	56	16.5	

4. In the header enter: `your name` and an `automatic date`.
5. Save the spreadsheet using the file name `crackers`.
6. *TOTAL SALES* for each variety of crackers is calculated by adding the figures for *OCTOBER*, *NOVEMBER* and *DECEMBER*.
7. Use the SUM function to calculate the *TOTAL SALES* for *SUPREME* crackers.

8. Replicate this formula to show the *TOTAL SALES* for all other cracker varieties.

9. Insert a new column entitled **PRICE PER CRACKER** between *VARIETY* and *OCTOBER*.

10. *PRICE PER CRACKER* is calculated by dividing the *PRICE OF BOX* by 12. Calculate the *PRICE PER CRACKER* for *SUPREME* crackers.

11. Replicate this formula to show the *PRICE PER CRACKER* for all varieties of cracker.

12. Save the spreadsheet keeping the file name **crackers**.

13. Make sure all data is displayed in full and all the figures have been updated as a result of these changes.

14. Print one copy of the spreadsheet on one page in landscape orientation, showing the figures, not the formulae.

Task 2

1. The manufacturers of *PREMIUM* crackers have gone out of business. Delete the entire row of data for these crackers without leaving any blank cells.

2. Apply the following alignments:
    - Right align all column headings except *VARIETY*.
    - Format the *PRICE PER CRACKER* and *PRICE OF BOX* columns to currency. Make sure you display a £ sign and two decimal places.

3. Add a single outside border around the row headings starting with *SUPREME* and ending with *FAMILY*.

4. Save the spreadsheet using the new file name **income**.

Task 3

1. Make the following changes to the spreadsheet file called *income*:
    - The *PRICE OF BOX* for *DELUX* crackers should be £45.
    - The DECEMBER sales of KIDS crackers should be 69.
    - The name DELUX should be spelt **DELUXE**.

5. Add a new column headed **INCOME**. The *INCOME* is calculated by multiplying the *TOTAL SALES* by the *PRICE OF BOX*.

6. Enter a formula to calculate the *INCOME* for *SUPREME* crackers.

7. Replicate this formula to calculate the *INCOME* for all varieties of cracker.

8. The *INCOME* column should be formatted to currency but integer format (i.e. 0 decimal places.)

9. Add a new row heading **AVERAGE** and calculate the average cost of a box of crackers in the *PRICE OF BOX* column using the AVERAGE function.

10. Make sure this figure is displayed with a currency symbol and zero decimal places.

11. Save the spreadsheet keeping the file name **income**.

12. Make sure gridlines and row and column headings will be displayed on the printout.

13. Print one copy of the spreadsheet on one page in landscape orientation showing the figures, not the formulae.

14. Display the formulae. Make sure the formulae are displayed in full.

15. Make sure the page orientation is landscape and that the spreadsheet fits on one page.

16. Make sure that gridlines will be displayed when printed.

17. Save the spreadsheet formulae using the file name `crackerform`.

18. Print the entire spreadsheet on one page in landscape orientation showing the formulae.

19. Make sure all formulae are displayed in full and are readable on your printout.

20. Close the file *crackerform*.

21. Close all open files.

Task 4

1. Using suitable software for creating graphs, open the datafile *overseas* which contains data on the sale of crackers abroad.

2. Create a comparative line graph showing the sales in *FRANCE* and *GERMANY* from *JUNE* to *AUGUST* inclusive.

3. Display the months along the x-axis.

4. Give the graph the heading `Cracker Sales Overseas`.

5. Give the x-axis the title `Month`.

6. Give the y-axis the title `Sales figures`.

7. Use a legend to identify each line. Make sure that the lines and/or data points are distinctive and can be clearly identified when printed.

8. Display the values (numbers) for each data point on both lines.

9. Make sure that the graph is created on a full page on a sheet that is separate from the source data.

10. Set the y-axis range from 15 to 95.

11. In the header enter `your name` and an `automatic page number`.

12. Save the file using the file name `sales`.

13. Print one copy of the line graph.

14. Close the file and exit the software securely.

Task 1 Step 14

	A	B	C	D	E	F	G
1	VARIETY	PRICE PER CRACKER	OCTOBER	NOVEMBER	DECEMBER	PRICE OF BOX	TOTAL SALES
2	SUPREME	2.083333333	16	22	36	25	74
3	DELUX	2.8325	28	40	45	33.99	113
4	PREMIUM	2.375	17	26	50	28.5	93
5	STANDARD	1.375	9	18	25	16.5	52
6	KIDS	0.999166667	26	34	47	11.99	107
7	FAMILY	1.375	29	45	56	16.5	130

Task 3 Step 13

	A	B	C	D	E	F	G	H
1	VARIETY	PRICE PER CRACKER	OCTOBER	NOVEMBER	DECEMBER	PRICE OF BOX	TOTAL SALES	INCOME
2	SUPREME	£2.08	16	22	36	£25.00	74	£1,850
3	DELUXE	£3.75	28	40	45	£45.00	113	£5,085
4	STANDARD	£1.38	9	18	25	£16.50	52	£858
5	KIDS	£1.00	26	34	69	£11.99	129	£1,547
6	FAMILY	£1.38	29	45	56	£16.50	130	£2,145
7	AVERAGE					£23		

Task 3 Step 18

	A	B	C	D	E	F	G	H
1	VARIETY	PRICE PER CRACKER	OCTOBER	NOVEMBER	DECEMBER	PRICE OF BOX	TOTAL SALES	INCOME
2	SUPREME	=F2/12	16	22	36	25	=SUM(C2:E2)	=G2*F2
3	DELUXE	=F3/12	28	40	45	45	=SUM(C3:E3)	=G3*F3
4	STANDARD	=F4/12	9	18	25	16.5	=SUM(C4:E4)	=G4*F4
5	KIDS	=F5/12	26	34	69	11.99	=SUM(C5:E5)	=G5*F5
6	FAMILY	=F6/12	29	45	56	16.5	=SUM(C6:E6)	=G6*F6
7	AVERAGE					=AVERAGE(F2:F6)		

Task 4 Step 13

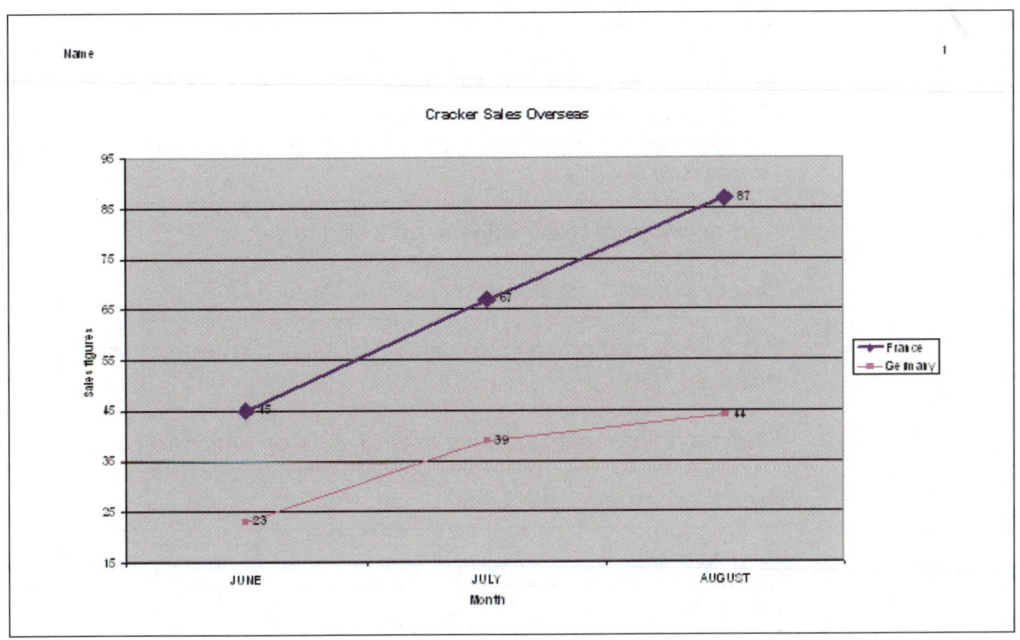

Self-assessment checklist

I feel confident that I can now:	✓
Understand the use of spreadsheet software	
Open a spreadsheet application	
Locate a cell by its address, and move round a spreadsheet	
Enter and format text	
Enter and format numeric data	
Amend and delete entries	
Use appropriate formulae and functions to perform calculations	
Copy (replicate) formulae down columns or along rows	
Widen columns	
Insert and delete columns and rows	

Print a spreadsheet

Set page orientation

Print a spreadsheet to display underlying formulae

Print displaying gridlines and row and column headings

Save a workbook

Open a workbook saved previously

Close a workbook

Understand the use of charting software

Understand the different chart types

Create bar, column and pie charts

Create line graphs

Add and format axes, titles, labels and legends

Deleted unwanted elements such as legends

Produce comparative charts and graphs and format elements so that data is clearly distinguished

Select single or comparative sets of data on which to base a chart or graph

Rescale chart or graph axes

Add data labels

Create charts and graphs on separate sheets

Print a chart or graph

Save a chart or graph

Close the file

Exit the application

Summary of critical errors

- Incorrect numerical data as a result of data entry or incorrect formula results
- Failure to insert specified rows or columns
- Failure to delete data in specified rows or columns
- Failure to display data in full
- Missing or incorrect data/values on a graph
- Using a stacked chart
- Not identifying data clearly on a chart or graph

- **What is a database?** 96
- **Opening Access** 97
- **Creating a database file** 97
- **Opening a table** 98
  Tables 98
  Data types 99
  Properties 99
  Saving tables 100
  Renaming tables 101
  Primary key 101
- **Starting a new file** 102
- **Closing a file** 102
- **Opening a database** 103
- **Entering records** 103
  Spelling 104
- **Widening columns** 104
- **Amending records** 105
- **Printing a table** 105
  Orientation 105
  Print preview 105
  Printing headings 106
- **Deleting records** 107
- **Finding and replacing** 107
- **Sorting records** 109
- **Queries** 111
  Selecting field names 111
  Expressions 113
  Running a query 114
  Saving a query 114
  Sorting records in a query 115

Showing and hiding fields 116
Printing a query 116
- **Adding personal details** 117
- **Reports** 117
  Creating an AutoReport 117
  Reports using the wizard 118
  Report orientation 119
  Naming a report 120
  Displaying data in full 120
  Headers and footers 121
  Saving a report 121
- **Exiting the application** 122
- **Self-assessment checklist** 125
- **Summary of critical errors** 126

What is a database?

A database contains information that is stored in a systematic way, allowing it to be easily sorted and searched. Well-known examples that you might meet in everyday life include address books, seed catalogues and estate agents' house details. In database applications such as Microsoft Access, the basic data are stored in *tables*, with all the details about any one item forming a complete *record*.

You will be asked to carry out the following tasks:

- Open a database file
- Open a named table
- Replace words
- Add new records
- Delete records
- Rename a table
- Set table orientation
- Print a table showing field (column) headings
- Amend records
- Search for records meeting specific criteria
- Display only specified fields
- Sort records
- Save a query with a specified name
- Print a query
- Create and print a report
- Save a report with a specified name
- Display headers and footers
- Close a database file
- Exit the application

To pass Unit 3 you must be able to:

- Select and use appropriate software
- Open a database file
- Open a named table of data
- Enter new records
- Amend records
- Delete records
- Replace entries
- Print records
- Sort records
- Design queries to search for records meeting specific criteria
- Print queries
- Create and print reports
- Save tables, queries and reports with a specified name
- Set table, query and report orientation

- Display headers and footers
- Close the database file
- Exit the application

Opening Access

Double-click the **Access** icon 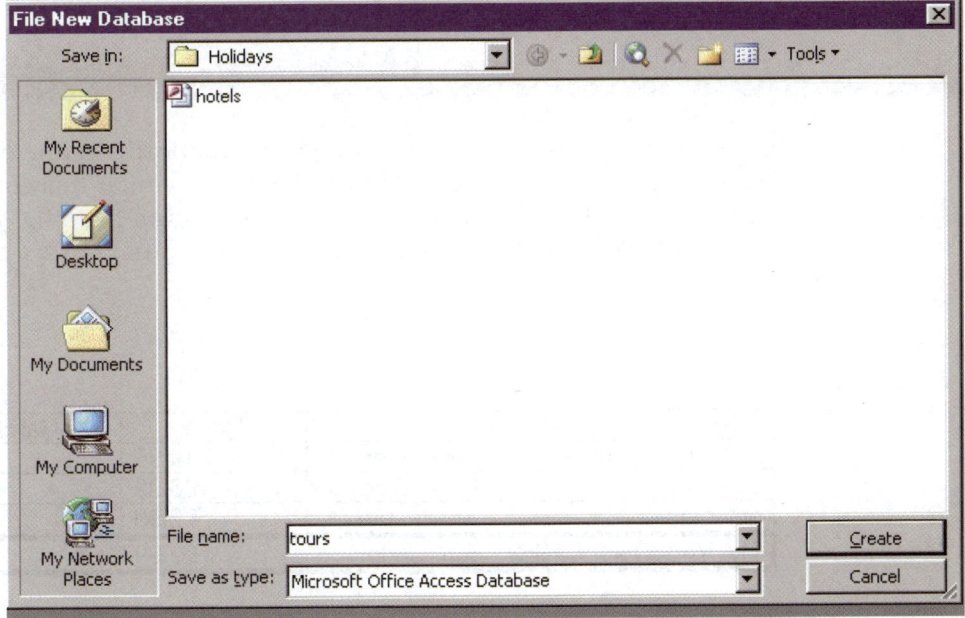 if it is visible on the desktop, or find Microsoft Access from the **Start/All Programs** menu.

Creating a database file

When you first open the application, you can open database files that have been created previously or create a new database. New CLAIT does not require you to create a database file or table of data, but it is difficult to understand the application without learning how to do so. It is also useful to be able to create databases if you want to practise on your own data.

Unlike other applications, Access requires you to create and name a database file *before* you can add any data.

After you select the **Blank Access database** option in the *Task* pane you will open a window very much like the *Save as* window used to save your work in other Microsoft applications. Decide where to save the new file, enter an appropriate file name and then click **Create**.

When the file opens, it is usually displayed as a restored window – see the next diagram. On the left are a series of tabs which you must click before working on any of the objects. For New CLAIT, you will work with the *Tables*, *Queries* and *Reports* tabs.

Opening a table

Once an object such as a table has been created, you can open it by double-clicking its name or clicking the **Open** button at the top of the database window. You can also view its structure by selecting **Design**.

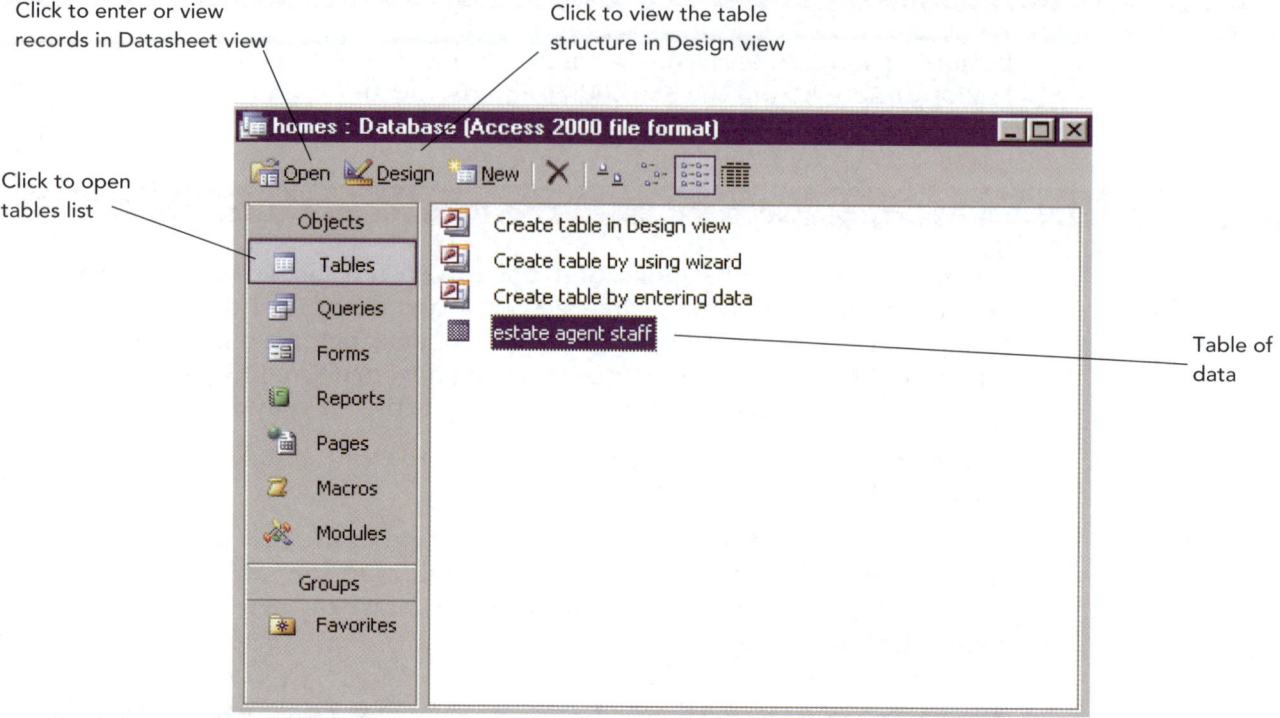

Click to enter or view records in Datasheet view

Click to view the table structure in Design view

Click to open tables list

Table of data

Tables

Information in a database file is stored systematically in one or more tables. When working with the data, the display looks similar to a spreadsheet. An entry in any cell is known as a *field* and the column headings are known as *field names*. All the information about one item is held in a single row and is referred to as a *record*.

Field

Title	Author	Price	Hardback	Category
Alice in Wonderland	Lewis Carroll	£14.95	Yes	Children
Unless	Carol Shields	£6.99	No	Fiction
Macbeth	Shakespeare	£2.99	No	Play
The Very Quiet Cricket	Eric Carle	£9.99	Yes	Children

One record

Before any records can be added to a table, its structure has to be established. To design the table, double-click the option to **Create table in Design view**.

Data types

For each field, only one specified type of data is allowed. For example, a *Name* field will usually hold text, an *Age* field will hold numbers and a *Price* field will hold currency. Where the data type is number, currency or date/time, the computer can perform calculations, search for larger or smaller entries, or search for dates that occur before or after one that is specified. Therefore it is important to select the correct data type. You also have the option to set a *Yes/No* data type where appropriate.

Having decided on the first field for the table, type its name in the first *Field Name* box. Now use the **Tab** key, or click with the mouse to move to the *Data Type* box and select an appropriate data type. Text is offered automatically, but a drop-down arrow allows you to find alternatives. You could also start typing the data type and it will appear in the box.

No *Description* is necessary for New CLAIT, so move to the next row and enter the second and subsequent field names and their data types.

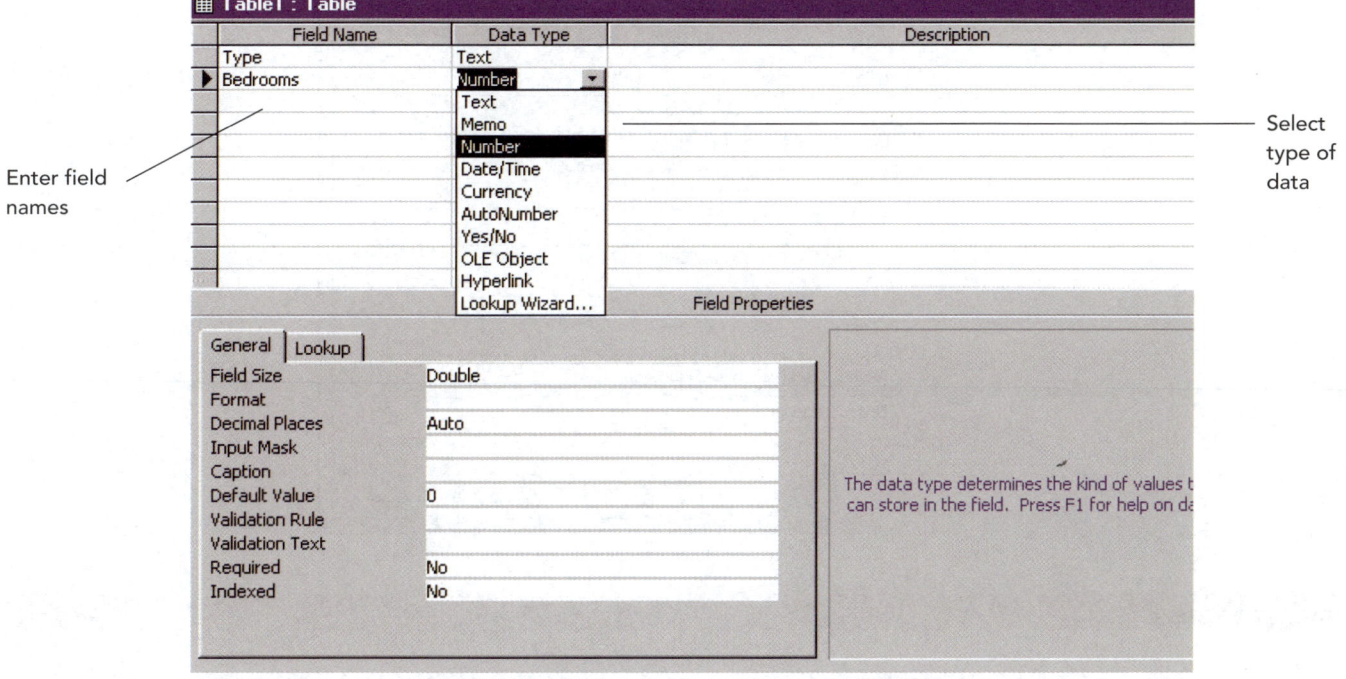

Enter field names

Select type of data

Properties

As you start entering a field name, a second window will open in the lower part of the screen labelled *Field Properties*, in which you can set various formats and rules for the field. Common changes include amending the automatic or default style of number or date, and decreasing the amount of space set aside for any entries.

- *Currency* – the default usually shows a £ symbol and two decimal places.
- *Numbers* – the default is usually set at *Long Integer*, which will suppress any decimals. To display decimals, change the entry to **Double** and then set the number of decimals in the *Decimal Place*s box.
- *Dates* – the range of formats includes *Short* (e.g. 21/5/06) and *Long* (e.g. 21st May 2006).

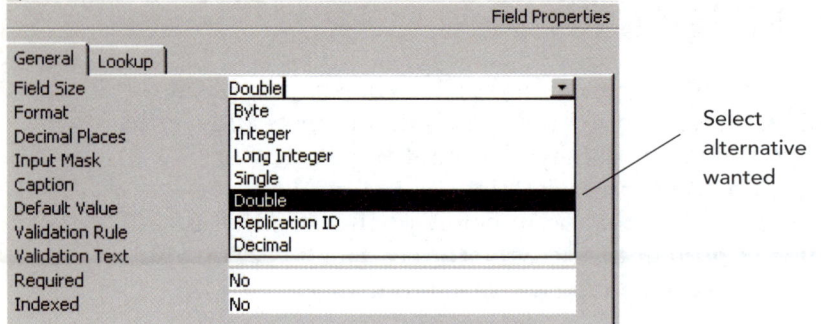

Select alternative wanted

Choose preference

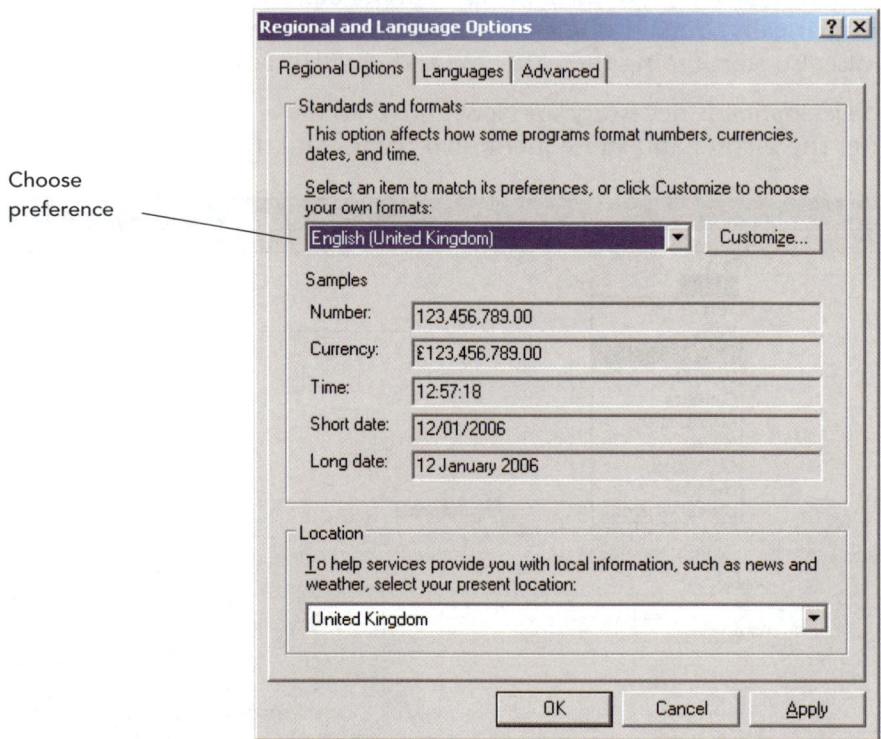

Saving tables

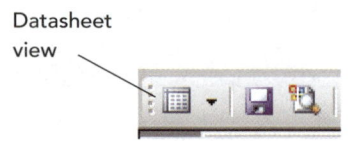

Datasheet view

When the table structure is complete, click the **Datasheet view** button to start entering records, or the **Close** button ⊠ on the table to return to the main database window.

You will first need to save the table, so click **Yes** when asked.

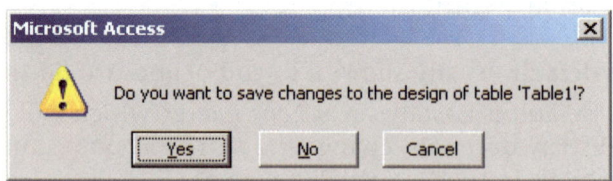

Type a name for your table in the *Save As* box. Table names should be relevant to the records they will contain but different from the main database file name. Finally, click **OK**.

Renaming tables

If you want to change a table name or correct a mistake in the naming, it is easy to rename any object created in Access. Right-click the closed table (or query or report) on the database window and select **Rename** from the menu that appears. Type in your new name and press **Enter** to complete the amendment.

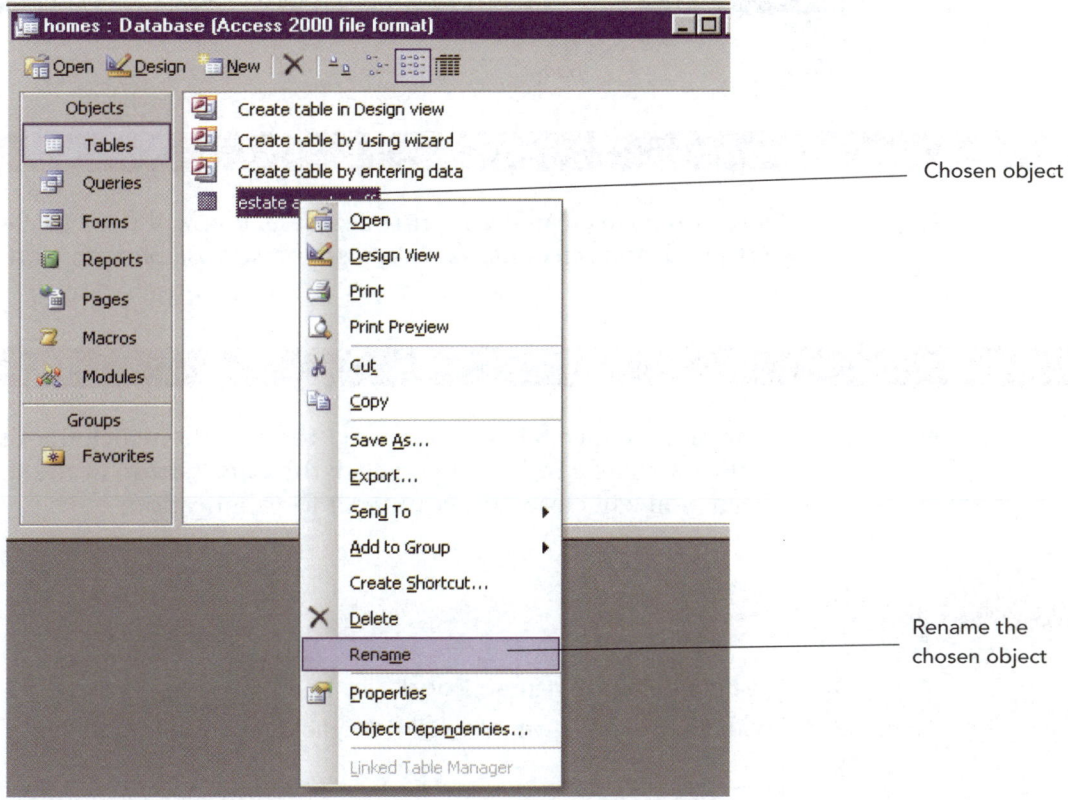

Chosen object

Rename the chosen object

Primary key

Before you can start entering records, you will see the following dialogue box.

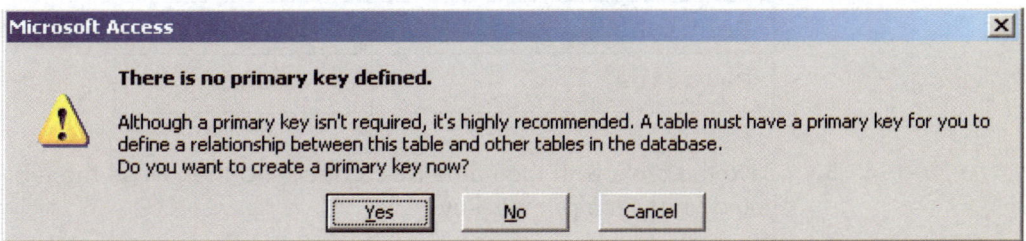

Microsoft Access is a *relational* database, which means that several tables can be linked for more sophisticated manipulation of data. This can only take place if one field in a table is assigned a *primary key*. For the purposes of New CLAIT no table will have a primary key, so at this stage always click **No**.

If you click **Yes** by mistake, you will find that a new field has been added to your table, labelled *ID* and with an *AutoNumber* data type. This means that each new record will be numbered 1, 2, 3 etc. To remove the field, return to *Design view* by clicking the button on the toolbar ![toolbar icon], select the **ID** row by clicking the grey box to the left of the field name and then press the **Delete** key.

Click to select ————

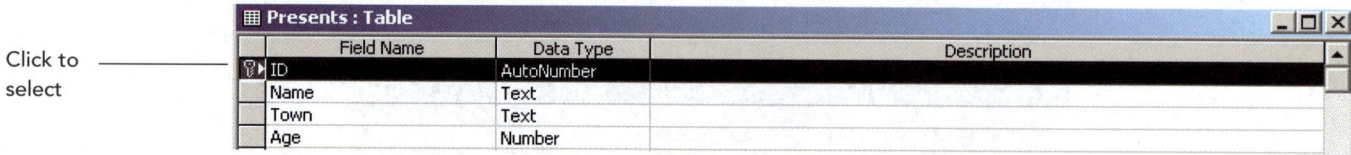

Starting a new file

Once you have created your first database, you will need to click the **New** button 🗋 and select **Blank Database** in the *Task* pane to start a new one.

Closing a file

If the table is open, click its **Close** button and then click the **Close** button on the database window. If you click the *Close* button at the top of the screen, you will close Access and exit the application.

Exercise 1

1. Create a database named **Food**.

2. Design a new table with the following field names and data types.

FIELD NAME	DATA TYPE
Main food	Text
Title	Text
Cooking time (mins)	Number
Portions	Number
Calories	Number

3. Save the table with the name **Recipes**, and then close the table, making sure you do not set a primary key.

4. Close *Food.*

Answer

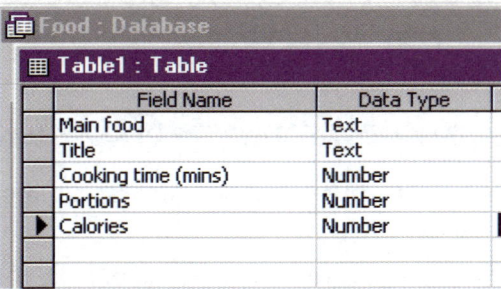

Opening a database

Click the **Open** button 📂 and browse through your files to locate the specified file name. Select it in the window and click **Open** or press the **Enter** key.

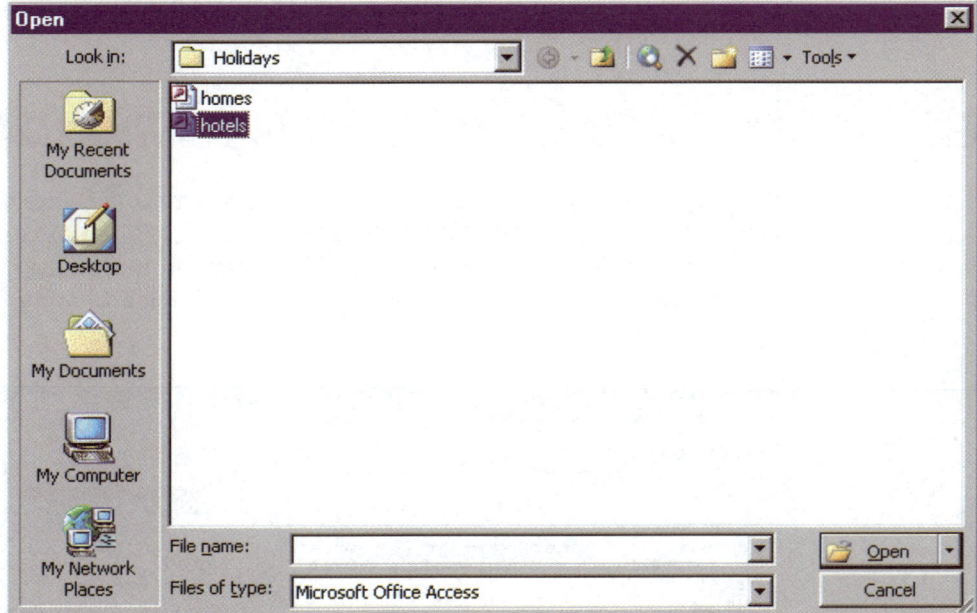

Entering records

Open a table showing on the database window by double-clicking or selecting it and clicking the **Open** button. If you are in *Design view*, click the **Datasheet view** button on the toolbar.

The field names will be visible across the screen on a grey background, and the first empty row will be displayed. Click into the first box and enter the first data entry. Then use the **Tab** or **arrow** keys to move across the row to enter all other data. Where number formats have been set, you will see a 0 (zero). Type over this to enter your data but do not add any letters or punctuation.

A new empty row will appear, ready for the next record. You will not be able to insert a record *between* those already present – always add new records at the end of the table.

Once you have added a number of records, scrollbars will appear to allow you to move around the table.

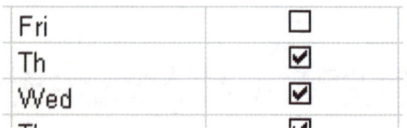

A quick way to repeat the entry of the data in the record above is to hold down **Ctrl** and press the **2** key.

If the table has any *Yes/No* fields, boxes may be offered instead of text. Click inside to add a tick for *Yes* or leave empty for *No*.

Spelling

Proofread your entries and use the spellchecker to make sure there are no errors. To spellcheck the table, click the **Spelling** toolbar button to open the *Spelling* box. Any errors can be corrected manually, or you can select an alternative from the *Suggestions*: list. Click a **Change option** to update the table.

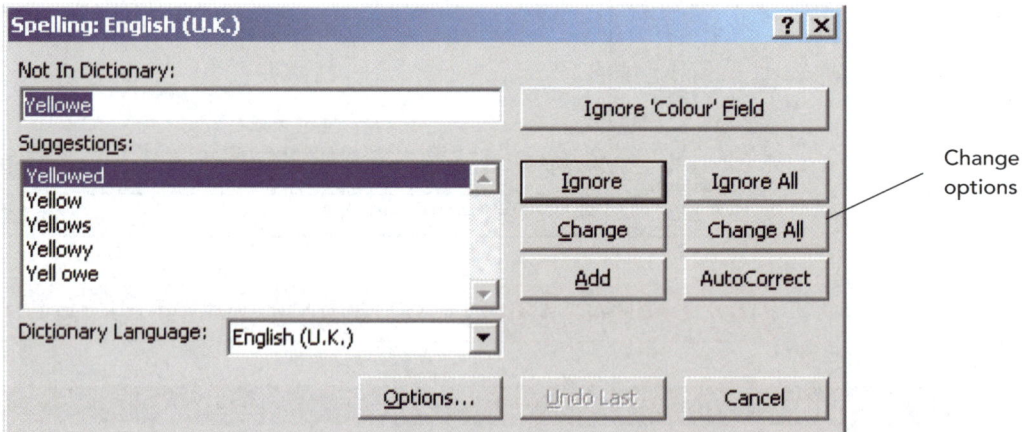

Change options

Widening columns

Original boundary position

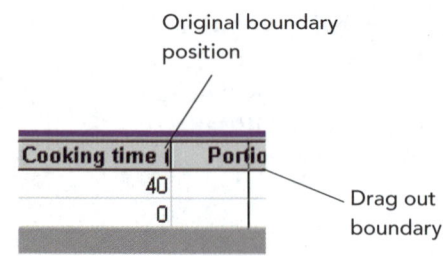

Drag out boundary

If a field name or entry is too wide and is hidden by a neighbouring entry, widen the column to display it in full. Position the pointer over the vertical line between field names in the grey area. When it changes to a two-way arrow, click and drag the column boundary to the right, or double-click to adjust the width to fit the longest entry exactly.

Amending records

To amend a field entry, either click in it with the mouse and make your changes, or move there using the **Tab** or **arrow** keys and double-click or press **F2** to put the cursor inside the cell.

Printing a table

Click the **Print** button 🖨 to print one copy of the open table.

Orientation

Access tables will print in portrait orientation by default. Therefore if you have a wide table, some fields may print on a second page. To change to landscape orientation, select this option on the *Page* tab after opening the **File/Page Setup** menu. Note that this orientation may revert back automatically – e.g. if you close and then reopen the table.

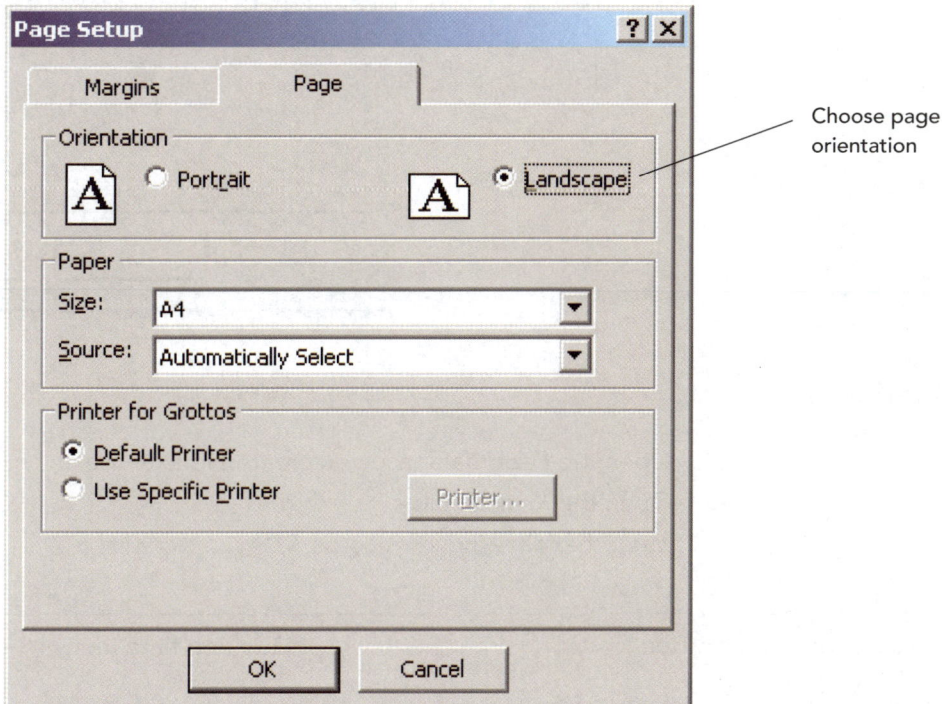

Choose page orientation

Print preview

To make sure that all your data are displayed fully, click the **Print Preview** button 🔍 to see what your printout will look like. Click the **Close** button on the toolbar to return to the table to carry out any corrections, or print directly when in this view.

Printing headings

You will need to print the field names as well as the records in the table. If they do not appear in *Print Preview*, open **Page Setup** and click the checkbox on the *Margins* tab.

Headings on/off

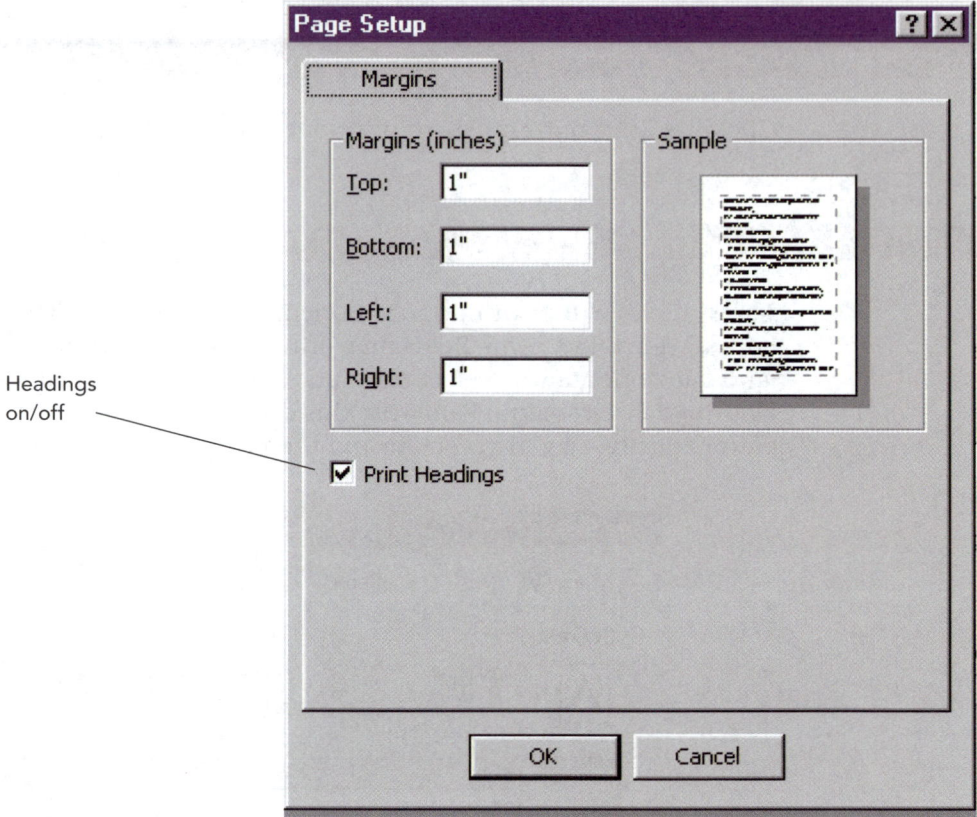

Exercise 2

1. Open the *Food* database you created in Exercise 1.
2. Open the *Recipes* table.
3. Enter the following six records.

Main food	Title	Cooking time (mins)	Portions	Calories
Cod	Fish pie	40	6	193
Lentils	Chilli	90	8	120
Aubergine	Roast vegetable soup	45	4	250
Banana	Tea bread	90	6	295
Eggs	Chocolate souffle	45	6	385
Pasta	Spaghetti bolognese	120	7	210

4. Print a copy of the table in landscape orientation ensuring that all data, including field names, are fully displayed.

5. Now make the following amendments:
   - ◾ *Fish pie* takes 50 minutes;
   - ◾ The *Tea bread* provides `eight` portions;
   - ◾ The *souffle* should be `Lemon`; and
   - ◾ There are 228 calories in one portion of *Spaghetti bolognese*.

6. Add the following three recipes:
   - ◾ `Hotpot` takes 180 minutes to cook, provides 10 portions, and uses `lamb` as the main food. Each portion contains 165 calories;
   - ◾ `Crumble` has `rhubarb` as the main food, takes 75 minutes to cook, contains 220 calories per portion and will provide 5 portions;
   - ◾ `Spanish omelette` takes 25 minutes to cook. Each portion contains 175 calories. The main ingredient is `eggs`. The recipe will feed 4 people.

7. Save these changes and print a second copy of the table making sure it is still in landscape orientation and that you display field names as well as the records.

Answer

Recipes : Table

Main food	Title	Cooking time (mins)	Portions	Calories
Cod	Fish pie	50	6	193
Lentils	Chilli	90	8	120
Aubergine	Roast vegetable soup	45	4	250
Banana	Tea bread	90	8	295
Eggs	Lemon souffle	45	6	385
Pasta	Spaghetti bolognese	120	7	228
Lamb	Hotpot	180	10	165
Rhubarb	Crumble	75	5	220
Eggs	Spanish omelette	25	4	175

Deleting records

Select the entire record to be deleted by clicking the grey box at the start of the row. Then press the **Delete** key or click the **Delete** button ▶✕ . You will have a chance to cancel the operation, but once accepted it cannot be reversed.

Common mistake

Deleting the wrong record or deleting only part of a record, leaving empty cells.

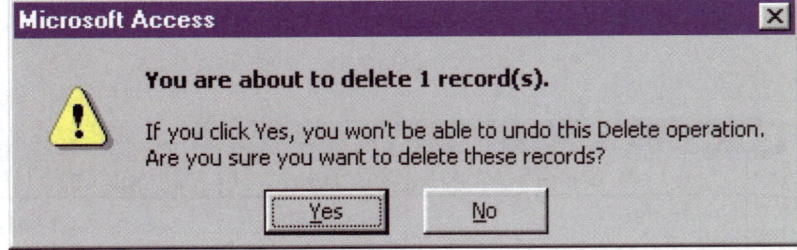

Microsoft Access

You are about to delete 1 record(s).

If you click Yes, you won't be able to undo this Delete operation. Are you sure you want to delete these records?

[Yes]   [No]

Finding and replacing

Databases can contain thousands of records, so you need a quick way to amend entries – e.g. if names change or errors are discovered. As with most Microsoft applications, Access makes use of the *Find and Replace* tool available from the *Edit* menu. However, it is set to search only the selected field (i.e. wherever the cursor is positioned) unless the option to search the entire table is selected.

To replace entries, open the **Edit/Replace** dialogue box and type the text that you want to find in the *Find What:* box. Type the replacement text in the *Replace With:* box and check that the correct field, or whole table, is to be searched.

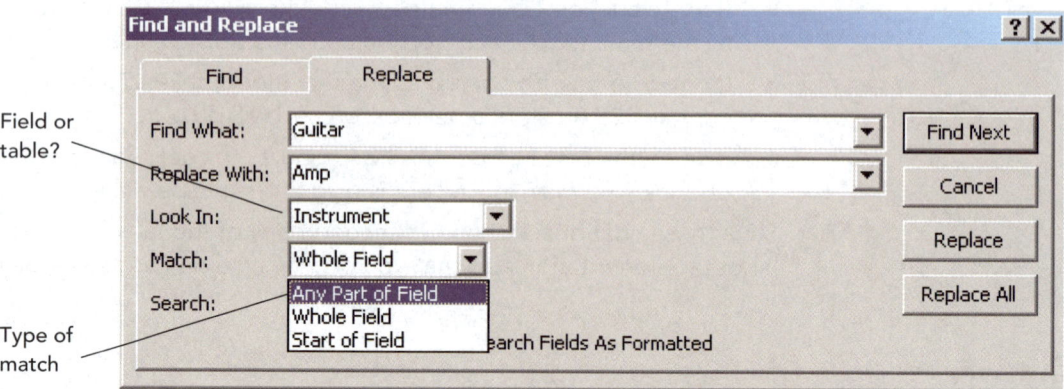

To complete the replacement throughout the table, click **Replace All**. To control the process, find the first matching entry by clicking **Find Next** and then click **Replace** or skip to another match by clicking **Find Next** again. Note: the process will not work if you actually position the cursor on the only example of a matching entry.

Common mistake

Replacing entries manually and missing out one or more replacements.

Common mistake

Not finding part of a field, rather than an entire entry, because the option has not been selected in the *Match* box.

Exercise 3

1. Open the file *Christmas* and the table *Grottos* from the CD or create your own version using the following data.

Grottos : Table

Shop	Town	Maximum age	Opening date	Opening hour	Closing hour
Dewburies	Manchester	11	01/12/2004	10:00:00	16:30:00
Hansomes	Bradford	14	10/12/2004	11:30:00	16:30:00
Bakewells	Leeds	10	04/11/2004	12:30:00	16:30:00
Salsbury Department Store	Bradford	9	15/11/2004	11:30:00	15:30:00
Maynards Store	Bradford	12	15/11/2004	11:30:00	16:00:00
Deralds	Leeds	9	10/11/2004	11:00:00	15:00:00

2. Print a copy of the table.

3. Now make the following amendments:

- Replace all entries for *Bradford* with `Birmingham`.
- Delete the record for *Bakewells.*
- Add the following two entries:

Shop	Town	Maximum age	Opening date	Opening hour	Closing hour
Saxons	Manchester	13	01/12/2004	10:30:00	16:30:00
Jerry's Toyshop	Leeds	11	14/12/2004	12:30:00	14:30:00

4. Print a copy of the amended table and then close the file.

Answer

Grottos : Table					
Shop	Town	Maximum age	Opening date	Opening hour	Closing hour
Dewburies	Manchester	11	01/12/2004	10:00:00	16:30:00
Hansomes	Birmingham	14	10/12/2004	11:30:00	16:30:00
Salsbury Department Store	Birmingham	9	15/11/2004	11:30:00	15:30:00
Maynards Store	Birmingham	12	15/11/2004	11:30:00	16:00:00
Deralds	Leeds	9	10/11/2004	11:00:00	15:00:00
Saxons	Manchester	13	01/12/2004	10:30:00	16:30:00
Jerry's Toyshop	Leeds	11	14/12/2004	12:30:00	14:30:00

Sorting records

To sort (reorder) the records in a table, decide which field will form the basis for the sort – e.g. by *Price*, or by *First Name* etc. – and then click any entry in that field.

To sort in ascending order – e.g. from lowest to highest numbers, or alphabetically from A to Z – click the ⬆ button. To sort in descending order, click the ⬇ button.

You do not have to select the whole table before sorting when using Access as records are never split during a sort.

> **FOR ANYONE USING A SPREADSHEET AS A DATABASE, A SORT THAT RESULTS IN DATA LOSING ITS INTEGRITY BECAUSE RECORDS HAVE BEEN SPLIT WILL BE PENALIZED AS A CRITICAL ERROR.**

Sometimes after working, closing and then reopening a table, the records will appear to have been reordered automatically. As long as the correct sort is carried out and printed when instructed, there is no penalty if records later appear in a different order.

1. Open the file *College* from the CD and then open the *Classes* table. If you prefer, create a file named `College` and then design a `Classes` table and enter the following records.

Class	Room	Day	Time	Cost	Start Date
Watercolour	Hall	Tuesday	Evening	£30	12/9/03
Yoga	Hall	Thursday	Morning	£20	28/9/03
French	C7	Tuesday	Evening	£45	12/9/03
Computing	A4	Wednesday	Afternoon	£80	03/1/04
Sculpture	Hall	Monday	Evening	£65	08/1/04
Spanish	C7	Thursday	Evening	£45	21/9/03
Keep Fit	Hall	Wednesday	Afternoon	£20	10/1/04
Drawing	A4	Tuesday	Morning	£30	19/9/03
Bee-keeping	Annexe	Monday	Evening	£50	08/1/04
German	C7	Monday	Morning	£45	25/9/03

2. It has been decided to display the *Time* in code form. Use **Edit/Replace** to amend the entries to show the following codes:
   - *Evening* should become **EV**
   - *Morning* should become **MO**
   - *Afternoon* should become **AFT**
3. The *Sculpture* class has no applicants, so delete the entire record for this class.
4. Add a further class: `Business`, taking place on `Wednesday evenings` in room `A4` and costing `£75`. The start date is `10 January 2004`.
5. Now sort the records in descending order of cost.
6. Print a copy of the table in landscape orientation, making sure all entries and field names are displayed clearly.
7. Save any changes and close the table.
8. Close the *College* file.

Answer

⊞ Classes : Table					
Class	**Room**	**Day**	**Time**	**Cost**	**Start date**
Computing	A4	Wednesday	AFT	£80	03/01/04
Business	A4	Wednesday	EV	£75	10/01/04
Bee-keeping	Annexe	Monday	EV	£50	08/01/04
German	C7	Monday	MO	£45	25/09/03
Spanish	C7	Thursday	EV	£45	21/09/03
French	C7	Tuesday	EV	£45	12/09/03
Drawing	A4	Tuesday	MO	£30	19/09/03
Watercolour	Hall	Tuesday	EV	£30	12/09/03
Keep Fit	Hall	Wednesday	AFT	£20	10/01/04
Yoga	Hall	Thursday	MO	£20	28/09/03

Queries

To answer questions such as 'How many classes run on Thursdays?', or 'Which classes start in January?' you must design search objects known as *queries*, which will find all the records matching your specific criteria. These searches can only be run when a table is closed, but they can be saved and then run repeatedly to take account of any new records added to the table.

Selecting field names

Records found as a result of a search do not have to display entries in all fields. Select which fields you want to be displayed and the order in which they should appear, if you want to limit the information that is displayed.

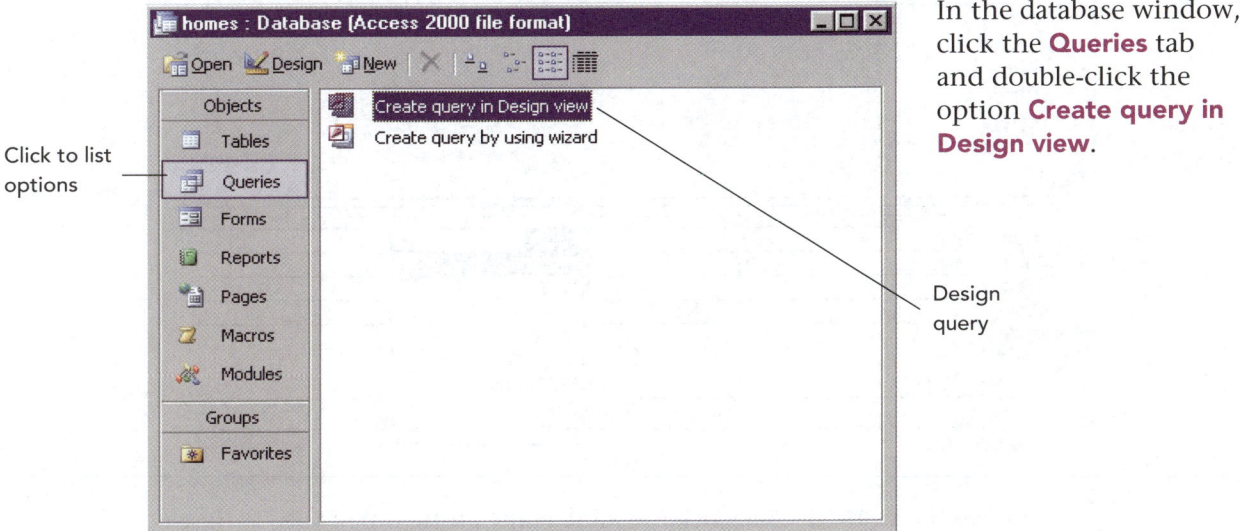

Click to list options

Design query

In the database window, click the **Queries** tab and double-click the option **Create query in Design view**.

Select the table that you want to search from the *Tables* tab in the *Show Table* dialogue box and click **Add** to place it at the top of the *Query* window. Then close the *Show Table* window. (If the *Show Table* window does not appear or is closed by mistake, open it from the *Query* menu.)

If you accidentally click the *Add* button twice, select and delete the extra table before continuing.

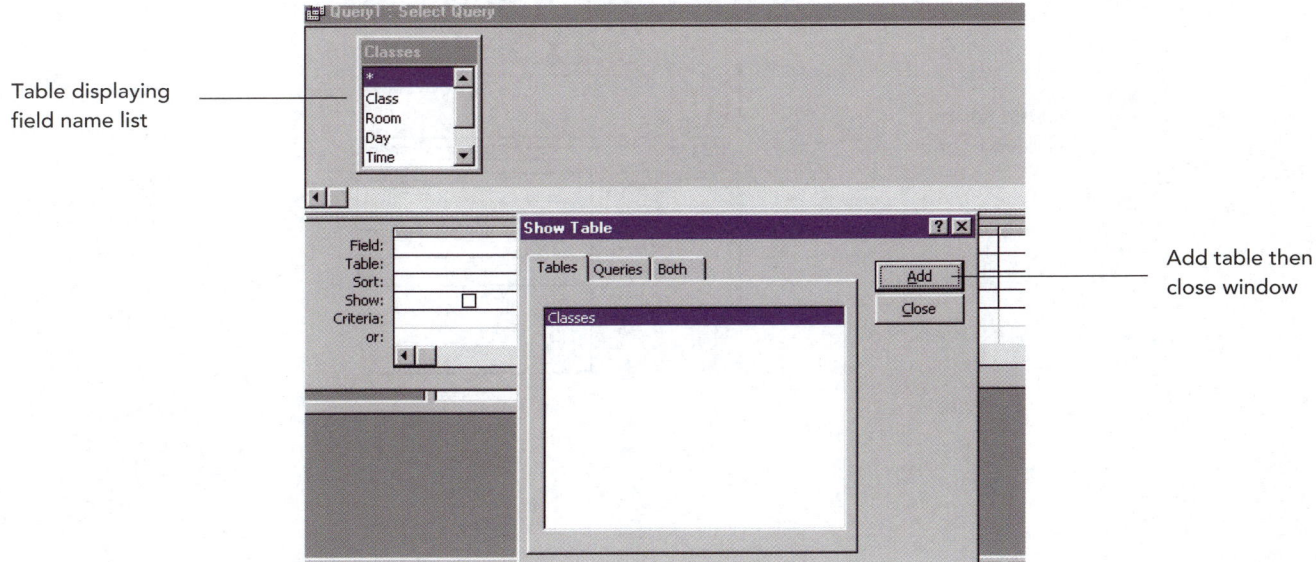

Table displaying field name list

Add table then close window

Decide which fields you want to display and position them along the *Field* row at the bottom of the query.

Use any of these methods to add fields individually to the query grid:

- double-click the name in the *Field name* list
- click a field name in the list and drag it to the next empty *Field* cell on the grid
- click on the grid and select a field name from the drop-down list in the *Field* row.

The source table will appear automatically underneath each field name.

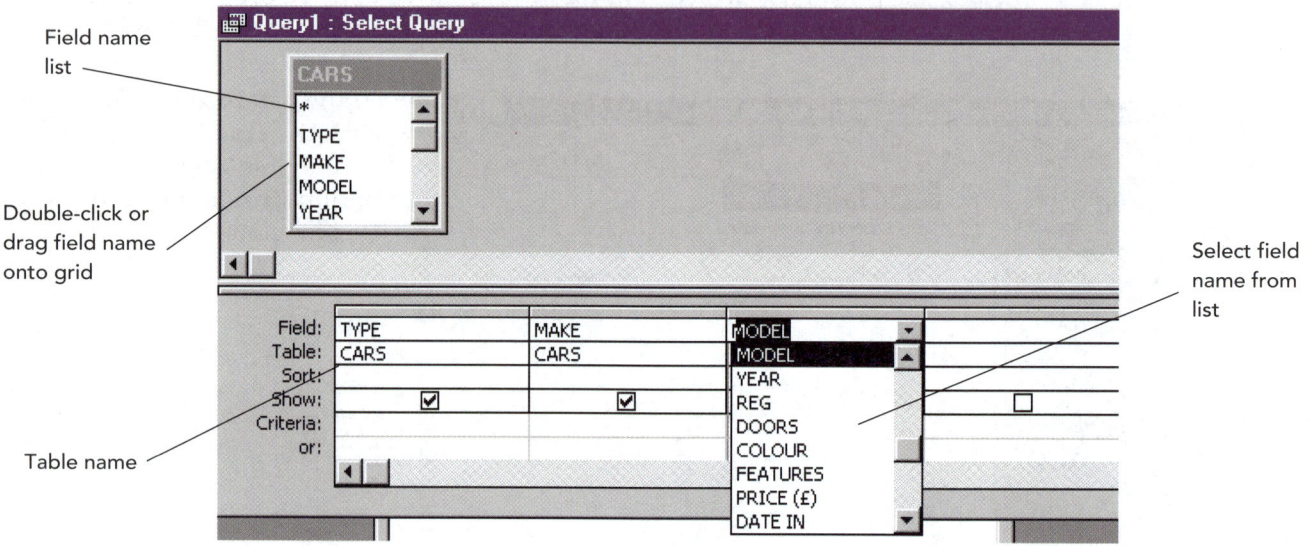

To add *all* the fields, double-click the table name at the top of the list to select all the names, then drag the block of names onto the first cell on the grid.

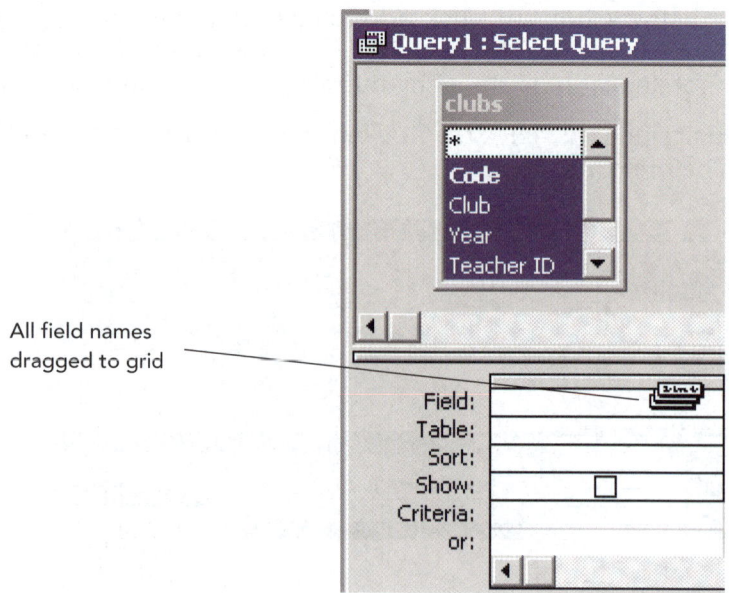

To search for specific records, you need to enter the criteria for one or more fields in the bottom row of the grid. The accepted format for these expressions must be used, and Access will then search for matching entries in that particular field.

For example, in the following database to find all *red* cars you would type the word `red` in the *Criteria* row under the *COLOUR* field name. To find cars delivered in June 2002, you would type `Between 1/6/02 and 30/6/02` in the *Criteria* row under *DATE IN*.

After pressing **Enter** or moving to another field, the computer adds quote marks to text entries, # symbols to date entries and nothing to number entries, indicating that the data types have been recognized.

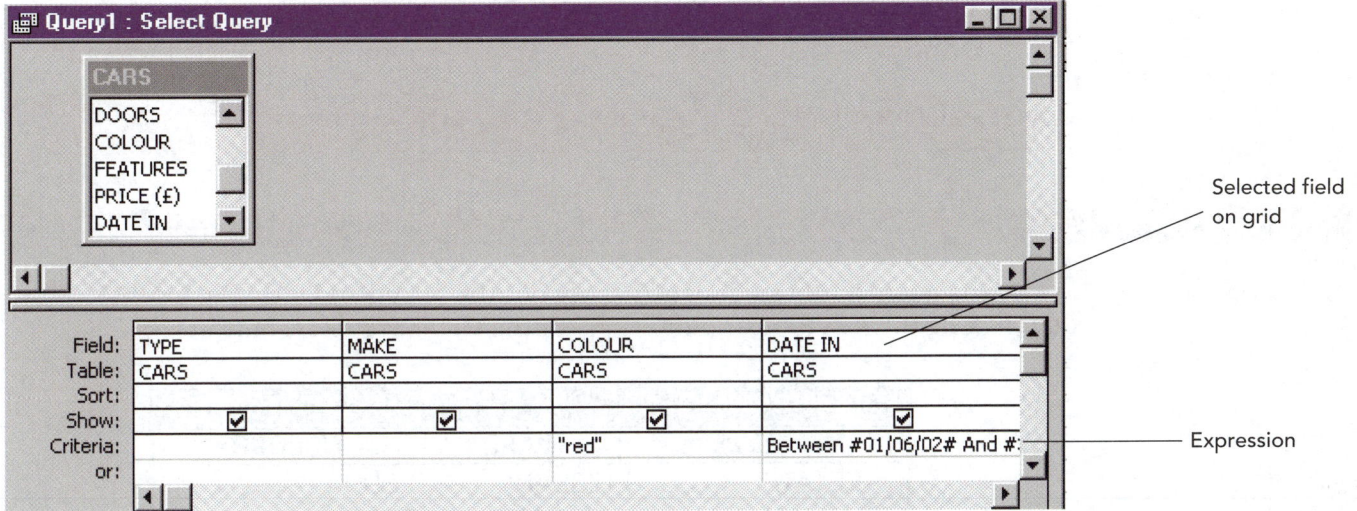

Selected field on grid

Expression

A wide range of expressions are accepted as search criteria. Here are the expressions you might need in order to carry out a search.

- To match an entry exactly – type the full word, date, time or number; e.g. `red`
- To find a numerical entry that is larger than, or (for dates/time) later than – use the greater-than symbol; e.g. `>100`
- To find a numerical entry that is smaller than (or before a date or time) – use the less-than symbol; e.g. `<1 Jan 2004`
- To find a numerical entry that is equal to or greater than – use >=; e.g. `>=11` will find 11 and all higher numbers
- To find a numerical entry that is equal to or less than – use <=; e.g. `<=11` will find 11 and all lower numbers
- To find a numerical entry that is not equal to – use <> or Not; e.g. `<>54` or `Not 54`
- To find either one entry or another – use OR; e.g. `London OR Bristol`
- To find an entry that begins with a particular letter or number – use * for the unknown characters; e.g. `P*` will find *Peter*, *Penny* and *Pat*
- To find an entry containing particular numbers or letters – use * for the unknown characters; e.g. `*34*` will find 12345 and 1348
- To find an entry between two dates or numbers – use *Between*; e.g. `Between 10 and 100`
- To find an entry where the table displays Yes and No checkboxes – type the word `Yes` or `No` as appropriate on the *Criteria* row.

Only type figures (e.g. 250 or 1467, not £250 or 1,467) when typing expressions.

AN INCORRECT SEARCH RESULT DUE TO THE USE OF THE WRONG CRITERIA IS A CRITICAL ERROR.

NOT PRINTING THE SPECIFIED FIELDS IS A CRITICAL ERROR.

Running a query

Once the query has been designed, carry out the search and view the results by clicking the **Run** toolbar button ❗ or the **Datasheet view** button.

Query1 : Select Query

TYPE	MAKE	COLOUR
ESTATE	NISSAN	RED
SALOON	RENAULT	RED
HATCHBACK	FORD	RED
4x4	VAUXHALL	RED
SALOON	NISSAN	RED

If the records do not appear as expected, return to the *Design view* by clicking the toolbar button and check all entries before running the query again.

Saving a query

Closing the query or clicking the **Save** button will offer a saving box in which to type the query name – e.g. *Red Cars*.

Exercise 5

1. Open the *College* database you worked on in Exercise 4.
2. Design a query to find all classes held on *Mondays*, and display all the fields.
3. Save as `Monday classes`.
4. Now design a new query to find all classes that cost less than *£25*. Display only the following fields: *Class*, *Day*, *Time* and *Cost*.
5. Save as `Cheap classes`.
6. Close the *College* file.

Answers

Monday classes : Select Query

Class	Room	Day	Time	Cost	Start date
▶ Bee-keeping	Annexe	Monday	EV	£50	08/01/04
German	C7	Monday	MO	£45	25/09/03

Cheap classes : Select Query

Class	Day	Time	Cost
▶ Yoga	Thursday	MO	£20
Keep Fit	Wednesday	AFT	£20

Sorting records in a query

As well as using the A–Z buttons to sort records when viewing the results of a query, you can select a sort order for any field during its design.

Click the relevant box in the *Sort* row and select **Ascending** or **Descending**.

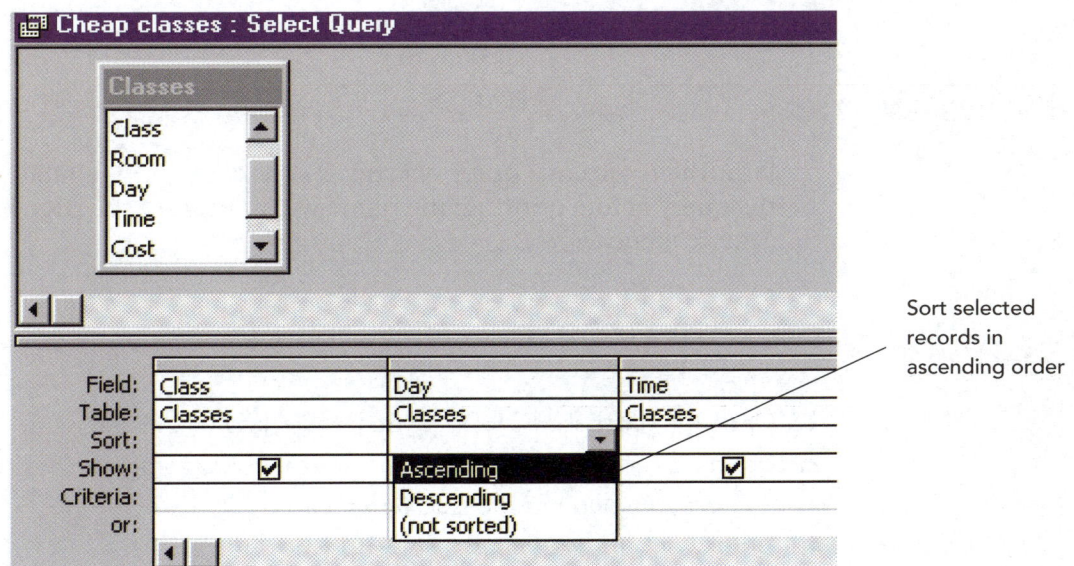

Sort selected records in ascending order

Showing and hiding fields

You may find that the fields that you must display after searching a table do not include the field(s) on which a search is based. To design an effective query, you must have these searchable fields on the *Field* row and enter expressions in the *Criteria* row. However, before running the query, click the **tick** off in the *Show* checkbox so that the field entries will not be displayed.

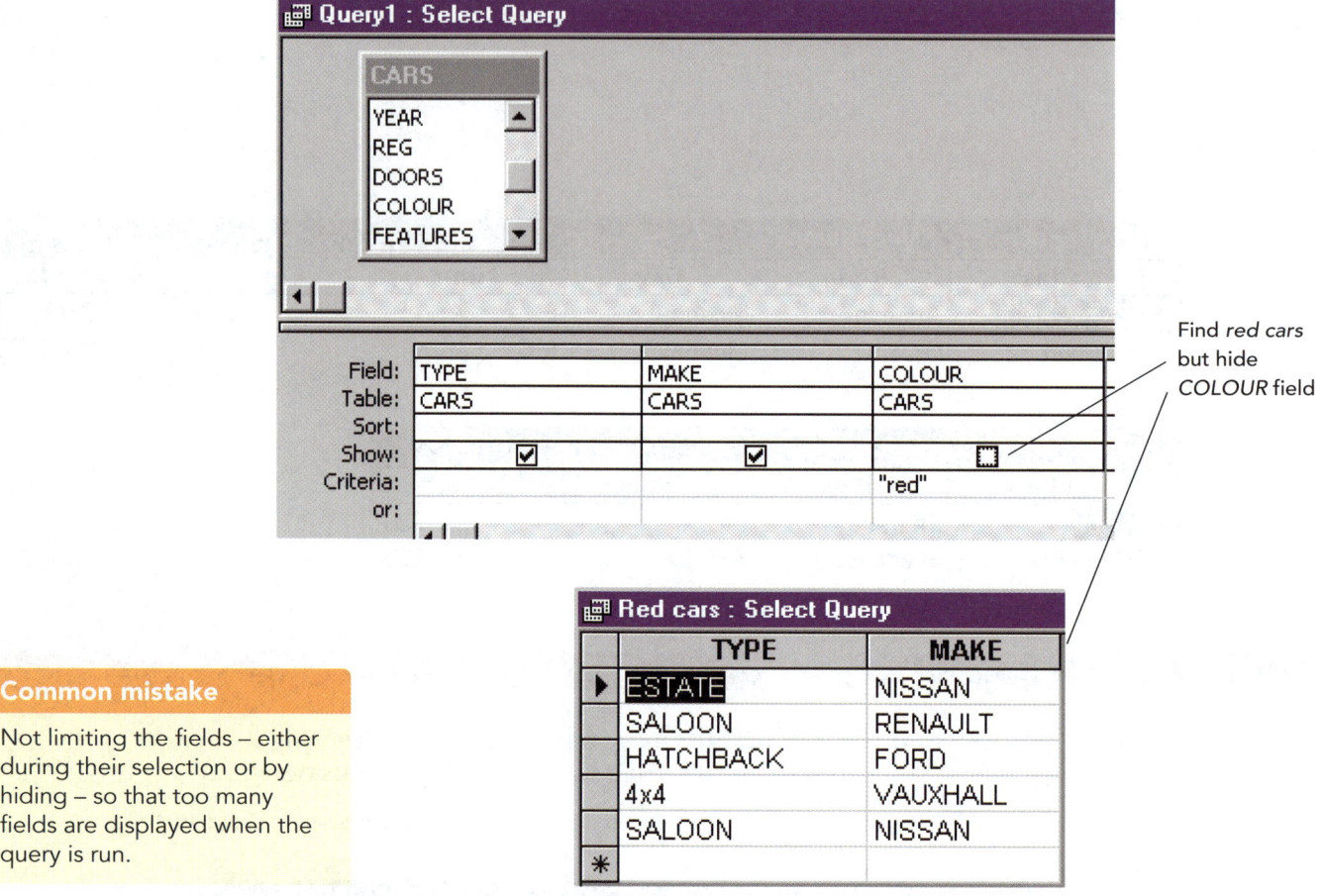

Find *red cars* but hide *COLOUR* field

Printing a query

Print the results of a query exactly as you would print a table. If you save the query before printing, the name will appear on the page instead of the generic name *Query1*.

Exercise 6

1. Open the database *Food* that you last worked on in Exercise 2.
2. Design a query to display all the recipes that have *eggs* as the main ingredient.
3. Sort in ascending order of *cooking time*.
4. Display only the *recipe title*, *cooking time* and *calories*.
5. Save as `Egg recipes` and print a copy.
6. Close *Food*.
7. Reopen the database *College* that you last worked on in Exercise 5.

8. Design a query to find all the afternoon classes that start in *2004* (i.e. after 31/12/03).
9. Sort the records in ascending order of cost.
10. Display only the following fields: *Class*, *Day* and *Cost*.
11. Save as `Afternoon Classes 2004`.
12. Print a copy of the records and then close the file.

Answer

Step 5

Egg recipes : Select Query		
Title	**Cooking time (mins)**	**Calories**
Spanish omelette	25	175
Lemon souffle	45	385

Step 12

Afternoon Classes 2004 : Select Query		
Class	**Day**	**Cost**
Keep Fit	Wednesday	£20
Computing	Wednesday	£80

Adding personal details

Every row in a database table is seen as *a record*. Therefore, you must not add your name, date and centre number on a new row because they will be incorporated into sorts and searches. Instead, write your details on any printouts by hand. In large classes, or when instructed to do so during an assessment, add your name or initials to the query, table or report name during a save or when renaming, to help you identify your own printouts.

Reports

To display your data more attractively than in a table, you can create an object known as a *report*. There are two quick methods for creating reports: selecting an *AutoReport* option from the menu or using the *Report Wizard*.

Creating an AutoReport

Select the **Report** tab and then click the **New** button. From the list, click a style of report – e.g. **AutoReport: Tabular** – and then choose a named table or query on which to base the report from the drop-down list. Click **OK** and wait a few moments for the report to appear.

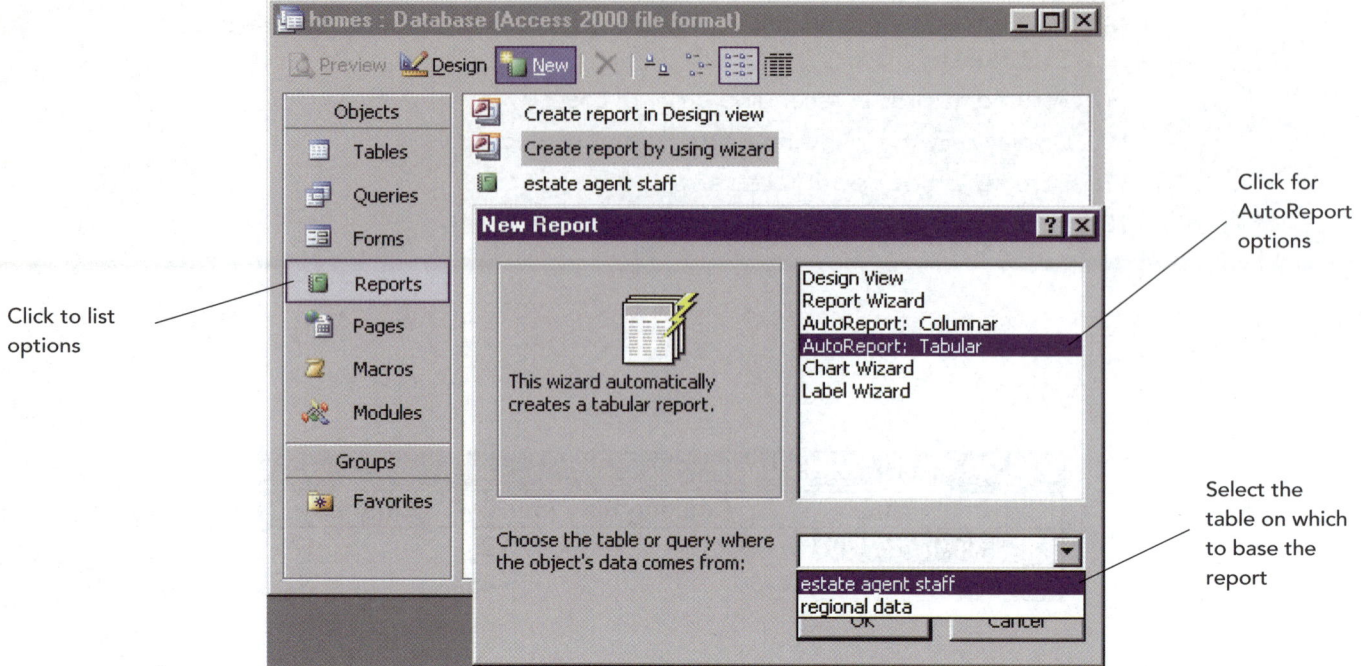

Click to list options

Click for AutoReport options

Select the table on which to base the report

A typical tabular report looks like this.

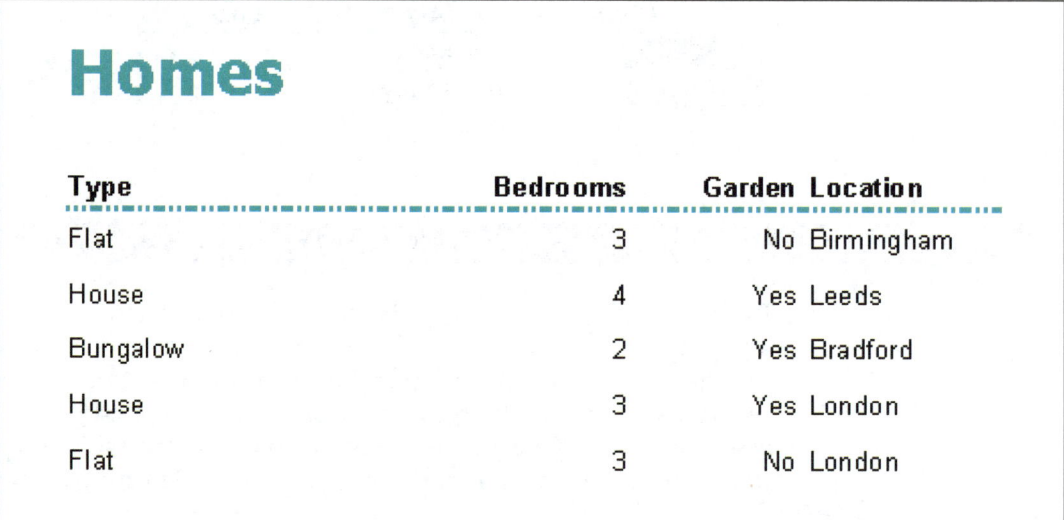

Homes

Type	Bedrooms	Garden	Location
Flat	3	No	Birmingham
House	4	Yes	Leeds
Bungalow	2	Yes	Bradford
House	3	Yes	London
Flat	3	No	London

Reports using the wizard

For more control over the appearance of the report, double-click the option on the *Report* tab to **Create report by using wizard**. You can now take the following steps to create a report based on your chosen table or query, clicking **Next** to move on.

- Click the **double arrow** button to add all the fields in their original order, or select individual fields and click the **single arrow**. You can now add fields to the report in your chosen order and leave some out of the report altogether.

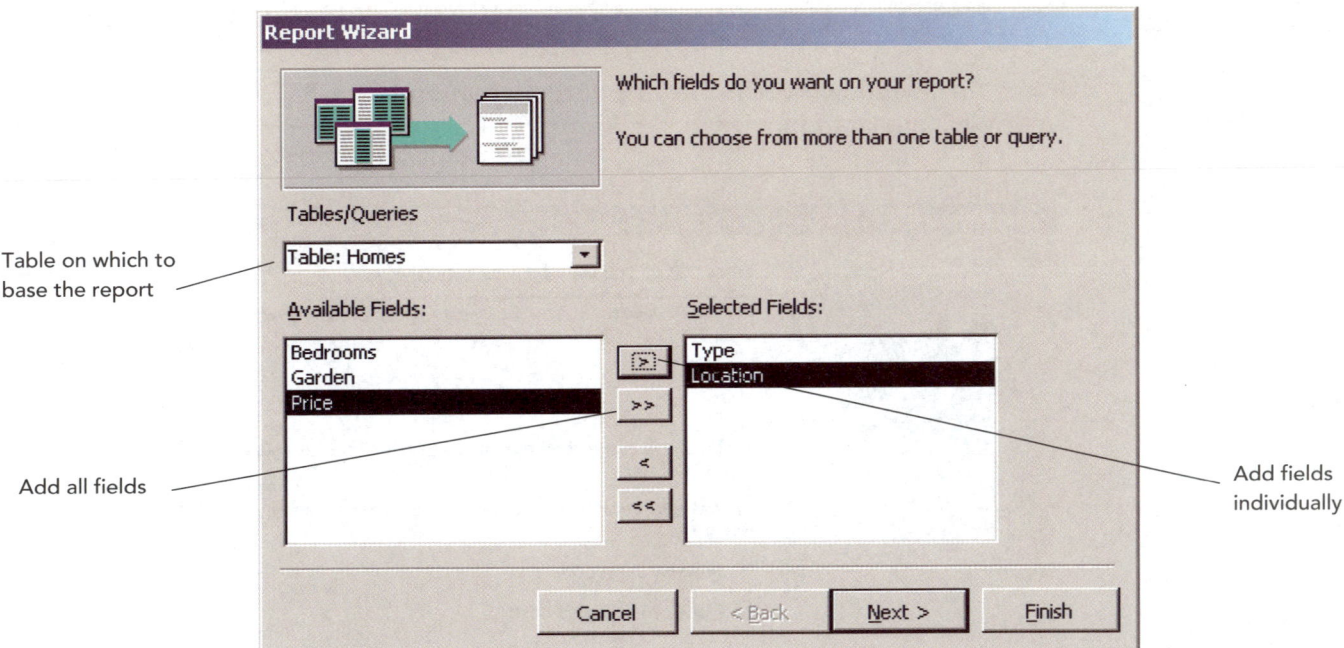

Table on which to base the report

Add all fields

Add fields individually

Extra steps not required for New CLAIT are available from the wizard:

- you can choose one field by which to group records – e.g. homes by *type*, or classes by *day*
- you can select fields on which to sort the records
- if you click **Summary Options**, you can add calculations – e.g. totals or averages for any fields containing numerical data.

Report orientation

At one stage during the creation of a report, you can click an alternative orientation if you do not want the report in portrait format. You can also select a preferred layout.

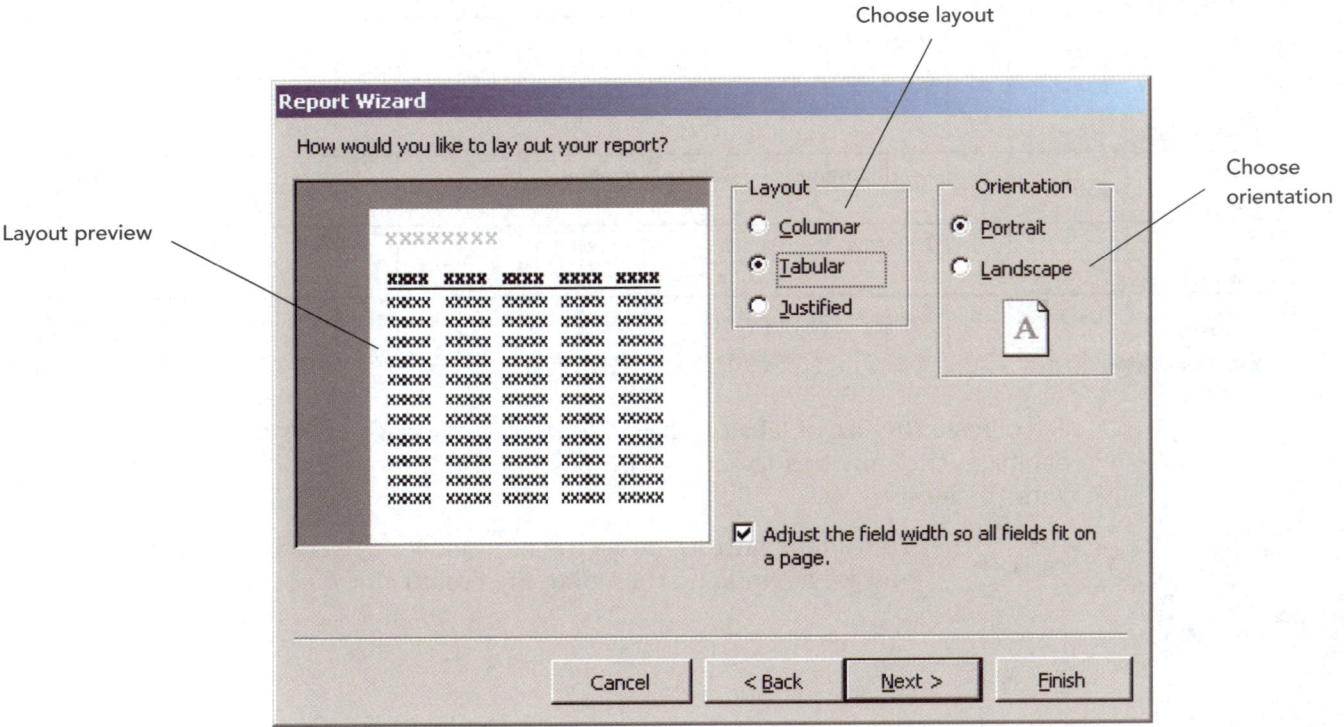

Choose layout

Choose orientation

Layout preview

Naming a report

In the final window, type in the *title* of the report and click **Finish**. The report will appear in preview.

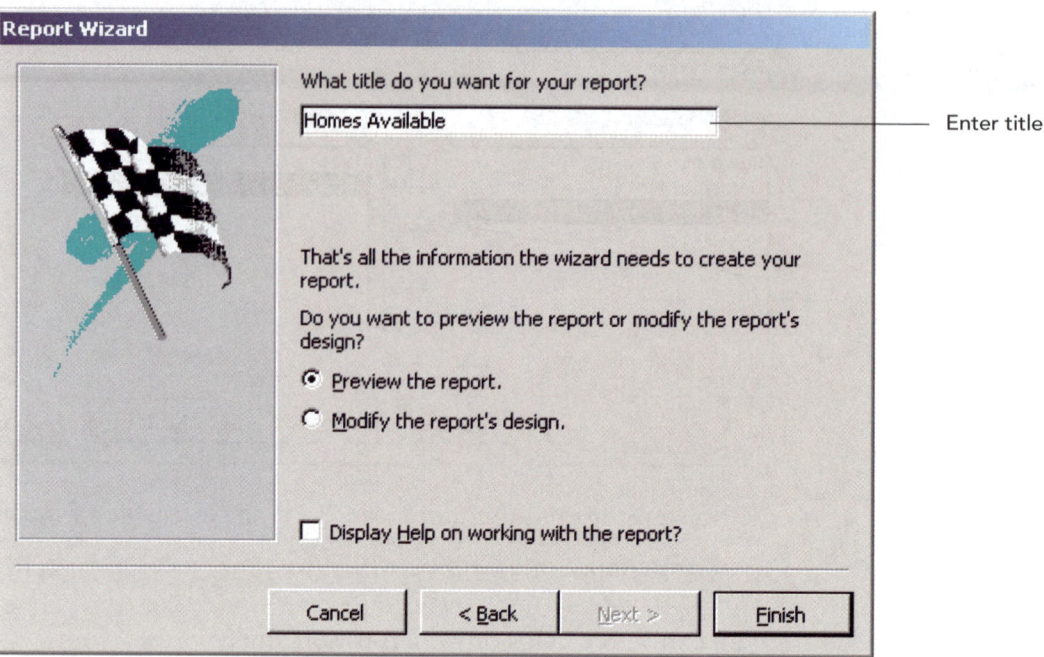

Enter title

Displaying data in full

Sometimes, report entries are too close together or labels are truncated. To improve the appearance of the report, click the **Design view** button.

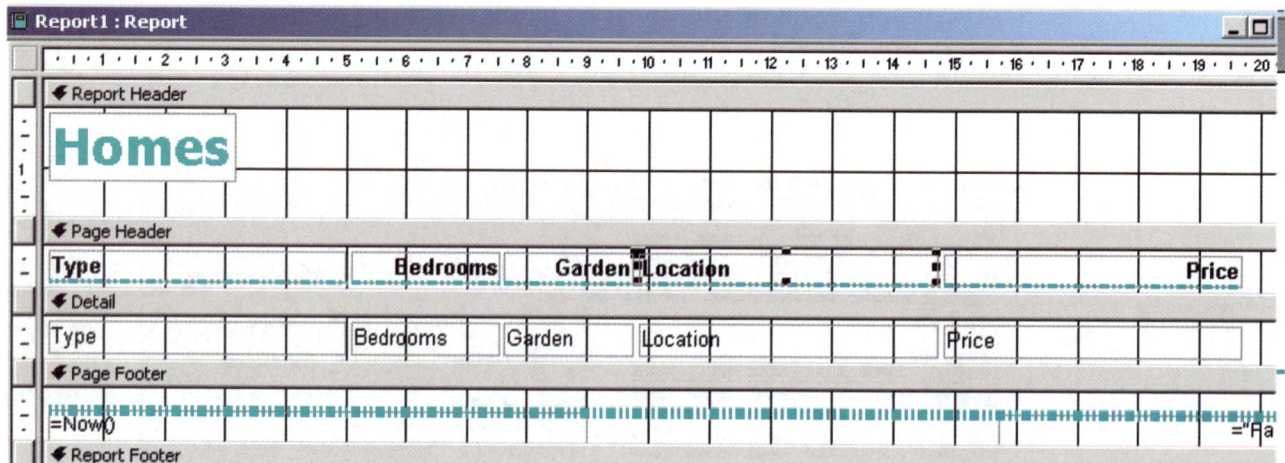

To increase the size of labels or boxes (*controls*) showing entries from the database, click any box to show *sizing handles* and then drag the border out with the mouse.

To realign controls, move the mouse over a selected box until you see a hand and then drag the box to a new position.

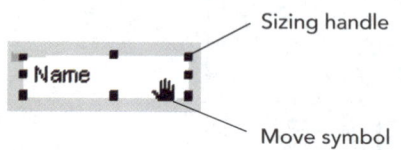

Sizing handle

Move symbol

Headers and footers

At the top and bottom of the report are areas for page or report headers and footers. Some entries will appear automatically.

In *Design view*, today's date shows as (*=Now*) and page numbers as = *"Page" & [Page]*.

To add them if they are missing, or have been deleted by mistake, open the **Insert** menu, choose **Page Numbers** or **Date and Time** and select the preferred style and position for the entry before clicking **OK**.

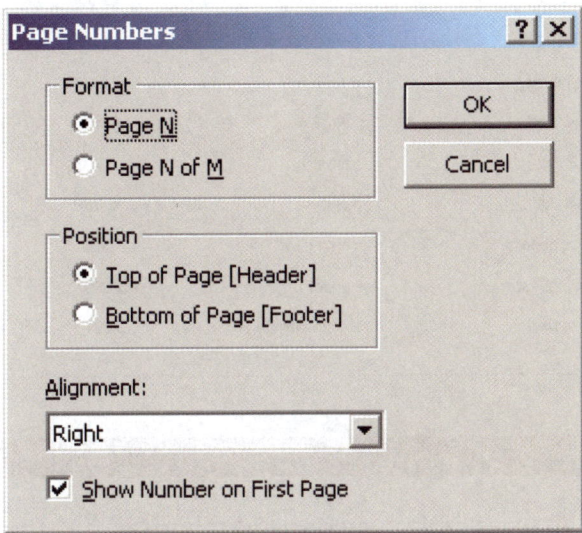

Saving a report

If you are using the wizard, the report will be saved automatically with the title that you choose. For an *AutoReport*, you will be asked to save the report and can enter a name into the *Save As* window.

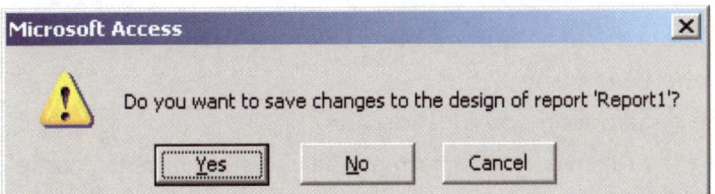

To change the name of a saved report, right-click the closed report in the database window and select **Rename**.

Exercise 7

1. Open the database *Music* from the CD.
2. Create a tabular report based on the *Instruments* table.
3. Set to portrait orientation.
4. Give the report the title: `Instruments in Stock`
5. Save the report with the name `In stock`.

6. Make sure that the date and page number are showing in the footer.
7. Check that all the data is fully displayed.
8. Print one copy.
9. Save and close the file.

Instruments in Stock

Instrument	Make	Price	In stock	Model
Guitar	Les Paul	£2,000	3	2005
Guitar	Fender Strat	£1,560	10	2004
Keyboard	Casio	£190	6	2006
Keyboard	Yamaha	£149	4	2005
Drum kit	Yamaha	£1489	2	2004
Drum kit	Roland	£2089	5	2006
Bass guitar	Fender	£310	10	2005
Bass guitar	Fender	£389	6	2005
Bass pad	Squier Affinity	£237	3	2006

Exiting the application

Close all open tables, queries and reports and then click the uppermost **Close** button showing in the top right-hand corner of the screen. You could also select **File/Exit**.

Exercise 8 – full assignment

Task 1

1. Open the database *Garden Centre* from the CD.
2. Open the table *Plants*.
3. Set the page orientation to landscape.
4. Print all the records in table format, making sure all data and field headings are fully visible.
5. Close the table.
6. Rename the table `Plant Varieties`.
7. Open *Plant Varieties*. Add the following three plants to the table:

Variety	Colour	Price	Season	Berries	Type	In stock
Petunia	Purple	£5.45	Summer	No	Annual	150
Rose	White	£20.50	Summer	Yes	Perennial	20
Snowdrop	White	£1.25	Spring	No	Bulb	185

8. Delete the entire record for *Iris*.
9. Replace the *Type* entries with the following codes using **Edit/Replace**:
   - Annual — `A`
   - Perennial — `P`
   - Bulb — `B`
   - Tree — `T`
10. Now make the following changes:
    - The foxglove is `purple`
    - Petunias cost `£4.75`
    - Holly berries appear in the `winter`.
11. Print all the data in landscape orientation, making sure that all data and field headings are displayed in full.
12. Make sure fields are wide enough to display all data in full on the printout.

Task 2

1. Create a query to find all perennial plants.
2. Sort them in alphabetical order of variety.
3. Display only the fields *Variety*, *Price* and *In stock*.
4. Save the query as `Perennials (your initials)` and print a copy in landscape orientation.
5. Create a second query to find all plants of which there are 15 or more in stock.
6. Display only the fields *Variety*, *Season* and *Price*.
7. Sort in descending order of numbers *In stock*.
8. Save as `Well stocked (your initials)` and print a copy.

Task 3

1. Create a final query to find all white or purple plants that have no berries.
2. Display only the fields *Variety*, *Colour*, *Type* and *Price*.
3. Sort in ascending order of type.
4. Save as `No berries (your initials)` and print one copy.

Task 4

1. Create a tabular report in landscape orientation displaying all the plants in the *Plant Varieties* table.
2. Name the report `All the Plants`.
3. Save the report with the same name.
4. Check that the page number and date are visible.
5. Print one copy of the report making sure all data is fully displayed.
6. Close the file.

Answer

Task 1 Step 4

Variety	Colour	Price	Season	Berries	Type	In stock
Foxglove	Pink	£2.45	Spring	☐	Perennial	30
Dahlia	Orange	£4.00	Autumn	☐	Annual	25
Holly	Green	£15.50	Autumn	☑	Tree	7
Iris	Yellow	£8.75	Spring	☐	Bulb	15
Crocus	Blue	£0.95	Spring	☐	Bulb	200
Lavender	Purple	£12.75	Spring	☐	Perennial	15
Magnolia	White	£26.50	Spring	☐	Tree	4
Rose	Yellow	£6.45	Summer	☑	Perennial	10

Task 1 Step 11

Variety	Colour	Price	Season	Berries	Type	In stock
Foxglove	Purple	£2.45	Spring	No	P	30
Dahlia	Orange	£4.00	Autumn	No	A	25
Holly	Green	£15.50	Winter	Yes	T	7
Crocus	Blue	£0.95	Spring	No	B	200
Lavender	Purple	£12.75	Spring	No	P	15
Magnolia	White	£26.50	Spring	No	T	4
Rose	Yellow	£6.45	Summer	Yes	P	10
Petunia	Purple	£4.75	Summer	No	A	150
Rose	White	£20.50	Summer	Yes	P	20
Snowdrop	White	£1.25	Spring	No	B	185

Task 2 Step 4

Variety	Price	In stock
Foxglove	£2.45	30
Lavender	£12.75	15
Rose	£20.50	20
Rose	£6.45	10

Task 2 Step 8

Variety	Season	Price
Crocus	Spring	£0.95
Snowdrop	Spring	£1.25
Petunia	Summer	£4.75
Foxglove	Spring	£2.45
Dahlia	Autumn	£4.00
Rose	Summer	£20.50
Lavender	Spring	£12.75

Task 3 Step 4

Variety	Colour	Type	Price
Petunia	Purple	A	£4.75
Snowdrop	White	B	£1.25
Lavender	Purple	P	£12.75
Foxglove	Purple	P	£2.45
Magnolia	White	T	£26.50

Task 4 Step 5

All the Plants

Variety	Colour	Price	Season	Berries	Type	In stock
Foxglove	Purple	£2.45	Spring	☐	P	30
Dahlia	Orange	£4.00	Autumn	☐	A	25
Holly	Green	£15.50	Winter	☑	T	7
Crocus	Blue	£0.95	Spring	☐	B	200
Lavender	Purple	£12.75	Spring	☐	P	15
Magnolia	White	£26.50	Spring	☐	T	4
Rose	Yellow	£6.45	Summer	☑	P	10
Petunia	Purple	£4.75	Summer	☐	A	150
Rose	White	£20.50	Summer	☑	P	20
Snowdrop	White	£1.25	Spring	☐	B	185

Self-assessment checklist

I feel confident that I can now:	✓
Understand the use of database software	
Open a database application	
Open a database file	
Open a table of data	
Enter new records	
Amend entries	
Use Edit/Replace to amend entries	
Delete entire records	
Widen columns to display data fully	
Set table orientation	
Print a table	

Save a table with a specified name

Sort records

Design queries to search for specific records

Print a query

Save a query

Create a report

Display all fields in a report

Set report orientation

Print a report showing headers and footers

Save a report

Close a database file

Exit the application

Summary of critical errors

- Not using the database provided
- Incorrect search results
- An incorrect sort that renders the database unusable
- Specified fields not printed

4

Producing an
e-publication

■ What is desktop publishing? 128

■ Opening Publisher 129

■ Starting point 129

■ Page orientation 130

■ Margins 131

■ Saving a publication 132

■ Saving a file as a different version 132

■ Opening an existing publication 132

■ Viewing a publication 132

■ Adding text 133
Resizing a text box 133
Moving a text box 133
Deleting text 133

■ Closing a publication 134

■ Formatting text 135
Font types 136

■ Alignment 136

■ Indents and spacing 137

■ Printing a publication 138

■ Inserting a text file 138
Columns 139

■ Borders 142

■ Spelling 142

■ Drawing objects 143

■ Pictures 145
Inserting a picture 145
Manipulating pictures 147

■ Headers and footers 150

■ Exiting the application 150

■ Self-assessment checklist 154

■ Summary of critical errors 155

What is desktop publishing?

Desktop publishing (DTP) is the production of professional-looking publications such as calendars, cards, posters, leaflets and brochures. Rearranging text and graphics to create a publication can be carried out using a word processing application, but it is far easier with a dedicated desktop publishing package such as Microsoft Publisher. Although there are a range of templates available in the Publisher catalogue that can be customized with personal details and preferred contents, this unit will develop and test your ability to produce a simple, one-page publication that contains columns of text and a picture.

You will be asked to carry out the following tasks:

- Select and use appropriate desktop publishing software
- Create a single page publication
- Set page orientation
- Set margins
- Save a publication
- Use text boxes to add text
- Apply serif and sans serif fonts
- Format text
- Divide frames into columns
- Import a text file
- Check spellings
- Insert a picture
- Print a copy of the publication
- Add borders
- Add drawing objects
- Resize and move a picture
- Crop, rotate or flip a picture
- Change text alignment and spacing
- Balance columns of text
- Indent paragraphs
- Close a publication
- Exit the application

To pass Unit 4, you must be able to:

- Select and use appropriate software to create a publication
- Create a new, blank publication
- Amend margins and layout
- Create text frames
- Add and format text
- Understand text types
- Check spelling
- Insert and manipulate pictures
- Insert text files

- Create columns of text
- Insert and format drawing objects
- Save a publication
- Print a publication
- Close a publication
- Exit the application

Opening Publisher

Double-click the Publisher icon on your desktop or launch Microsoft Publisher from the **Start/All Programs** menu.

Starting point

The opening screen offers various options:

- *New from a design:* you can choose from a range of blank publication sizes or select *Publications for Print* and customize brochures, newsletters, business cards etc. that have been professionally designed
- *New:* where you can choose to start an A4 blank publication or web page or customize an existing publication
- *Open:* open a publication you have saved previously.

For New CLAIT, click **Blank Print Publication** in the *Task* pane and a new blank page will be displayed.

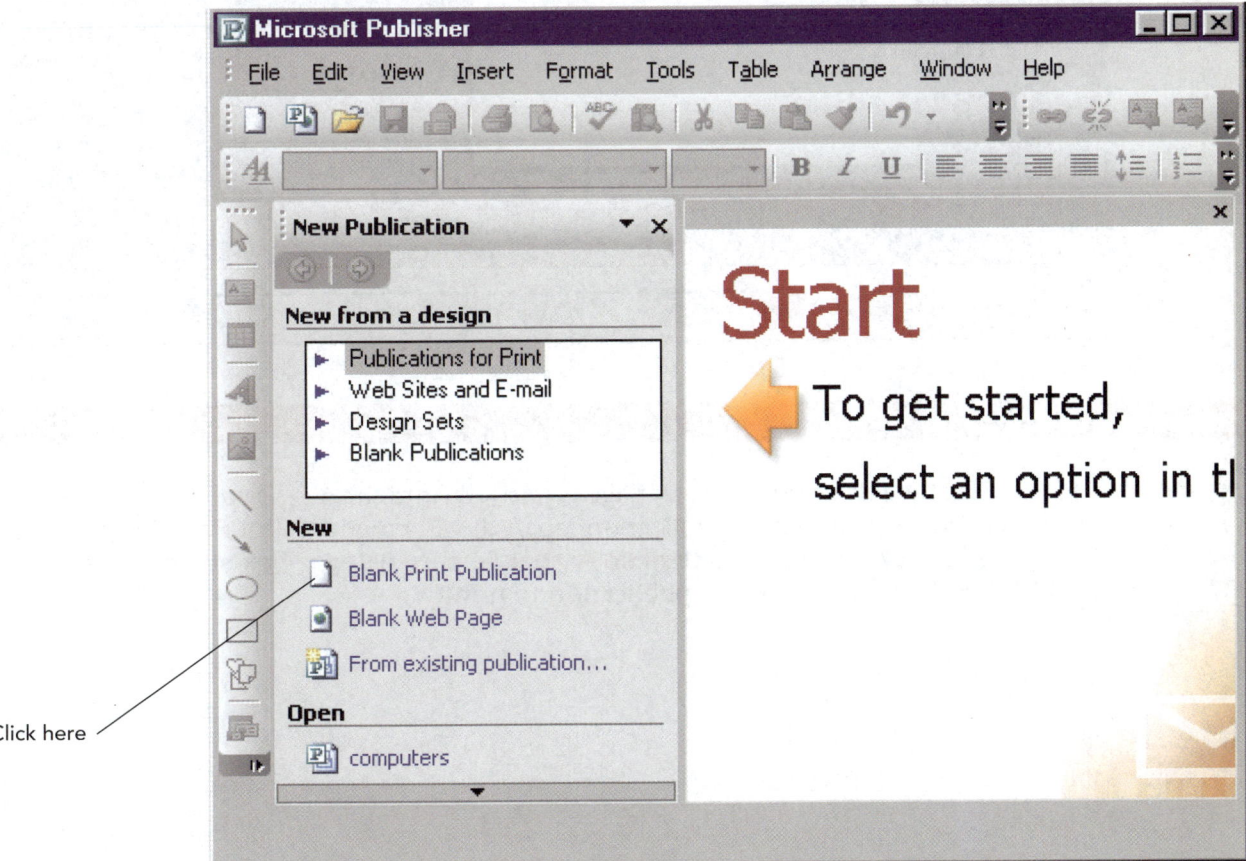

When the page opens, part of the screen will be taken up with the *Task* pane. This is not needed for New CLAIT so click the **Close** button to give yourself more room.

Exit Publisher

Object toolbar offers tools for adding text and images

Page orientation

The default layout for each page is portrait (upright A4). If you are asked to produce a landscape publication, open the **File** menu, select **Page Setup** and click the appropriate **radio button**. In this dialogue box you can also select a different size of publication to print.

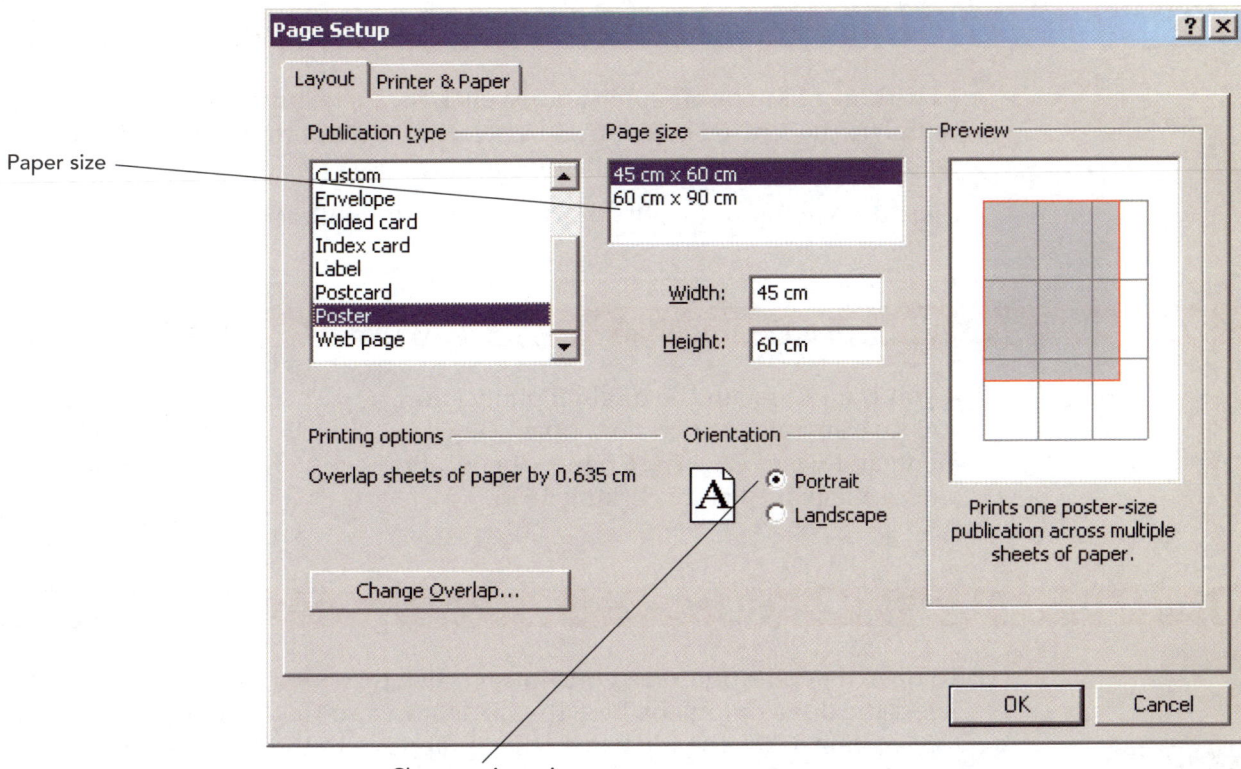

Paper size

Change orientation

Margins

Changing the page margins is carried out from the *Arrange* menu. Select **Layout Guides** and enter a new measure, or use the **up** or **down arrows** in the correct *margin* box to change from the default settings.

If the unit of measure is wrong – e.g. inches instead of centimetres – type **"** or **cm** in the box after the numbers and Publisher will convert your publication to the appropriate units.

For New CLAIT, you are allowed tolerances as follows:

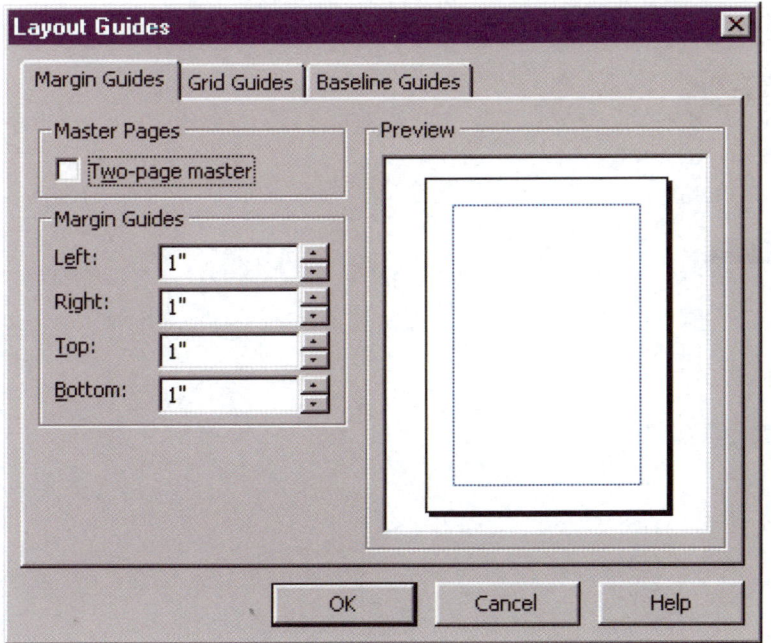

- top margin 8 mm
- bottom margin 4 mm
- left and right margins a total 6 mm tolerance.

On the page, coloured margin and grid guides will be visible. They will not print but they help you to position objects.

Saving a publication

As with most Microsoft applications, click the **Save** button 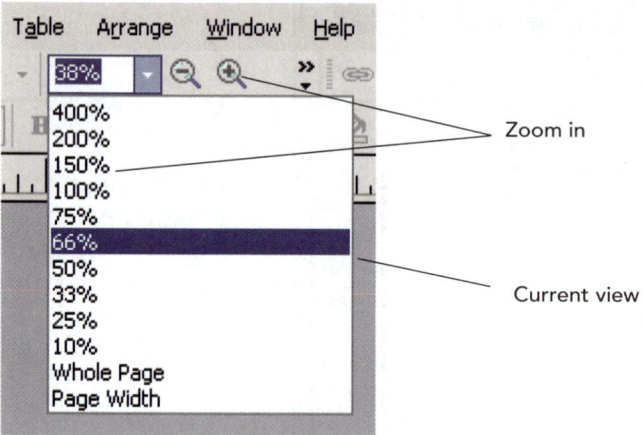 and complete the *Save in*: box entries by selecting the appropriate location and typing in a name for the file before clicking **Save**.

Click the *Save* button regularly to update your publication as you work.

Saving a file as a different version

If you want to retain the original publication and save an amended version, open the **File** menu and select **Save As**. Change the location and/or file name before clicking **Save**.

Common mistake

Overwriting the original publication rather than saving a new version.

Opening an existing publication

To open a publication saved previously, click the **Open** toolbar button. Select the drive or folder where the file is stored so that it is displayed in the *Look in*: box. Click the file name when it appears in the window and then click **Open**.

Viewing a publication

You may find that you are viewing your publication at a very low magnification. This is useful for placing images and text over the whole page.

To zoom in quickly when working on details, press the **F9** key at the top of the keyboard. Zoom out by pressing **F9** again.

You can also change the magnification in the *Zoom* box by selecting from the drop-down list or typing over the measure, or by clicking the **+ Zoom In** or **– Zoom Out** buttons.

Adding text

In Publisher, text and images are normally added to a page by inserting them into a frame or box, although images can also be placed directly on the page.

Click the **Text Box** tool 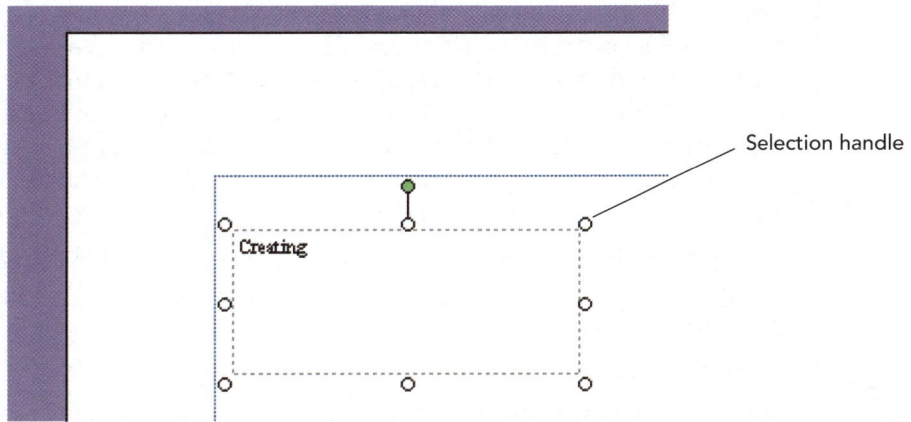 on the *Objects* toolbar and then move the mouse pointer over the page. It will show a cross which you can click and drag to create a text box.

When you let go the mouse, the cursor will be flashing inside and you can start typing your text. The white circles round the border of the box (*selection handles*) show that it is selected.

Selection handle

Make sure that any boxes do not encroach beyond the blue guides, otherwise the page may not print correctly.

Resizing a text box

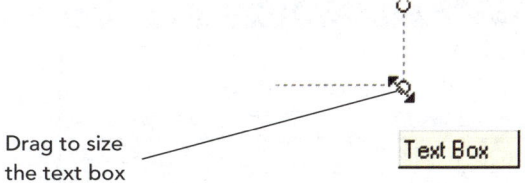

Drag to size the text box

To make room for a second box, or another frame on the page, you may need to reduce the text box size. Click on the text to select the box and move the mouse pointer over any *selection handle*. When it shows a two-way arrow drag the boundary inwards.

Moving a text box

Drag the box to a new position by moving the pointer around near a border until it shows four arrows. Click and drag the box across the page.

Deleting text

To delete letters or words, click in the text and then use the **Backspace** or **Delete** keys as normal. To delete a block of text, select it and press the **Delete** key. To remove the whole text box, select it and then either press the **Delete** key, or open the **Edit** menu and select **Delete Object**.

Closing a publication

Close the current publication by selecting **File/Close**. If you click the **Close** button, you will exit the application.

Exercise 1

1. Open Publisher and start a blank publication.

2. Set the left and right margins to 3 cm.

3. Create a text box and enter the following text as a heading: `Flowers for Sale`

4. Underneath this heading, create a second text box and enter the following text: `Fresh garden flowers flown all the way from Jersey will be on sale at half price. Come along to Plovers Garden Centre, Mill Lane, Selsey, Billingham on Saturday, 26th August from 8.30 am — 11.30 am to take advantage of this amazing offer. First come first served, so don't be late!`

5. Add a third text box below this text and enter your name and today's date.

6. Proofread your text, correct any spelling mistakes and save the file as `Flower sale`.

7. Close the file.

8. Now reopen *Flower sale* and make the following amendments: *Jersey* should be changed to `Guernsey`; the address of the garden centre is `Plover` Lane; and the date of the sale is now `1st August`.

9. Save the publication as a new version with the file name `Guernsey flowers`.

10. Close the file.

Answer

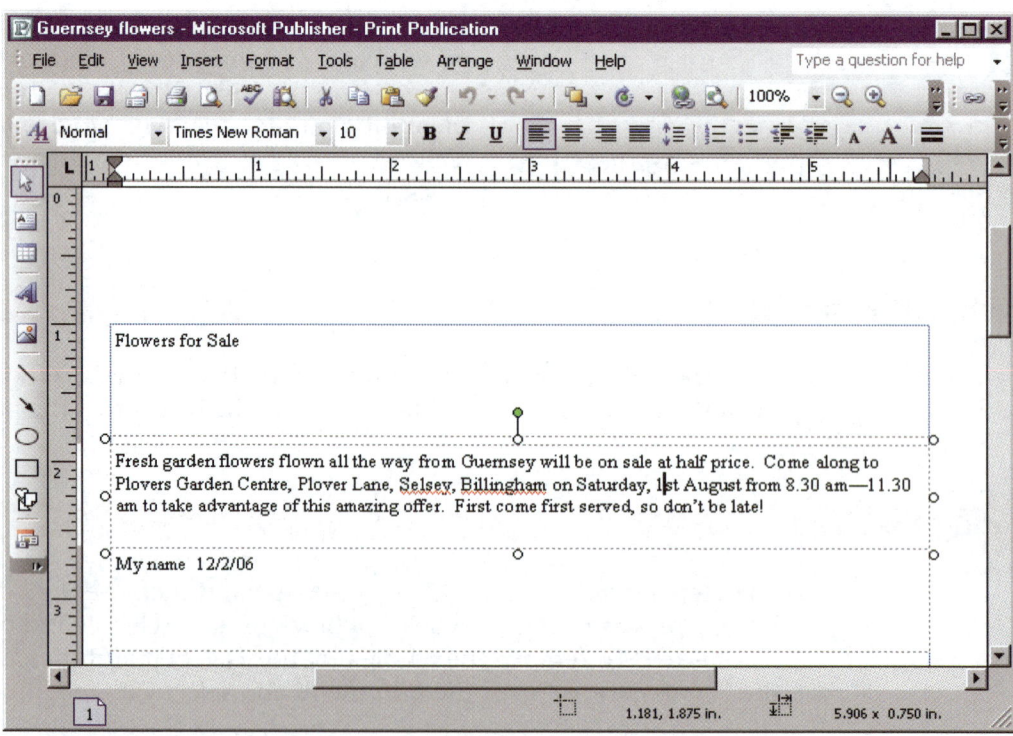

Once your text is in place, you can select it using the mouse pointer and then apply a different font type or size or add emphasis by using the formatting toolbar buttons. Click the **arrows** in the boxes to find alternative fonts and sizes, or type an exact size over the measure visible in the *Font Size* box and then press **Enter**. Note that you will not be able to access the toolbar unless the text box is selected.

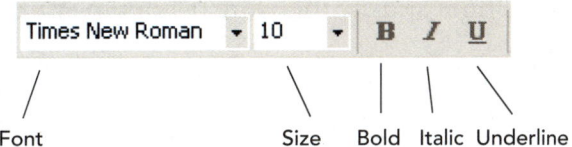

To increase or decrease the font size in visible steps, click the **Increase** or

Decrease Font Size buttons . These are particularly useful if you want to increase the text size slowly so that you fill a box with a heading. You can also stretch the text across the width of the box by selecting **Format/ Character Spacing** and applying different letter spacing (kerning) options.

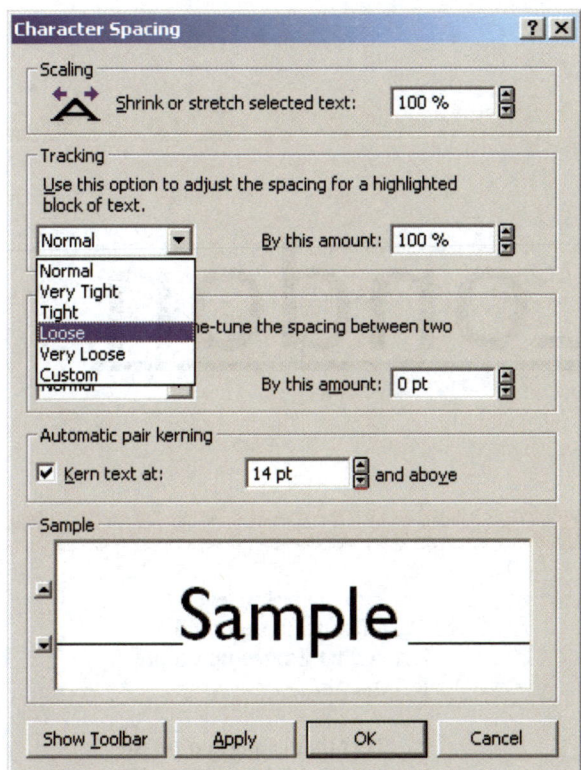

USING ILLEGIBLE FONTS IS A CRITICAL ERROR.

Common mistake	Common mistake
Not adjusting a heading to fill the width of the page.	Not adjusting the size of selected text so that headings, subheadings and main (body) text differ by at least two font sizes – e.g. body text at 14, subheadings at 18 and heading at 24 would be adequate, but sizes of 11, 12 and 13 would not.

Font types

There are two main types of font that can be chosen which will produce different effects when applied to the various elements of a publication.

- *Serif* fonts such as Times New Roman or `Courier New` have tiny lines – serifs – at the ends of the characters.
- *Sans serif* fonts such as **Tahoma** and Arial do not have these lines and are therefore plainer in appearance.

Exercise 2

1. Start a new blank publication and select landscape orientation.
2. Set all the margins to 3.5 cm.
3. Create a text box and enter the heading `Going to London`
4. Apply a sans serif font.
5. Increase the size of the text so that the heading stretches across the width of the publication.
6. Underline the word *London* in the heading.
7. Close without saving.

Answer

Going to <u>London</u>

Alignment

Text boxes can be moved round the page so that you can place text in different parts of the publication, but also the words can be positioned inside the box in different ways – on the left or right, centred or justified (often known as fully justified). Select the text and then click the appropriate toolbar button.

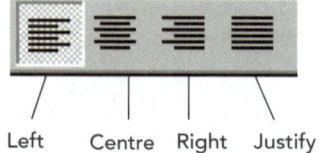

Left   Centre   Right   Justify

Text that is aligned on the left so that it lines up on the left margin.

　　　Text that is aligned on the right so that it lines up on the right margin.

Text that is centre aligned so that it is positioned centrally in the publication.

Text that is fully justified so that it fills the space evenly but may add gaps.

You may want to begin each new paragraph a few centimetres in from the edge of the box. You can also change spacing between lines. Make these changes by selecting the text, opening the **Format** menu and clicking **Paragraph**.

Change the preset style of indent and alter measurements in the *Left*: and *Right*: boxes to set in the whole paragraph or block of text, or change the indent in the *First line*: box to set in the first line of each paragraph by an exact amount.

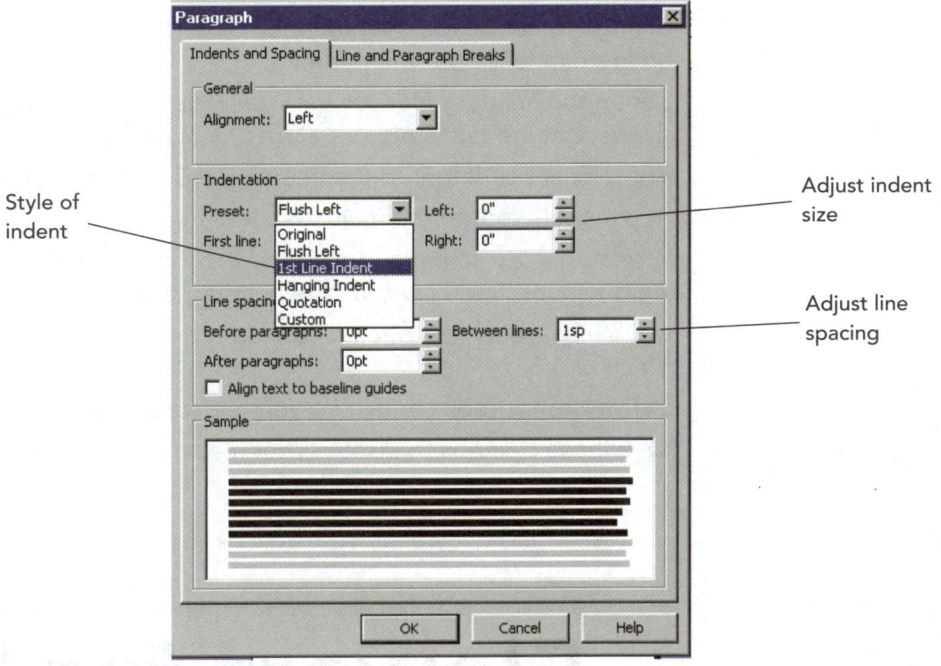

Style of indent

Adjust indent size

Adjust line spacing

You can also add bullet points and numbers to lists by using the normal toolbar buttons or by selecting this option from the **Format** menu.

To increase the spacing between lines, click a *Spacing* toolbar button or select **Paragraph** on the **Format** menu. Increase the measurement in the *Between lines*: box.

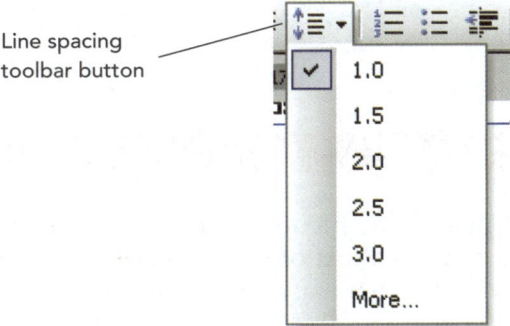

Line spacing toolbar button

Shortcuts are also available from the keyboard: use **Ctrl** and **2** for double line spacing (2 sp), **Ctrl** and **1** for single line spacing (1 sp) and **Ctrl** and **5** for $1\frac{1}{2}$ line spacing (1.5 sp).

Printing a publication

Click the **Print** toolbar button 🖨 to print one copy of your publication. You may be asked to print a composite copy of your publication. For commercial publishing, this means a copy where all the colours in your publication will print on the same page. It should not require any special print instructions and you are not expected to print in colour.

Exercise 3

1. Reopen the *Guernsey flowers* publication you created in Exercise 1.
2. Change to landscape orientation and, if necessary, move or resize any boxes to bring them fully onto the page.
3. Centre the heading *Flowers for Sale*, widen the text box and increase the font size so that the text stretches across most of the width of the page.
4. Apply a sans serif font to the heading and format to bold and underlined.
5. Apply a serif font to the main text.
6. Format this text to italic and amend the font size so that the text is clearly legible, but still smaller than the heading text.
7. Double space the main text and indent the first line of the paragraph by about $\frac{1}{2}$ inch or 1.3 cm.
8. Delete the text box containing your personal details.
9. Save these changes to update your file and print a copy of the publication.

Answer

Flowers for Sale

Fresh garden flowers flown all the way from Guernsey will be on sale at half price.

Come along to Plovers Garden Centre, Plover Lane, Selsey, Billingham on Saturday, 1st

August from 8.30 am – 11.30 am to take advantage of this amazing offer.   First come first

served, so don't be late!

Inserting a text file

Many publications are built up by incorporating documents created elsewhere. To add text saved as a text or word processed file, draw a text box and then open the **Insert** menu and click **Text File**.

Browse through the files on your computer to find the file, select it and click **OK**.

If the text box is not large enough to contain all the text, you will see an error message:

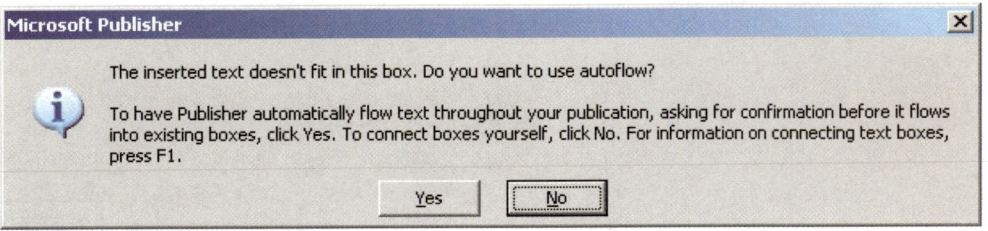

If you click **Yes**, Publisher will create further text boxes, often on one or more new pages, and the extra text will be added to them.

Clicking **No** will return you to your publication. The missing text will not be visible but will be retained by the computer and you will see the overflow symbol [A - - -] instead.

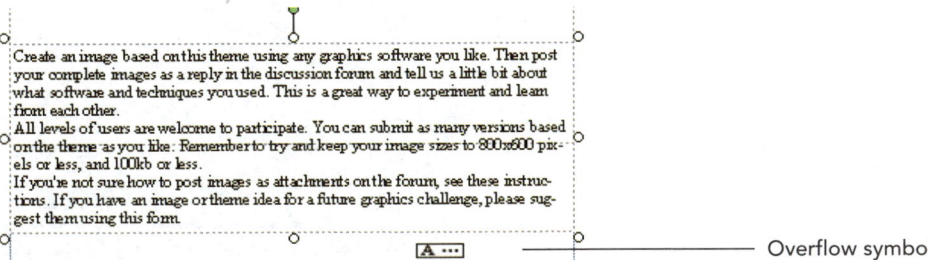

Overflow symbol

For New CLAIT, always click **No** so that you can keep the text within the single text box on your page. Make room for the extra text in one of two ways:

- increase the size of the text box
- select the visible text and apply a smaller font size.

Columns

You will need to display your imported text in two (or more) columns on the page, and make sure that they balance at the bottom of the page. Although you could create two identical text boxes and add half the text to each one, it is much more sensible to create two columns within a single box. This allows the text to wrap round the columns as you amend font sizes or add images in order to balance their contents.

Either before or after you insert a text file, right-click in the text box and select **Format Text Box**.

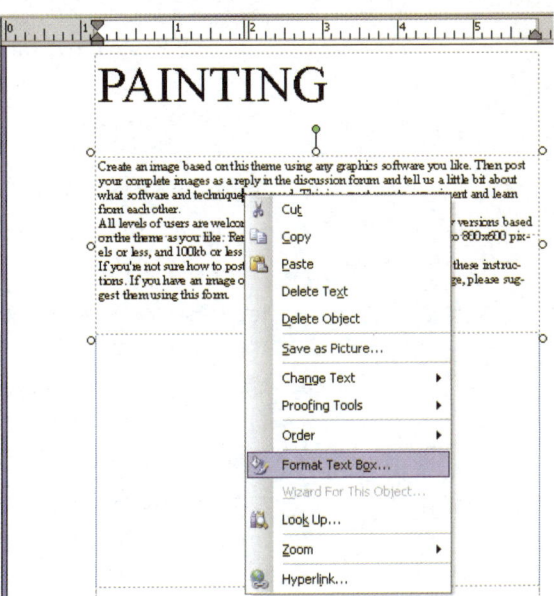

Click the **Text Box** tab and then the button labelled **Columns**.

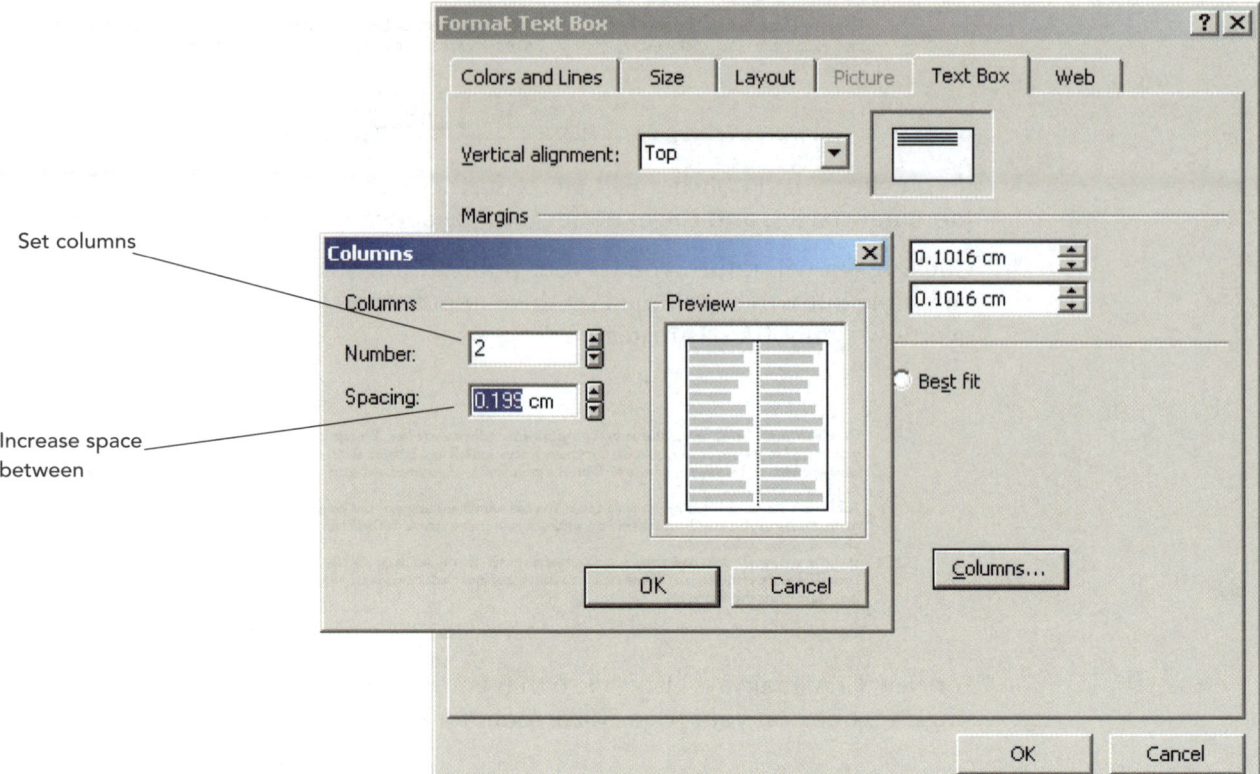

In the dialogue box, increase the number of columns, e.g. to 2. You may also need to increase the amount of space between the columns. Use the **up arrow**, or type an exact measure into the box and press **Enter**.

Back in your publication, select the main text and use the **Increase** and **Decrease Font Size** buttons to amend the font size very slowly until the columns balance at the bottom of the page.

Common mistake

Not balancing the text within the columns carefully enough. There should be no more than two lines difference between them.

Exercise 4

1. Start a new publication in landscape orientation.
2. Set all the margins to 4 cm.
3. Create a page-wide heading and enter the text: `Beating Stress`
4. Increase the size of the text so that the heading stretches across the width of the page and apply a serif font.
5. Create a second text box and insert the text file called *Stress* from the CD, or enter the text given on the next page.
6. Display the text in two columns, separated by a space of 2 cm.
7. Format the text so that the first line of each paragraph is indented by 1.5 cm.
8. Increase the size of the main text until the columns are balanced at the bottom of the page.
9. Save as `Beating Stress`.
10. Print a copy and then close the publication.

Text of file:

There is no such thing as a stress-free existence and experts agree that a certain amount of stress can be good for you because it motivates you and keeps you on your toes.

Stress becomes a problem when pressures start to pile up and you are unable to control or cope with the extra demands.

Certain life events are known to be highly stressful including the death of a member of the family, personal injury or illness, losing your job, retirement or moving house. When more than one of these events happen at the same time, it is extremely difficult for anyone to cope well.

Symptoms of stress are well known. They include excessive sweating, indigestion, nausea, palpitations, feeling tired and drained, headaches, lying awake at night worrying and loss of interest in life.

There are certain things you can do to reduce or eliminate stress from your life. Firstly, you need to examine what exactly is causing the stress and then decide whether you can do anything about them or not. Sometimes nothing can be done, but at least you can build up your resilience. Do it in three ways: change your lifestyle to a healthier one, take more physical exercise and practise relaxation techniques. You will find that over time you are coping much better and feel far less stressed.

Answer

Beating Stress

There is no such thing as a stress-free existence and experts agree that a certain amount of stress can be good for you because it motivates you and keeps you on your toes.

Stress becomes a problem when pressures start to pile up and you are unable to control or cope with the extra demands.

Certain life events are known to be highly stressful including the death of a member of the family, personal injury or illness, losing your job, retirement or moving house. When more than one of these events happen at the same time, it is extremely difficult for anyone to cope well.

Symptoms of stress are well known. They include excessive sweating, indigestion, nausea, palpitations, feeling tired and drained, headaches, lying awake at night worrying and loss of interest in life.

There are certain things you can do to reduce or eliminate stress from your life. Firstly, you need to examine what exactly is causing the stress and then decide whether you can do anything about them or not. Sometimes nothing can be done, but at least you can build up your resilience. Do it in three ways: change your lifestyle to a healthier one, take more physical exercise and practise relaxation techniques. You will find that over time you are coping much better and feel far less stressed.

Borders

Emphasize a text box or other object by adding a border round it.

Border

After selecting the object, click the **Line/Border Style** button or open the **Format** menu, select **Format Text Box** and change settings on the *Colours and Lines* tab. You can select one of the line styles visible, or click **More Lines** to open the dialogue box offering a wider range of options, including *Border Art* (a border in the form of small pictures).

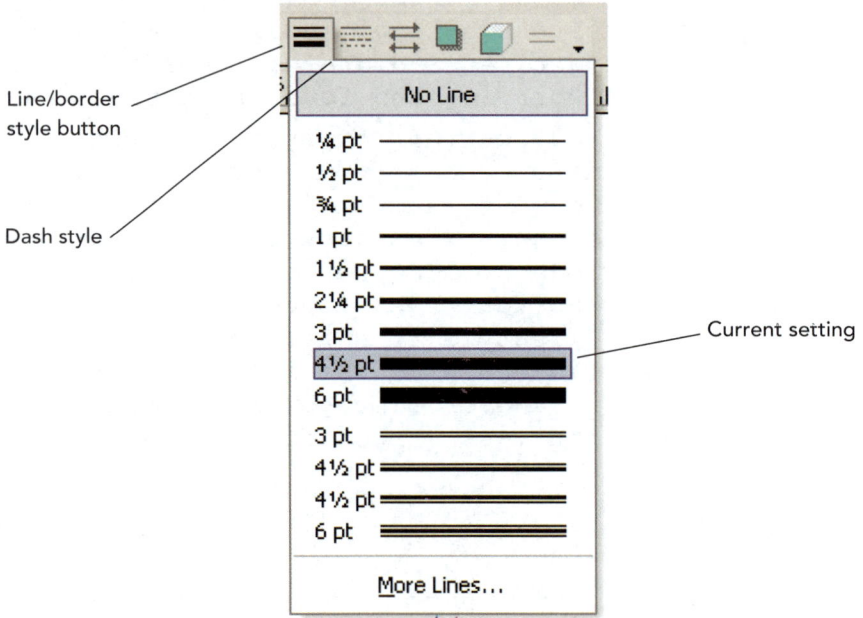

Line/border style button

Dash style

Current setting

Spelling

To check your publication for spelling mistakes, either right-click a red wavy line that appears under a word to select from alternatives that will be presented or click the **Spelling** toolbar button to open the spellchecker box. You could also go to **Tools/Spelling/Spelling**. For any word identified, select an alternative or change it manually in the box. Click a **Change** option to update your publication, or click **Ignore** to continue checking the next word. Return to your publication by clicking **Close**.

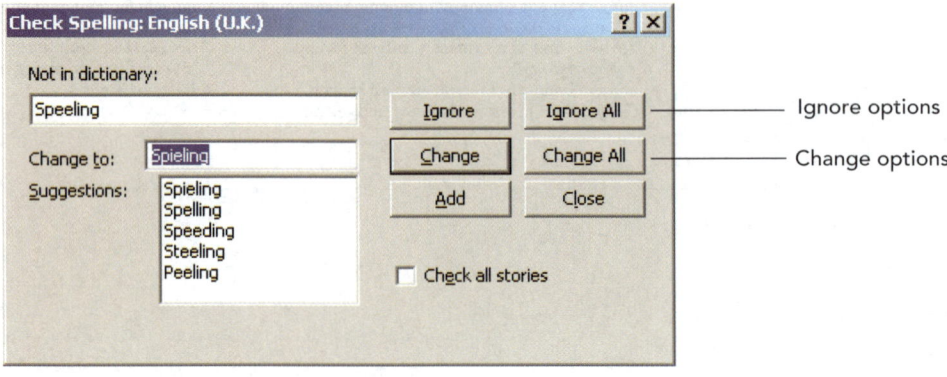

Ignore options

Change options

Don't forget to proofread in non-exam situations as the spellchecker will not pick up words spelt correctly but out of context.

Drawing objects

Publisher has a wide range of shapes that can be drawn on the page including circles, rectangles, lines and custom shapes such as hearts, arrows and stars. Once they're on the page, the lines of the shapes can be emphasized and coloured.

Click any **shape** button and then draw the object on the page in the same way that you would draw a text box, with the mouse pointer showing a cross. Let go the mouse and the selected drawing that appears can be resized or moved and the border or line thickened using a **Line/Border Style** option.

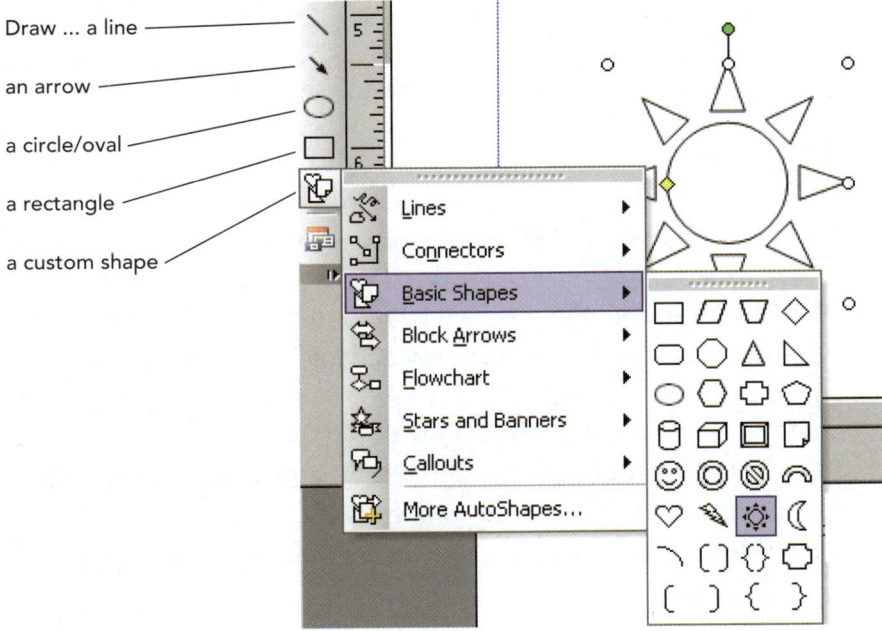

To keep a line straight (or a circle round, or a rectangle square), hold **Shift** as you drag the pointer across the page.

Exercise 5

1. Start a new, blank publication in portrait orientation, and set all the margins to 3 cm.

2. Create a page-wide heading by inserting the following text using a large, sans serif font: `Renting a Room`

3. Centre the heading and border the text box with a thick line.

4. Insert the text file *Renting* from the CD into a text box that fills the rest of the page. If you prefer, use a text editing or word processing application to create and save the file first. The text is as follows:

Homeowners struggling to meet high mortgage repayments can supplement their incomes by renting a room and benefiting from tex relief, while at the same time making affordable rented accommodation available for local people.

In the Government's "rent a room" scheme, homeowners can charge rent of up to £4,250 tax free, within a tax year. But in some areas this figure dis not reflect the true market rental value. Although the scheme is a step in the right direction, and also helps those looking for affordable homes, it does not go far enough for some critics. They believe the threshold should be raised to a figure nearer £6,000 a year to reflect the rise in property values over the past 5 years since the rate was set.

Just one word of warning if you are thinking of rinting out a room. Do take advice as you need to be aware of the possibility of creating a liability to capital gains tax if you are not letting your property in the correct manner.

5. Save the publication as **Renting**.

6. Correct the three spelling mistakes you will find in the text.

7. Format the main text box to display two columns and increase the spacing between them to 0.45 cm.

8. Apply a serif font to the main text.

9. Draw a solid line down the centre of the box to divide the two columns of text.

10. Increase the font size and fully justify the main text. Make sure the columns of text are balanced at the bottom of the page.

11. Ensure that the heading text is clearly larger than the main text.

12. Update the publication to save these changes.

13. Print a copy of the publication on one page.

14. Close the file.

Renting a Room

Homeowners struggling to meet high mortgage repayments can supplement their incomes by renting a room and benefiting from tax relief, while at the same time making affordable rented accommodation available for local people.

In the Government's "rent a room" scheme, homeowners can charge rent of up to £4,250 tax free, within a tax year. But in some areas this figure does not reflect the true market rental value. Although the scheme is a step in the right direction, and also helps those looking for affordable homes, it does not go far enough for some critics. They believe the threshold should be raised to a figure nearer £6,000 a year to reflect the rise in property values over the past 5 years since the rate was set.

Just one word of warning if you are thinking of renting out a room. Do take advice as you need to be aware of the possibility of creating a liability to capital gains tax if you are not letting your property in the correct manner.

Pictures

When working with Publisher, there are two main types of picture you might want to include in your publication:

- pictures in the *Clip Art Gallery*, which is accessible from the toolbar
- images, drawings and photos stored on your computer or on a disk.

For New CLAIT, you will be provided with an image that you must insert into the publication.

Inserting a picture

Clip art

Picture Frame tool

Clip Art

Picture from File

Empty Picture Frame

From Scanner or Camera...

Click **Picture Frame** tool to offer a short cut to *Clip Art*, or go to **Insert/Picture/Clipart** to open the *Clip Art* task pane. Type your choice of subject into the box and click the **Search** button to find appropriate pictures.

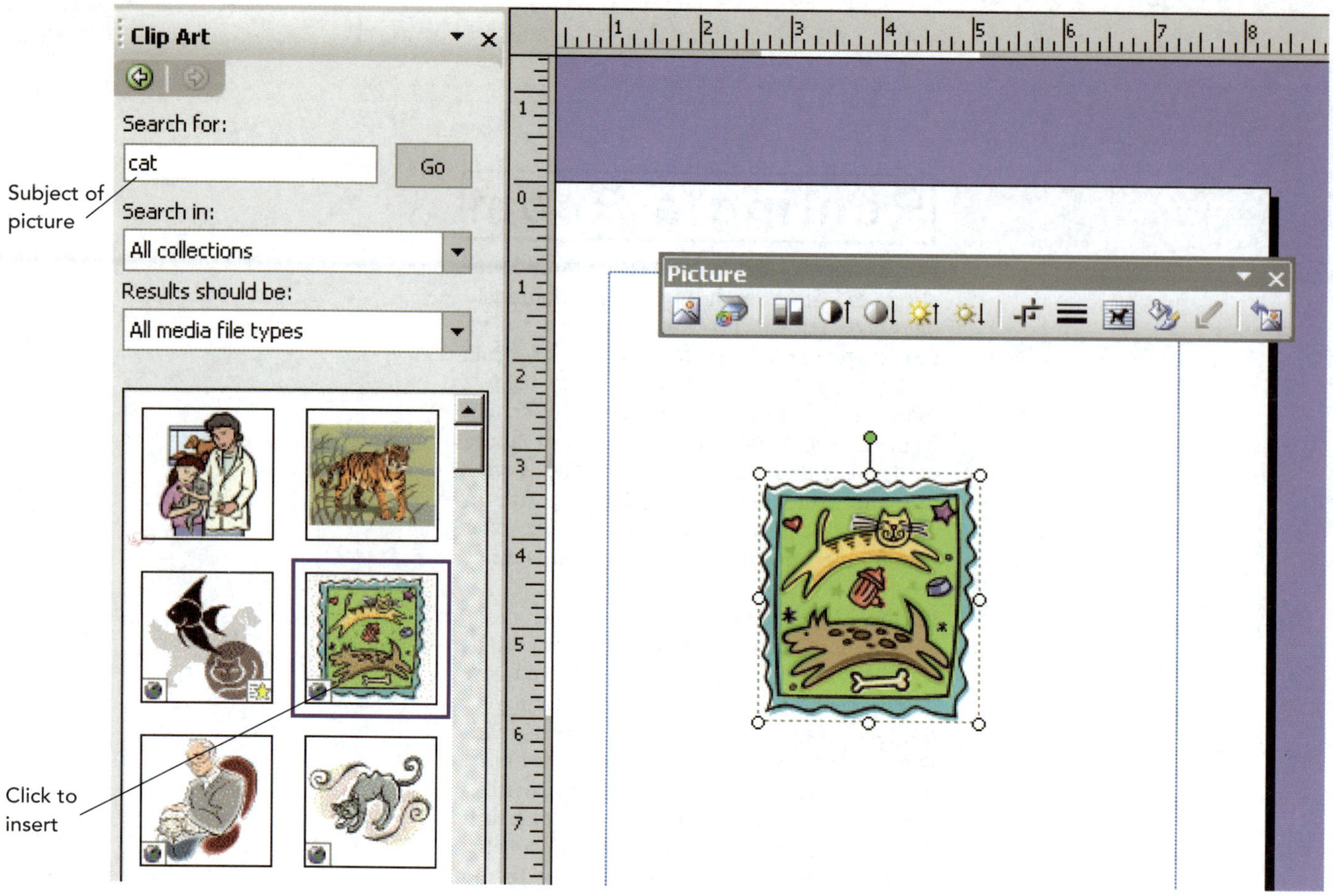

Clip Art ▼ ✕

Search for:

| cat | | Go |

Subject of picture

Search in:

| All collections | ▼ |

Results should be:

| All media file types | ▼ |

Click to insert

Click any picture to add it to your publication.

To add a picture into a column of text, first click the **Picture Frame** tool, select **Empty Picture Frame** and draw a frame inside the column. Then insert the picture into this frame.

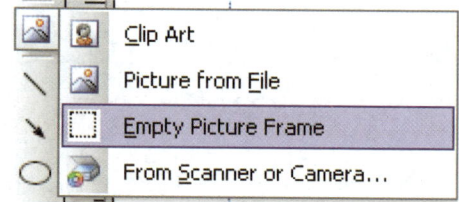

		Clip Art
		Picture from File
		Empty Picture Frame
		From Scanner or Camera...

From file

For other pictures, use the *Picture Frame* tool or open the **Insert** menu, select **Picture/From File** and draw a frame on the page. You will then be able to browse for the picture file. Click **Insert** to add it to your publication.

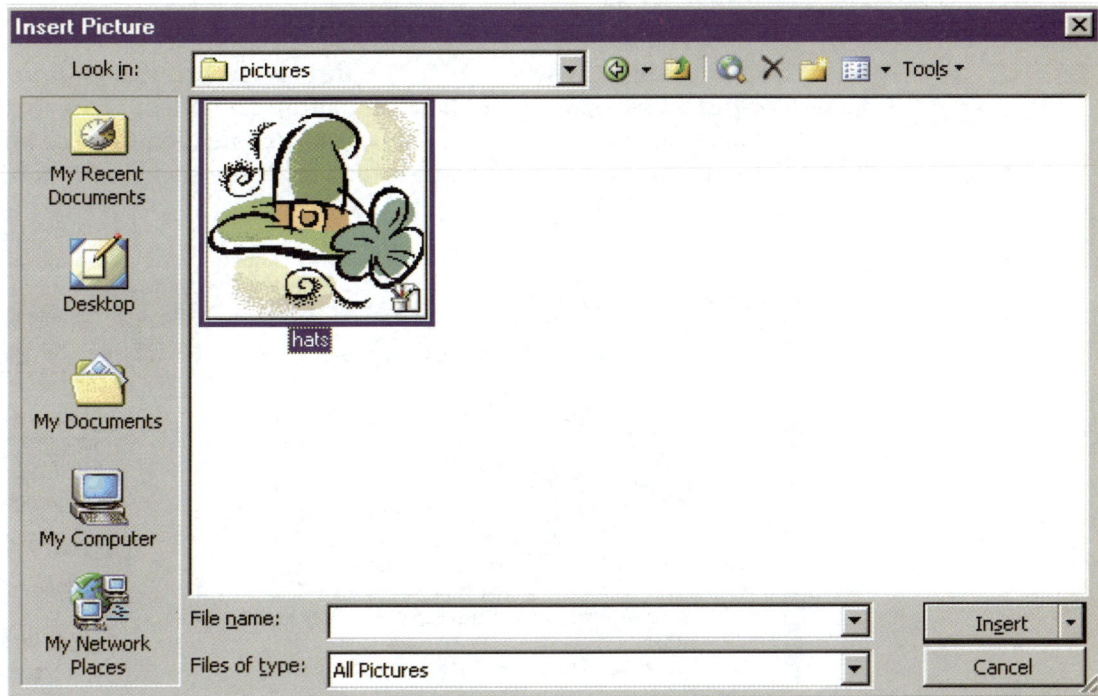

If there is already text in the box taking up most of the space, reduce the font size first, so that the text does not overflow when the picture is added.

INSERTING THE WRONG IMAGE OR FAILING TO INSERT THE SPECIFIED IMAGE IS A CRITICAL ERROR.

Manipulating pictures

The picture will appear selected so that you can resize or move it in the same way that you can amend text boxes. To keep the picture in proportion, resize by dragging a white circle from a *corner*, not from the centre of any border.

Don't drag from here

Resized out of proportion

Drag from here

For New CLAIT you will be asked to resize a picture during the assignment. Make sure that the larger image is quite sizeable. This will give you more room for manoeuvre when working with the smaller image. Otherwise, you may end up with a tiny second image and it will be harder to readjust the balance of text within your publication.

Text wrapping

You can change the way a picture is displayed within a column of text by selecting a *text wrap*. Right-click the picture and select **Show Picture Toolbar** if the toolbar does not appear automatically. Choose one of the following text wrapping options: *Tight* to fit the text closely to the picture, *Square* or *Top and Bottom*.

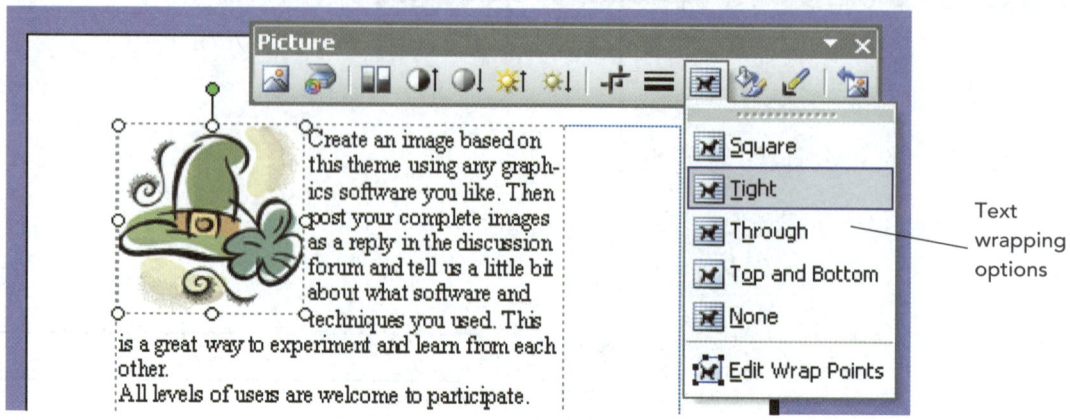

Text wrapping options

Cropping

You can remove part of an image by *cropping*. With the picture selected, click the **Crop** toolbar button and then move the mouse pointer over the side nearest to the part of the image you want to remove. Drag the border inwards and, when the unwanted area is outside the dotted line, let go. That section will disappear. Reverse the crop if you make a mistake.

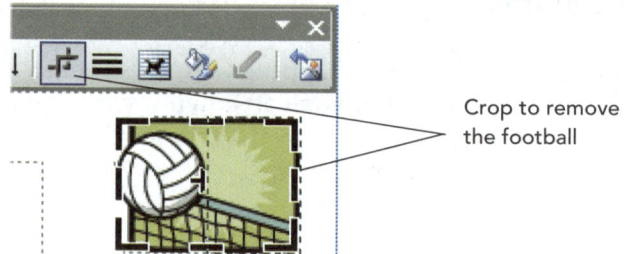

Crop to remove the football

Flip or rotate

To change the orientation of the picture, you can drag round the green circle at the end of the rotate arm when the pointer positioned over it shows a circle. The dotted lines show the new position for the image.

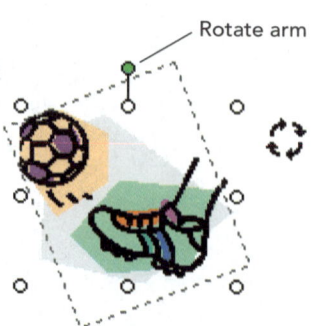

Rotate arm

You can also select an option from the drop-down list next to the **Free Rotate** toolbar button.

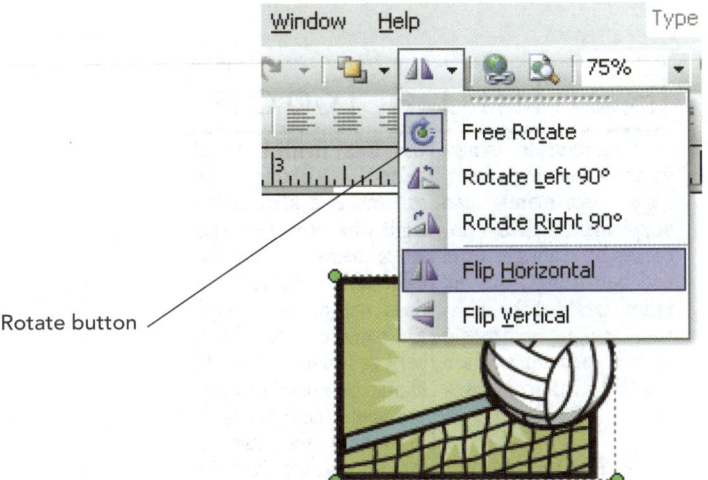

Rotate button

Exercise 6

1. Reopen the *Renting* publication you created in Exercise 5.

2. Insert the image *house* from the CD.

3. Increase its size in proportion, so that it fills about a quarter of a column, and position it at the bottom of the left-hand column of text. Make sure the image does not obscure any text.

4. Indent the first line of each paragraph.

5. Adjust the font or text box size so that no text is lost and the columns are balanced at the bottom of the page.

6. Save a new version of the publication with the file name `Renting2` and print a copy, making sure the publication fits one page.

Renting a Room

Homeowners struggling to meet high mortgage repayments can supplement their incomes by renting a room and benefiting from tax relief, while at the same time making affordable rented accommodation available for local people.

In the Government's "rent a room" scheme, homeowners can charge rent of up to £4,250 tax free, within a tax year. But in some areas this figure does not reflect the true market rental value. Although the scheme is a step in the right direction, and also helps those looking for affordable homes, it does not go far enough for some critics. They believe the threshold should be raised to a figure nearer £6,000 a year to reflect the rise in property values over the past 5 years since the rate was set.

Just one word of warning if you are thinking of renting out a room. Do take advice as you need to be aware of the possibility of creating a liability to capital gains tax if you are not letting your property in the correct manner.

Headers and footers

When you want to add extra text, such as your name or a page number, to your publication, do this by creating a text box above (header) or below (footer) the margin guides. This will then not affect the layout of the publication.

Exiting the application

Click the **Close** button or go to **File/Exit**.

Task 1

Before you begin this task make sure you have the text file *computer safety* and the image *computer* from the CD.

1. Create a new single-page publication.

2. Set up the master page or template for the page as follows:
    - page size A4
    - page orientation portrait/tall
    - left margin 2 cm
    - right margin 2 cm
    - top margin 2.5 cm
    - bottom margin 2.5 cm.

3. In the bottom margin area key in your name.

4. Set up the page layout in a newsletter format, to include a page-wide heading above two columns of text:
    - column widths equal
    - space between columns 1 cm.

5. Enter the heading **WORKING SAFELY WITH COMPUTERS** at the top of the page.

6. Format the heading in a sans serif font (e.g. Arial).
    - Make sure the heading text extends across both columns and fills the space across the top of the page. You may increase the character spacing (kerning) and/or font size to achieve this.
    - Make sure there is no more than 1 cm of white space to the left or right between the heading and the margins.

7. Save the publication with the file name `computing1`.

Task 2

1. Import the text file *computer safety* from the CD.
    - The text should begin at the top of the left-hand column below the heading. It should fill the first column then flow under the heading into the second column. Increase the font size but make sure it is not larger than the heading text.
    - Make sure all the text has been imported and is visible on the page.

2. Spellcheck the text and correct the three spelling errors. Do not make any other amendments to the text file.

3. Import the image *computer* from the CD.

4. Place it below the heading at the top of the second column.
    - Make sure the image does not overlap any text or extend into the margin or column space.
    - Make sure the image is in proportion.

5. Format all the imported body text to be left-aligned.

6. Format the imported body text in a serif font (e.g. Times New Roman).

7. Make sure your publication fits onto one page.

8. Save your publication keeping the file name *computing1*.

9. Print a composite copy of the publication on one page.

Task 3

1. Flip the *computer* image horizontally.
2. Reduce it in size. Make sure you keep the original proportions of the image.
3. Move the image to the top of the first column below the heading.
4. Make sure that the image does not overlap any text or extend into the margin or column space.
5. Change the subheading to `SAFE WORK WITH COMPUTERS`
6. Draw a line below the heading to separate the heading from the text. The line must extend from the left margin to the right margin but not into the margin area.
7. Make sure the line does not touch or overlap any text.
8. Save your publication using the new file name `computing2`.

Task 4

1. Continue working on the publication *computing2*.
2. Change the body text to be fully justified.
3. Increase the size of the subheadings: *Be Comfortable, Breaks* and *Eyes* so that the subheadings are the same size, and are larger than the body text but smaller than the heading.
4. Format the subheadings in a sans serif style that is different to the heading (e.g. Comic Sans).
5. Format the subheadings to be left-aligned.
6. Format the body text so that each paragraph has a first line indent. Make sure that you do not insert a clear linespace between paragraphs and that the subheadings are not indented.
7. Change the size of the body text so that both columns are balanced at the bottom of the page.
8. Make sure that the heading, subheadings and body text are still different sizes.
9. Make sure all the original text is still displayed on the page and your publication fits onto one page.
10. Save your publication keeping the file name *computing2*.
11. Print a composite copy of the publication on one page.
12. Close the publication and exit the software securely.

Task 2 Step 9

WORKING SAFELY WITH COMPUTERS

When working with computers, there are common sense precautions you can take that will ensure you minimise any risk to your health and welfare.

Be Comfortable
Make sure that your chair is at a comfortable height and has a back that supports your spine and can be adjusted easily. Check that your eyes are broadly in line with the top of the monitor – you may need to angle the screen or place the monitor on a box for extra height. There should be ample space around your work area for papers and notes, and you may find it helpful to use a document holder. Ensure there is plenty of room for your legs to move freely, and support them with a footstool if that feels more comfortable. Hold the mouse lightly rather than gripping it too fiercely, and make use of a wrist rest to limit the possibility of developing repetitive strain injury (RSI). The keyboard should be positioned at a sensible height too.

Breaks
It is vital that you take regular breaks, to stop you sitting in the same position for extended periods of time. Move around the room and take regular, short breaks from your work. However, always ensure that cables are tucked away and no bags or coats are left on the floor, in case they cause accidents.

Eyes
If you find yourself suffering from headaches when you use your computer, adjust the screen settings for colour and contrast and move the monitor or draw curtains. If necessary, visit an optician in case you need to wear glasses.

My Name

SAFE WORK WITH COMPUTERS

When working with computers, there are common sense precautions you can take that will ensure you minimise any risk to your health and welfare.

Be Comfortable

Make sure that your chair is at a comfortable height and has a back that supports your spine and can be adjusted easily. Check that your eyes are broadly in line with the top of the monitor – you may need to angle the screen or place the monitor on a box for extra height. There should be ample space around your work area for papers and notes, and you may find it helpful to use a document holder. Ensure there is plenty of room for your legs to move freely, and support them with a footstool if that feels more comfortable. Hold the mouse lightly, rather than gripping it too fiercely, and make use of a wrist rest to limit the possibility of developing repetitive strain injury (RSI). The keyboard should be positioned at a sensible height too.

Breaks

It is vital that you take regular breaks, to stop you sitting in the same position for extended periods of time. Move around the room and take regular, short breaks from your work. However, always ensure that cables are tucked away and no bags or coats are left on the floor, in case they cause accidents.

Eyes

If you find yourself suffering from headaches when you use your computer, adjust the screen settings for colour and contrast and move the monitor or draw curtains. If necessary, visit an optician in case you need to wear glasses.

My Name

Self-assessment checklist

I feel confident that I am able to: ✓

Understand the use of desktop publishing software

Open a desktop publishing application

Create a new, blank publication

Change page orientation

Set margins

Add and format text

Distinguish between serif and sans serif fonts

Align and indent text

Insert text files

Set text in columns

Use the spellchecker

Add and format drawing objects

Insert, resize and move images

Crop, rotate or flip images

Add borders

Print a publication

Save a publication

Open a publication saved previously

Close a publication

Exit the application

Summary of critical errors

- The image is missing
- The text file is missing, incomplete or amended
- Using illegible fonts

unit 5

Creating an e-presentation

- What are presentations? 158
- Opening PowerPoint 159
  Slide layout 159
- New presentation 160
- Views 160
- Working with text 160
- Closing a presentation 161
- Exiting PowerPoint 162
- Formatting text 162
- Deleting text 163
- Text alignment 163
- Saving a presentation 163
  Saving a new version 164
- Promoting and demoting text 165
- Inserting and deleting lines of text 166
- Bullets 166
- Opening a presentation saved earlier 167
- Images 168
  Clip art gallery 168
  Inserting a picture from file 169
  Formatting pictures 170
- New slides 171
  On the *Outline* or *Slides* tab 171
  In *Normal* view 171
- Changing slide order 173
- Spelling 173
- Drawn shapes 174
- Page orientation 175

- Slide Master 175
- Edit and replace 176
- Headers and footers 177
- Printing 178
- Backgrounds 181
- Self-assessment checklist 186
- Summary of critical errors 186

What are presentations?

Applications such as Microsoft PowerPoint can bring talks and presentations to life by helping you produce professional-looking slides that emphasize your main points. The slides making up a presentation can have colourful backgrounds, images, sound and movement, tables of data and various types of chart. They can be printed out or run as a slide show on the computer. You can also create audience handouts and speaker's notes to accompany the presentation.

You will be asked to carry out the following tasks:

- Open appropriate presentation software
- Create a three-slide presentation
- Set text styles in Slide Master view
- Add headers and footers
- Apply a background colour
- Add text to a slide
- Add an image
- Save a presentation
- Insert a new slide
- Add and fill a drawn shape
- Demote or promote text
- Change slide order
- Print selected slides
- Delete text
- Replace words
- Print handouts (audience notes)
- Print an outline of the presentation
- Close the presentation
- Exit the software

To pass Unit 5, you must be able to:

- Select and use appropriate software to create a presentation
- Understand the different views in which to work
- Insert, delete and format text
- Demote and promote text to different levels
- Use the master slide to add or format text or objects appearing on every slide
- Add or remove bullets
- Use the spellchecker
- Insert and format images
- Insert and fill drawn shapes
- Add new slides
- Change slide order
- Replace text entries automatically
- Set background colour
- Save a presentation

- Save a presentation with a different file name
- Print selected slides, handouts and outlines
- Close a presentation and exit the application

Opening PowerPoint

Double-click the **PowerPoint** icon 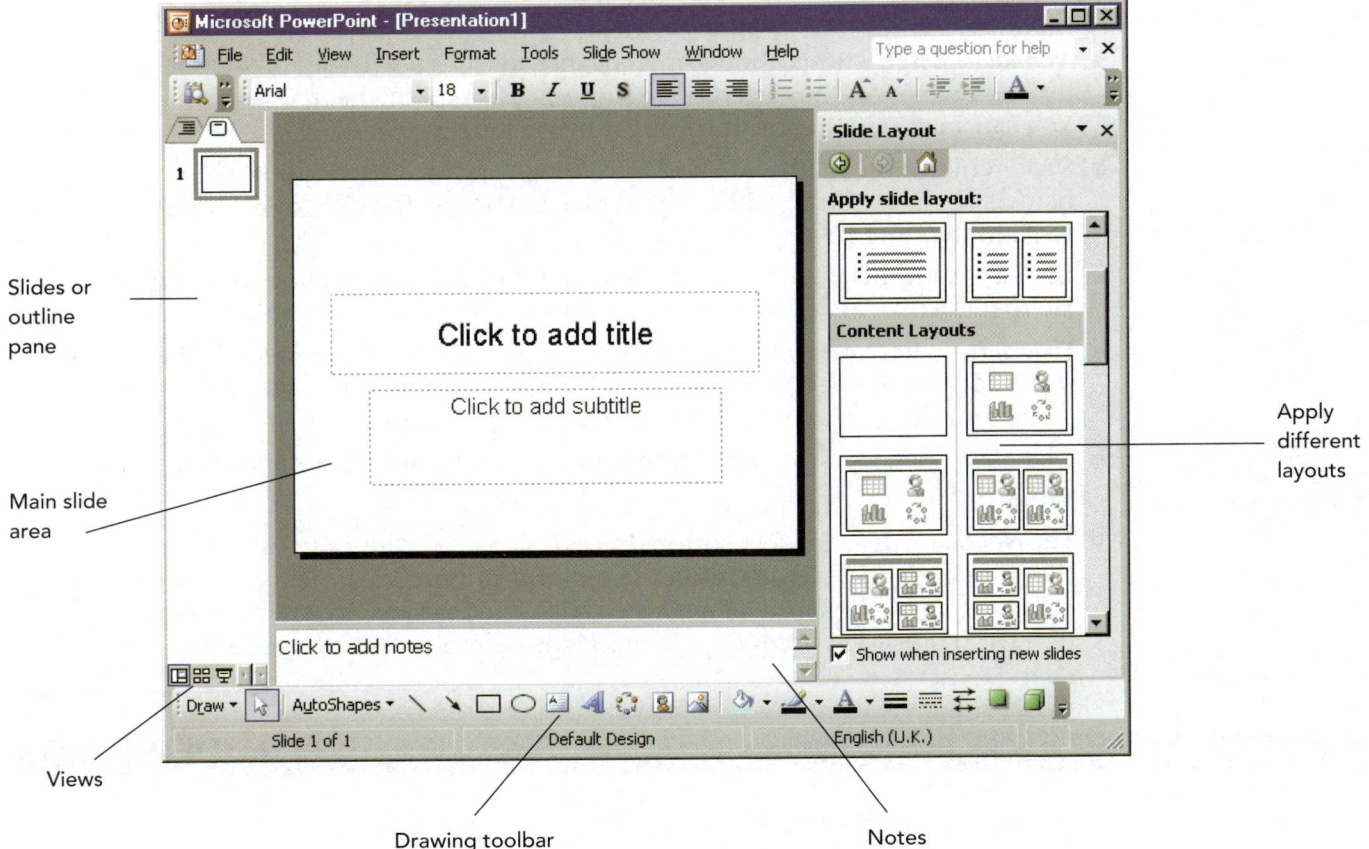 or launch the application from the **Start/All Programs** menu. A new blank slide will be displayed in *Normal* view.

Slide layout

Whenever you start a new presentation or insert new slides you will be offered a slide layout automatically. However, you can apply other layout styles to a slide at any time. Go to **Format/Slide Layout** to open the *Layout* pane. Each layout is labelled, so click one and it will be applied.

One slide, the *Title* slide, behaves differently from the rest. It is offered as *Slide 1* but should not be selected for other slides in the presentation.

Select a slide layout showing boxes in place that may include columns, images or charts if you think you will want shortcuts to these objects. The boxes are known as *placeholders*. They can be deleted or you can add further objects to any blank areas on a slide.

New presentation

Once you have started work in PowerPoint, click the **New** button ⬜ to create a new presentation.

Views

Your main working area is a slide, but you can view your work in different ways. Several working views can be reached via a shortcut button in the bottom left-hand corner of the screen or a tab at the top of the left-hand pane.

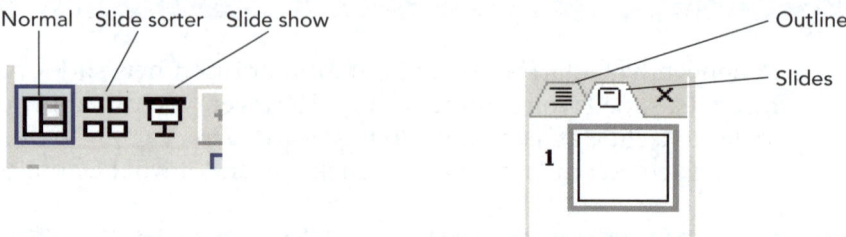

- *Normal* – presentations always open in this view. You will see three different panes on the screen: *slide/outline*, *notes* and the *main slide* area. You can start work in any of the areas by clicking in place.

- *Slide* – enlarge the main slide area in *Normal* view by dragging out the pane borders so that you can add text and images and see the effects of coloured backgrounds and fills.

- *Outline* – concentrates on the textual content of the presentation only. This alternates with a *Slides* tab that shows thumbnails of your presentation.

- *Slide Sorter* – lets you view small thumbnail pictures of all the slides in the presentation together. This is a good view for changing slide order and seeing how designs affect the overall look of the presentation.

- *Slide Show* – lets you run the presentation without the toolbars and menus being visible.

The *Notes Page* has no view button, but you can type your notes directly into the pane in *Normal* view or select the option from the *View* menu. This view offers a thumbnail picture of a selected slide and text area in which you can type word processed notes for use as an aide-mémoire when giving a talk.

Working with text

In *Outline* view, click next to a slide image and start typing.

If you have selected a layout with placeholders for text, you can also click and type in the boxes visible in *Normal* view.

To add text to any blank areas, click the **Text Box** button on the *Drawing*

toolbar visible below the slide ![button]. When you move your mouse over the slide, the pointer will display a cross; you can click and drag to draw the shape of a box. The cursor will be inside the box and you can type as normal. Note that if you click somewhere else first, the box will disappear and you will need to redraw it.

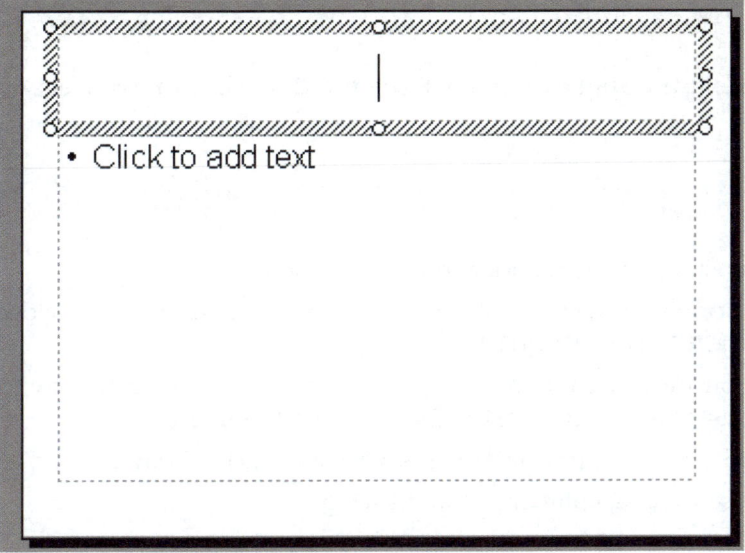

You will not be able to draw a very large box, but it should expand as you add more text; text will wrap down the box if the box is narrow. To enter text on a new line within the box, move the cursor to the end of the line and press **Enter**.

To move a text box, position the pointer over a border. When it shows four arrows, hold down the mouse button and drag the box to a new position.

To resize a text box, position the pointer over one of the white circles (*sizing handles*) round the edge. When it shows a two-way arrow, hold down the mouse button and gently drag the border in or out.

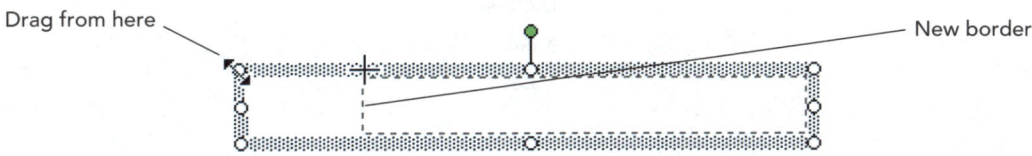

Note that text added in a text box will not be displayed in *Outline* view or on an outline printout.

Closing a presentation

A quick way to close the presentation is to click the lower **Close** button in the top right-hand corner of the window. You can also open the **File** menu and select **Close**.

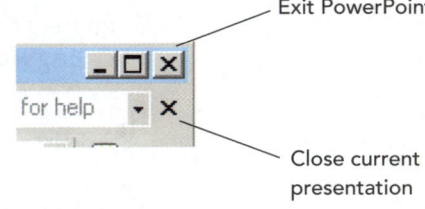

Exiting PowerPoint

To exit the application, click the top **Close** button or select **File/Exit**.

Exercise 1

1. Launch PowerPoint and start a new presentation.
2. In Normal view, click in the Title placeholder and type the following:
   CRICKETING COUNTIES
3. Below this, type the following, pressing **Enter** after each entry to make a list:
   Somerset, Essex, Middlesex, Kent, Sussex
4. Add a final text box and enter your name and the date.
5. Close the presentation without saving.

Answer

CRICKETING COUNTIES

Somerset

Essex

Middlesex

Kent

Sussex

My Name 1/11/04

Formatting text

To change the look of text, select the words with your mouse. Now use the following toolbar buttons:

B **Bold**

I *Italic*

<u>U</u> <u>Underline</u>

You can change the size of characters by selecting an alternative measure in the *Font Size* box, or you can increase or decrease the selected text in steps by clicking the **Increase Font Size** or **Decrease Font Size** buttons.

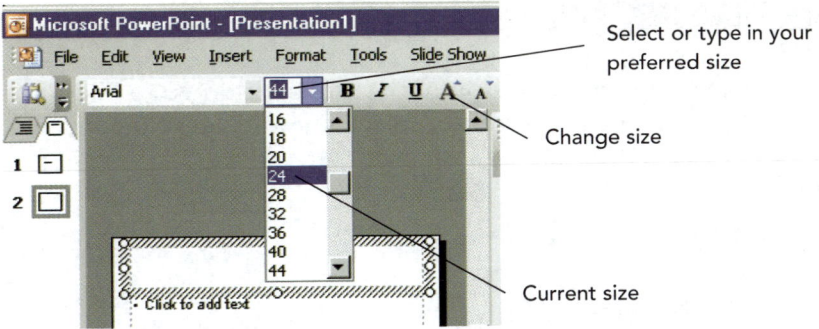

Select or type in your preferred size

Change size

Current size

If the exact font size you want is not offered, for example 15 pt, click any number in the box to select it and then replace it by typing in the new measure. Press **Enter** to accept the new size.

Deleting text

To remove text, select it with the mouse and press the **Delete** key. You may need to close up lines in a list using the **Backspace** key.

To delete an unwanted placeholder or text box, click the border and press **Delete**.

Text alignment

Place the text within a text box on the left, centre or right by selecting the box and clicking one of the alignment buttons.

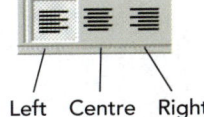

Left   Centre   Right

Saving a presentation

A single PowerPoint file contains all the slides in your presentation. Save this at any time by clicking the **Save** button . Select an appropriate location and file name for the file before pressing **Enter** or clicking the **Save** button.

Select location

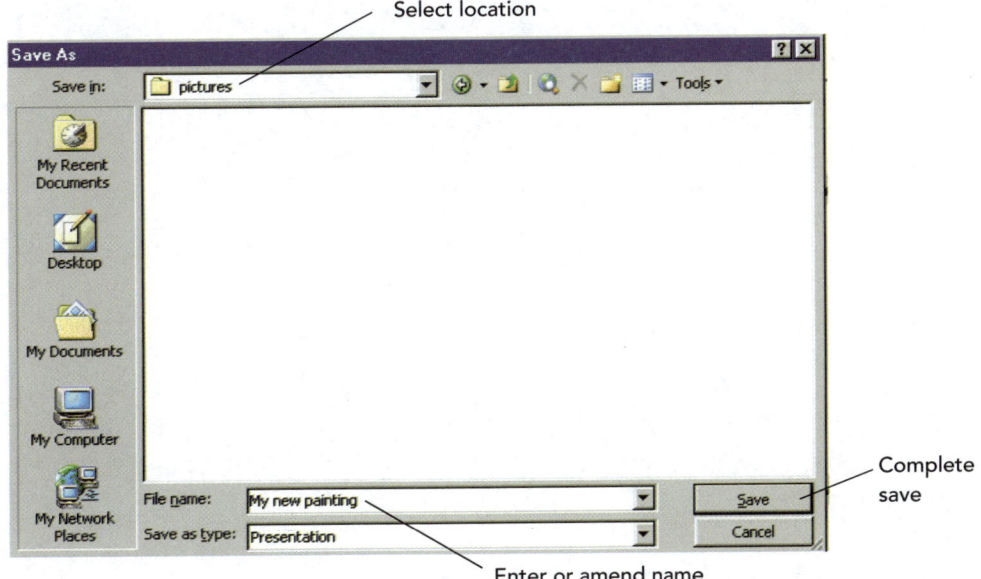

Complete save

Enter or amend name

To save a different version of the presentation go to **File/Save As** and amend the file name and/or select a new location before clicking **Save**.

1. Start a new presentation.
2. Select a slide layout with a bulleted list placeholder e.g. *Title and Text*.
3. In Normal view, click in the Title placeholder and type the heading:
   `Transport`
4. Centre the heading and make it bold.
5. Click in the **Bulleted List** placeholder. Add the following text as a list:
   `Little Energy Needed`
   `Car`
   `Bus`
   `Good for You`
   `Walk`
   `Bicycle`
6. Change to Outline view and insert the following list items between *Bus* and *Good for You*:
   `Train`
   `Plane`
7. Amend the title to read: `Transport Methods`
8. Check in Normal view and, if necessary, move the text boxes up a little to ensure no text is off the slide.
9. Save the presentation as `Transport` and close the file.

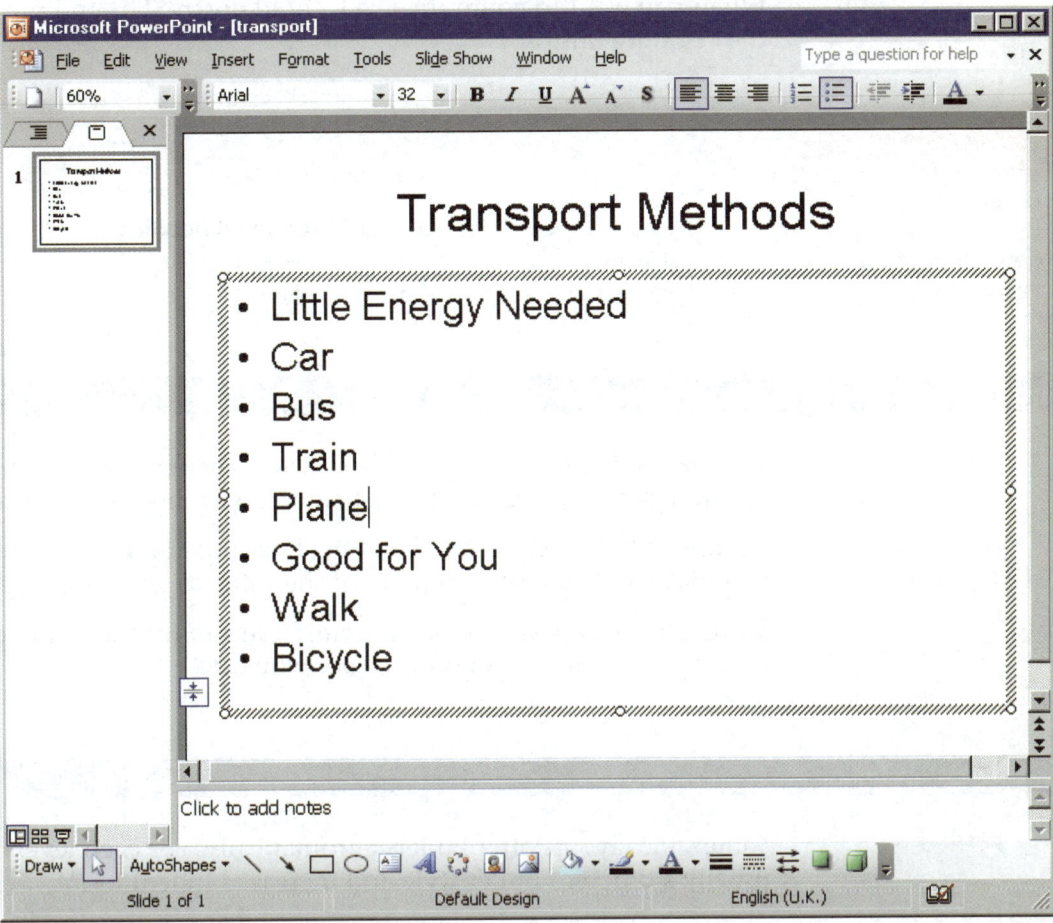

Promoting and demoting text

After entering text on a slide, you might decide that you want to change the organization of paragraphs or insert extra lines. One way to do this is to change the *level* of a particular line of text. Any line can be *promoted* up to the top level, which creates a new slide, or *demoted* down to a low level, such as a sub-bulleted item in a complex list.

When you start a new presentation and work in *Outline* view, you will see *Slide 1* with the cursor flashing next to it.

Start typing to add text, which will be at the top or title level. Press **Enter** and you will create *Slide 2*. If you want to add extra text at a lower level on *Slide 1*, you must now press the **Tab** key or click the **Demote** button. This will take the line down a level.

To display the **Demote** button, select **View/Toolbars** and click **Outlining**. This adds the *Outlining* toolbar to the side of the screen.

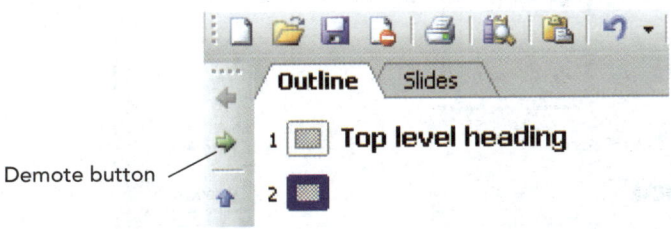

To type more entries at the same level, press **Enter**.

When you want to go up the levels, hold down **Shift** and press **Tab**, or click the **Promote** button.

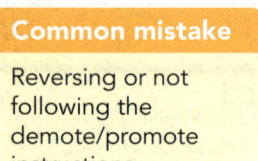
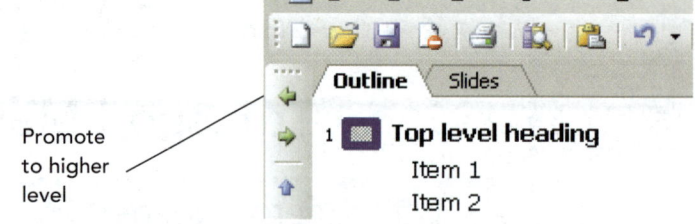

Promote to higher level

Inserting and deleting lines of text

To delete a line within a list, simply select the text, press **Delete** and close up the space, making sure the list adjusts with lines still at the correct level.

To insert a line, click at the end of the line above and press **Enter**. You may then have to demote or promote this new line to set it at the appropriate level.

To adjust the appearance of list items, you can increase or decrease line spacing from the option on the *Format* menu.

Bullets

Some slide layouts offer bullets automatically. For each level of text, there is usually a different bullet style and increased indentation.

- **Click to edit Master text styles**
  - **Second level**
    - Third level
      - Fourth level
        - » Fifth level

Change the look of the bullets by selecting the bulleted text, opening the **Format** menu, clicking **Bullets and Numbering** and selecting an alternative style.

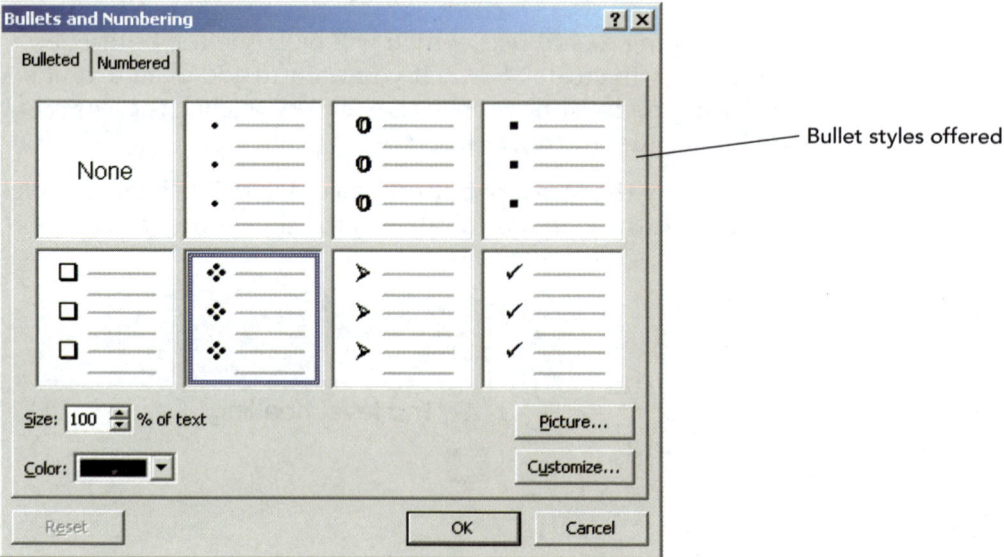

Bullet styles offered

To remove unwanted bullets, select the line or block of text and click off the **Bullets** toolbar button 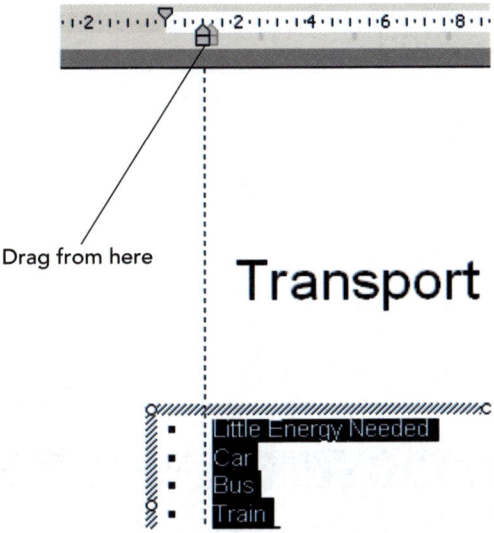. To add bullets, select the lines and then click the button on.

If the text is too close to the bullet, use the ruler to drag the line of text along.

Drag from here

Transport

- Little Energy Needed
- Car
- Bus
- Train

Opening a presentation saved earlier

Click the **Open** button and browse through the files on your computer to find the named presentation. Select it in the window and click **Open** or press **Enter**.

Exercise 3

1. Reopen *Transport* which you created in Exercise 2.
2. In Outline view, demote the list items *Car, Bus, Train, Plane, Walk* and *Bicycle* to level 2.
3. Now delete *Train* but do not leave a gap in the list.
4. Change to Normal view.
5. Remove bullets from the level 1 subheadings: *Little Energy Needed* and *Good for You*.
6. Underline the subheadings and format the list items to italic.
7. Save your presentation with the name `Transport2` to update these changes and then close the file.

Transport Methods

Little Energy Needed
- *Car*
- *Bus*
- *Plane*

Good for You
- *Walk*
- *Bicycle*

Images

You can add pictures to any slide from the *Clip Art Gallery*, which is available within Microsoft applications. You can also insert images that have been saved on your computer or provided on disk.

> **INSERTING THE WRONG IMAGE OR FAILING TO INSERT THE SPECIFIED IMAGE IS A CRITICAL ERROR.**

Clip art gallery

Click the **Insert Clip Art** toolbar button on the *Drawing* toolbar or select this option from the **Insert/Picture** menu.

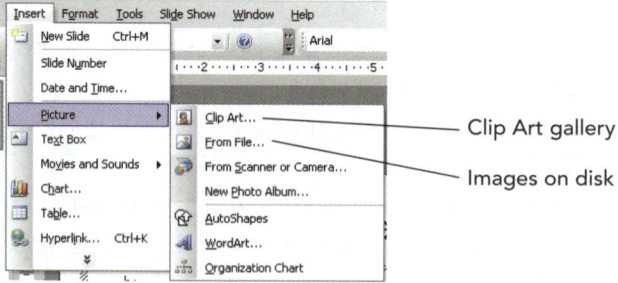

When the *Clip Art* search pane opens, enter your search word in the box and click the **Search** button. Browse through the selection of pictures and click one to add it to your slide.

If you search for images using a shortcut *Clip Art* placeholder, click **OK** to add a selected image to the slide and close the gallery.

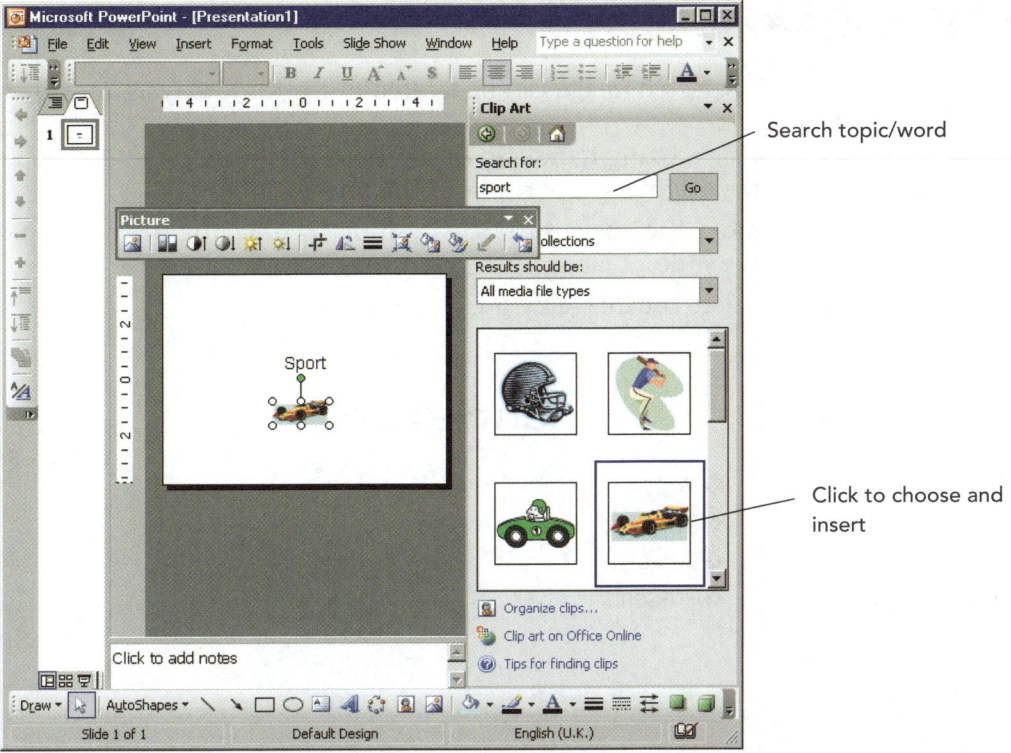

Search topic/word

Click to choose and insert

Inserting a picture from file

Open the **Insert** menu and select **Picture/From File** or click the **Insert Picture** toolbar button ![button]. This will allow you to browse through your files to locate the image. Select it in the window, click **Insert** and the picture will appear on your slide.

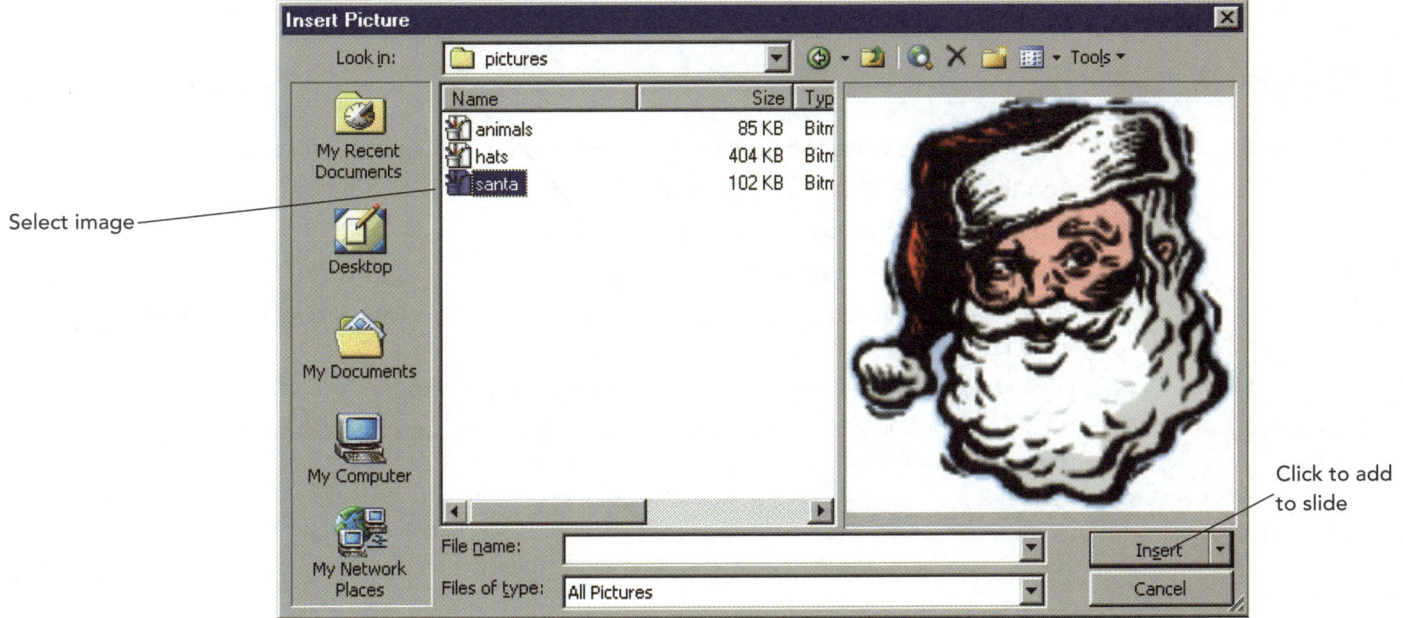

Select image

Click to add to slide

A selected image can be treated in the same way as a text box:

- drag a sizing handle in or out to resize it (use *corner* sizing handles to retain the original proportions of the image)
- move the image to a new position by dragging the whole picture across the slide
- delete the image by pressing the **Delete** key.

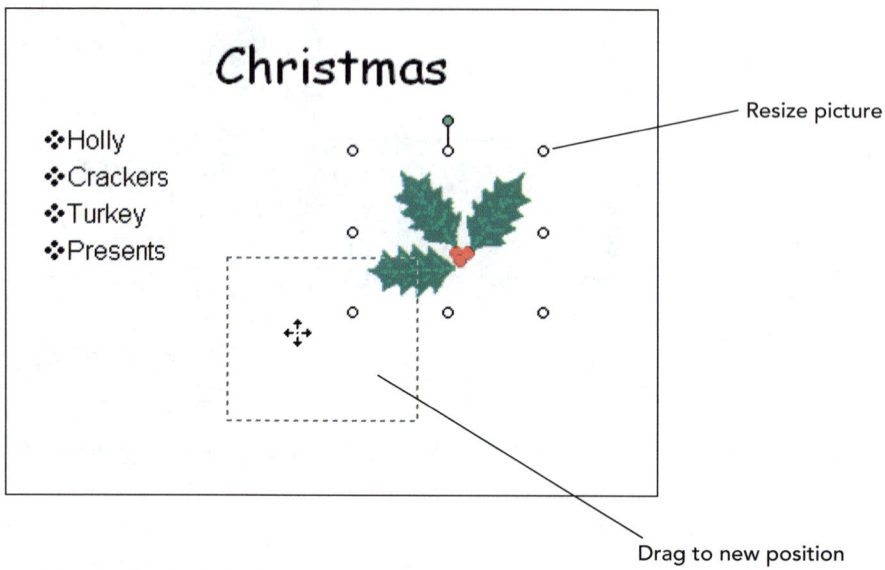

Common mistake

The image overlaps and hides some of the text, or the image is placed in the wrong position.

Exercise 4

1. Start a new presentation and apply a layout with a placeholder for an image.
2. Add the text **ANIMAL PICTURES** and centre it in the middle of the slide.
3. Use the shortcut to open the Clip Art Gallery.
4. Select any picture of an animal.
5. When it appears, reduce it to half the original size and move it to the top right-hand corner of the slide.
6. Now reopen the gallery from the toolbar and select another animal picture.
7. When it appears, increase it to twice the original size and move it to the opposite corner.
8. Save the slide as **Animals** and close the file.

New slides

For New CLAIT you will be asked to create a three-slide presentation and then add a fourth slide.

There are two simple methods for adding new slides.

On the *Outline* or *Slides* tab

Click a slide image on the tab and press **Enter**. On the *Outline* tab, click at the end of any text if some has already been added. You may need to promote the line to reach the top level, i.e. a new slide.

Move between slides simply by clicking the numbered slide.

In *Normal* view

With a slide open on screen, click the **New Slide** toolbar button 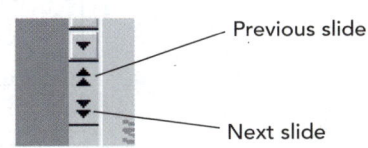 or select this option from the **Insert** menu. The new slide will open on screen as the *following* slide in the presentation.

To move through your presentation, press the **Page Up** or **Page Down** keys or click the **Next Slide** or **Previous Slide** navigation arrows on the right-hand side of the slide.

Previous slide

Next slide

A message at the bottom left of the screen will tell you which slide is currently being viewed.

Slide 4 of 4

1. Start a new presentation and select a blank slide layout.

2. In the Outline pane: enter the following text as a heading: `Food Shopping on the Internet`

3. Now add the following text at a lower non-bulleted level:

   `You can find food and other items in two ways: searching using key words or browsing the virtual aisles once you have opened a retail Website on your screen.`

4. Add a new slide 2 and enter the title: `What You Can Buy`

5. Working in Normal view, insert the image *house* (from the CD). Position it in the bottom left-hand corner of the slide.

6. Now open the Clip Art Gallery and find and insert a picture of any household object such as a chair, bed or computer. Resize this image so that it is double the size of the house, keeping it in proportion, and place it in the opposite corner of the slide.

7. Add the following text in the centre of the slide: `If you have the money, you can buy practically anything online.`

8. Add a final slide with the heading: `Security` and the following text: `Don't forget to keep a note of your order number in case there is a problem.`

9. Save the presentation as `Shopping`.

10. Navigate through the presentation and format all text to a font that differs from the default – e.g. Arial, Times New Roman or Comic Sans MS. Make the headings bold and underlined, and all other text italic. Amend alignment and font sizes if necessary so that all text is clearly visible.

11. Update the file to save these changes and then close the presentation.

Answer

Food Shopping on the Internet

You can find food and other items in two ways: searching using key words or browsing the virtual aisles once you have opened a retail Website on your screen.

1

What You Can Buy

If you have the money, you can buy practically anything online.

2

Security

Don't forget to keep a note of your order number in case there is a problem.

3

Changing slide order

Click **Slide Sorter** view or the **Slides** tab in *Normal* view to see thumbnails of all the slides. To move any slide, click it and drag it to its new position. The pointer will show an arrow with a small box attached, and a vertical line will show the position of the slide at any time. When you let go the mouse, the slide will drop into place.

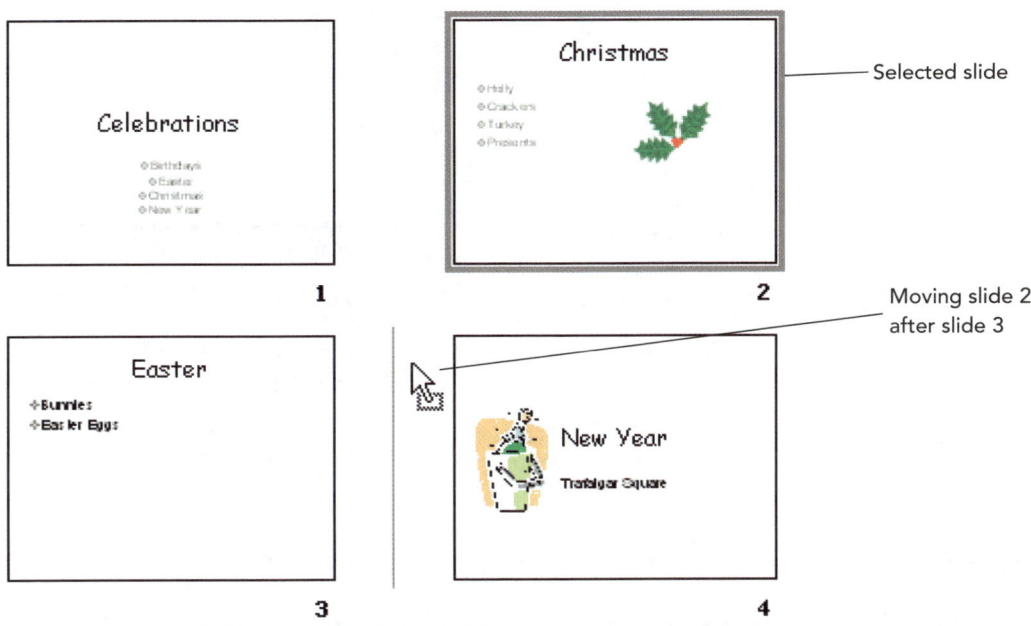

Selected slide

Moving slide 2 after slide 3

Spelling

Checking spelling is the same in PowerPoint as other Office applications. You can right-click a wavy line under a word to be offered an alternative or go to **Tools/Spelling** to open the spellchecker box. Click an alternative in the *Suggestions* box and then click **Change** to correct highlighted words, or click **Ignore** to leave it unchanged.

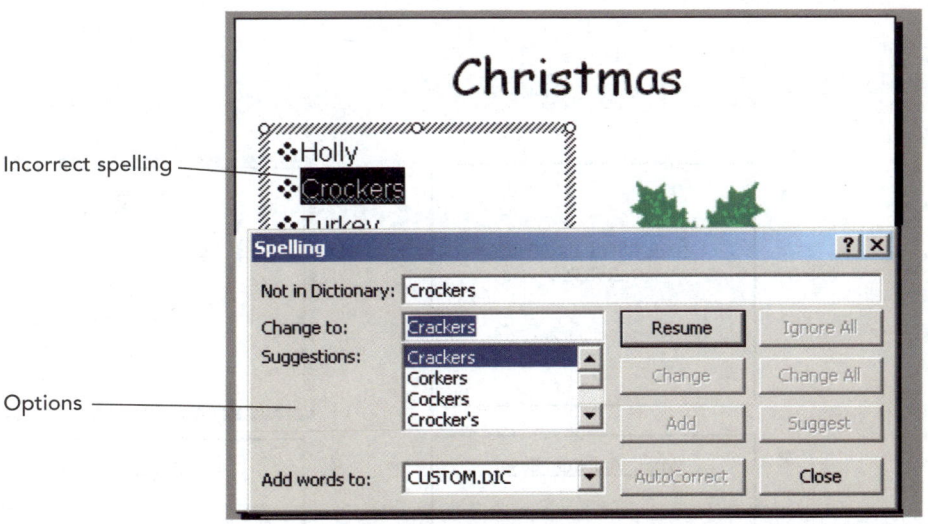

Incorrect spelling

Options

Drawn shapes

To draw a shape onto a slide, click the appropriate *AutoShape* button and then drag the mouse across the slide when it shows a cross. The shape or line will appear. For a circle, hold **Ctrl** as you draw an oval, and for a square hold **Ctrl** as you draw a rectangle.

Change line style and width, or fill the selected shape with colour by choosing from the *Line and Fill Colour* options. (See Unit 6.)

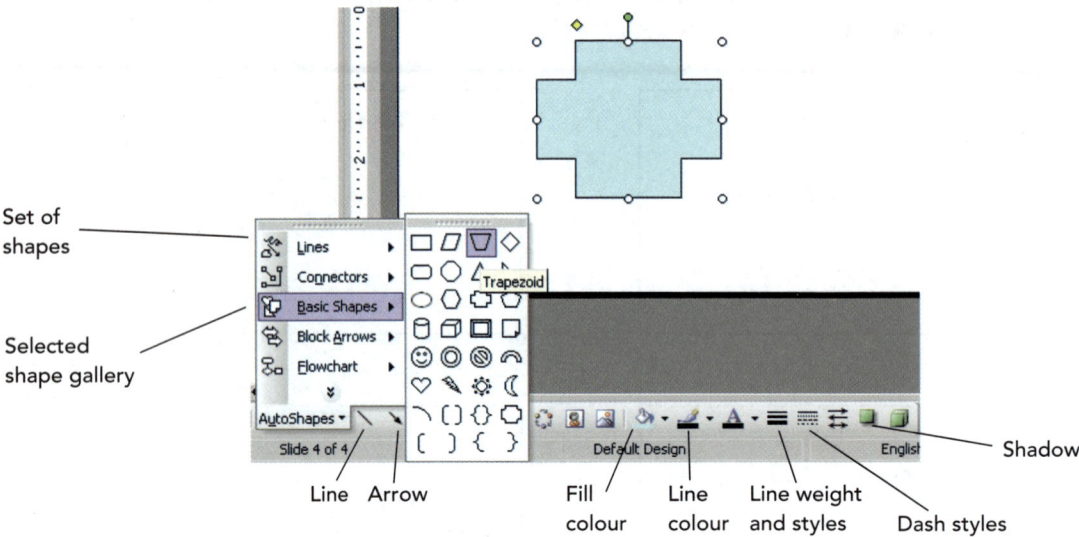

Set of shapes

Selected shape gallery

Line   Arrow

Fill colour

Line colour

Line weight and styles

Dash styles

Shadow

Exercise 6

1. Reopen the *Shopping* presentation you created in Exercise 5.
2. Create a new slide 4 with the heading `Prices`
3. Add a drawn shape of a star, fill it with yellow and apply a thick border.
4. Add the following text in a text box: `If you use the Web to compare prices, you can save a great deal of money.`
5. Move this slide so that it becomes slide 3.
6. Format the text so that it is the same on all slides.
7. Save the presentation as `Shopping2`.
8. Close the file.

Answer

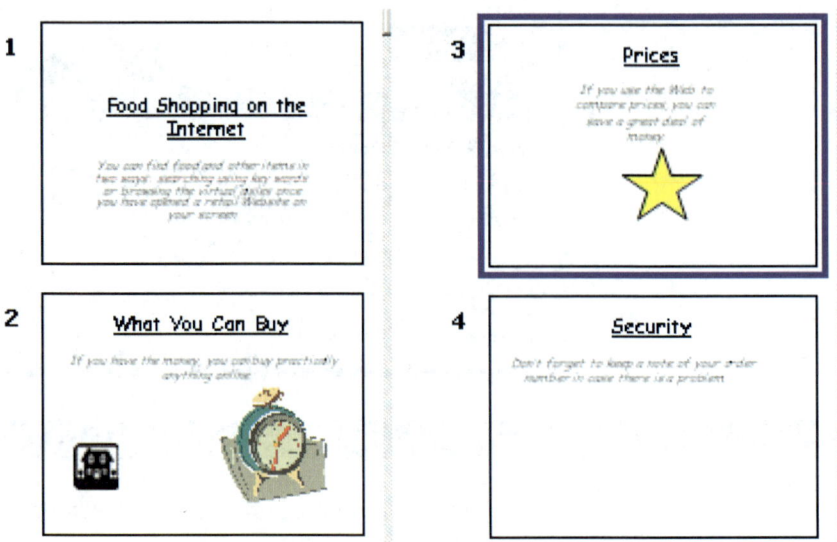

Page orientation

Slides are automatically displayed in landscape orientation. To change to portrait (upright A4), go to **File/Page Setup** and click the appropriate **radio** button. You can also decide what type of printout you want – e.g. 35 mm slides or A3 paper, and set the exact width and height of your printout by changing the measurements in the boxes.

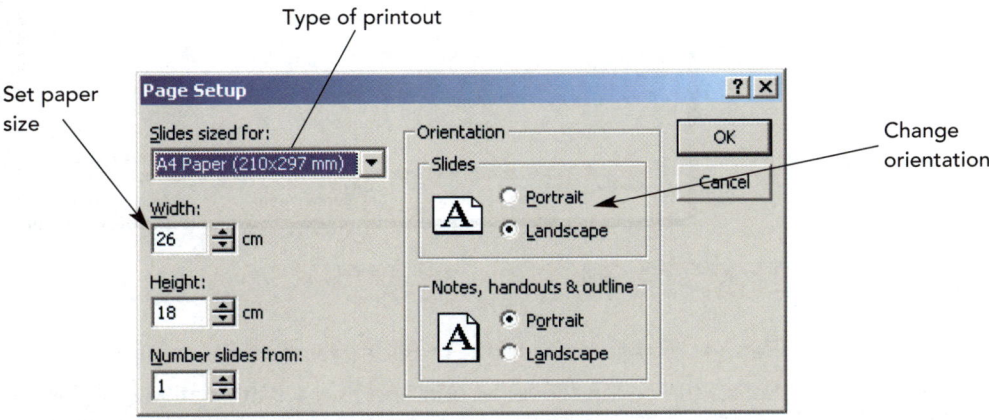

Set paper size · Type of printout · Change orientation

Slide Master

To save time when formatting a long presentation, PowerPoint comes with a special slide called the *Slide Master* which is accessed from the **View/Master** menu. Changing or adding elements here will change all the slides in the presentation, so that you don't have to alter every slide manually. Click **Close Master View** or **Normal View** button to return to your slides.

Here are some of the changes you may want to make.

- *Add pictures and text* – images and text boxes can be inserted on the *Slide Master* as normal, but they need to be sized and positioned so that they don't interfere with other slide objects. To change these additions, you must always return to the *Slide Master*.

> **Common mistake**
>
> Positioning an object on the Slide Master that interferes with text or objects on one or more slides.

> **Common mistake**
>
> An object is not inserted on the Slide Master and is inconsistently displayed when added manually to different slides.

- *Format text* – if you haven't altered the basic title, list item or other text fonts in *Normal* view, you can select an alternative to apply throughout the presentation. Different font types and sizes will have been preset for each level of text so you must pick the appropriate level before changing them.

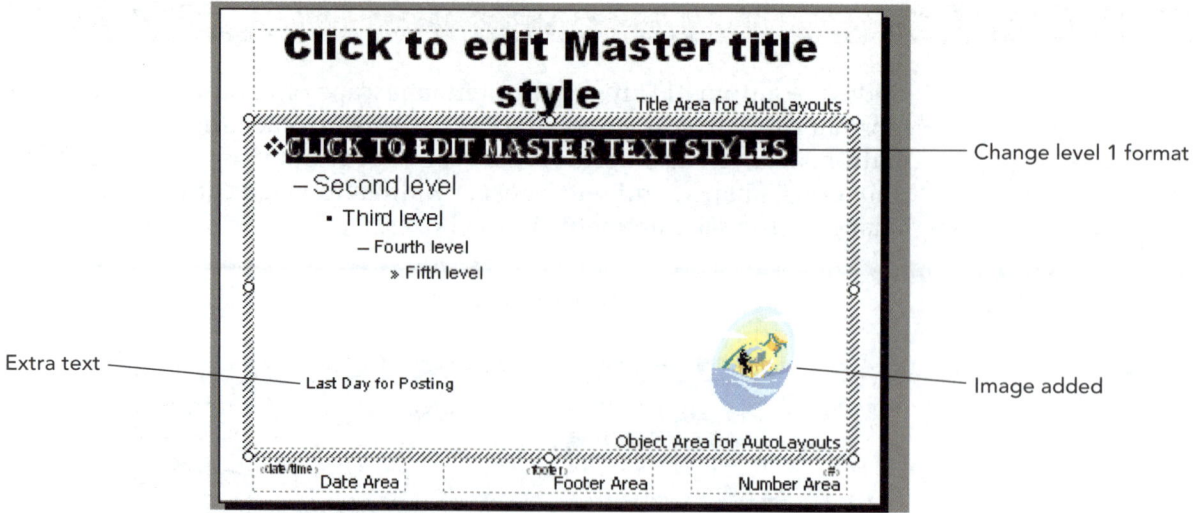

	Change level 1 format
Extra text	Image added

1. Reopen *Transport2* and go to Slide Master view.
2. Select the second level of text and find an alternative style of bullet.
3. Insert the image *bike* (from the CD) and resize if necessary.
4. Position the image at the top of the slide, on the right of the heading. Make sure that it will not overlap any heading text.
5. Add a text box at the bottom of the slide and add your name and today's date. Format the text to font size 10, centre aligned.
6. Save this as a new version of the presentation with the name **New Transport** and then close the file.

Answer

Transport Methods 🚲

Little Energy Needed
  ➢ Car
  ➢ Bus
  ➢ Plane
Good for You
  ➢ Walk
  ➢ Bicycle

My name 02/606

Edit and replace

To replace one word with another throughout the presentation, you can use the *Search and Replace* tool available from the *Edit* menu.

Go to **Edit/Replace** and type the word you want to change in the *Find what*: box. Type the replacement word in the *Replace with*: box. You can also click the various checkboxes to match whole words (rather than replacing parts of words), or to replace only words that contain specific upper or lower case letters.

To control the process, click **Find Next** to highlight the first matching word and then either click **Replace** or leave the original in position and move on to the next match by clicking **Find Next** again. Click **Replace All** only if you are certain the replacements will be acceptable.

Common mistake

Not matching the case or not amending replacements where these should have initial capital letters.

Headers and footers

To add automatic headers or footers to any slides or printouts, go to **View/ Header and Footer** and click the **Slide** or **Notes and Handouts** tab. You can also open the dialogue box from the **Insert** menu by selecting **Date and Time** or **Page Number**.

Click in the boxes for dates/times and page numbers and type in your text for a header or footer. Items will appear in preset positions on the slides but you can move them in the same way that you move text boxes.

On slides, you can add footers to a single slide by clicking **Apply**, or to all the slides in a presentation by clicking **Apply to All**. You can also add footer text to all your slides in *Slide Master* view by clicking and typing into the placeholder.

To add today's date to any slide or printout, select **Update automatically**. You can choose your preferred style of date and/or time from the box. If you want a fixed date, type it into the *Fixed* box.

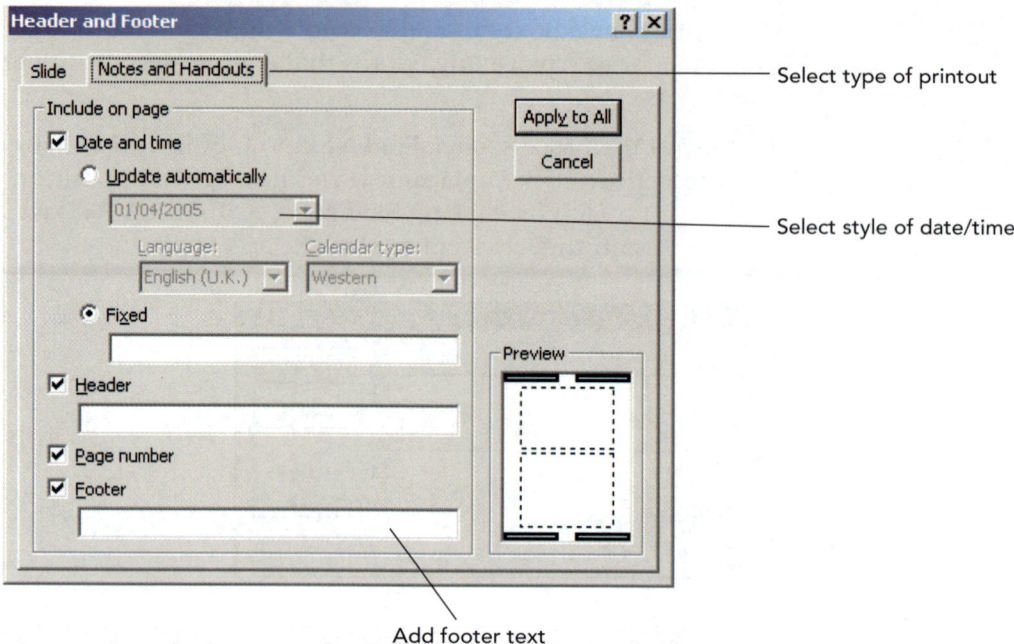

Select type of printout

Select style of date/time

Add footer text

Printing

If you click the **Print** toolbar button , you will print out one set of slides – each one on a separate page.

You can print different aspects of the presentation:

- *notes page* – used as a speaker's aide which contains reminders under a small picture of the slide
- *handouts* (audience notes) – with up to nine thumbnail pictures of the slides to a page
- *individual slides* – identify which to print if you don't want them all; e.g. 1–3 or 2, 5, 7
- *outline* – just the text content of the presentation.

To set the options, go to **File/Print** and select the appropriate item from the *Print what*: box. If handouts are selected, set the number of slide pictures that will print on a single page.

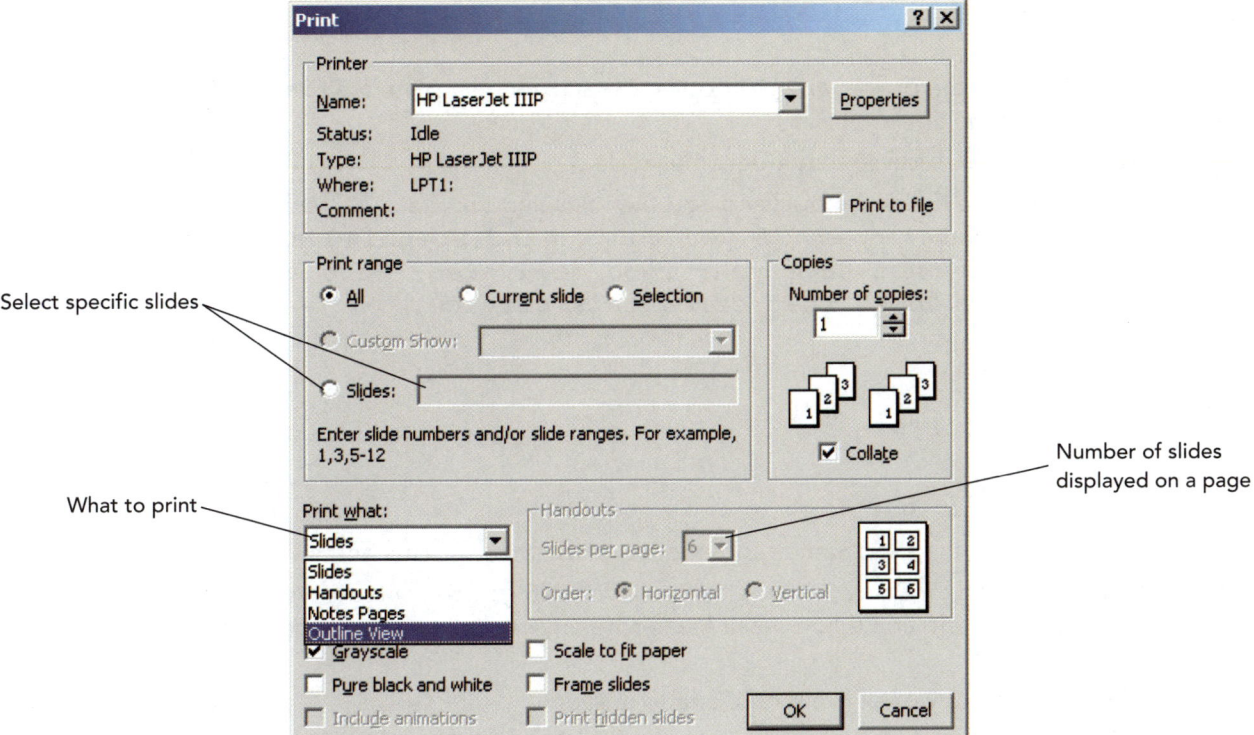

Select specific slides

What to print

Number of slides displayed on a page

If you click the **Preview** button in the *Print* box, you have another chance to set various options – e.g. add headers or footers or choose how many slides to display on a handout.

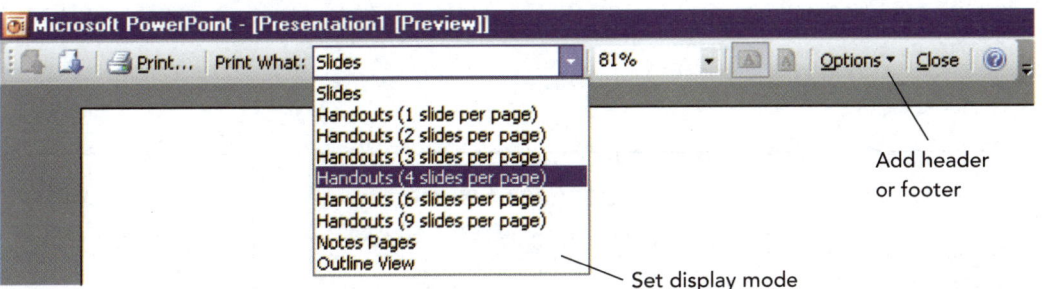

Add header or footer

Set display mode

FAILURE TO DISPLAY ALL SLIDES ON THE HANDOUT OR OUTLINE IS A CRITICAL ERROR.

Common mistake

Printing a handout with the wrong number of slides displayed.

Common mistake

Not checking which slides will print – e.g. for an outline – after limiting a printout for handouts or slides.

Common mistake

Using a text box for titles or main text, rather than typing on the Outline tab or into a placeholder. This text will not show on any printouts.

1. Reopen the presentation *Shopping2* which you completed in Exercise 6. Add a new slide 5.

2. Move this slide so that it becomes slide 3.

3. Enter the heading **Food** and add the following text below it, removing any bullets if they appear: `If you don't mind spending an extra £5, why not have your food delivered? Here are some of the shops that offer this service:`

   `Waitrose`

   `Tesco`

   `Sainsburys`

   `Iceland`

   `Marks & Spencer`

4. Demote the shop names and add bullets to the list items only.

5. Using *Edit/Replace*, change the word *food* to **goods** wherever it appears in the presentation (four times). Make sure any capital letters are readjusted correctly.

6. Print a copy of all five slides, one to a page.

7. Now print a handout displaying all the slides on one page.

8. Finally, print an outline of the presentation with the date as a header or footer.

9. Update the presentation and close the file.

Answer

Step 6

![Slide 1: Goods Shopping on the Internet — You can find goods and other items in two ways: searching using key words or browsing the virtual aisles once you have opened a retail website on your screen]

1

![Slide 2: What You Can Buy — If you have the money, you can buy practically anything online.]

2

![Slide 3: Goods — If you don't mind spending an extra £5, why not have your goods delivered? Here are some of the shops that offer this service: - Waitrose - Tesco - Sainsburys - Iceland - Marks & Spencer]

3

![Slide 4: Prices — If you use the Web to compare prices, you can save a great deal of money.]

4

![Slide 5: Security — Don't forget to keep a note of your order number in case there is a problem.]

5

Step 8

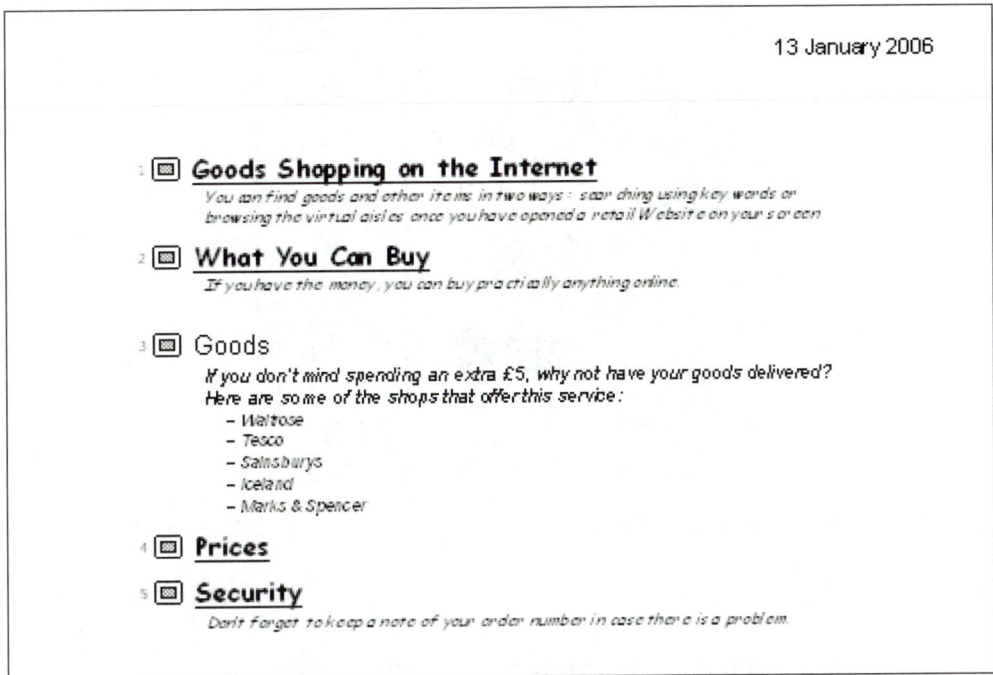

13 January 2006

1. **Goods Shopping on the Internet**
   You can find goods and other items in two ways: searching using key words or browsing the virtual aisles once you have opened a retail Website on your screen

2. **What You Can Buy**
   If you have the money, you can buy practically anything online.

3. Goods
   If you don't mind spending an extra £5, why not have your goods delivered? Here are some of the shops that offer this service:
   - *Waitrose*
   - *Tesco*
   - *Sainsburys*
   - *Iceland*
   - *Marks & Spencer*

4. **Prices**

5. **Security**
   Don't forget to keep a note of your order number in case there is a problem.

Backgrounds

To add a coloured background to one or more slides in your presentation, choose from those available in the **Format/Background** menu.

Click the **down arrow** in the empty window to open the menu.

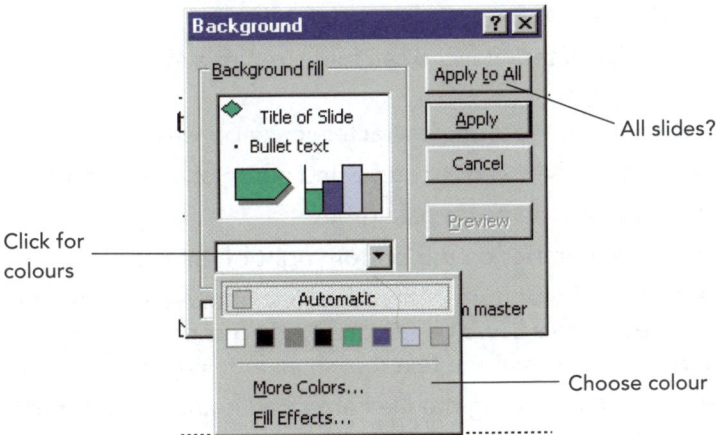

Select one of the eight coloured boxes and apply to one or all of the slides in the presentation. Click **More Colors** to open the colour palette and choose from a wider range or click **Fill Effects** to apply a textured or patterned background.

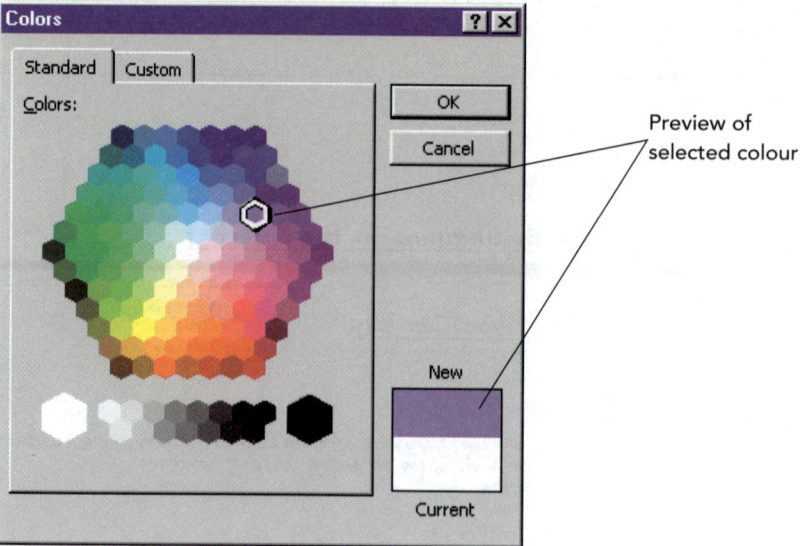

Preview of selected colour

Exercise 9 – a full assignment

Task 1

1. Produce a short presentation of three slides.

2. Set up a master slide as follows. This master slide layout must be used for all slides.
   - Set the slide orientation to landscape.
   - Use a placeholder (text frame) for the title towards the top of the slide.
   - Use a placeholder (frame) for the main slide content.

3. Set up the text styles as follows:
   - *Title* – bold, large font, centred.
   - *1st level* – no bullet, medium size, left aligned.
   - *2nd level* – bulleted, italic, small font size left aligned and indented from 1st level.

4. Make sure there is at least one character space between the bullets and the text.

5. In the footer enter the word **Nature** and automatic fixed date.

6. Format the background to be pale green.

7. Display the slide number on the bottom right of the slide.

8. Add a text box at the bottom of the slide, just above the footer, that contains the words **Tickets available from Reception** followed by your name shown in brackets. Format the text to a small font size and centre it in the box.

9. Save the presentation using the file name **talk** and use it for the rest of the assignment.

Task 2

1. Create slide 1 and enter the title **Birds and their Habitats**

2. Enter the following text on three lines in the main placeholder (frame), at level 1:
   Talk by Professor Jane English
   University of East Anglia
   Saturday 12 September at 8.30 pm

3. Insert the image *butterfly* from the CD and position it at the top of the slide on the left, between the title and main text. You may resize this image.
   - Make sure you maintain the original proportions of the image.
   - Make sure the image does not touch or overlap any text.
4. Create slide 2 and enter the title: `Birds Around Britain`
5. Add the following text at level 1:

   `Waders`

   `Domesticated Birds`

   `Reptiles, frogs and toads`
6. Create slide 3 and enter the title `Signs of Pollution`
7. On this slide, add the following text at the levels shown in brackets:

   `The lichen test` (level 1)

   `None — bad air` (level 2)

   `Small amounts — slightly better` (level 1)

   `Long and shrubby — clean country air` (level 2)

   `Lifeless water` (level 2)

   `Sewage` (level 2)

   `Oil` (level 2)

   `Dead birds` (level 2)
8. Use the spellcheck facility to check the accuracy of the text.
9. Save the slide show keeping the file name *talk*.
10. Print out each of the three slides, one per page, in landscape orientation.

Task 3

1. Replace the word *birds* with the word `animals` wherever it appears in the presentation (4 times), and ensure you retain initial capitals in any titles.
2. On slide 3:
   - demote the line beginning *Small amounts …* to level 2
   - promote the phrase *Lifeless water* to level 1.
3. Create slide 4 and enter the title: `Literature available soon`
4. Draw a cube using an AutoShape and shade it dark green.
5. Make sure the shape does not touch or overlap any text.
6. Save the presentation using the new file name `nature`.
7. Print slides 2, 3 and 4 as *handouts* with three slides on one page.

Task 4

1. In your presentation called *nature* change the order of the slides so that slide 4 becomes slide 2.
2. On slide 4, *Signs of Pollution*, delete the list item *Sewage*, leaving no gap.
3. Save the amended presentation as `leaflets`.
4. You need to print an outline of the presentation. Enter your name as a header or footer for this printout, and print the presentation in Outline view to display the text on all four slides.
5. Close the presentation and exit the software securely.

Task 2 Step 10

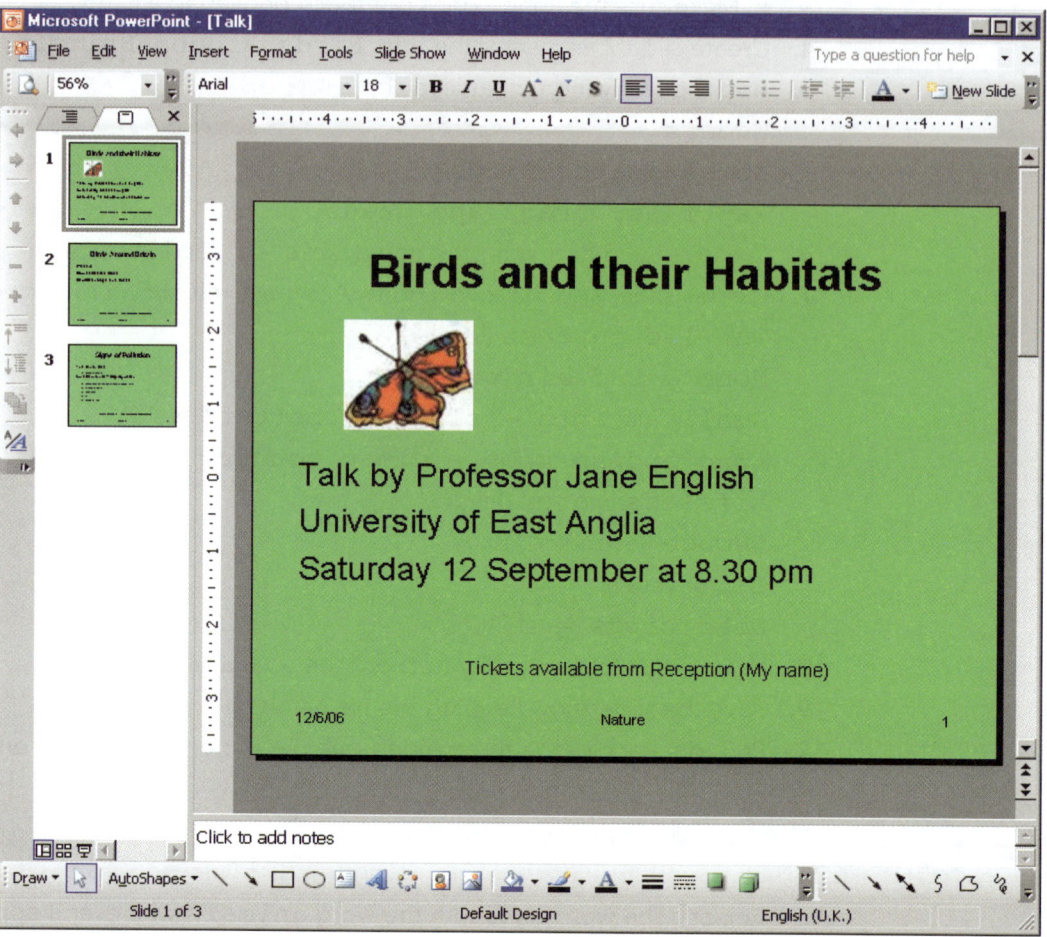

Task 3 Step 7

Animals Around Britain

Waders
Domesticated animals
Reptiles, frogs and toads

_____
_____
_____
_____
_____
_____
_____

Signs of Pollution

The lichen test
  – None – bad air
  – Small amounts – slightly better
  – Long and shrubby – clean country air
Lifeless water
  – Sewage
  – Oil
  – Dead animals

_____
_____
_____
_____
_____
_____
_____

Literature available soon

_____
_____
_____
_____
_____
_____

Task 4 Step 4

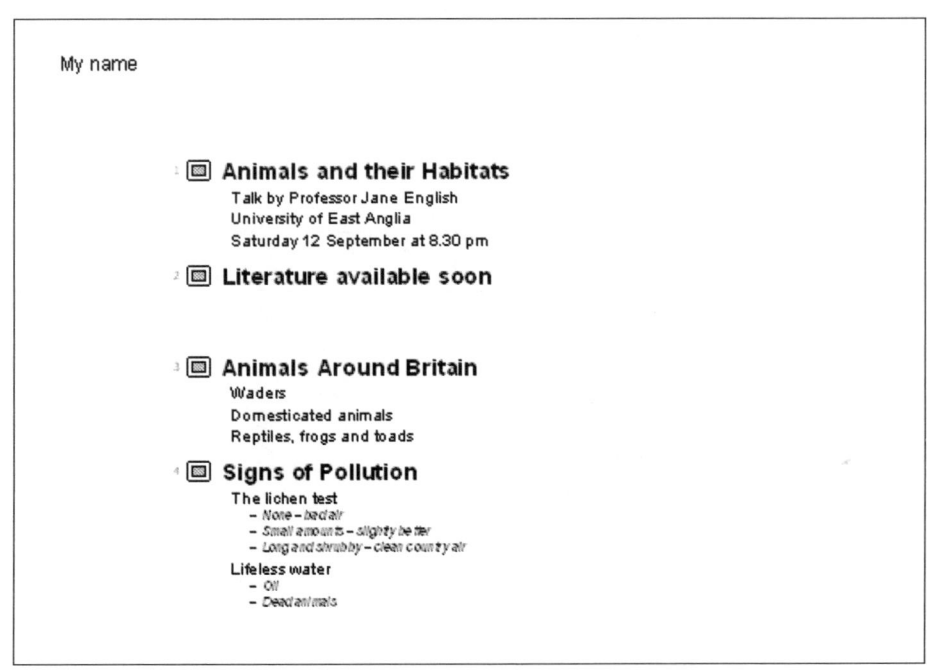

My name

1. ▣ **Animals and their Habitats**
     Talk by Professor Jane English
     University of East Anglia
     Saturday 12 September at 8.30 pm

2. ▣ **Literature available soon**

3. ▣ **Animals Around Britain**
     Waders
     Domesticated animals
     Reptiles, frogs and toads

4. ▣ **Signs of Pollution**
     The lichen test
       – None – bad air
       – Small amounts – slightly better
       – Long and shrubby – clean country air
     Lifeless water
       – Oil
       – Dead animals

Self-assessment checklist

I feel confident that I can now: ✓

Understand the use of presentation software

Work in different views

Open a presentation application

Set page orientation

Enter and format text

Insert and format images

Demote or promote text

Add or remove bullets

Add new slides to a presentation

Change slide order

Use a spellchecker

Add drawn shapes

Shade or fill shapes

Use Edit/Replace to amend entries

Use the master slide to add or format text or objects appearing on every slide

Set a background colour

Add headers or footers

Print slides

Print handouts

Print an outline of the presentation

Save a presentation file

Open a presentation saved previously

Close a presentation

Exit the application

Summary of critical errors

- Specified image is missing
- Missing slide on any printout

6

e-image creation

- **What is computer art?** 188
- **Selecting appropriate software** 189
- **Using Microsoft Word** 189
- **AutoShapes** 189
  Straight lines 190
  Squares and circles 191
- **Closing artwork** 191
- **Working with AutoShapes** 192
  Colours and borders 192
  Layers 193
  Transparency 194
  Adding text 194
  Copying AutoShapes 194
  Rotating AutoShapes 195
  Deleting AutoShapes 196
  Working with multiple shapes 196
- **Saving artwork** 196
- **Setting the size of artwork** 196
- **Picture files** 198
- **Importing an image** 198
- **Flipping or rotating an image** 199
- **Moving an image** 199
- **Cropping an image** 202
- **Resizing an image** 202
- **Text** 203
  Stretching text 204
  Rotating text 205
- **Printing in colour or black and white** 207
- **Using Paint Shop Pro** 210
- **Launching the program** 210
- **Toolbars** 210
- **Measurement units** 211
- **New file and artwork size** 211
- **Selecting** 212
- **Pictures** 213
  Cropping 213
  Rotating and flipping 214
  Layers 214
  Resizing 215
  Moving an image 216
- **Saving a file** 216
- **Working with colours** 218
- **Vector objects** 219
  Flood fill 220
  Lines 220
  Preset shapes 220
  Formatting 221
  Text 222
  Copying shapes 223
- **Printing** 224
- **Digital camera images** 224
  Image resolution 225
  Text on an image 226
  Printing a camera image 226
- **Self-assessment checklist** 226
- **Summary of critical errors** 227

What is computer art?

It is possible to create attractive artwork using your computer, even if you have never thought of yourself as 'good at drawing'. Ready-made shapes are available that can be added to your page with a few clicks of the mouse, and these can then be filled with colours from a large palette or bordered with various styles and widths of coloured lines. If you add in images from the gallery, or from any other pictures that have been saved on your computer, together with text that can be formatted in different styles and sizes, you can build up professional-looking pictures that can be used for a range of different purposes.

This unit will develop and assess your ability to create a piece of artwork incorporating text, shapes and images and then print it in colour. There are a number of dedicated software programs that allow you to work with images, but the tools required for New CLAIT are also available in Microsoft applications such as Word, PowerPoint and Paint. However, you will have to be able to use image editing software to download and work with digital camera images.

You will be asked to carry out the following tasks:

- Open appropriate software
- Add drawn shapes such as lines, rectangles and circles
- Set the size for a piece of artwork
- Add background colour
- Import images
- Use the cropping tool to remove part of an image
- Flip or rotate images
- Resize images
- Move images
- Format shapes
- Copy shapes
- Delete shapes
- Add and format text
- Size text
- Amend text
- Save an artwork file
- Print artwork in colour
- Download images from a digital camera
- Add text to camera images
- Change image resolution
- Print in black and white

To pass Unit 6 , you must be able to:

- Select appropriate software to produce artwork
- Set artwork size
- Import images
- Flip or rotate images

- Crop images
- Resize images
- Move images
- Add and format AutoShapes
- Copy AutoShapes
- Delete AutoShapes
- Add and format text
- Save artwork
- Print artwork in colour
- Download camera images
- Change image resolution
- Add text to an image
- Print in black and white

Selecting appropriate software

The first part of this unit shows you how to use Microsoft Word to carry out most of the tasks. The second part will cover the graphics editor Paint Shop Pro, but you could use alternative programs such as Photoshop or CorelDraw as they work in very similar ways.

You will need to turn to the section on Paint Shop Pro for coverage of working with digital camera images.

Using Microsoft Word

Word is covered in detail in Unit 1 and it may be helpful to work through that before using that package to create and format your artwork.

AutoShapes

Having opened Word and started a new document, you will be asked to set the size of the artwork. To do this, you will need to add a circular or rectangular shape to the page from the *AutoShape* options and insert any images, text or drawn objects inside. If necessary, change the page from portrait to landscape orientation by selecting the option from the **File/Page Setup/Paper Size** dialogue box.

Lines, squares, circles and more complex shapes can be found on the *Drawing* toolbar or from the *AutoShape* menus. If the toolbar is not visible, click the **Drawing** toolbar button or right-click any empty part of a toolbar and select **Drawing** from the list.

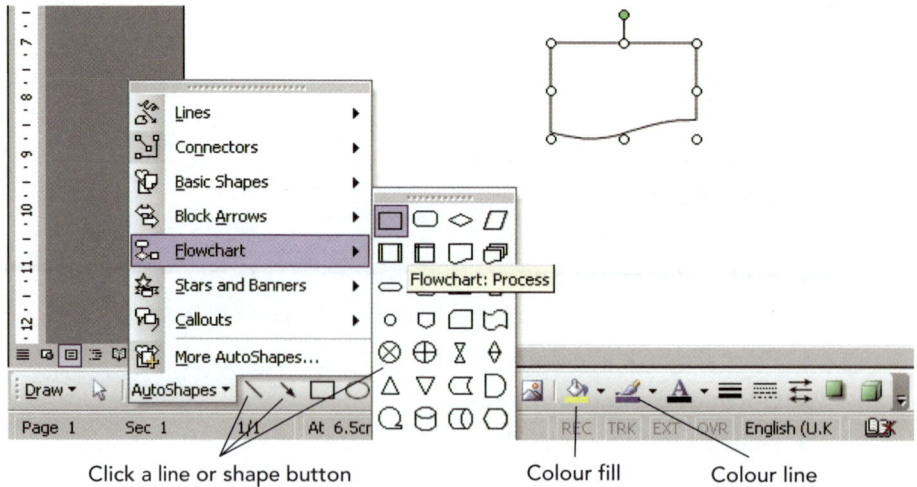

Click a line or shape button   Colour fill   Colour line

Select a line or shape by clicking its toolbar button, and then move the mouse pointer over the page. It will show a cross. Click and drag the pointer across the page to create the shape you have chosen and let go the mouse button when you have finished. Freeform lines and curves behave slightly differently as clicking allows you to create more complex shapes or shapes that bend – double-click the mouse to finish drawing.

To draw several similar shapes, double-click the toolbar button to keep it turned on, and then click it off when you have finished drawing.

Drawn shapes will appear selected, displaying white circles known as *sizing handles*. These handles can be dragged in or out when the pointer shows a two-way arrow to alter the size of the shape. Always use a corner sizing handle to maintain a shape's proportions. When you first start drawing in Word 2003 you will find that you are provided with a special area, the *drawing canvas*. This can cause complications so remove it by going to **Tools/Options** and taking off the tick in the box labelled 'Automatically create drawing canvas' on the *General* tab.

You can drag round the green circle at the end of the extended arm to rotate the shape, and exaggerate one aspect by dragging the yellow diamond that may also be visible.

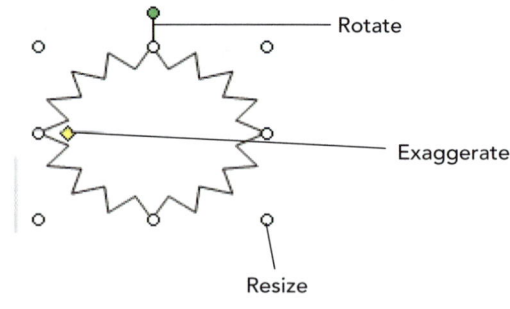

Move the selected shape to a different part of the page by clicking inside it and dragging it to a new position when the pointer shows a four-way arrow.

Take off the selection by clicking on a blank part of the page – the white circles will disappear.

Straight lines

If you are trying to draw a line, you may find that if you draw it with the mouse the line is kinked. Keep lines straight by holding down the **Shift** key as you drag the mouse. To move or resize a line, click it to show the sizing handles and then treat it like any other shape.

Squares and circles

When using the *Rectangle* tool, hold down **Shift** as you drag out the shape and it will form a square. In the same way, draw circles by holding down **Shift** as you use the *Oval* tool.

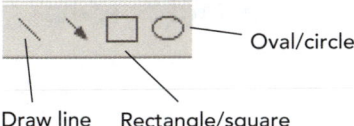

Draw line Rectangle/square Oval/circle

Closing artwork

Click the lower **Close** button or go to **File/Close**. If you click the top **Close** button or select **File/Exit** you will exit the application.

(Closing a Word document and exiting the application are covered more fully in Unit 1.)

Exercise 1

1. Launch Word and start a new document.
2. Insert the following shapes anywhere on the page:
   - a large rectangle
   - a large oval
   - a small square
   - a small circle.
3. Join two of the shapes with a straight line.
4. Add a more complex shape – e.g. a star – from the AutoShape menu and stretch it by dragging the yellow diamond.
5. Close the document without saving.

Answer

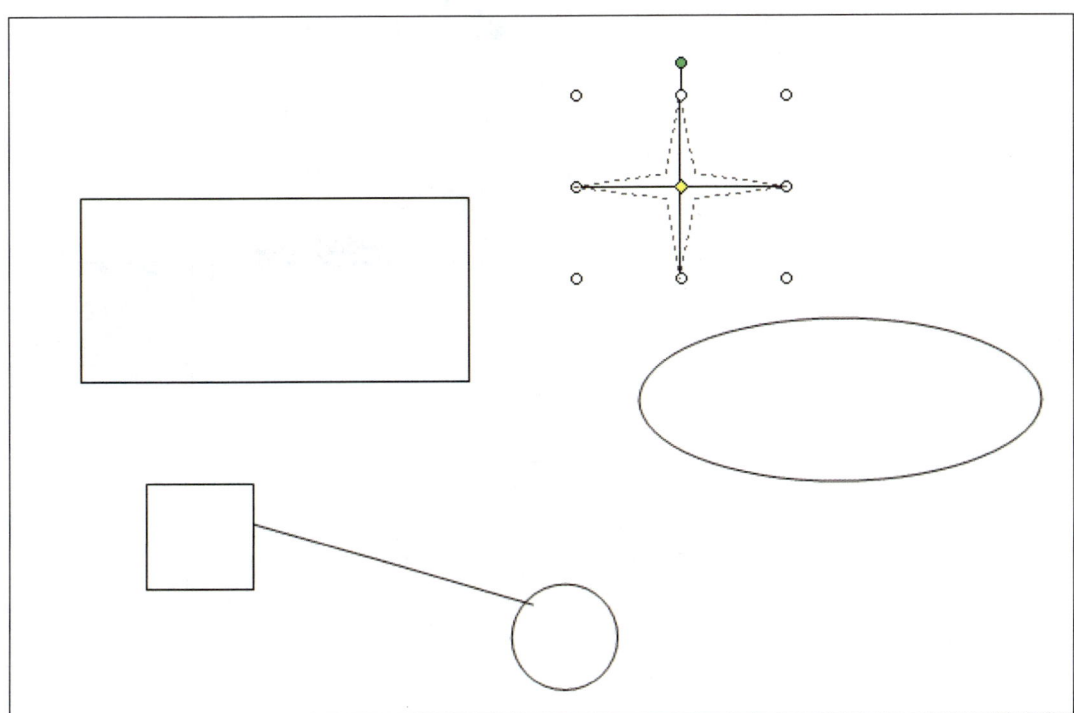

Colours and borders

When the shape first appears, it may have a coloured fill or border. To remove unwanted colour, click the **arrow** next to the *Fill Color* or *Line Color* toolbar button and select **No Fill/Line**.

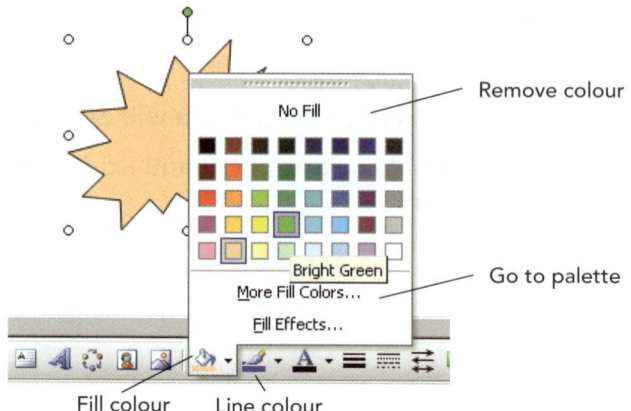

Change or add colours by selecting the shape and then filling with colour from the *Fill Color* button or colouring the line or border from the *Line Color* button. Click the **arrow** next to either button and select from the coloured boxes.

Click **More Fill/Line Colors** to choose from a wider palette.

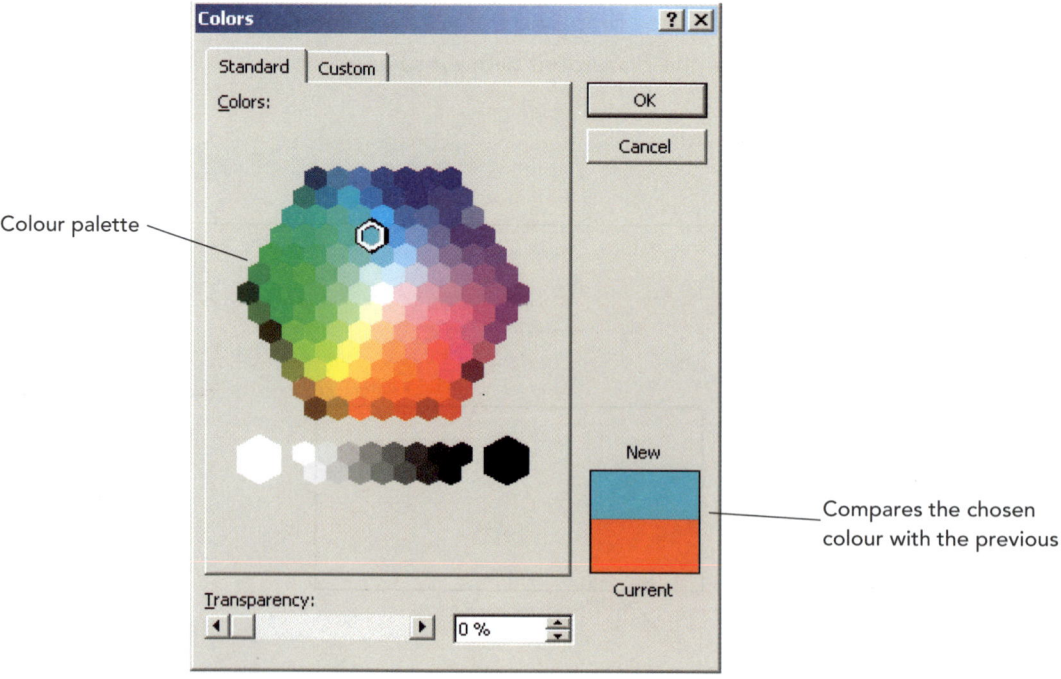

Choose a different style or weight of line or border, and add shadow or 3-D effects by selecting from the toolbar options.

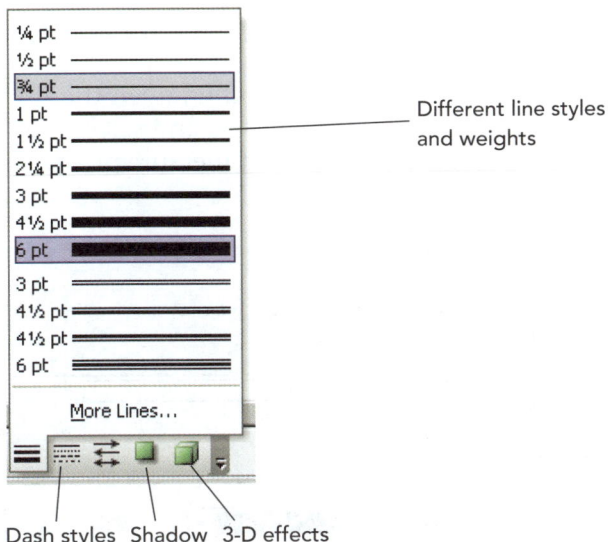

Different line styles and weights

Dash styles   Shadow   3-D effects

Layers

Objects such as *AutoShapes* can be layered on top of one another, but this may mean you obscure part or all of an underlying object. To reorder any object, select it and then go to **Draw/Order** on the *Drawing* toolbar. Options include sending it behind text, sending it back one layer, sending it behind all the layers, and bringing it forward.

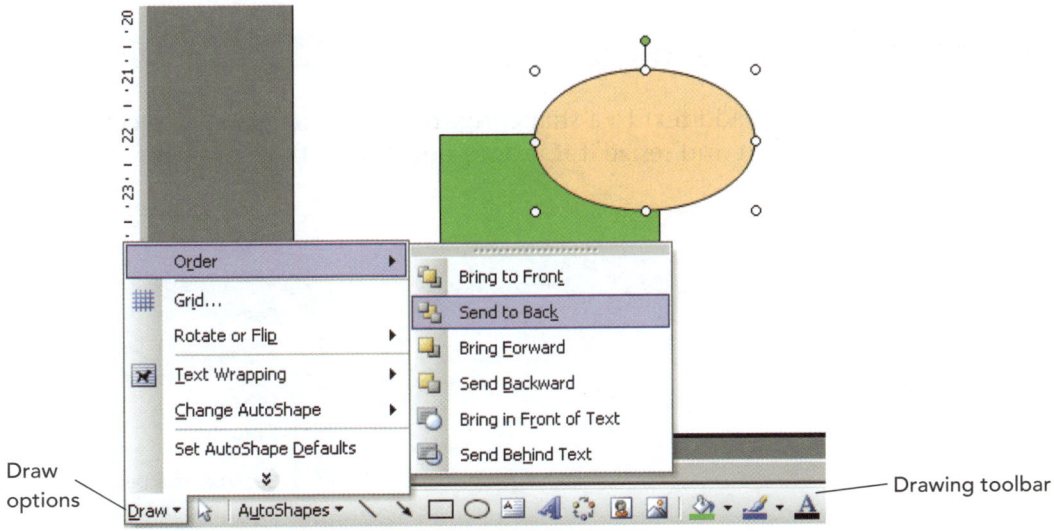

Draw options

Drawing toolbar

The *No Fill* option (see previous section) can also be used to display objects underneath an 'empty' shape or text box that may actually have a white fill, or if you need to show a coloured background.

Shape added

Background now visible

Transparency

To layer coloured shapes on top of one another, open the **Fill Color/More Fill Colors** palette or go to **Format/AutoShape** and select the **Colors and Lines** tab. Increase the transparency to a set measure or alter it by eye by dragging the slider to a new position.

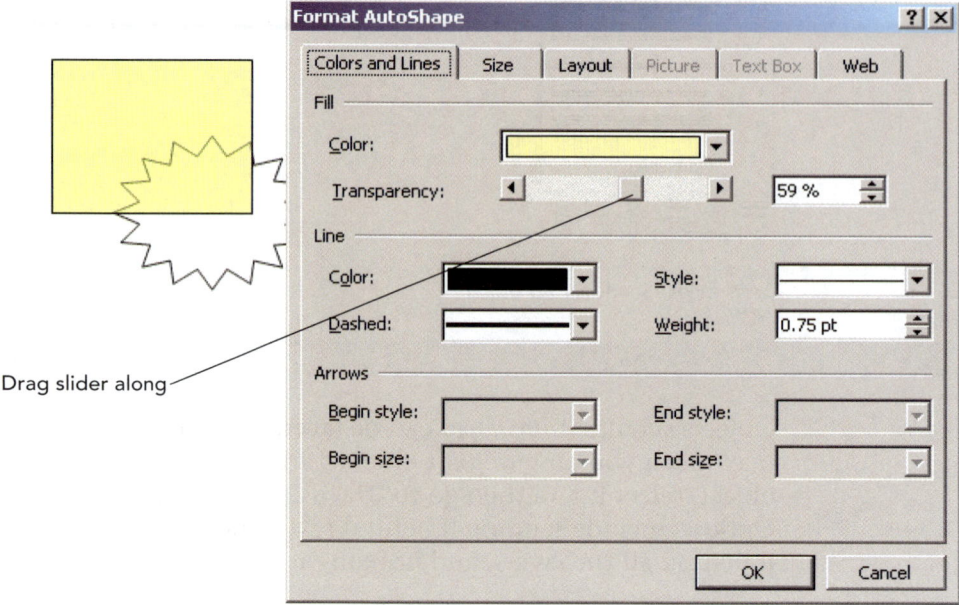

Drag slider along

Adding text

To add text to a shape, right-click the shape and select **Add Text**. Enter the text and resize it if it does not fit the shape exactly.

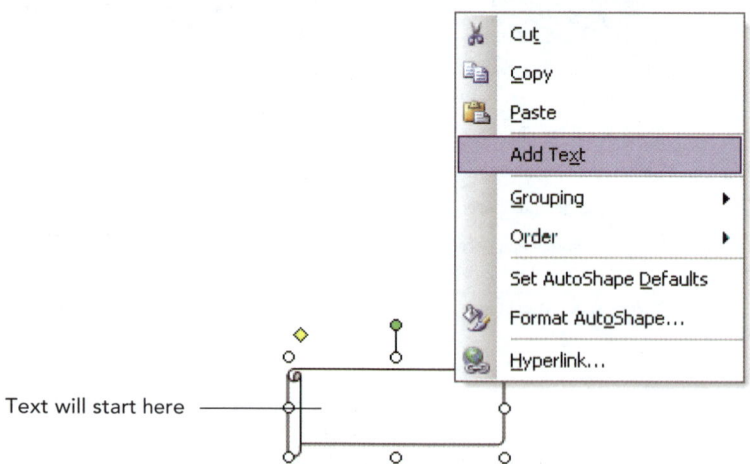

Text will start here

Copying AutoShapes

Having drawn and formatted one shape, you can make exact copies by selecting it and then clicking the **Copy** toolbar button . Click somewhere else on the page to take off the selection and then click **Paste** . Drag the copied shape to the position you want it in. Keep pressing **Paste** to add as many copies as you need.

An alternative way to copy shapes is to hold down **Ctrl** as you drag a selected shape to a new position. The mouse pointer will display a + sign to show it is making a copy.

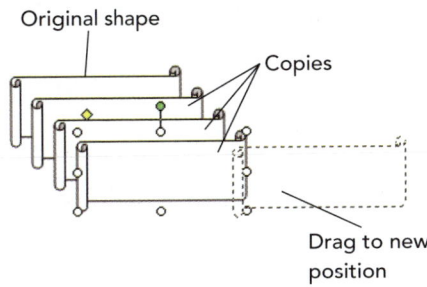

Rotating AutoShapes

As well as dragging the green *free rotate* button on the arm of any shape, or dragging the *sizing handle* to rotate a line, you can select various options from the *Draw/Rotate or Flip* menu. Flip or rotate shapes horizontally or vertically by selecting one of the options.

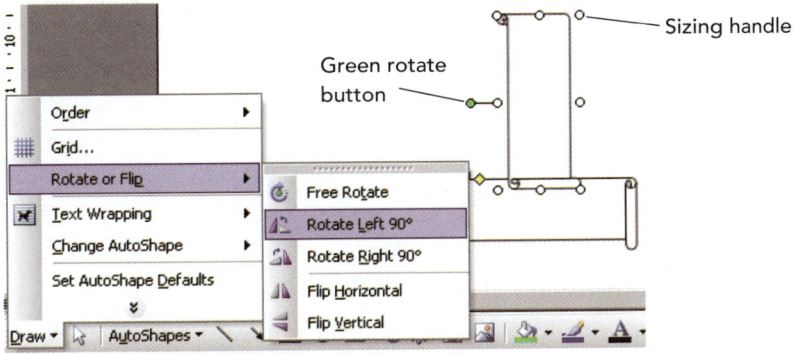

Note that you cannot rotate text boxes.

Exercise 2

1. Start a new document.
2. Insert a large circle.
3. Fill it with yellow.
4. Copy this shape and position the copy to the right of the original circle.
5. Fill the second circle with red.
6. Join the two shapes with a thick, black straight horizontal line.
7. Now rotate the line so that it is vertical, and position it between the two circles.
8. Close the document without saving.

Answer

Deleting AutoShapes

To remove an unwanted shape, select it and press the **Delete** key.

Working with multiple shapes

If you want to select more than one shape – e.g. to apply the same format or delete them all – either hold down **Shift** as you click each in turn, or draw round them after clicking the *Select Objects* arrow.

Draw ▾ ——— Select several shapes

Saving artwork

When you are creating artwork, it is a good idea to save regularly. As the artwork is part of a Word document, save the file in the same way that you would save a typed Word document: click the **Save** button, select the appropriate location and accept or amend the file name before clicking **Save**.

Exercise 3

1. Start a new document.
2. Add a rectangle shape of any size.
3. Fill the shape with light green, and border it with a thick, dark green line.
4. Make three copies of the rectangle and arrange all four shapes in a line across the page.
5. Resize the copied shapes so that they are all different sizes.
6. Change the line style of the border of one shape to dotted lines.
7. Change the colour fill of another shape to blue.
8. Join up the shapes with single lines, making sure the lines are straight.
9. Delete one of the green shapes that has a solid border.
10. Save the artwork as `Rectangles` and then close the file.

Answer

Setting the size of artwork

Having launched the program and started a new document, you must set the size of the artwork at the start by creating the appropriately sized *AutoShape* – e.g. a square or circle – on the page. You then insert the various elements of the artwork inside this shape.

Fix the size of any shape by double-clicking or going to **Format/AutoShape** and then clicking the **Size** tab. Type the width and height measurements in the relevant boxes and click **OK**.

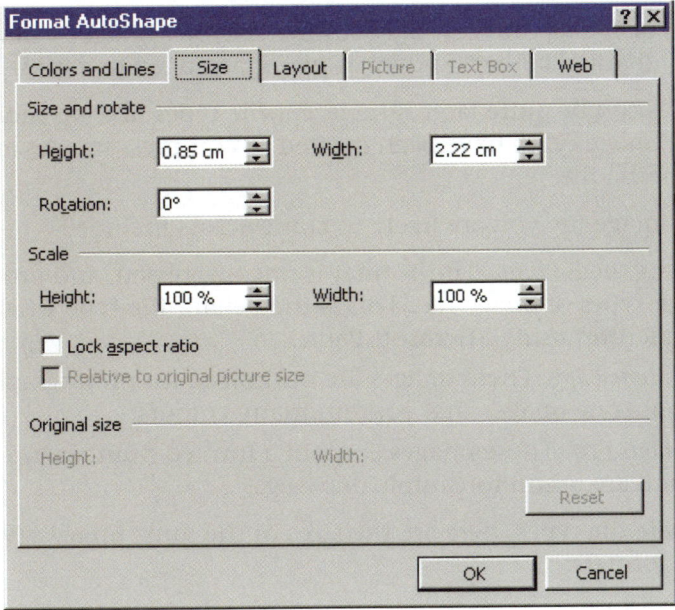

Exercise 4

1. Start a new document and create a piece of artwork 10 cm high and 15 cm wide.

2. Insert two small circles into the artwork, one in each of the top corners. Colour one red and one yellow.

3. Now add a white rectangle taller than it is wide and centre it in the middle of the artwork.

4. Copy the shape and rotate it to the right so that it is wider than it is high. Move this shape to the bottom left-hand corner and colour it black.

5. Save the artwork as `Black shape` and close the file.

Answer

Picture files

You will be provided with one or more images that you must insert into your artwork.

They will be *bitmap* images – also known as *raster* images – made up of tiny dots of individual colour, known as *pixels*, arranged in a grid.

Image files can be quite large, and larger file types take up more disk space. Different image types have been created to compress images and cut down the size of the file.

Types of image file you are likely to come across include:

- *bitmap* – e.g. *house.bmp*. This format is uncompressed, and produces one of the largest types of image file. This is the default file type when you are creating pictures using Microsoft Paint.
- *jpeg* – e.g. *house.jpg*. These images are optimized for photographs and similar continuous-tone images that contain many colours.
- *gif* – e.g. *house.gif*. These images contain a limited number (up to 256) of colours and are useful for simple drawings.

To compare file types, here are the sizes of the same image saved in different formats:

- gif file – 2.13 KB
- jpg file – 4.73 KB
- black & white bitmap – 6.9 KB
- 256-colour bitmap – 55.8 KB

Importing an image

<table>
<tr><td>FAILURE TO IMPORT THE SPECIFIED IMAGE IS A CRITICAL ERROR.</td></tr>
</table>

Either click the **Insert Picture** toolbar button or open the **Insert** menu and select **Picture/From File**. Then browse through your folders to locate the picture you want to add to your artwork. Select its name when it appears in the *Insert Picture* window and click the **Insert** button.

When browsing, it can be useful to see a preview of the picture files. Change the view if necessary by clicking the **down arrow** next to the *Views* button and selecting **Preview** or **Thumbnails**.

View options button

Flipping or rotating an image

In Word 2003, you can flip or rotate an image directly. Select the picture and choose the correct flip or rotate option from the **Draw/Rotate or Flip** menu.

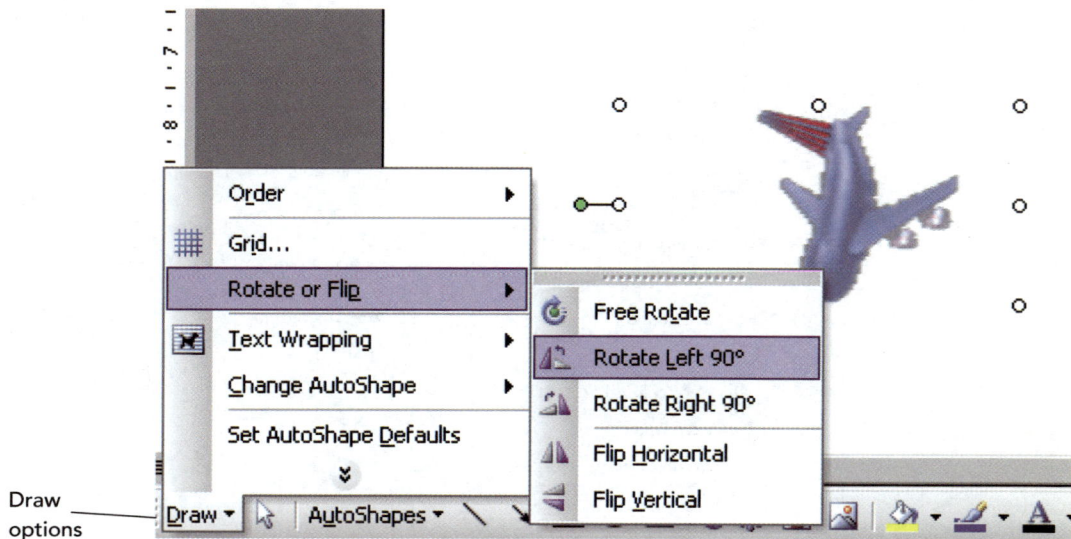

Draw options

Common mistake

Flipping vertically instead of horizontally or vice versa, or rotating incorrectly.

Moving an image

When a picture has been selected and shows black sizing handles, you can use the Word alignment buttons to centre it on the page or align it to the left or right (see Unit 1 for more information).

In order to drag a picture around the screen and position it accurately in your artwork, you need to change its format. Do this by applying text wrapping. You can open the **Format/Picture** menu and select a style from the **Layout** tab, but it is easier to use the *Picture* toolbar.

If this is not displayed above the main window when the inserted picture appears or is selected, open it in one of two ways:

- right-click an empty part of any toolbar and select **Picture** from the list
- right-click the picture itself and select **Show Picture Toolbar**.

The *text wrap* options are normally used to determine how text wraps around a picture on the page, but the effect also allows pictures to be treated like drawn objects and these will show white sizing handles.

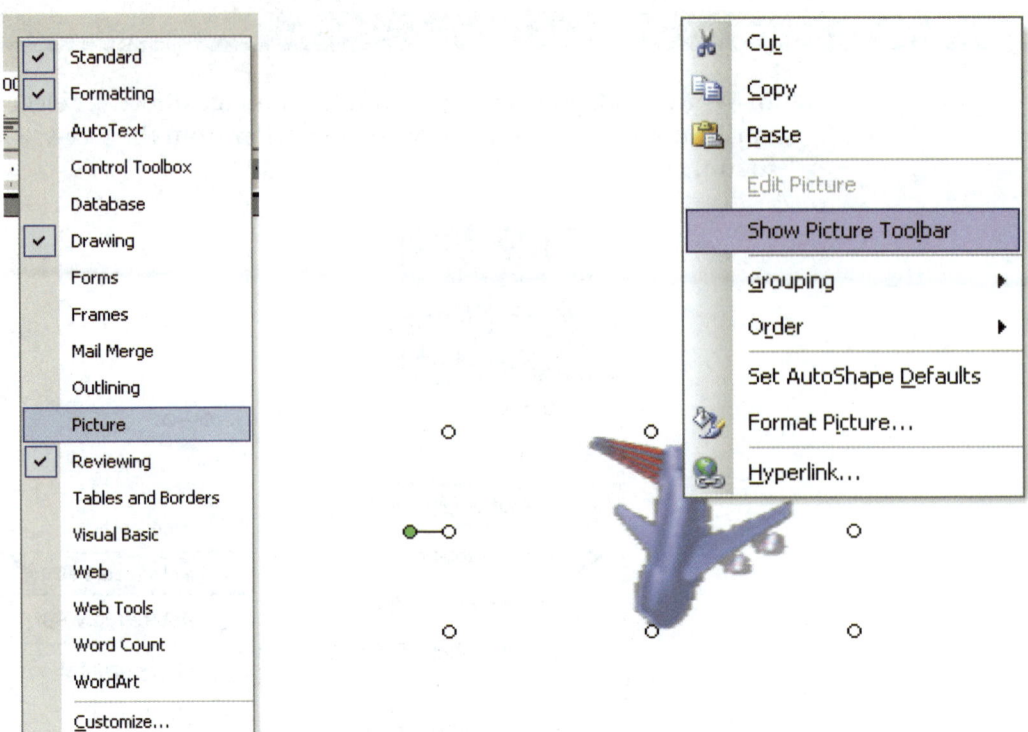

Select the picture, click the **Text Wrapping** button on the *Picture* toolbar (it shows a picture of a dog) and select an option such as *Tight*. Let go and then use the mouse pointer when it shows a cross ✛ to drag the picture into position.

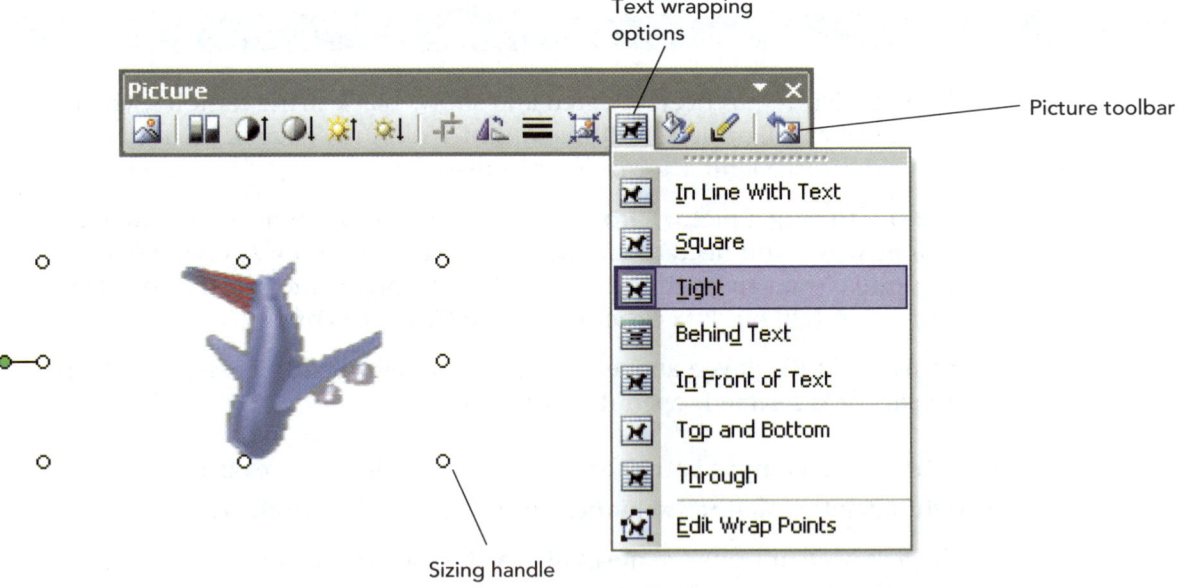

For New CLAIT, you must position your amended picture within the *AutoShape* that sets the size for the artwork. Drag the picture into the shape and adjust its size carefully until it fills the required space. You may need to apply a *Draw/Order* option such as bringing the picture *Forward* so that it can be seen clearly.

Picture obscured in artwork behind the shape

Exercise 5

1. Start a new document.
2. Set a rectangular piece of artwork 9 cm high and 12.5 cm wide.
3. Create a small square and colour it blue.
4. Copy this shape three times and line up the squares across the top of the artwork.
5. Open the image file *bird.gif* from the CD.
3. Rotate it 90 degrees anticlockwise so that the bird faces to the right.
6. Insert the picture into your artwork below the squares.
7. Save as `Bird Square`.
8. Close the file.

Answer

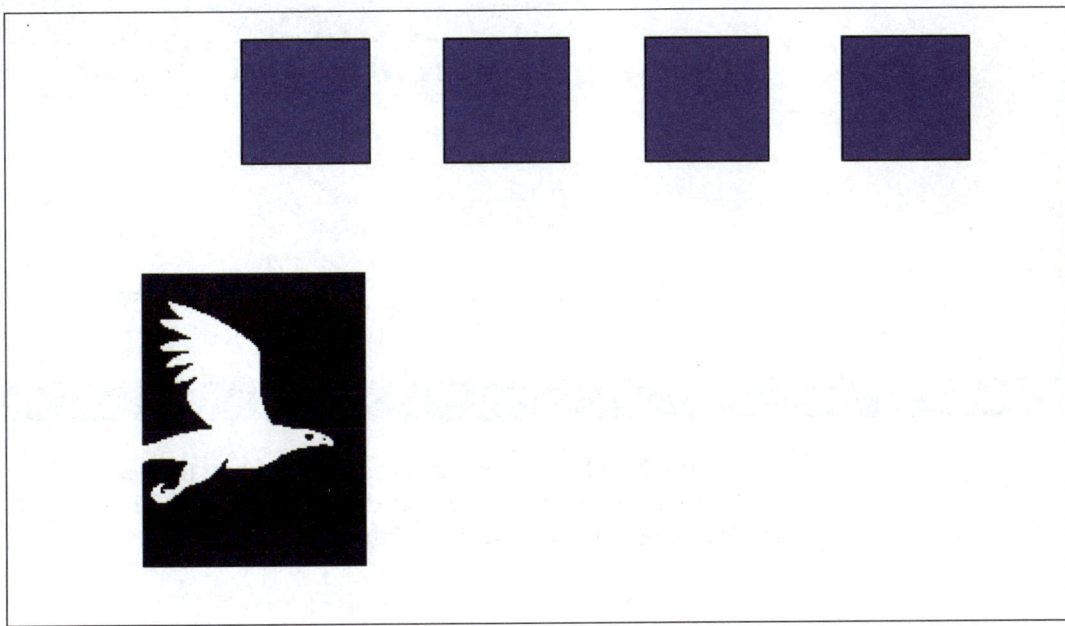

Cropping an image

Pictures often have unwanted parts that need to be trimmed off. Remove these areas using the *Cropping* tool on the *Picture* toolbar.

Click on the **Crop tool** button ⌁ and then move the pointer, which will now display the cropping image over the edge nearest to the unwanted part. Click and hold down the button over a sizing handle on the border, the pointer will change to a ⌐ , and then drag the border inwards. When the unwanted part of the image has been left *outside* the dotted edge, let go the mouse. That area will disappear.

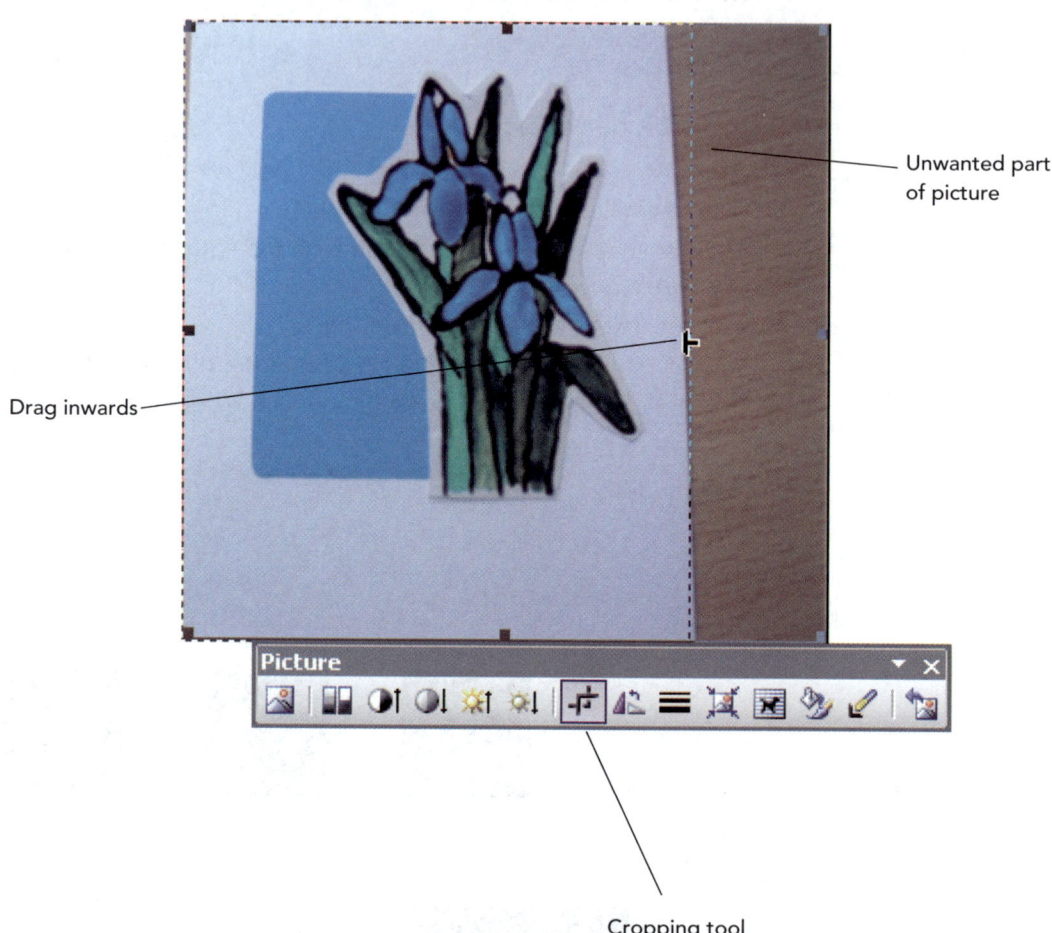

Unwanted part of picture

Drag inwards

Cropping tool

Resizing an image

The sizing handles can be dragged in or out to increase or decrease the size of the picture. Over a sizing handle, the pointer will change to a two-way arrow. Drag from a corner to maintain the picture's proportions.

New picture size

Border dragged inwards

Dragging started here

To resize a picture in one dimension to an exact measure – e.g. to fit your artwork – you can open the **Format** menu or right-click and select **Format Picture**. Click the **Size** tab and enter new measurements in either the *Height* or the *Width* box. Click the **Lock aspect ratio** checkbox to keep the picture in proportion.

Exercise 6

1. Start a new document and set a new piece of artwork 15 cm wide and 9 cm high.
2. You need to insert the picture *sunshine* from the CD.
3. Flip the picture horizontally so that the sun is on the left.
4. Crop it to remove the top of the picture showing the clouds.
5. Place the picture in the centre of your artwork, and resize it so that it fills most of the space but still leaves a white border.
6. Save your work as **Sunny Day**.

Answer

Text

As this unit is asking you to create artwork, you won't be carrying out normal word processing tasks but you will need to place text in a text box. This can then be positioned correctly on the page.

Click the **Text box** button found on the *Drawing* toolbar and click and drag across the page to create a box. The cursor will be flashing inside the box, so start typing as normal.

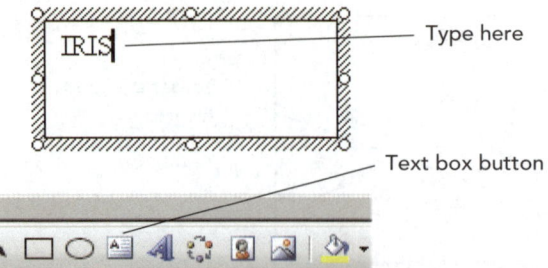

Type here

Text box button

To add text on a new line within the box, press **Enter**. You can format the text box border by right-clicking on it and selecting **Format Text Box**. Use the **Line Colour** options, or remove the border by selecting **No Line**. Display coloured backgrounds behind the box by selecting **No Fill** from the **Fill Color** options.

To change the font style or size, select the text and use the normal Word toolbar buttons (see Unit 1).

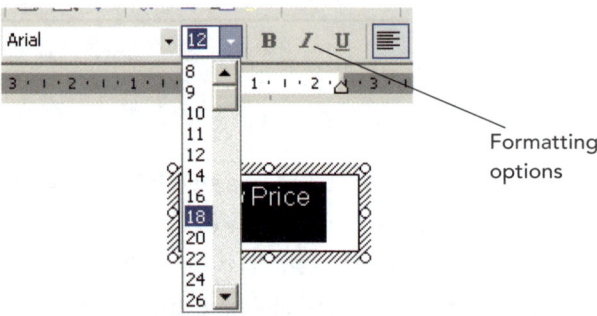

Formatting options

There is a *Font Color* button to apply colours to the text. You can also find this option in the *Format/Font* dialogue box.

Stretching text

To fill the width of the page with text, drag the boundary of the text box outwards and then increase the font size. To add extra space between letters, go to **Format/Font/Character Spacing** and set this to **Expanded** with an increased point size.

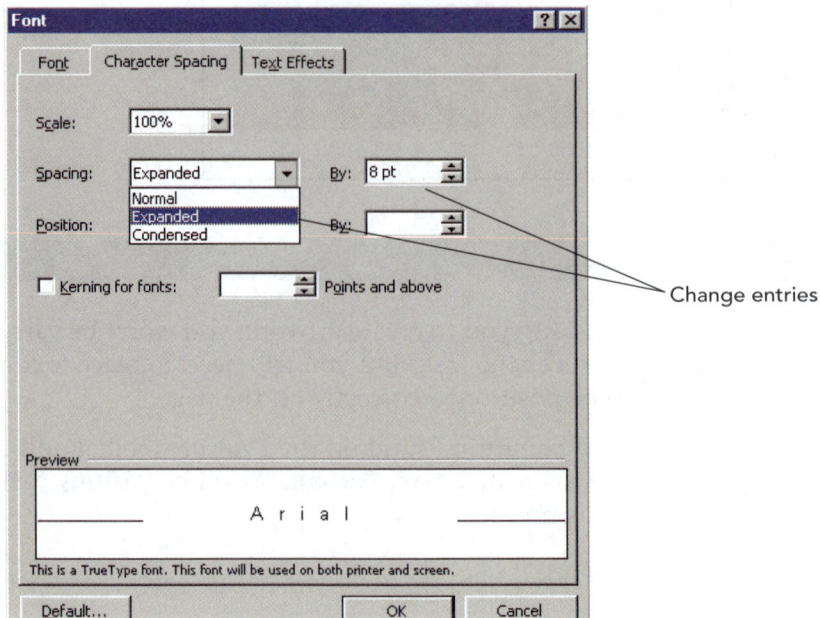

Change entries

1. Reopen the *Sunny Day* file you created in Exercise 6.
2. Type the following text in a text box: `What a Lovely Day`. Format the text to bold, italic.
3. Reduce the size of the picture to leave more space underneath it.
4. Position and resize the text box so that it stretches across the width of the artwork under the picture. Increase the font size so that the text fills the box.
5. Remove the text box border.
6. Update the file to save these changes, and then close the file.

Answer

Rotating text

A selected text box cannot be angled on the page using the *Draw/Rotate or Flip* option from the toolbar, so you must resize the box and change the direction of the text inside. To swap between vertical and horizontal, use the **Format/Text Direction** command.

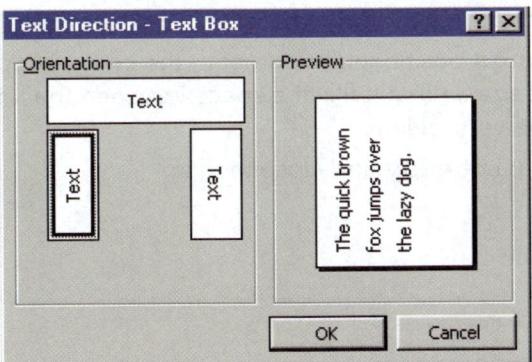

Common mistake

Rotated text is angled in the wrong direction.

After rotating horizontal text 90° clockwise, it will read from the top down. Rotating 90° anticlockwise will make it read from the bottom up.

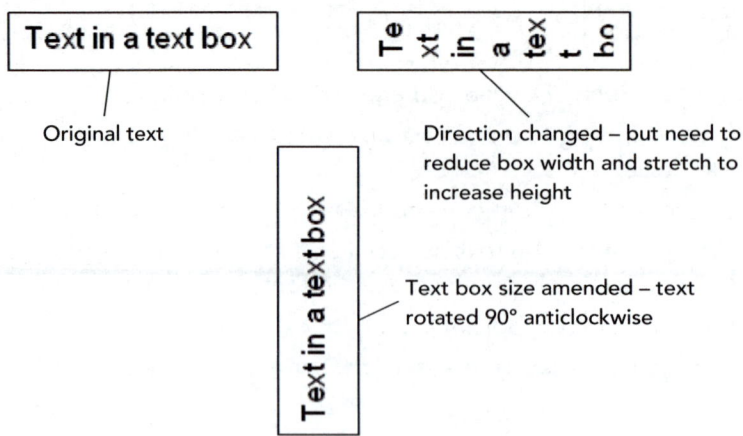

Original text

Direction changed – but need to
reduce box width and stretch to
increase height

Text box size amended – text
rotated 90° anticlockwise

Exercise 8

1. You have been asked to design a cover for a party song CD (see the answer for the layout of the design).

2. Create a new piece of artwork and set the shape as a 9 cm diameter circle.

3. Fill the entire background with a pale blue colour.

4. Insert the image *Cake* (from the CD) and apply the following changes:
   - crop the image to remove the fork
   - flip the image horizontally
   - resize the image in proportion so that it is 3 cm high, and place it in the centre of the artwork.

5. Centred above the image, insert a rectangular shape 2.5 cm wide and 0.5 cm high, and colour it red.

6. Copy this shape twice, colour one black and the other yellow. Position them underneath one another.

7. Add the text **HAPPY BIRTHDAY** in black, positioned as shown so that it reads vertically down the artwork on the right of the image. Make sure it is sized to fill the space.

8. Draw a thick vertical black line to divide the image and rectangles from the text.

9. Now add the text **Songs** positioned underneath the image. Apply a red font and increase the text size so that it fills the space between the left-hand edge of the artwork and the vertical line.

10. Save your artwork as **Birthday** and close the file.

Printing in colour or black and white

To print one copy of a Word document, you normally simply click the **Print** button. However, Unit 6 is the only New CLAIT unit that requires you to print in colour.

For colour prints, you need to check that *Color* has been selected. Go to **File/Print**, click the **Properties** button or appropriate tab depending on your printer, and make sure you have chosen the **Color** option.

When you need to produce a black and white printout, just change the settings in the *Print* box before printing.

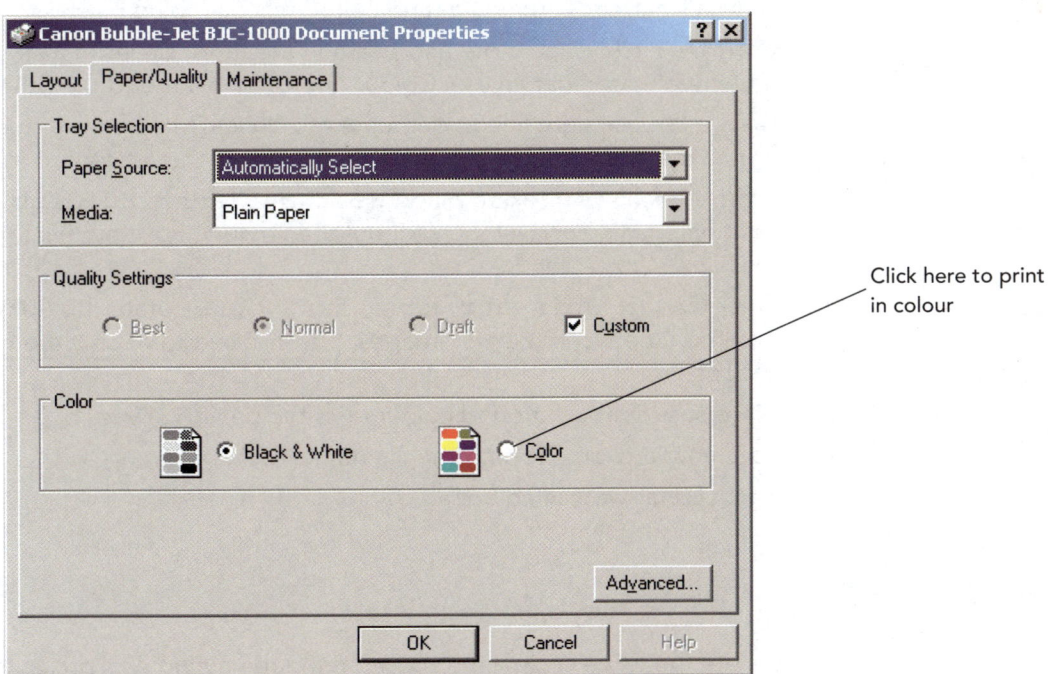

FAILURE TO PRINT ARTWORK DISPLAYING THE CORRECT COLOURS IS A CRITICAL ERROR.

You will need to work through the section on digital cameras starting on page 224 before you can attempt this exercise.

Task 1

Before you begin this task make sure you have the image files *boat* and *water* from the CD.

1. You are going to produce a draft design for a mouse mat commissioned by a yachting club.
2. Create a new piece of artwork that is 8 cm high and 10 cm wide.
3. Fill the background with a light blue colour.
4. Open the image *boat*.
5. Crop the image to remove the boat, leaving just the sails.
6. Flip the image horizontally.
7. Resize the image in proportion and move it so that it fills the top left-hand quarter of the artwork.
8. Save your artwork using the file name `Yachting`.
9. Open the image *water*.
10. Crop it to remove the boat.
11. Resize so that it matches the *boat* image and position it on the right of the *boat* image.
12. Save your artwork keeping the file name *Yachting*.

Task 2

1. Draw a small circle 1cm high and colour this dark blue.
2. Copy the circle twice more and position the three circles in a straight line underneath the *boat* image. Colour one circle black and the other white.
3. Draw a thick straight line underneath the circles. Make sure it does not touch any image and stretches across the full width of the artwork.
4. Enter the following text in black: `Westway Yachting Club`. Size the text to fit on one line and fill the width of the artwork. Position this text underneath the line.
5. Enter the text `Join and have fun!` in red. Rotate this 90° clockwise and position it between the two images. Size this text to fit only the height of the images.
6. Make sure the background colour is visible behind any text.
7. Save your artwork keeping the file name *Yachting*.
8. Print your artwork in colour.

Task 3

1. Delete the white circle and reposition the remaining two circles to line up symmetrically under the *boat* image.
2. Change the text *Westway Yachting Club* to: `The Westway Yachting Club` and resize the text to stretch across the width of the artwork.

3. Change the red text for *Join and have fun!* to blue.

4. Save your artwork using the new file name `Club`.

5. Print your artwork in colour.

Before you begin this task make sure you have the following images:

- a black and white image of a room taken using a digital camera
- *cat.jpg* from the CD.

1. Open a suitable software package to enable you to download a picture taken using a digital camera.

2. Download a suitable picture of a room.

3. On the image, insert the text: `room`

4. You may position this text anywhere on the image. Make sure the text will be clearly readable on the printout.

5. Save the image using a suitable file name.

6. Print the picture in black and white.

7. Close the picture.

8. Open the image *cat*.

9. Change the resolution of this image to be 30 pixels/inch or 12 pixels/cm, but keep its width and height the same.

10. Save the changed image using the file name `catpic`.

11. Print the image *catpic*.

12. Close the file and exit the software.

13. Make sure you check your printouts for accuracy.

Answer

Task 2 Step 8

Task 3 Step 5

Using Paint Shop Pro

This section offers several new exercises for Paint Shop Pro but you can also practise all the other exercises, including the full assessment, introduced earlier in the unit.

Launching the program

If you don't have a shortcut on your desktop, find the *JASC Software* menu from **Start/All Programs** and click **Paint Shop Pro**. This unit shows examples using version 7.

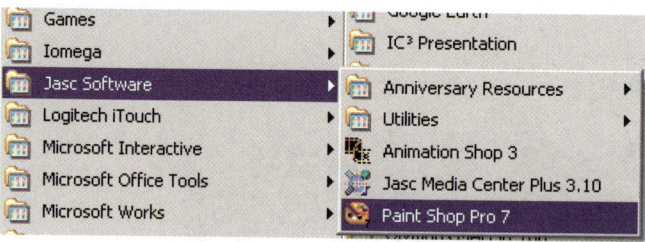

Close the *Tip of the Day* window if it appears, to view the toolbars and menus.

Toolbars

When using this package, you will find that numerous toolbar options are available. As always, if any buttons are 'greyed out' it means they cannot be used to carry out a task or with that particular part of the image.

To open a new toolbar or palette, right-click at the end of any toolbar to display the names of those available. Click the name to open its window. (Once you get to know the program, you can type the underlined letter to bring up a specific toolbar e.g. **O** for *Tool Options* and **L** for the *Layer Palette*, or click the icon if it is visible, as this will turn the toolbar either on or off.)

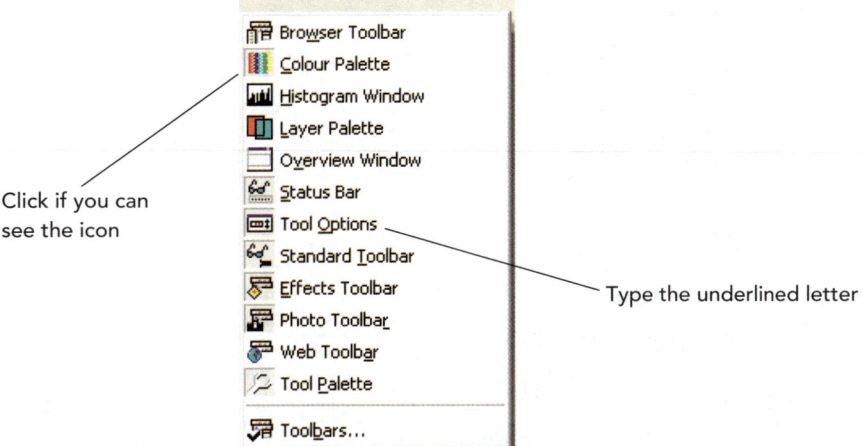

Click if you can see the icon

Type the underlined letter

Measurement units

To resize shapes and images more exactly, you may need to change the units on the ruler, e.g. from inches to centimetres. You can display a missing ruler from the **View** menu and set units by opening the **File** menu, selecting **Preferences** and clicking **General Program Preferences**. Click the **Rulers and Units** tab and select a different unit.

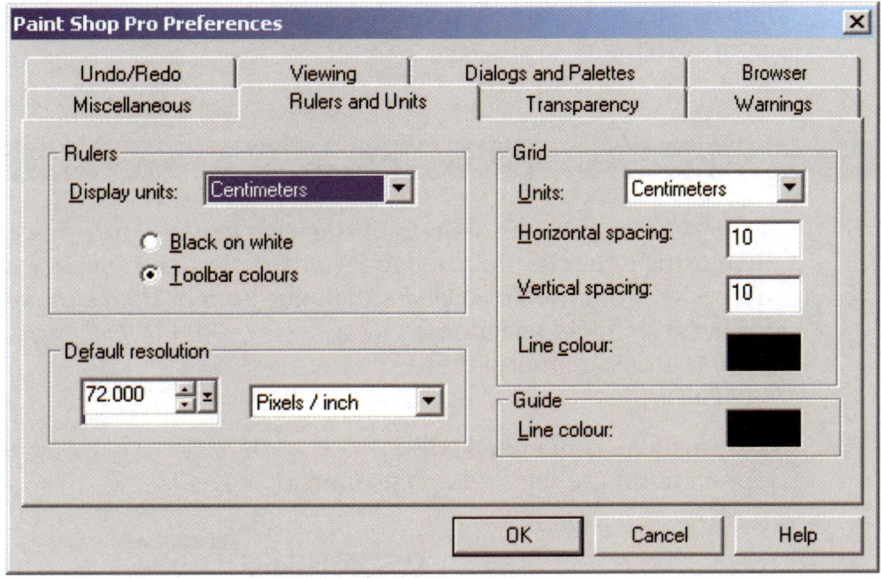

To create a shape of specified size, you can now draw it accurately next to the horizontal and vertical rulers.

New file and artwork size

To create a new file, click the **New** toolbar button ⬜ . This opens the *New Image* dialogue box where you can select measurements/units for the image and background colour. You can select *White, Transparent,* one of a limited number of colours specified or the foreground or background colour set in the colour palette. See *Working with colours* later in this unit to find out how to change these colours.

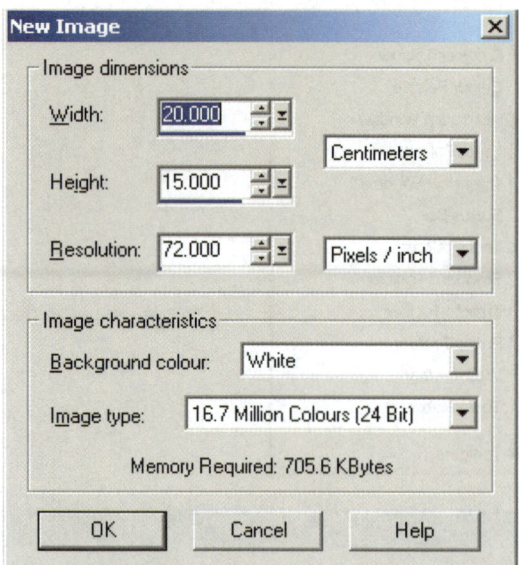

The image that opens is your *artwork canvas* – the starting point for a new picture. As you create images by adding layers, the 'bottom' layer is known as the *background*, so a new blank image will appear labelled *Image1* (*Background*).

If the required artwork is rectangular, use the background. However, if you are asked to create a circular piece of artwork, draw a circle of the required dimensions and insert your text and objects. (See later in the unit for more about working with shapes.)

Selecting

When selecting objects or areas of the page to work on, you can draw round them using either the *Selection* tool (for simple shapes such as circles and squares set from the *Tool Options* dialogue box) or the *Freehand* (lasso) tool (for more complex selections).

These buttons are found on the *Tool Palette*.

Selection tool —————— |⬚ ⌇| —————— Freehand

Flashing lines (a *marquee*) will appear round the selected image or area.

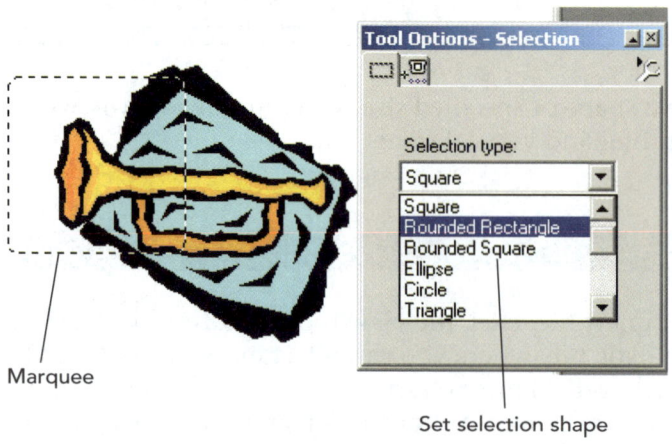

Marquee

Set selection shape

To remove the selection, double-click, hold down **Ctrl** and right-click, or go to **Selections/Select None**.

Pictures

To add a picture to your artwork, or to work on a picture or photo within the application, locate and open the image file. Use the normal **Open** button, or select **File/Browse** to view thumbnail pictures of the contents of any folder selected in the left pane. Double-click an image to open it on screen.

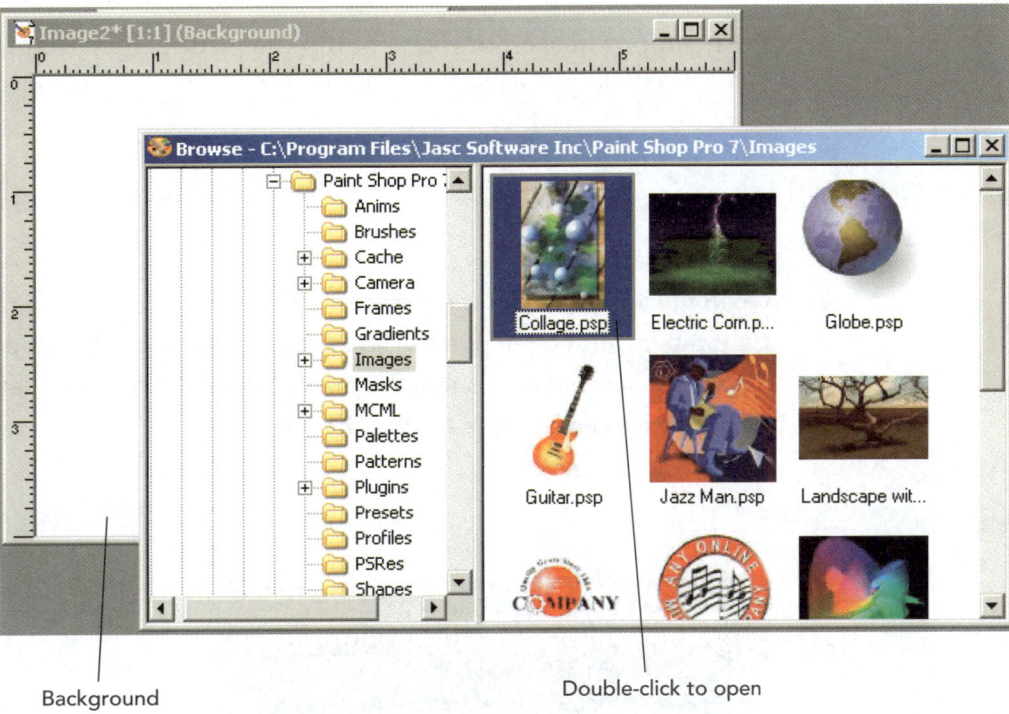

Background

Double-click to open

Cropping

To remove unwanted parts of the image, select the area to be retained by clicking a *Selection* tool and then drawing round it. Now go to **Image/Crop to Selection** to remove the unwanted areas.

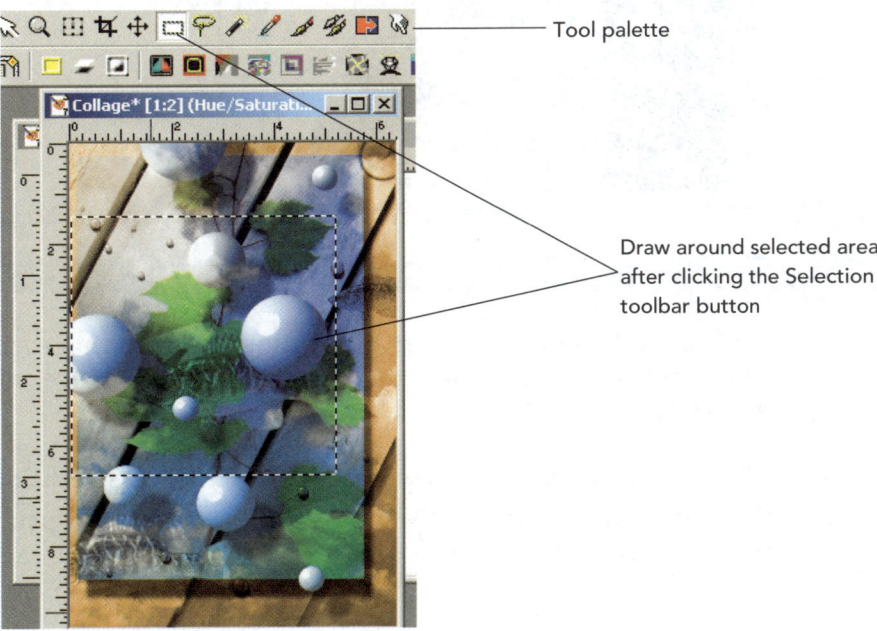

Tool palette

Draw around selected area after clicking the Selection toolbar button

You could also click the **Crop** tool  and then draw around the area you want to keep. Double-click *inside* the area to retain this part of the picture only.

Rotating and flipping

Create mirror images, or rotate or flip the picture, by selecting the appropriate option from the *Image* menu.

Exercise 10

1. Open Paint Shop Pro.
2. Open the image file *band.jpg* from the CD.
3. Crop the picture to remove the figure on the left wearing a striped suit.
4. Create a mirror image, so that the man in black is now on the left.
5. Close the file but do not save the changes.

Answer

Layers

You will build up your artwork by creating layers, so that each can be edited independently. Once you have started a new image, add pictures as new layers.

1. Click the picture title bar to select it, right-click and select **Copy**.
2. Click the background to activate this window and then open the **Edit** menu. Select **Paste/As New Layer**.

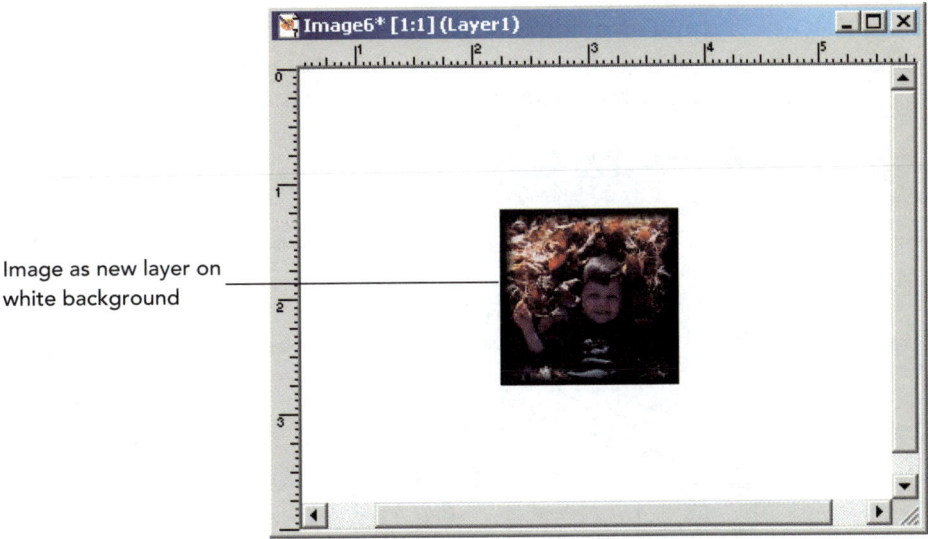

Image as new layer on white background

3. Once you have added several layers to your artwork, you will need to select the correct layer before you can carry out any editing. To view the layers, open the *Layer* palette by clicking the **Toggle** button.

Click button

4. Rest the mouse on any layer in the *Palette* window to see its contents.

5. Rename a layer for ease of working by right-clicking, selecting **Rename** and typing in the new name.

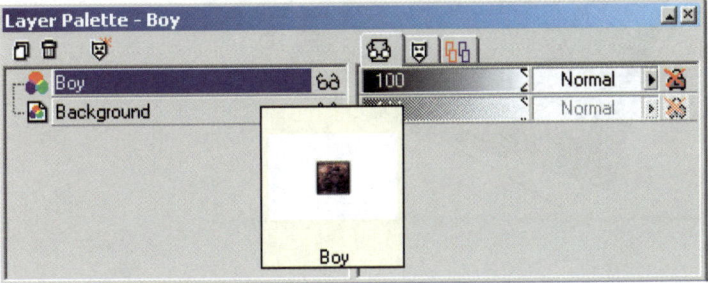

Resizing

To change the image size, drag the corners. Use the right mouse button to retain the original proportions.

If the image is not selected, click the correct layer in the *Layer Palette* and then click the **Deformation** tool . This will add the deformation handles and guides. If the image is too large to work with, drag it across the artwork until you find a corner, then drag this inwards until the whole image is visible on screen.

You could also double-click the tool and change the X and Y positions to 0 in the *Settings* box that opens. This will position the left-hand corner of the picture in that corner of your image window.

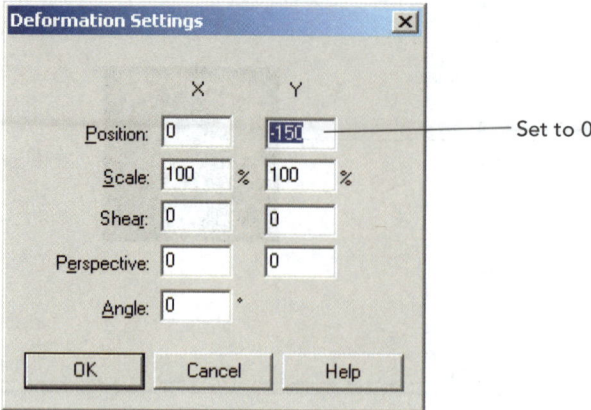

To rotate the selected image, drag the centre bar when the pointer shows curved arrows.

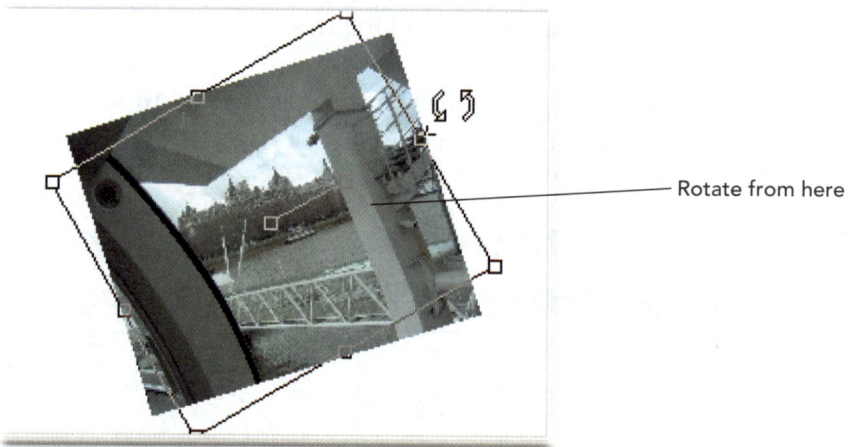

Moving an image

Click the **Move** tool and drag the picture around with the mouse, or drag the picture after clicking the **Deformation** tool.

For smaller steps, select the image and then hold down **Shift** and **Ctrl** as you press an arrow key. The image will be nudged across the page in the direction of the arrow.

Saving a file

Graphics editing programs create unique file types that retain the layers, but you can also save your work in a range of image file types. If possible, save in the application's own format to preserve the layers to work on later.

Click the **Save** button and select the location and rename the file before clicking **Save**.

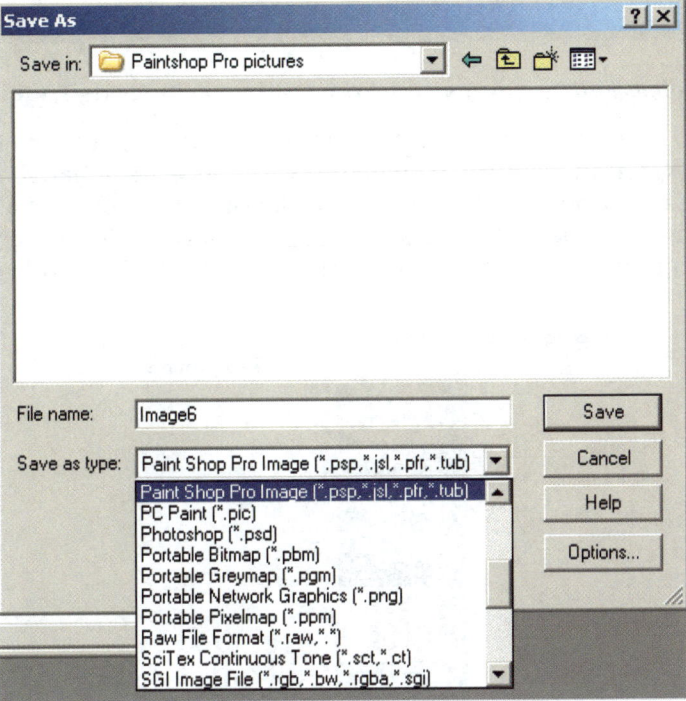

Exercise 11

1. Start a new file and set your artwork size as 8 cm wide by 10 cm high.

2. Select a blue background.

3. Open the image file *trumpet.jpg* from the CD.

4. Rotate it 90° to the right.

5. Crop it to remove most of the white surround.

6. Add the image to the background layer and then resize it so that it is about 2 cm square.

7. Move it to the top of the artwork.

8. Save your artwork as `Trumpet on Blue`.

Answer

Working with colours

If the *Colour Palette* is not visible, open it by clicking the **Toggle** button ▮▮▮ .

The two solid colour boxes at the top of the palette show the foreground and background colours that will apply as you work. Change the colours by clicking either box to open the *Colour* dialogue box offering a wider range. You can also click in the *Available colours* panel. The left mouse button sets the foreground colour and right button sets the background colour.

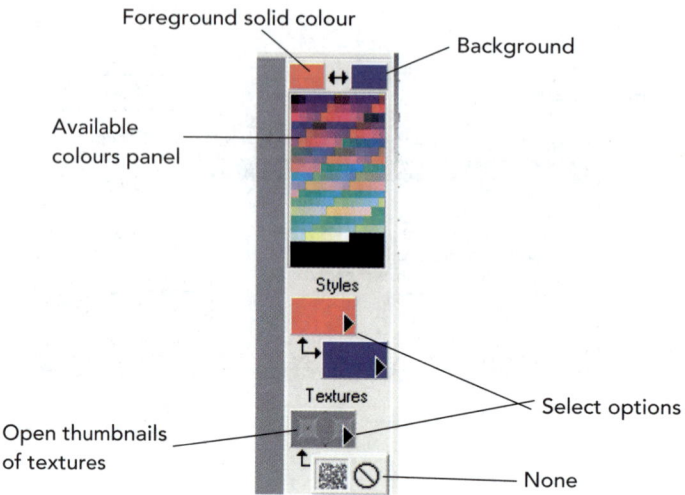

For each colour, you can also select and amend styles – solid colour, gradient, pattern – and textures by clicking the **arrow** in the relevant colour box, choosing the style or texture and then clicking the box again to display the range of options.

Click the button ⊘ if you don't require any style or texture.

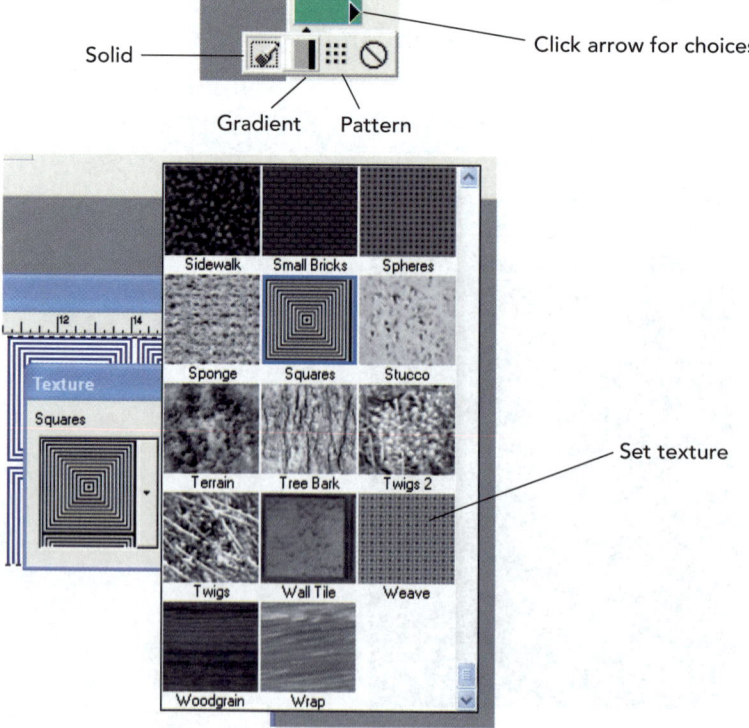

To create a black and white picture, simply select **Greyscale** from the *Colours* menu.

The picture files and many paint effects such as the *Paint Brush* and *Flood Fill* that you add to your artwork are bitmaps made up of coloured dots known as pixels. These only work on raster layers so you will only be able to add a paint effect to a raster layer.

Image editing programs also allow you to create mathematically constructed vector objects that behave differently and work on *vector* layers. You can create text, lines and shapes as vector objects so that they will retain their sharpness when rescaled and can be moved and edited independently.

Vector layers in the *Layer Palette* have a different symbol: click the **+** sign to display the contents.

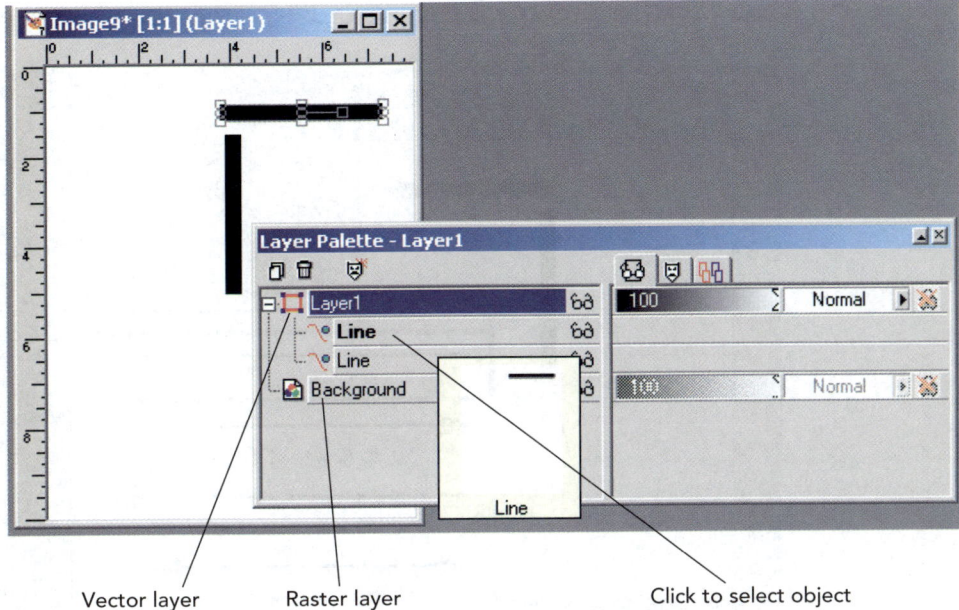

Vector layer   Raster layer   Click to select object

To create a paint effect on a raster layer, or add a vector object on a new layer, click the appropriate tool and, if necessary, click the **Toggle** button

▭ or press the **O** key to open the *Tool Options* window for detailed settings.

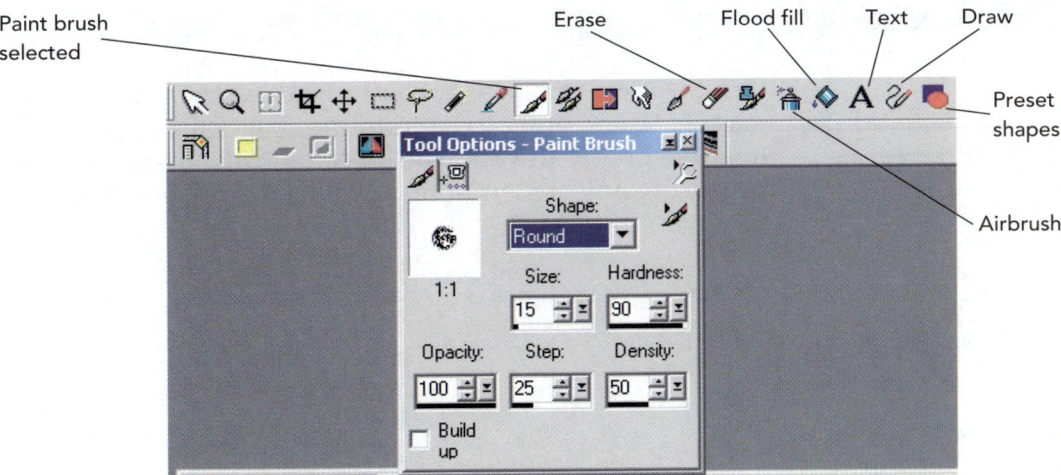

Flood fill

Mark out any area with a *Selection* tool, unless you want the whole area coloured, and then click the **Flood Fill** tool button 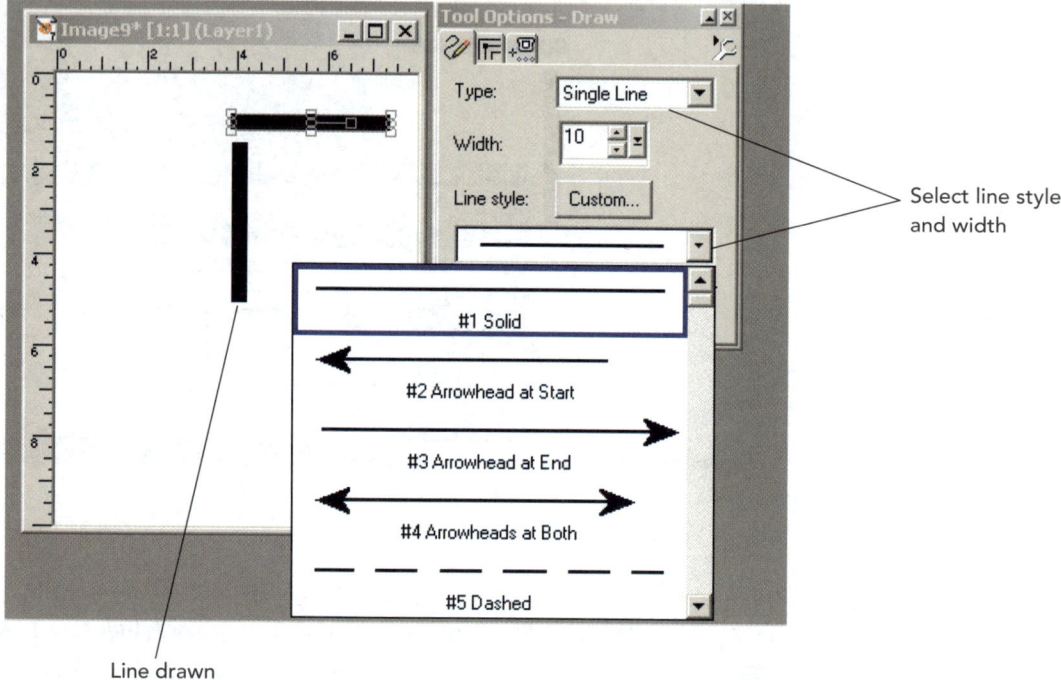. Left-click the selected area to flood with the foreground colour, style and texture that has been set, or right-click to flood with the background.

Lines

Use the *Draw* tool to add lines. Hold down **Shift** while using **Draw** to keep lines straight. Thin lines will have a width of 1 or 2, and you must have a stroke (foreground) style set – e.g. solid colour. (For New CLAIT, choose *Single Line* from the *Tool Options* window, rather than *Freehand* or *Bezier*.)

Select line style and width

Line drawn

Preset shapes

Click the **Preset Shapes** tool button and set the border width, line style, exact shape and other styles from the *Tool Options* window before drawing the shape on the artwork. The fill colour will be the background colour on the palette. Any borders or lines will be the stroke (foreground) colour.

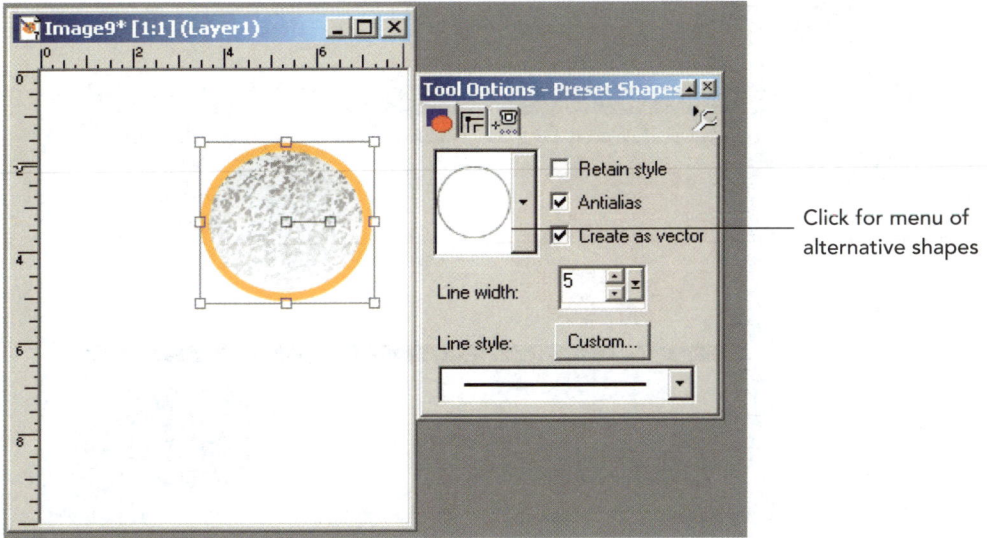

Click for menu of alternative shapes

Formatting

Vector objects can be reselected to move, rotate or resize them. You can change their appearance by double-clicking to open the *Properties* box. Select the object from the *Layer Palette* or click the vector **Object Selector** tool [icon] and then double-click the target object on screen.

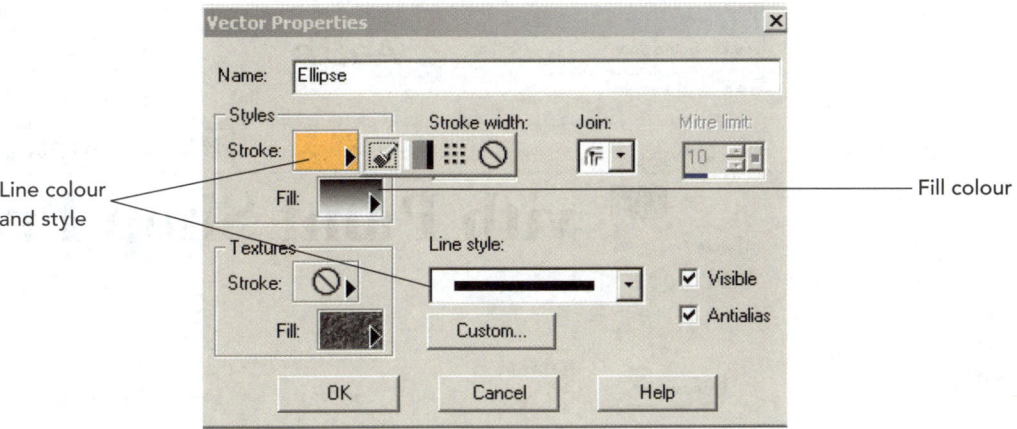

Line colour and style

Fill colour

Exercise 12

1. Start a new file and set the size at 15 cm wide by 8 cm high. Select a white background.

2. Add a red circle about 2 cm in diameter and position it in the top left-hand corner.

3. Now add a dark blue rectangle with a light blue border and place it in the top right-hand corner. Make it 2 cm wide and 4 cm high.

4. Draw a straight, thick black line underneath the shapes, stretching across the width of the artwork.

5. Rotate the rectangle so that it is now 2 cm in height.

6. Move the rectangle to the bottom right-hand corner.

7. Increase the size of the circle so that it is twice the original size.

8. Add the image *trumpet.jpg* (from the CD) and reduce it in size. Move it to the top right-hand corner of the artwork.

9. Save your artwork as Shapes.

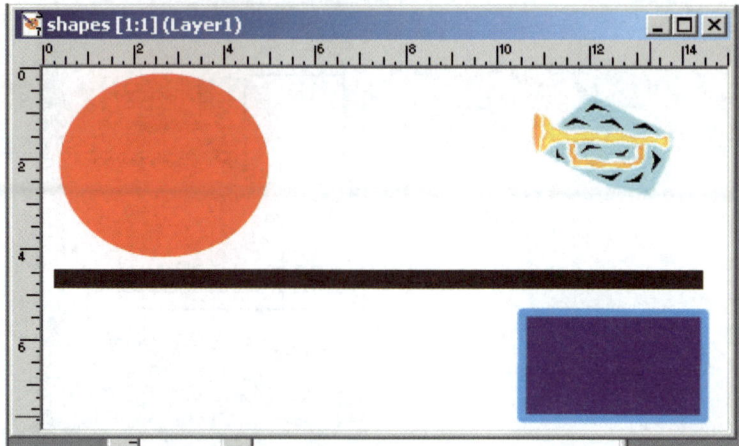

Text

Click the **Text** tool $\mathbf{A}$ and then click the image to open the *Text Entry* window. Type your text and select size, alignment, colour, font etc. Choose **Create as Vector** text so that you can edit it later.

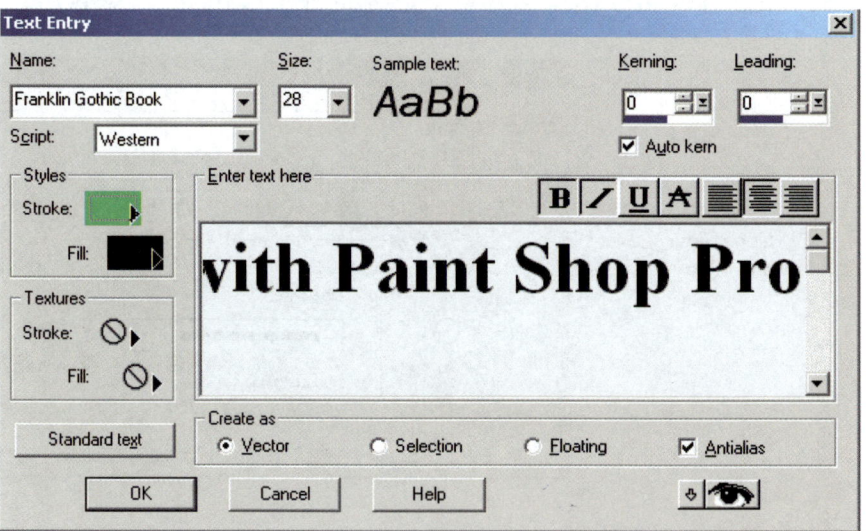

Once on the page, drag the text to a different position, or resize when it shows the sizing handles around the edge. Double-click the selected text in the *Layer Palette* or click the **Object Selector** arrow, click the appropriate text entry on the screen and then click the **Edit Text** button in the *Tool Options* window to return to the *Text Entry* dialogue box.

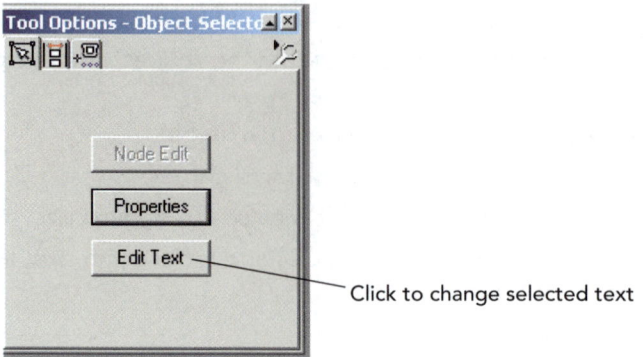

Click to change selected text

To rotate selected text – e.g. so that it is vertical on the page – drag the right-hand box on the central bar when the cursor shows curved arrows. Drag a corner box to stretch the text across the page.

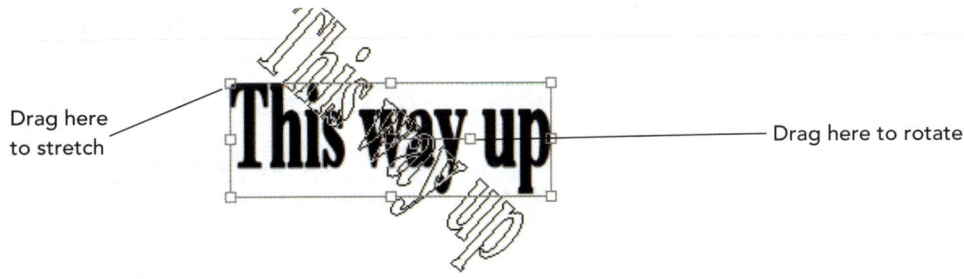

Drag here to stretch

Drag here to rotate

Exercise 13

1. Reopen *Shapes* whch you created in Exercise 12.
2. Add the text `Musical Shapes` in black, Times New Roman bold.
3. Position the text on the black line and stretch it so that it extends across the width of the artwork.
4. Now change the rectangle to green with a red border.
5. Increase the thickness of the black line.
6. Save and close the file.

Answer

Copying shapes

To create several similar shapes, select the first and click **Copy**. Then select **Edit/Paste as New Vector Selection** (or right-click and select this option from the menu that appears). Click the mouse to add each shape to your artwork and then select each shape individually to change its colour and size as required.

Printing

Click the **Print** toolbar button to print one copy of your artwork. If it does not look right, check in **File/Page Setup** or the **File/Print** properties that the colour option and correct paper sizes have been selected.

Check that
colour is selected

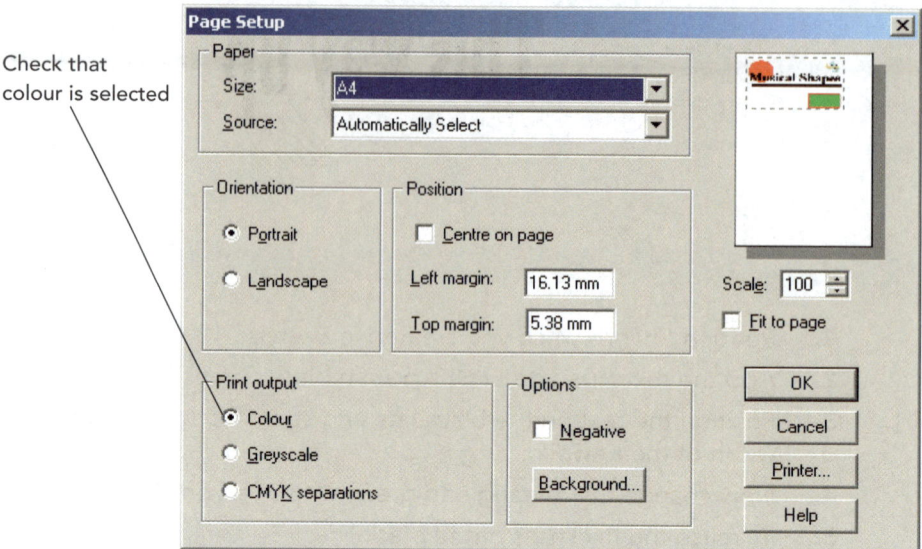

Digital camera images

Having connected a camera to your computer and switched it on, either click **My Computer** to display all the drives, or open your chosen image editing program and click **File/Open** or **Browse**.

Select the camera from the drives listed in the window (it will probably be labelled 'Removable Disk'), and the pictures should appear. You may have to open a subfolder to find the pictures.

List of drives
available

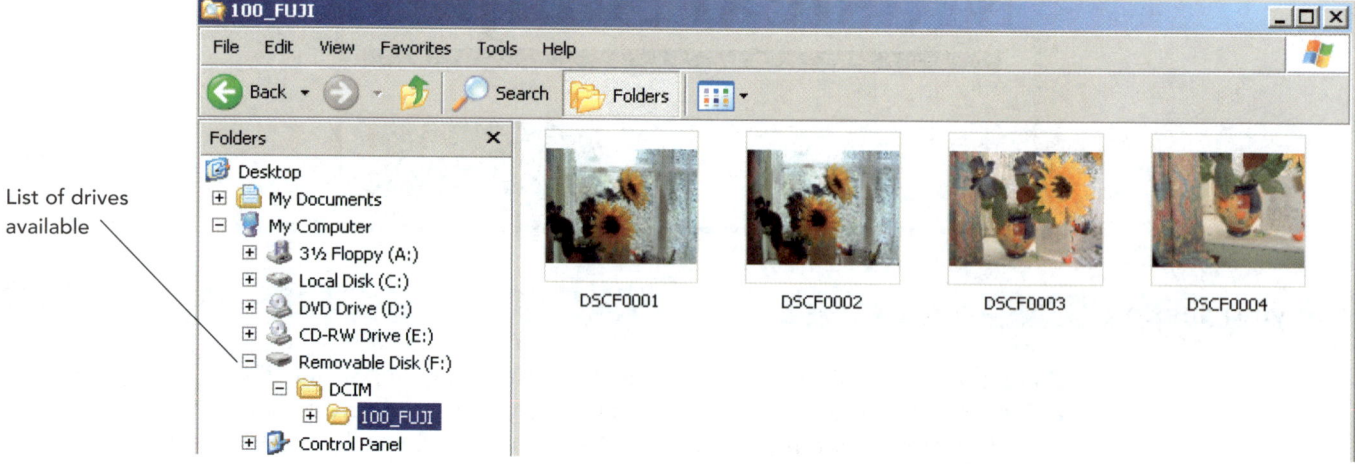

Open the pictures by double-clicking and save any that you want to keep in an appropriate folder on your computer. Make sure you rename them because they will have been numbered obscurely (e.g. *DSCF0001*) when the pictures were taken.

You can locate your saved images at any time by using the *Browse* facility in your image editing software and opening the folder in which they were saved. Double-click to open an image for editing.

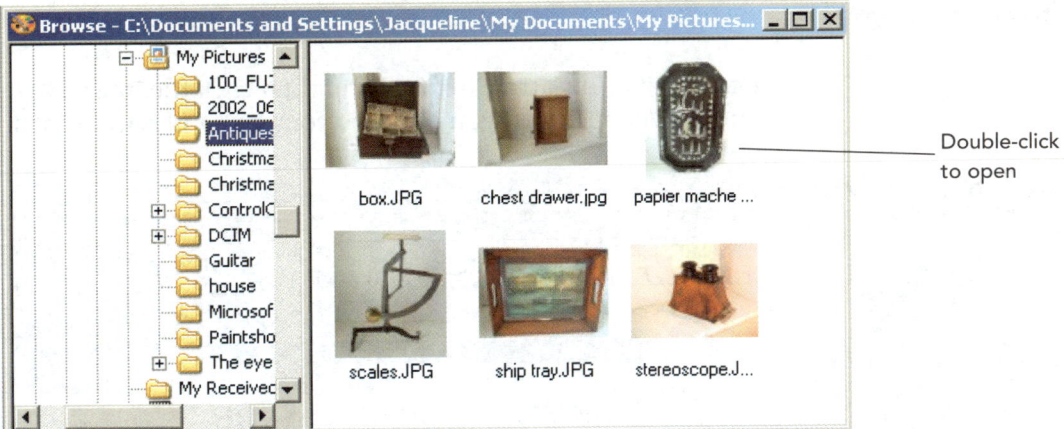

Double-click
to open

Image resolution

Resolution refers to the number of pixels (dots) in an image and is a measure of how closely together the pixels are displayed. For example, 300 dpi means there are 300 dots per inch (90 000 dots in a square inch). Higher resolution photos will produce nice crisp images, whereas a very low resolution photo will appear to be more blurred.

You need to remember that when printing pictures of different sizes, the number of pixels remains the same. A reasonable quality print of 240 dpi would have 240 distinct pixels for each inch in the print, either vertically or horizontally, so a 5" × 7" print would contain 2 016 000 pixels (2 megapixels) i.e. 1200 (5" × 240) × 1680 (7" × 240). A cheap camera with a resolution of 640 × 480 pixels could only create a 240 dpi print that is 2" × 3" in size, whereas a 6 megapixel camera could produce one 9" × 12".

To change the resolution of a picture, open it on screen and click **Image/Resize**. Check that resolution is in pixels per inch or per centimetre and amend the measurement in the *Resolution* box before clicking **OK**.

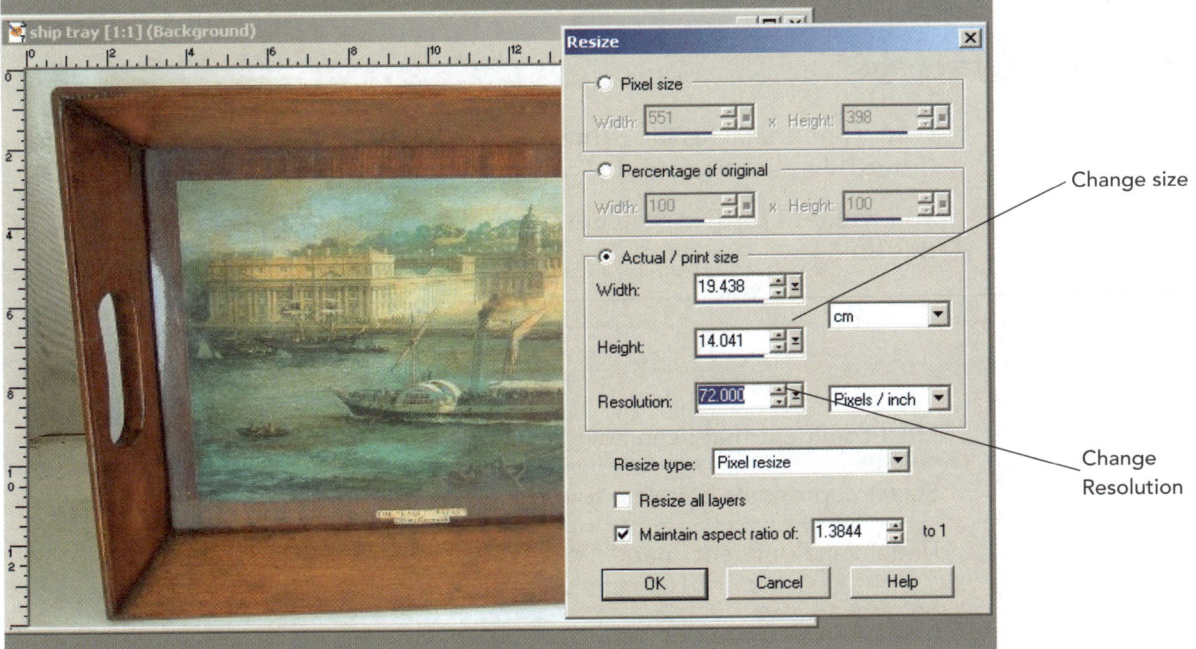

Change size

Change
Resolution

Text on an image

To add a title, click the **Text** tool and then click the image. A *Text Entry*
window will open and you can type your text and select font size and colours.

Text tool

Type in here

Click **OK** and then move or stretch the text on screen, or return to the
editing window to make other changes.

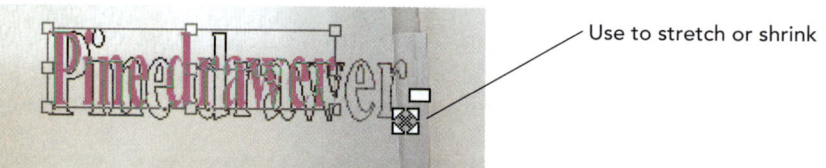

Use to stretch or shrink

Printing a camera image

Print as normal, checking that **Black & White** (or **Greyscale** if this is offered
instead) has been selected if you are asked to print without colour.

You will find further exercises, including a full assessment in Exercise 9 of
this unit.

Self-assessment checklist

I feel confident that I can now	✓
Select appropriate software to produce artwork	
Understand different image file types	
Set artwork size	
Import an image	
Flip or rotate images	

Crop images

Resize images

Move images

Add and format shapes

Copy shapes

Delete shapes

Add and format text

Resize text to fit

Change text direction

Save artwork

Save with a different file name

Download images from a digital camera

Change image resolution

Add text to a digital image

Print artwork or images in colour or black and white

Close an artwork file

Exit the application

Summary of critical errors

- Specified image is missing
- A block of text is missing
- Colours on the printout are not as specified

7

Web page creation

- What is web page authoring? 230
- Selecting the appropriate software 231
- Opening the software 231
- Views 231
- Entering text 232
- Formatting text 232
  Heading styles 233
- Saving web pages 233
- Opening web pages 235
- Closing web pages 235
- Links 235
  Internal links 235
  External links 237
  E-mail links 238
- Applying a background colour 239
- Printing a web page 240
  Printing a web page showing the source code 240
- Viewing web pages in a browser 242
  Printing from a browser 243
- Testing links 243
- Inserting a text file 244
- Importing and positioning images 245
- Exiting the application 247
- Self-assessment checklist 251
- Summary of critical errors 251

What is web page authoring?

Web pages on the World Wide Web may contain text, pictures, sounds and moving images. They are normally written in the code known as *HyperText Markup Language* or *HTML*. Usually they are created with the help of one of many software programs available and are then published on the Internet for others to access and read. To view web pages and move from one page to another, you need to have special software known as a *browser* on your computer and to be connected to the Internet.

Unit 7 develops and tests your ability to use appropriate software to create and link web pages containing text and images, and to view the pages using a browser.

You will be asked to carry out the following tasks:

- Name a folder and use it for all your web pages
- Create a web page using appropriate web authoring software
- Insert a text file
- Amend paragraph spacing
- Enter text
- Apply different text styles
- Change text alignment
- Save web pages
- Import and format images
- Add internal links
- Open web pages
- Create an external link
- Create an e-mail link
- Apply a background colour
- View web pages in a browser
- Test links
- Print web pages
- Print web pages showing the source code
- Close web pages
- Exit the application

To pass Unit 7, you must be able to:

- Select appropriate web authoring software
- Create new web pages
- Enter text
- Format text
- Apply different text styles
- Change text alignment
- Open web pages
- Insert a text file
- Import and format images
- Create the following links: internal, external and e-mail

- Apply a background colour
- Save web pages
- View web pages in a browser
- Test links
- Print web pages
- Print web pages showing the source code
- Close web pages
- Exit the application

Selecting the appropriate software

You do not need to be able to write HTML code in order to create web pages, although understanding how it works can be useful. You can turn word processed or desktop publishing (DTP) documents into web pages using applications such as Word or Publisher, but it is more sensible to use a dedicated web authoring package. There are a number of such programs available; the one used in this unit is Microsoft FrontPage.

The most common browser is Internet Explorer, but you could use an alternative such as Netscape, Mozilla Firefox or Opera.

Opening the software

Double-click the **FrontPage** icon , or launch the program via the **Start/All Programs** menu.

Views

When FrontPage opens, you will see a blank page and various toolbars. There are four ways to view your page as it develops. Click the tab at the bottom of the screen to switch between views:

- *Design* view is the working mode where you add and format the text and images.
- *Code* view will reveal the underlying code in which the page is written automatically.
- *Split* view allows you to see both code and design pages.
- *Preview* shows you how the page will appear when viewed by someone accessing it using a browser such as Internet Explorer or Netscape.

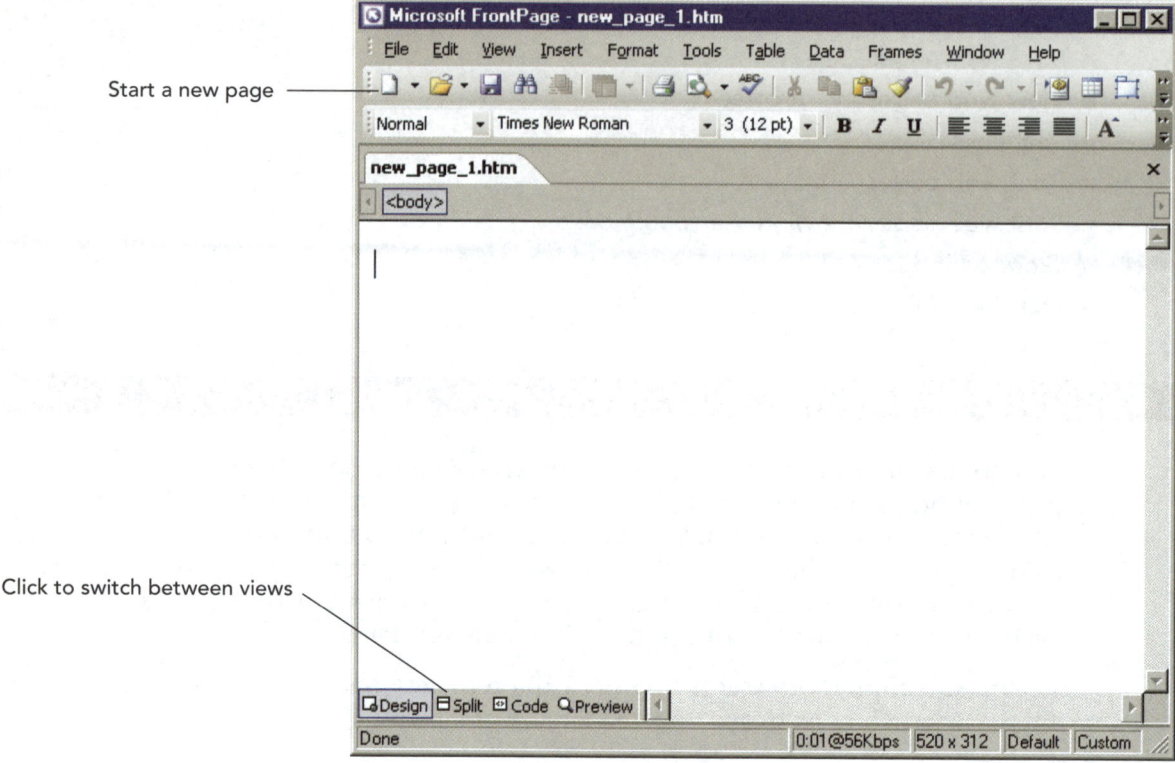

Start a new page

Click to switch between views

Entering text

Entering text on a web page is similar to using Word for word processing. However, when you press **Enter** you will normally move down *two* lines – i.e. the default setting is double-line spacing. To type text on the following line, hold down **Shift** as you press **Enter**.

FAILURE TO INCLUDE THE SPECIFIED TEXT IS A CRITICAL ERROR.

Formatting text

Select any text and use the formatting toolbar buttons to change the font type or size, or add emphasis such as bold or italic. You will notice that the font sizes are limited and expressed in numbers as well as points. You can also use the *Increase* or *Decrease Font Size* buttons.

Use one of the alignment buttons to left align, right align, centre or justify the text on the page.

Alignment buttons

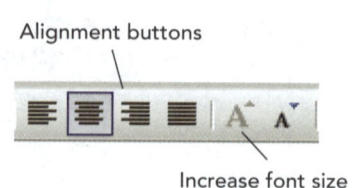

Increase font size

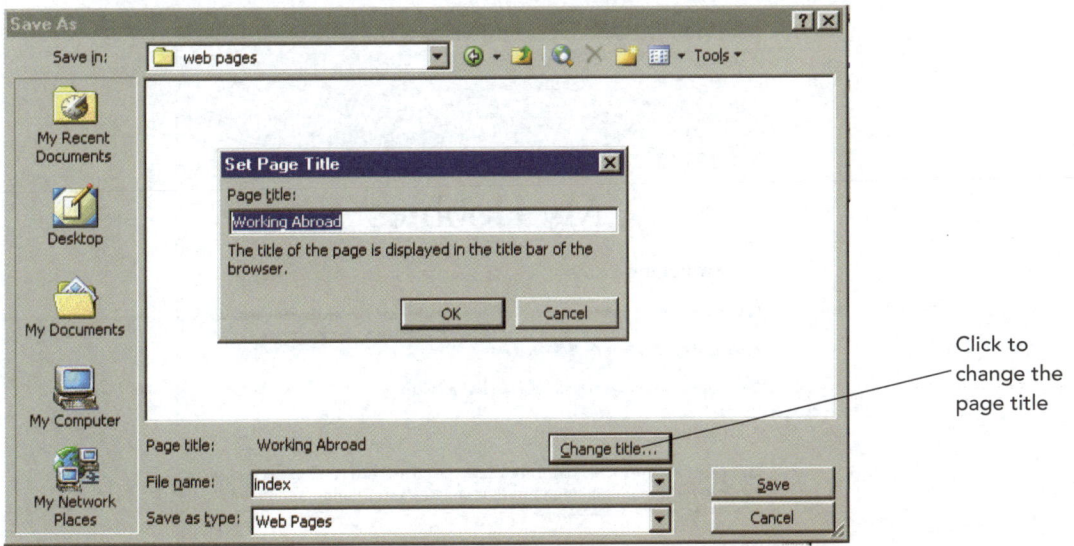

Select appropriate heading text

Font size

Heading styles

Browsers display text in different ways. When creating a web page, it is common to use a generic setting for styles of text that are then interpreted by the browser. The styles are arranged at different levels, with the top level having the largest font size.

Normally you work through the levels in a logical order – i.e. apply *Heading 1* to the main page heading and then pick lower-level headings 2–6 for subheadings and main text.

Saving web pages

Click the **Save** button to save your page. As well as deciding on the file name and location, you can accept or change the page title that will be displayed in the browser title bar. Click **Change title** to open the *Set Page Title* dialogue box if you are not happy with the name displayed automatically.

For the assignment, you will be asked to rename a folder and save all your work into this folder, so take care when selecting the location for your files.

Click to change the page title

Common mistake

Not saving with the specified file name into the correct folder, or introducing an error into the file name.

1. Open FrontPage and start a new, blank web page.

2. Type the following heading:

   My Hobbies

3. Centre the text and apply a large font size (e.g. 6 or 7).

4. Now add the following paragraphs:

   Bird watching

   I live in an area that is excellent for birds. There are waders and gulls around the coast, and the woods are a good place to find woodpeckers, nuthatches and other insect-eaters. Find out more about birds from the RSPB website.

   Click here to see a picture of the South coast near my house.

   Cooking

   Most people enjoy pasta, and I can make a number of different sauces. I particularly enjoy vegetarian food so many of these are based on tomato, pepper and onion. You will find a favourite recipe on my Cookery page.

   Sailing

   My family has a small sailing boat and we take it out in most weathers. My father and I like to race, but mum prefers a short sail to a quiet beach where we can swim, sunbathe and have barbecues.

   The Royal Yachting Association (RYA) runs a range of sailing courses, and will send you a list of these if you write to their headquarters.

5. Apply a medium size font (e.g. 4 or 5) to the subheadings.

6. Apply a small size font (e.g. 2 or 3) to the main text.

7. Save the page as Hobbies.

Answer

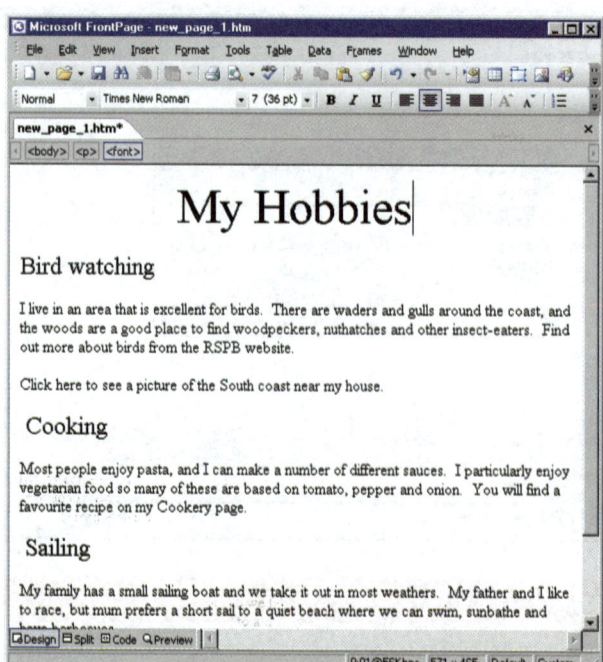

Opening web pages

Open a page saved previously by clicking the **Open** toolbar button 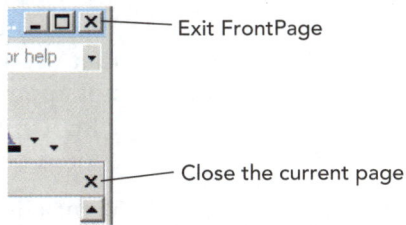 and browsing through the files on your computer. When the page file name is displayed in the window, select it and click the **Open** button.

If you try to open a named web page file from *My Documents* or a folder in which the pages are stored, double-clicking will open it into your browser rather than FrontPage. To edit a page using your authoring software, open FrontPage first of all and then open the page from here.

Closing web pages

To close a web page, click the lower **Close** button in the top right-hand corner or select **File/Close**. Clicking the top **Close** button will exit the application.

Exit FrontPage

Close the current page

Links

Web pages have special code embedded in them to create hyperlinks. When a hyperlink is clicked it will open a new page or e-mail message window. The new page will either be internal – i.e. on the same website – or external – on a separate website.

Any text or graphic can be made into a hyperlink. You will notice that hyperlink text is often coloured and underlined. When viewing web pages, you can tell that an element is a hyperlink because the mouse pointer positioned over it displays a hand 🖑 rather than an arrow.

To insert a hyperlink in your web page, type or locate the text you want as the 'clickable' text and select it, or select an image. Then click the **Hyperlink** button 🌐 or go to **Insert/Hyperlink** to open the *Create Hyperlink* dialogue box. You can also right-click the selected text or image and select **Hyperlink**.

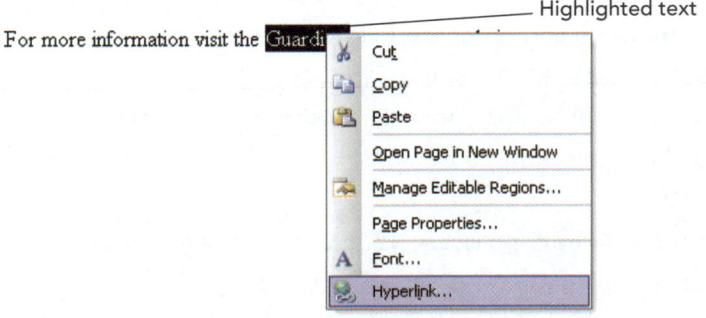

Highlighted text

For more information visit the Guardi...

Internal links

To insert an internal link that will open another page on your computer, check the files listed in the *Insert Hyperlink* window. If the target file is visible, click it and click **OK**. Otherwise, click the **up arrow** and search for the file on your computer.

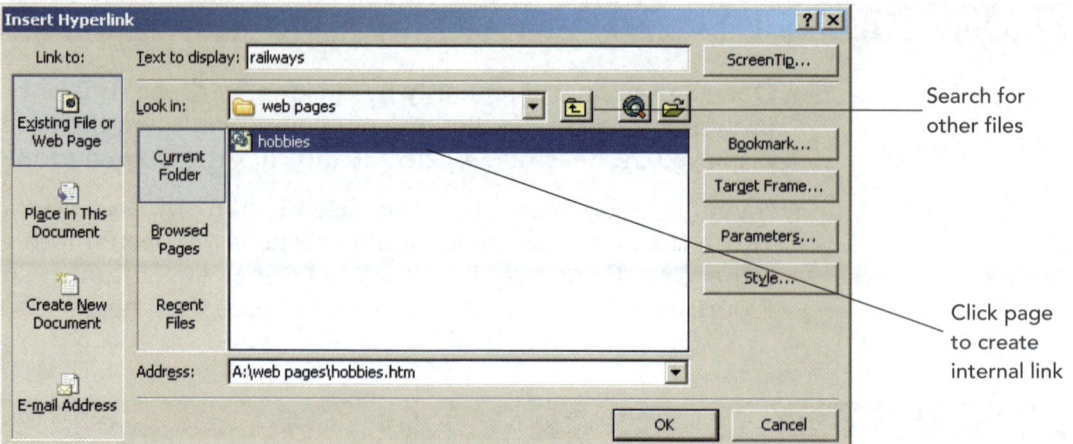

Search for other files

Click page to create internal link

When you select the file and click **OK**, you will return to your page and see that the selected text is now blue and underlined, although an image will not appear any different. Rest the mouse over the text or image and the URL (Uniform Resource Locator, i.e. the Internet address) for the link should be visible in the bottom left-hand corner of the screen.

Right-click the hyperlink and select **Follow Hyperlink** (or hold **Ctrl** as you click the mouse pointer) to check that the link works. The linked page should open on screen. Click the named tab to return to your original page.

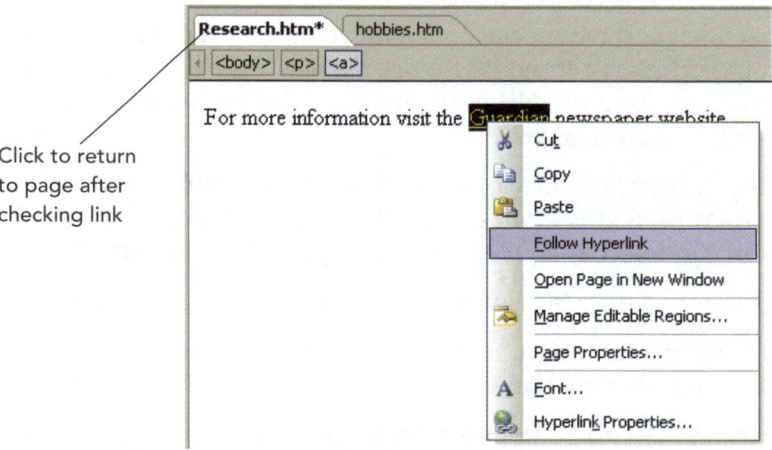

Click to return to page after checking link

Exercise 2

1. Start a new page and enter the following text:

   GAMES TO PLAY WHEN YOU GET OLD

2. Apply a top-level heading style (large size font) and centre align the text.
3. Now add the following paragraphs:

   CROQUET

   Learn the finer points of this ancient game

   TENNIS

   Keep fit and keep moving — we tell you how to do it safely

   BOULE

   Not just for the French, this is an exciting game at any age

4. Apply a lower-level heading style (medium size font) to the subheadings and an even lower heading style (small size font) to the main text.
5. Save the page as Games.

6. Start a new page and enter the heading: CROQUET

7. Apply a top-level heading style to this text and centre it on the page.

8. Below the heading, type the following paragraph:

   `This game was introduced into England in the 1850s and grew in popularity over the 60s and 70s. It spread to America and Russia and well-known celebrities such as Groucho Marx, Tolstoy and Dorothy Parker were known to have played at one time.`

9. Apply a lower-level heading style and format to italic.

10. Save the page as `Croquet`.

11. Now make a link to this page from *Games*. Use the subheading CROQUET as the link text.

12. Test that the link works and then close both pages.

Answer

GAMES TO PLAY WHEN YOU GET OLD

CROQUET
Learn the finer points of this ancient game

TENNIS
Keep fit and keep moving – we tell you how to do it safely

BOULE
Not just for the French, this is an exciting game at any age

External links

To link to a page on a website accessed via the Web, either type its URL directly in the box or click the **Web** button and connect to the Internet to locate the page using a search engine. (See Unit 8 for help with searching.) When you have accessed the website, return to FrontPage. The full URL will appear in the *Address* box. Click **OK** to establish the link in your page.

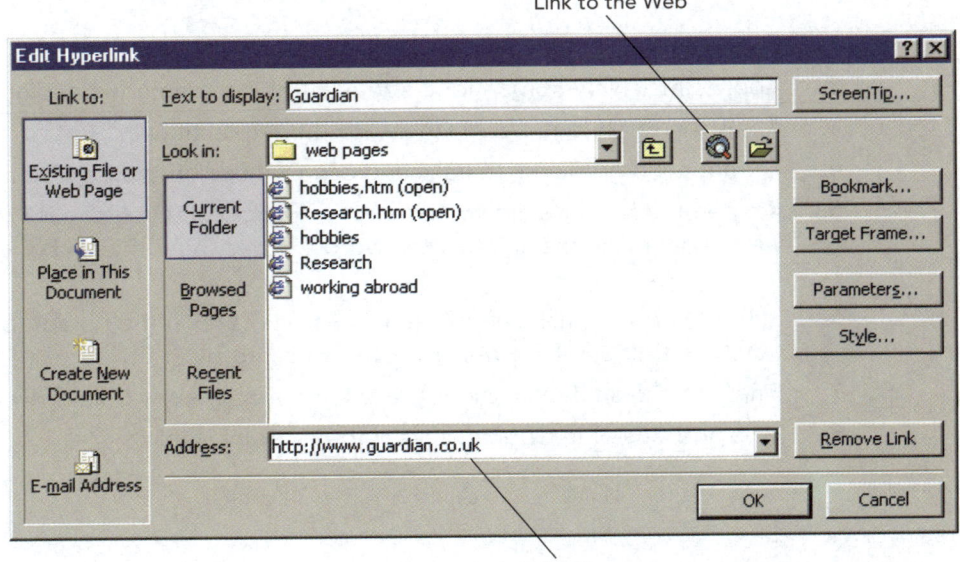

E-mail links

If you want web surfers to be able to click on a web page and send you e-mail messages directly, you can create an e-mail link.

Select the text to be clicked. In the *Hyperlink* dialogue box click the **E-mail Address** button. Type the full e-mail address into the box that opens. The address will appear in the box prefixed by *mailto*: which must be left in place to identify the type of link created. Click **OK** to return to the page.

Full e-mail address with prefix

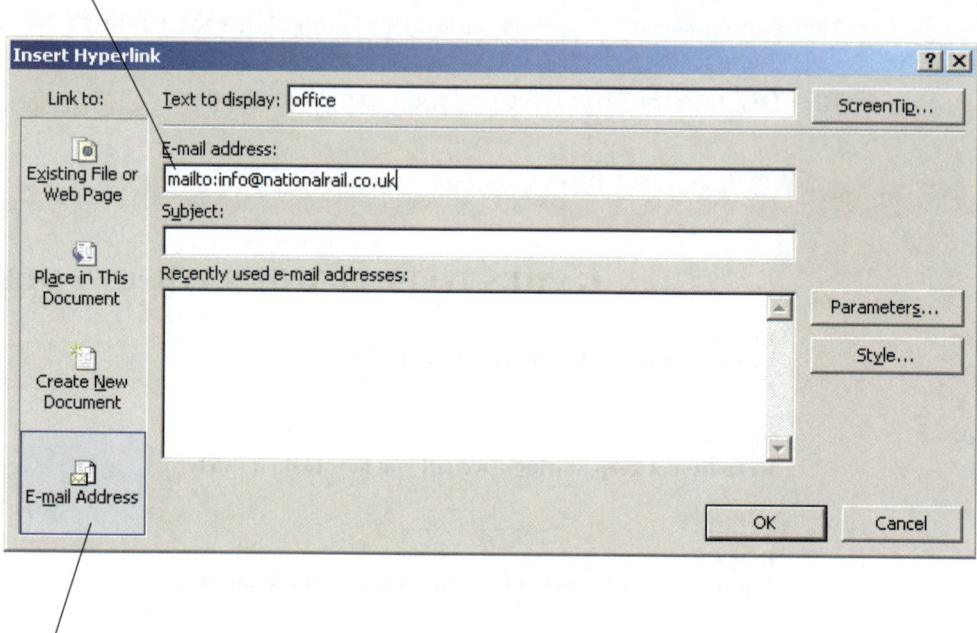

Click button to add e-mail link

FAILURE TO CREATE A LINK THAT WORKS CORRECTLY IS A CRITICAL ERROR.

Exercise 3

1. Open the web page *Cookery* from the CD.

2. Apply Times New Roman font, size 6 (24 pt.) to the page heading.

3. Apply the same font, size 4 (14 pt.) to the recipe title.

4. Format the ingredients to italic and centre these on the page.

5. Reopen the *Hobbies* file you created in Exercise 1. Create a link to the *Cookery* web page. Make the link text the word *Cookery* near the end of the paragraph headed *Cooking*.

6. Still on *Hobbies*, make an external link from *RSPB* in the paragraph on bird watching to the RSPB's website **www.rspb.org.uk**

7. Finally, make an e-mail link to the RYA. The address is **training@rya.org.uk**

8. Save and close the *Cookery* and *Hobbies* web pages.

Step 4

Cookery

Pasta is a wonderful food - filling, cheap and you can cook it with a range of different sauces. My favourites are tomato and pepper, minced meat (Bolognese) and cheese sauce.

Pasta with Tomato and Pepper Sauce

1 tin chopped tomatoes
1 red pepper, diced
1/2 onion, sliced
olive oil
A few chopped basil leaves

Gently fry the onion in olive oil for a few minutes, then add the other ingredients. Cook over low heat for about 10 minutes, until soft. Meanwhile, boil 4oz any pasta shapes for about 10 minutes. Drain the pasta, toss in the sauce and serve with grated cheese.

Step 7

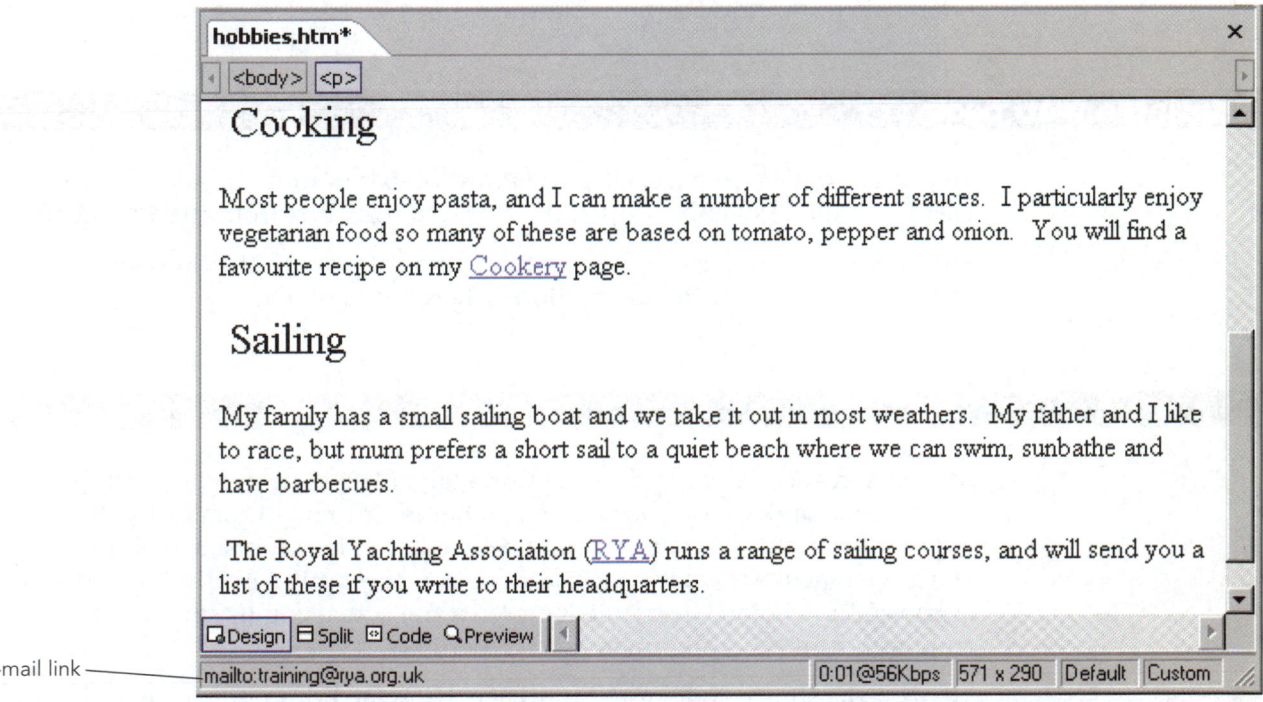

E-mail link

Applying a background colour

You can add coloured or picture backgrounds to web pages. Right-click the page and click **Page Properties Formatting**, or open the **Format** menu and select **Background**. On the **Background** tab, click in the **Background colour** box and select your preferred colour. You will also be able to set colours for hyperlink text before and after links have been accessed.

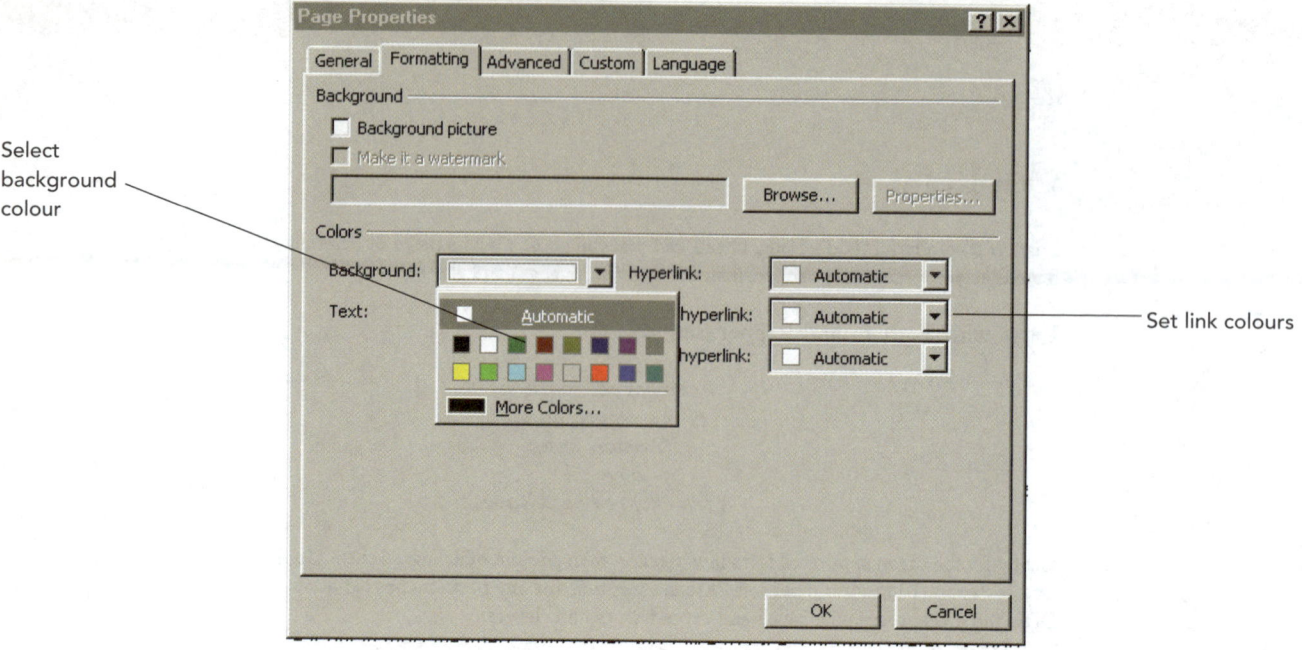

Select background colour

Set link colours

Printing a web page

To print a single web page, click the **Print** toolbar button. To select specific pages or number of copies, open the *Print* dialogue box from the **File** menu.

You can print your pages from the authoring software or the browser, so make sure you follow the instructions where this is stated.

Printing a web page showing the source code

In your software, you can click the **Code** tab at the bottom of the screen to see the code underlying your web page that is written automatically. It might look confusing, but you should be able to identify the actual text you have typed (shown in black) and various formatting instructions such as background colour (the code represents the actual colour chosen), emphasis, font type, alignment and hyperlinks.

To print the source code from FrontPage, click the **Print** button when the code is displayed on screen.

```
 1  <html>
 2
 3  <head>
 4  <meta http-equiv="Content-Language" content="en-gb">
 5  <meta http-equiv="Content-Type" content="text/html; charset=windows-1252">
 6  <title>Holidays</title>
 7  </head>
 8
 9  <body bgcolor="#CCFFFF">
10
11  <p><font size="7">Holidays</font></p>
12  <p><font size="5">England</font></p>
13  <p><font size="4"><a href="http://www.dorset.gov.uk">Bournemouth</a></font></p>
14  <p>If you like the seaside, this is the place to be.  It has seven miles of
15  golden sands and wonderful facilities.  Even in the rain there is the
16  <a href="http://www.aquarium.co.uk">aquarium</a> to visit.  </p>
17  <p><font size="4">Brighton</font></p>
18  <p><font size="5">Europe</font></p>
19  <p><font size="5">America</font></p>
20  <p><font size="5">India</font></p>
21
22  </body>
23
24  </html>
25
```

Title → line 6
Background colour → line 9
Text on page → lines 11–20
External link → line 16

Exercise 4

1. Reopen the *Games* page you created in Exercise 2.
2. Apply a pale blue background colour.
3. Print a copy of the page.
4. Print a second version of the page showing the source HTML code.
5. Close the page.

Answer

Step 4

```
<html>

<head>
<meta http-equiv="Content-Language" content="en-gb">
<meta name="GENERATOR" content="Microsoft FrontPage 5.0">
<meta name="ProgId" content="FrontPage.Editor.Document">
<meta http-equiv="Content-Type" content="text/html; charset=windows-1252">
<title>GAMES TO PLAY WHEN YOU GET OLD</title>
</head>

<body bgcolor="#99CCFF">

<h1 align="center">GAMES TO PLAY WHEN YOU GET OLD</h1>
<h2><a href="croquet.htm">CROQUET</a><br>
<span lang="EN-GB">Learn the finer points of this ancient game</span></h2>
<p class="MsoNormal"><span lang="EN-GB"> </span></p>
<h2><a href="croquet.htm" style="text-decoration: none"><font color="#000000">
TENNIS</font></a><span lang="EN-GB"><br>
Keep fit and keep moving - we tell you how to do it safely</span></h2>
<h2><span lang="EN-GB"> </span></h2>
<h2><span lang="EN-GB">BOULE<br>
Not just for the French, this is an exciting game at any age</span></h2>
<p> </p>

</body>

</html>
```

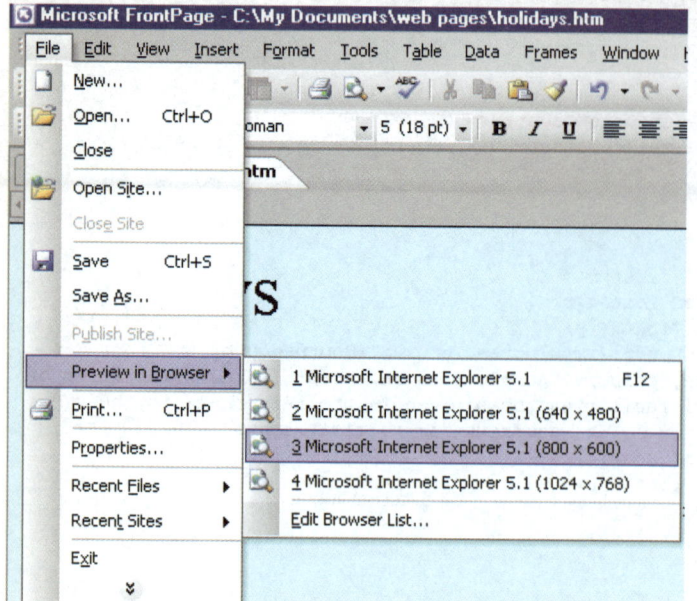

Although you can check your pages on the *Preview* tab, it is important to see how they are developing when viewed in your browser.

Save any changes made to the page and then open the **File** menu and click **Preview in Browser**.

Select the correct browser and resolution and a new window will open showing your web page.

Its file location will show in the *Address* box.

Return to your page by clicking the minimized **FrontPage** button on the taskbar, and continue to move between browser and FrontPage as you make any changes necessary.

If FrontPage is closed, find the file by opening the browser and clicking **File/Open** before searching your computer for the relevant file.

You must always save your page in FrontPage, and click the **Refresh** button on the browser toolbar to see the effects of the latest changes.

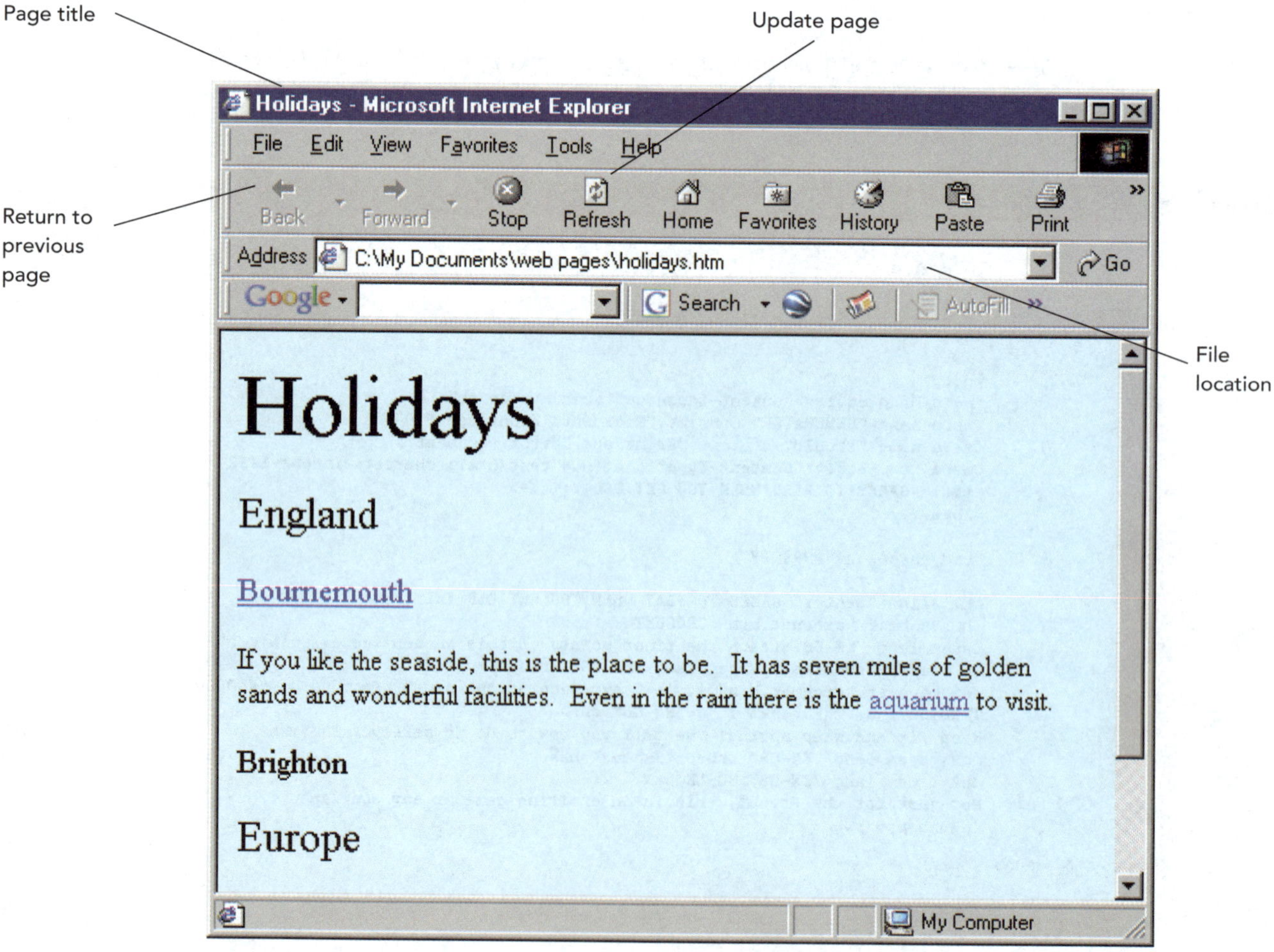

Page title

Update page

Return to previous page

File location

Holidays

England

Bournemouth

If you like the seaside, this is the place to be. It has seven miles of golden sands and wonderful facilities. Even in the rain there is the aquarium to visit.

Brighton

Europe

Printing from a browser

To print a page from the browser, click the **Print** button.

Your printout should show the URL pathway, including the web page file name and folder location. Check it is visible from **File/Print Preview**. If the information is missing, go to **File/Page Setup** and add &u in the *Header* box.

To print the code after displaying a page in the browser, open the **View** menu and select **Source**. This will open a new Notepad window and you can print from here by selecting **File/Print**.

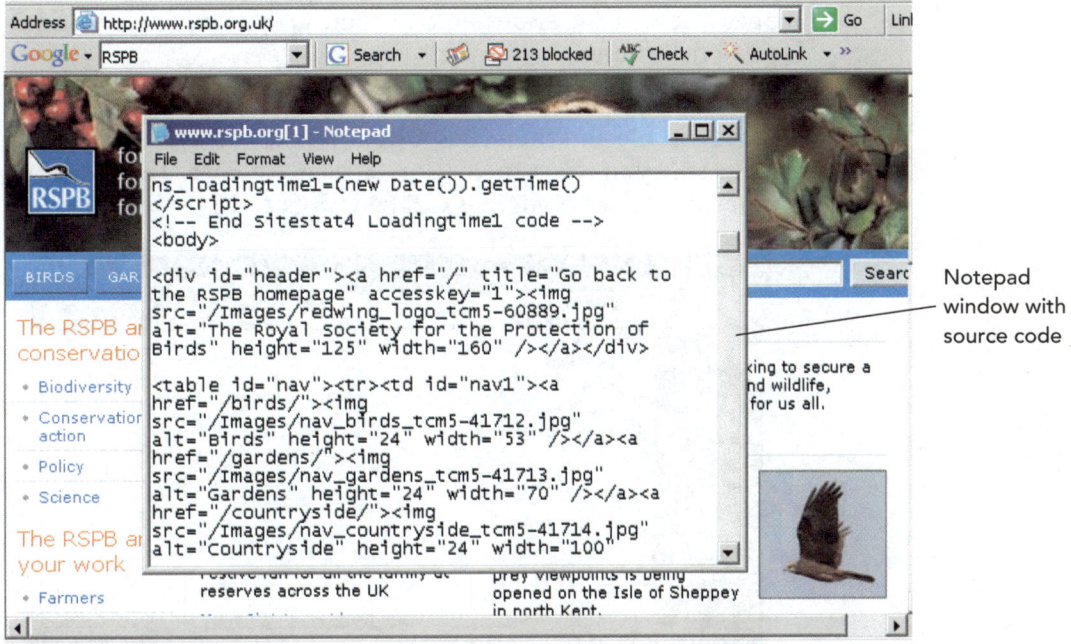

Notepad window with source code

Source: From The Royal Society for the Protection of Birds website (www.rspb.org.uk). Reproduced with permission

Testing links

To check that your external links are working properly, view the page in your browser and make sure you are connected to the Internet. When you click the hyperlink, the correct web page should open. Return to your page by clicking the **Back** button.

When clicking the e-mail link, a new message window will open only if your computer is set up to work with e-mails.

Exercise 5

1. Reopen the web page *Croquet* that you created in Exercise 2.

2. Add the following text at the bottom of the page: For full details of how to play contact Gerald Haigh.

3. Centre the text and apply a mid-level heading style.

4. Insert an e-mail link using *Gerald Haigh* as the link text. The address is g.haigh@croquet.com

5. Open *Games* and test the internal links and e-mail link in your browser.

6. Print a copy of *Games* from the browser.

Answer

Showing the amendment only.

For full details of how to play contact <u>Gerald Haigh</u>.

Inserting a text file

To use text already typed within a text editing or word processing application, you can start a new web page or open one already created, open the text file and then copy across the text using normal copy and paste techniques.

An alternative method is to go to **Insert/File**, browse for the text or word processed file and then click **Open**. When you are searching for the text, make sure you select the option to view **All Files**, **Text Files** or **Word 97-2000** otherwise only HTML files will be visible.

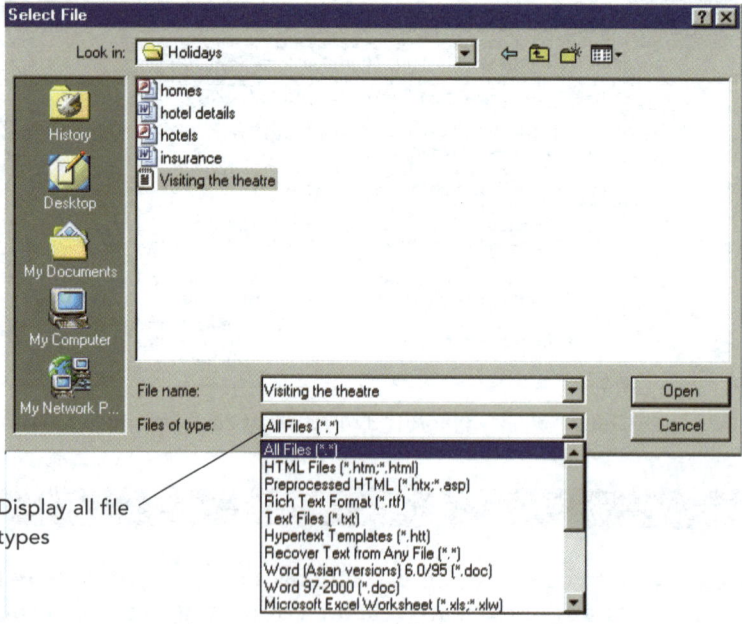

Display all file types

You will be offered various formats for the file so leave the default – formatted paragraphs – and click **OK**.

The text will appear on your page and you can edit and format it as normal.

> **NOT INSERTING THE CORRECT TEXT FILE OR MAKING CHANGES TO THE TEXT WHERE YOU ARE NOT INSTRUCTED TO DO SO IS A CRITICAL ERROR.**

Common mistake

Not following the instructions to insert clear line spaces or new paragraphs.

Common mistake

Changing font or other formats or amending the wording.

1. Start a new web page and insert the text file *south coast* from the CD.

2. Save the page with the name Coast.

3. Apply different formats to the heading and subheadings.

4. Reopen *Hobbies* from Exercise 1 and create an internal link to *Coast*. Use *Click here* in the second paragraph as the link text.

5. Now update the *Hobbies* page and view it in your browser.

6. Test all the links and, if necessary, return to FrontPage to make any corrections.

7. Print a copy of the web page *Coast* from your browser.

8. Print a copy of the source code from your browser.

Answer

Steps 7 and 8

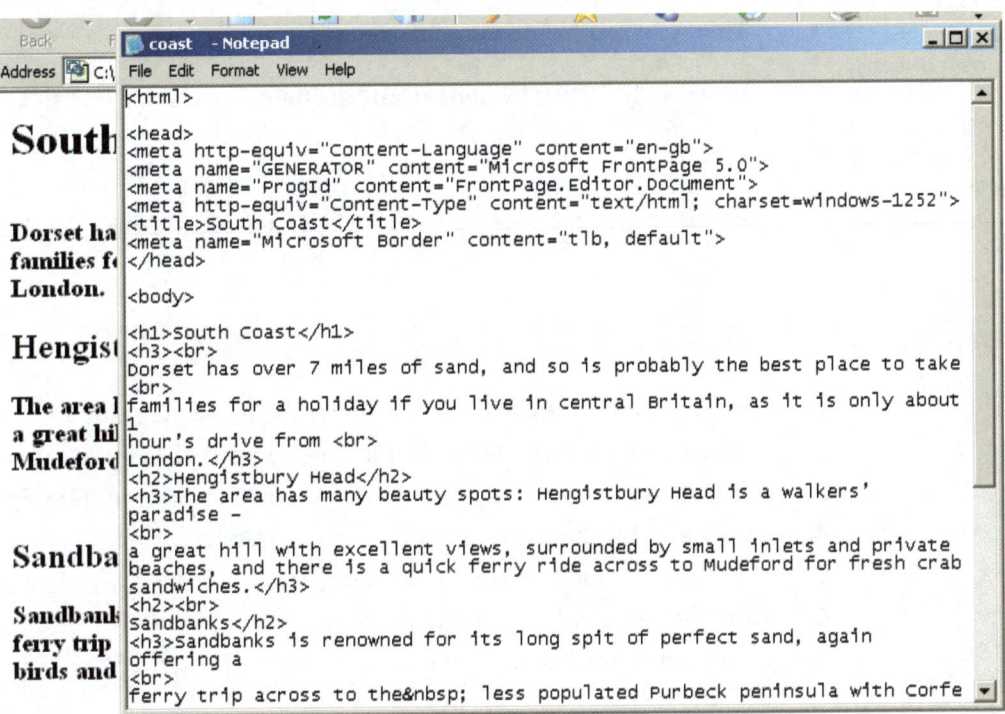

Importing and positioning images

To display a picture on your page, go to **Insert/Picture/From File**. Browse through your folders until you locate the file, select it and click **OK**.

When it appears, click it to select it and then, if necessary, reduce its size by dragging one of the corner sizing handles. (For help with working with images, see Unit 6.)

Drag the picture to a different part of the page with the pointer – a dotted vertical line will mark its progress. When the image is in the correct position, let go the mouse button and the picture will drop into place. You can then centre, left align or right align the picture using the normal toolbar buttons.

You can also right-click a picture and select **Picture Properties** to open a dialogue box where you can set its size or position more accurately.

RAILWAYS

It is easier to plan your journey if you visit the National Rail website.

Then you can follow your interest in railways.

Write to the office for further information.

FAILURE TO IMPORT THE CORRECT IMAGE IS A CRITICAL ERROR.

Exercise 7

1. Open *Coast* from Exercise 6 and insert the image *Coast picture* from the CD.
2. Reposition it so that it is below the heading but above the main text.
3. Reduce it in size and centre the picture and heading on the page.
4. Apply a yellow background colour to the page.
5. Update the page to save these changes and print a copy.
6. Now reopen *Cookery* from Exercise 3.
7. Insert the image *Pasta* from the CD so that it is right aligned underneath the list of ingredients.
8. Save the page and print a copy.
9. Close all web pages.

Step 5

South Coast

Dorset has over 7 miles of sand, and so is probably the best place to take families for a holiday if you live in central Britain, as it is only about 1 hour's drive from London.

Hengistbury Head

The area has many beauty spots: Hengistbury Head is a walkers' paradise - a great hill with excellent views, surrounded by small inlets and private beaches, and there is a quick ferry ride across to Mudeford for fresh crab sandwiches.

Step 8

Cookery

Pasta is a wonderful food - filling, cheap and you can cook it with a range of different sauces. My favourites are tomato and pepper, minced meat (Bolognese) and cheese sauce.

Pasta with Tomato and Pepper Sauce

1 tin chopped tomatoes
1 red pepper, diced
1/2 onion, sliced
olive oil
A few chopped basil leaves

Exiting the application

Click the upper **Close** button or go to **File/Exit**.

Exercise 8 – a full assignment

Task 1

1. Rename the folder *web files* (from the CD) containing all the files for this assignment with the name **mypages** and save all your work in this folder.
2. Open suitable software for creating and editing web pages. You are asked to create and format a new web page.
3. In your web page editing software, create a new document.

4. Enter the following text:

    Art

    We find at Smallwood College that adults love gaining artistic skills, and our newly built studios offer a wide range of opportunities for experimenting with art products and new technologies.

    Here are some of our courses:

5. Click at the end of the text and then insert the text file *Art.txt*.

6. Check that each paragraph is separated by at least one clear line space.

7. After the main text, insert a clear line space and add the following text:
    Contact Patricia for next term's prospectus.

8. Save your document using the file name `artcourses.htm`

Task 2

1. Apply Arial font, HTML size 6 (24 point) to the main heading, and Arial font, HTML size 4 (14 point) to the subheadings.

2. Format all other text as Arial font, HTML size 2 (10 point).

3. Format only the final sentence *Contact Patricia for next term's prospectus* to bold.

4. Insert the image *painting* from the CD and position this below the main heading but above the rest of the text.

5. Centre the image on the page.

6. Create a link in the *artcourses.htm* page to the homepage as follows:
    - Object to be linked: *painting* image
    - Link to: `smallwood.htm`

7. Check your web page for accuracy.

8. Save the web page keeping the name *artcourses.htm*.

9. Close the *artcourses.htm* page.

Task 3

1. Open the homepage *smallwood.htm* from the CD. Do not change the font on this page.

2. On a separate line below the text *four main skills* insert the following text as a list:

    Speaking and writing

    Computer literacy

    Making simple gifts in wood and paper

    Becoming more independent

3. Centre align this text.

4. Format this text as Arial font HTML size 4 (14 point).

5. Create an internal link: use the text *excellent courses* and link to the *artcourses.htm* page.

6. Save the amended *smallwood.htm* page.

7. Create an external link to the BBC website: **www.bbc.co.uk**. Use *BBC programme* as the link text.

8. Create an e-mail link using the name *Patricia* as the link text. The e-mail address is: p.wentworth@smallwood.ac.uk

9. Save the web page keeping the file name *smallwood.htm*.

Task 4

1. A background colour will improve the homepage.

2. Apply a background colour to the *smallwood.htm* page. Make sure the background colour is different from the text colour and that the text and images are clearly visible against the background colour.

3. Check your web page for accuracy.

4. Save the web page keeping the file name *smallwood.htm*.

5. Close all web pages and exit the web page editing software.

6. Load the *smallwood.htm* page into the browser and test the three links.

7. From the browser print the *smallwood.htm* page.

8. Display the HTML source code for the *smallwood.htm* page.

9. Print the HTML source code for this page.

10. Close the *smallwood.htm* page.

11. Load the *artcourses.htm* page into the browser and test the one link.

12. From the browser print the *artcourses.htm* page.

13. Display the HTML source code for the *artcourses.htm* page.

14. Print the HTML source code for this page.

15. Close the *artcourses.htm* page.

16. Exit the browser.

Answers

Task 2 Step 7

Art

We find at Smallwood College that adults love gaining artistic skills, and our newly built studios offer a wide range of opportunities for experimenting with art products and new technologies.

Here are some of our courses:

Watercolour

Learn about mixing colours, applying washes and which brush to use. Try your hand at simple still life or be more ambitious and attempt a landscape.

Pottery

Our kiln is always fired up and you can throw pots in stoneware or make vases, cups and other objects of use in the home. A wide range of glazes is available.

Photography

We have 2 dark rooms and technicians on hand to give their advice and show you how to get the best from

Task 4 Step 7

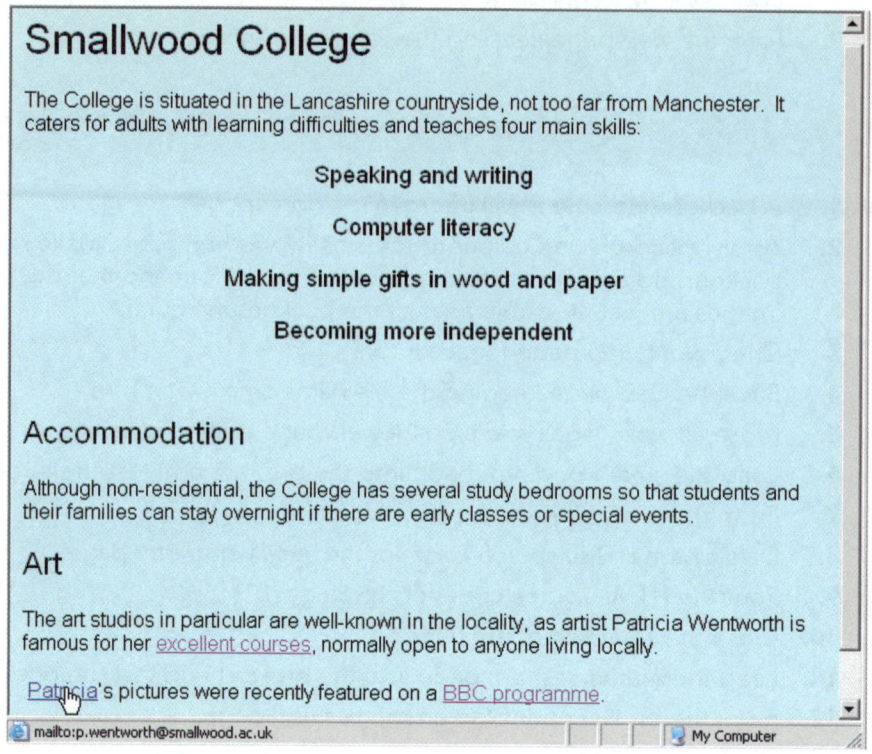

Task 4 Step 9

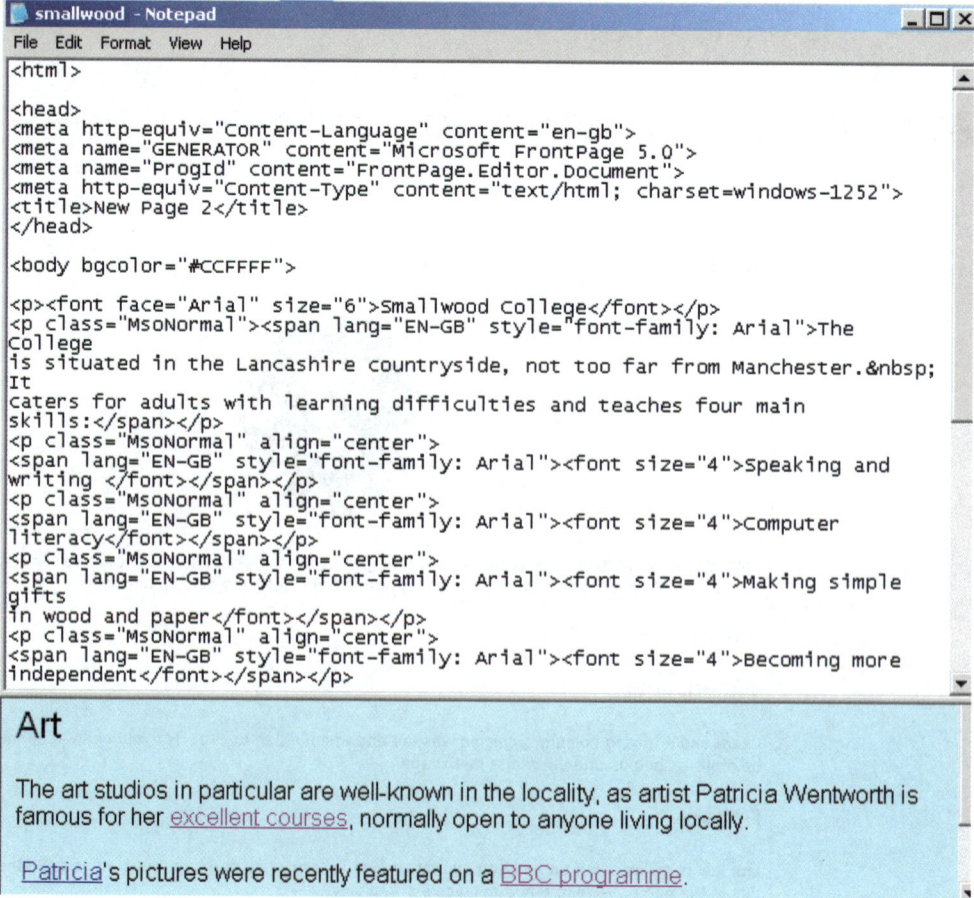

Self-assessment checklist

I feel confident that I can now:	✓
Select appropriate web authoring software	
Create a new web page	
Enter text	
Format text	
Apply different text styles	
Change text alignment	
Open web pages	
Create internal, external and e-mail links	
Save a web page	
View web pages in a browser	
Test links	
Print a web page	
Print a web page showing the source code	
Insert a text file	
Import and format an image	
Apply a background colour	
Close web pages	
Exit the application	

Summary of critical errors

- Links are missing or do not work
- A specified image is missing
- Specified text file is missing or amended

8

Online communication

- **What is online communication?** 254
  E-mail addresses 255
- **Opening Outlook** 255
  Folders 255
- **Reading e-mails** 257
- **Creating messages** 258
  Copying an e-mail 259
  Sending an e-mail 260
  Receiving an e-mail 261
  Replying to an e-mail 262
  Reply to All 262
  Forwarding an e-mail 262
  Deleting an e-mail 263
- **Printing e-mails** 263
- **Attaching files to e-mails** 264
  Opening attachments 266
  Saving attachments 266
  Printing attachments 267
- **Saving a draft e-mail** 267
- **Contacts (addresses)** 267
  Adding addresses automatically 269
  Retrieving a contact automatically 269
- **Help** 269
- **Exiting Outlook** 270
- **The World Wide Web** 270
- **Opening a browser** 271
  Browser window 271
  Hyperlinks 272
  URLs 273
- **Searching web pages** 274
  Index 274
  Search engines 274
  Keywords 275

- **Printing web pages** 276
- **Bookmarking web pages** 277
- **Saving from the Web** 279
  Web pages 279
  Images 279
- **Reading pages offline** 281
- **Netiquette** 281
- **Viruses** 281
- **Self-assessment checklist** 287
- **Summary of critical errors** 287

What is online communication?

You can use the telephone to talk to someone else across a telephone network. In the same way, one computer can communicate with another using the networks of computers known as the *Internet*. Messages sent from one computer to another electronically are known as *e-mails*.

There are two different e-mail systems that you may come across:

- software permanently available on your computer that will allow you to write and read messages offline – e.g. Outlook Express, Eudora, First Class and Outlook
- software that you can use after connecting to the Internet and registering at a website such as www.hotmail.co.uk or www.yahoo.co.uk

Both work in similar ways, but this unit is based on Microsoft Outlook.

This unit develops and tests your ability to use the Internet for sending and receiving e-mail messages, and for locating specific information on the World Wide Web.

You will be asked to carry out the following tasks:

- Open an e-mail system
- Open and read a specific message
- Add an e-mail address to your address book/contacts list
- Forward a message with its attachment
- Reply to a message
- Send a copy of an e-mail
- Save an attachment on your computer
- Delete a message
- Create an e-mail using an address from your address book
- Attach a file to an e-mail
- Print an e-mail showing header details
- Take screen prints of mailbox contents
- Open a browser
- Use a search engine to find specific information on the Web
- Bookmark a web page
- Open a web page using its URL/address
- Use the index on a web page to find specific information
- Save a web image
- Print a web page
- Exit the browser and e-mail applications

To pass Unit 8 you must be able to:

- Open e-mail software
- Open and read e-mails
- Create and send e-mails
- Copy e-mails
- Delete e-mails
- Forward e-mails

- Print e-mails
- Open and save attachments
- Attach files to e-mails
- Add an address to your address book/contacts list
- Open a browser
- Search the Web using a search engine
- Bookmark web pages
- Go directly to a web page using a URL
- Use the index on a web page to find specific information
- Save images from the Web
- Print web pages
- Exit browsers and e-mail systems

E-mail addresses

For you to send or receive e-mails, you must have an e-mail address. Your organization or college may provide this, or you will be set up with an address when you register with an Internet Service Provider (ISP). Your address will be in two parts joined by the @ symbol:

- your username (see Unit 1) e.g. *j.sherman* or *jackie_sherman*
- the address of your organization or e-mail provider's computer (known as a mail server) e.g. *hotmail.co.uk* or *pearson.com*

The address is then username@server (with no spaces)

e.g. *j.sherman@pearson.com*

When typing in e-mail addresses, every letter and punctuation symbol must be correct, but you can use either upper or lower case.

AN INCORRECT, INACCURATE OR OMITTED E-MAIL ADDRESS IS A CRITICAL ERROR.

Opening Outlook

Double-click the **Outlook** icon [icon] if it is available on the desktop, or open Microsoft Outlook from the **Start/All Programs** menu.

Folders

When the program first opens, you will see a list of folders for storing e-mails and a main window, which will display the contents of any open folder. Open a folder by clicking its name in the list. Any folder containing unread messages will show the number of messages in brackets next to the name.

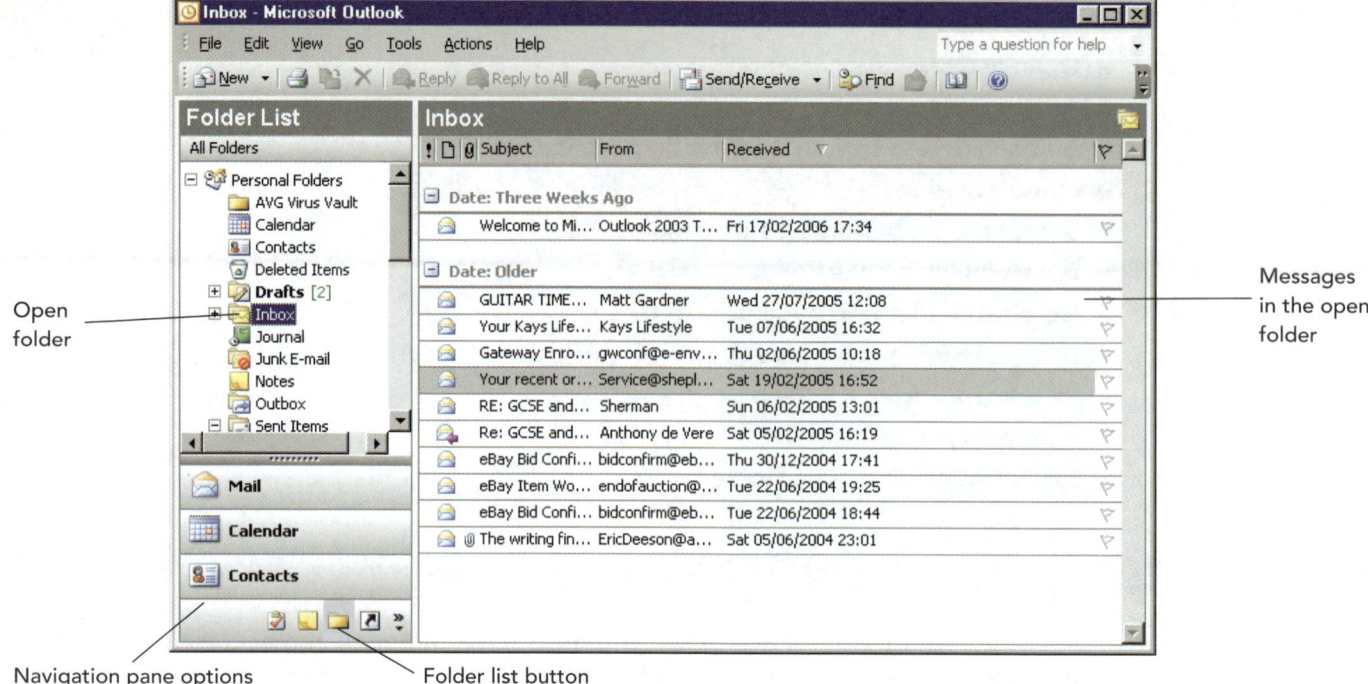

Open folder

Messages in the open folder

Navigation pane options

Folder list button

There are six folders that you will be working with for New CLAIT:

- *Inbox* – this is where all messages first appear when you receive them.
- *Outbox* – messages ready to send are stored here temporarily.
- *Sent Items* – copies of messages that you have sent are stored here.
- *Deleted Items* – if you want to remove e-mails from the system, they are stored in this folder until it is emptied – after this happens, the messages are no longer recoverable.
- *Drafts* – unfinished messages that are not ready to send are stored here.
- *Contacts* – the e-mail addresses of people you write to are stored here.

Many other folders will be visible in the Outlook folder list or *Navigation Pane*, but they are not needed for this unit. If the folder list is not visible, find it by clicking the **Folder List** button.

As well as just basic details about a message, you can click on **View/AutoPreview** to display some of the message details, or select a *Reading Pane* option where you can read a selected message in full in an extra window.

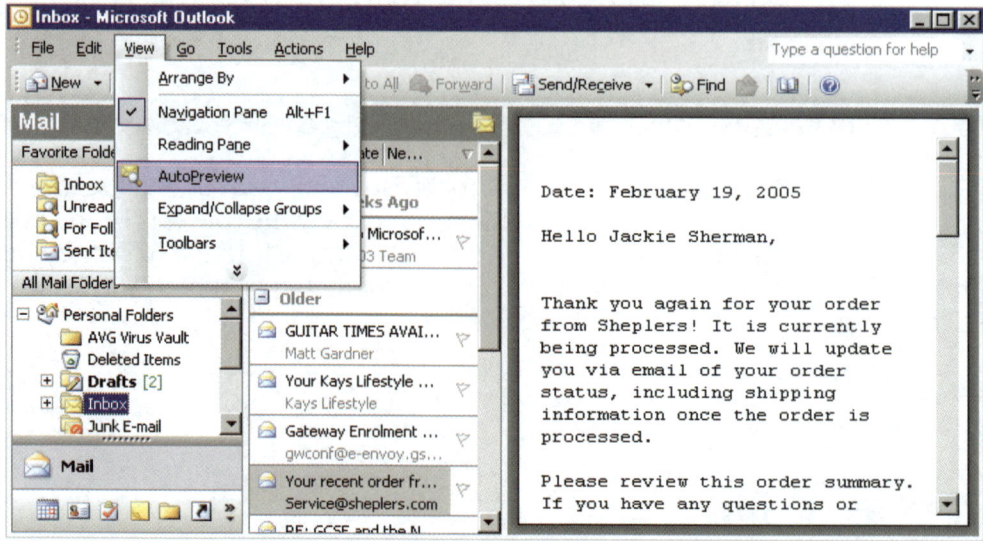

When a message arrives in the *Inbox*, some information about it will be displayed. Depending on how the computer is set up, you should see who the message is from, what it is about and when it was received. You may also be able to see whether it was copied to anyone else, its size and whether there is a file attached.

Right-click to change column headings

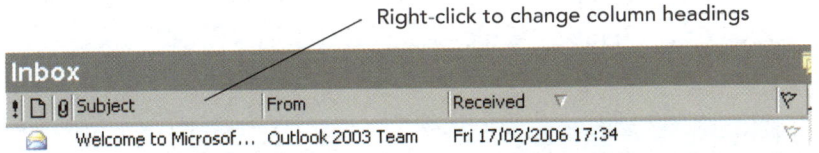

To change the column headings, right-click any heading and select **Customize Current View**. In the *View Summary* dialogue box, click the **Fields** button. This will open the *Show Fields* box. Select any column headings you wish to add and click the **Add** button, or remove unwanted column headings by selecting them and clicking **Remove**. Keep the changes by clicking **OK**.

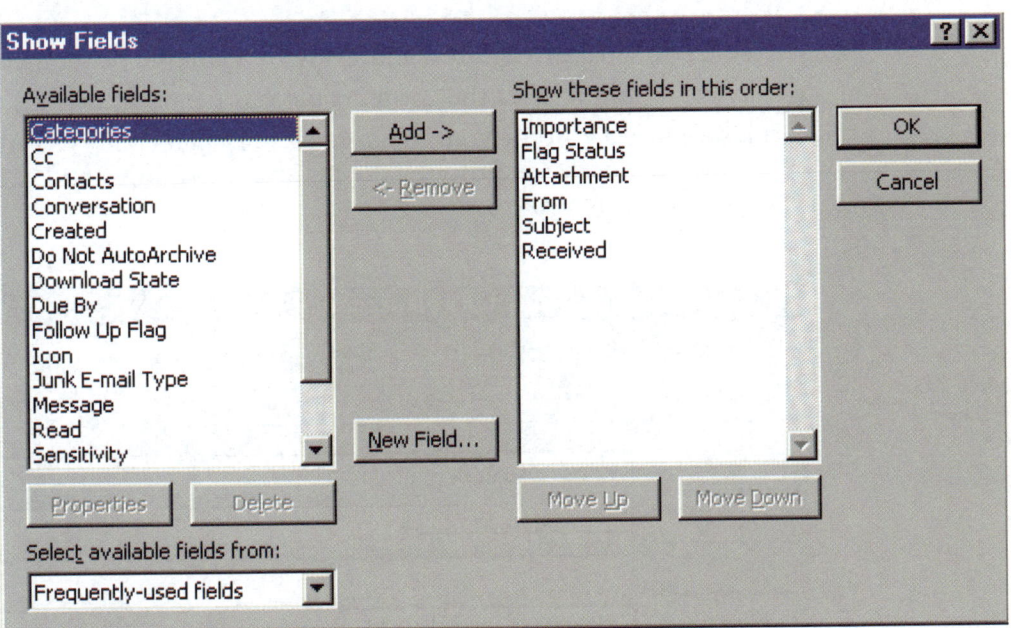

Any message in the *Inbox* can be read by double-clicking on it – this will open it in its own window. When fully open, the sender's information will be seen at the top of the message.

Sender

Close message

Read other messages in the folder

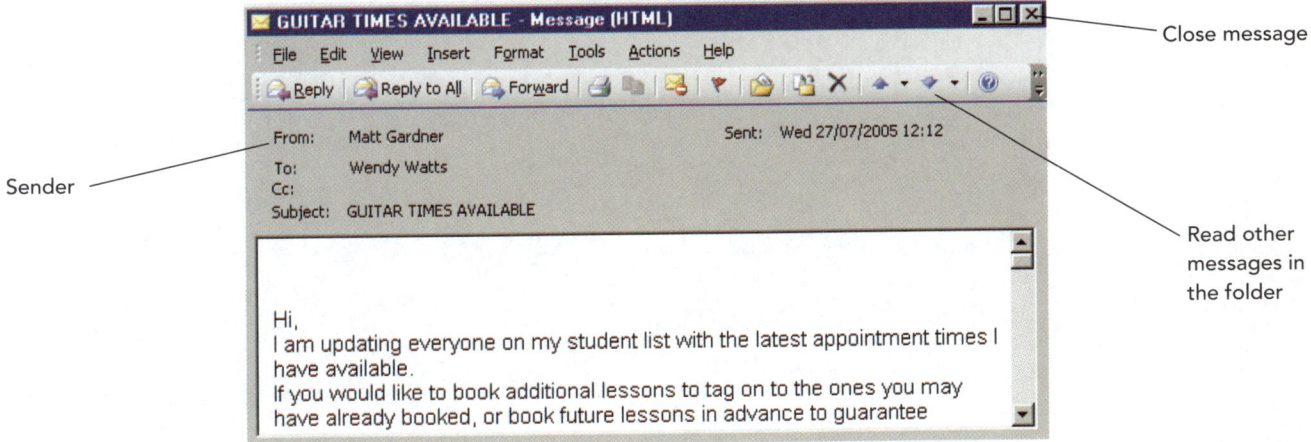

1. Open Outlook and click on **Inbox**.

2. You should see a message – e.g. a welcome from Microsoft or a message from a friend or colleague or company salesperson. Note the e-mail address of the sender, the date it was sent and any other information such as its size or the subject of the message.

3. Select the message and double-click it to open it in its own window.

4. Scroll down to read the message.

5. Close the message window and return to the *Inbox*.

Creating messages

To send a message, click the **New** button 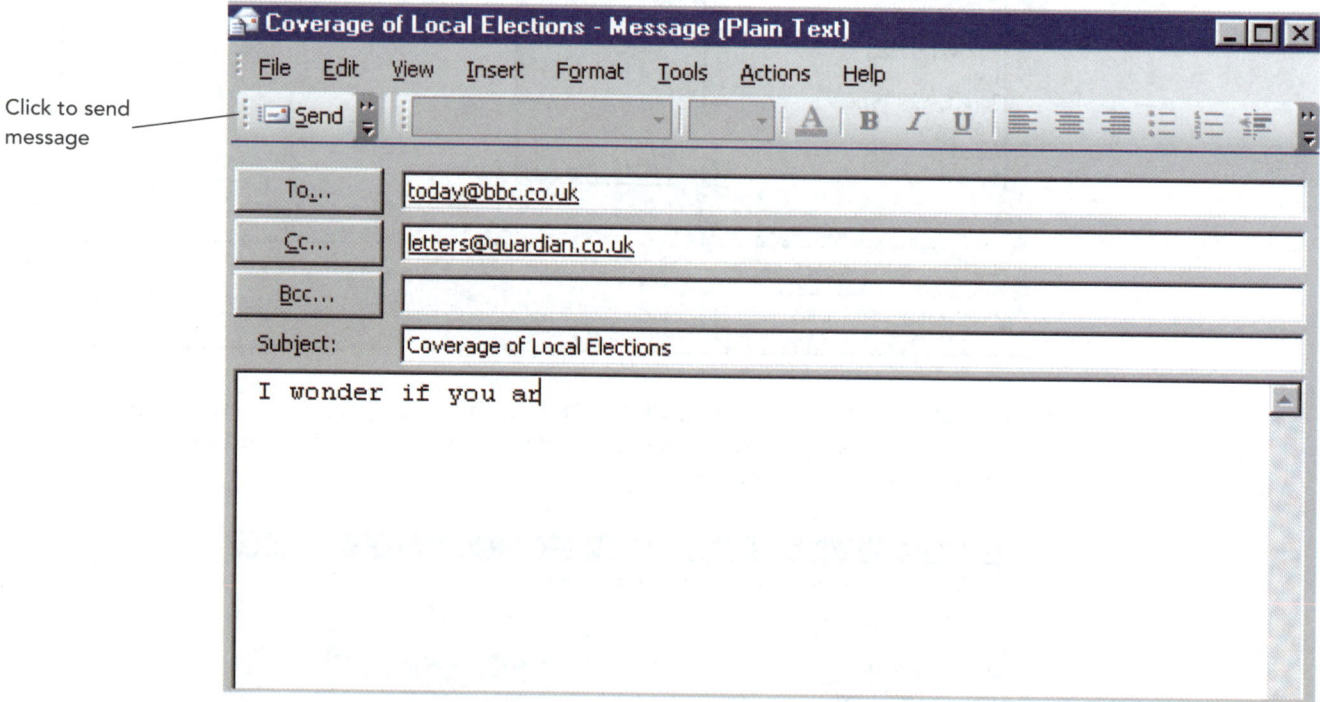 when an e-mail folder has been selected. If you are in another part of Outlook, click the **down arrow** next to the button and select **Mail Message**.

A composing window will open. You will need to complete these boxes:

- *To* – the full e-mail address of the person you are writing to. For several recipients, separate each full address with a comma or semi-colon.

- *Subject* – a summary of the contents of your message.

- *Message window* – type your message here. E-mails follow normal letter-writing conventions, although greetings and endings tend to be more informal in e-mails.

Although some people use abbreviations and leave mistakes in e-mails, formal e-mails and all New CLAIT messages should be typed accurately. Proofread on screen and make use of the spellchecker available from the **Tools/Spelling** menu. For any questionable word that is highlighted, amend your message by selecting the correct spelling and clicking **Change**, or leave the original by clicking **Ignore**.

When you check the message, you may find the text has been placed on new lines inconsistently. Don't worry about this as different systems display messages differently.

Sometimes you will see a formatting toolbar to add emphasis or change fonts and sizes. Often, e-mail messages are left unformatted in plain text. Open the **Format** menu to select your preferred option.

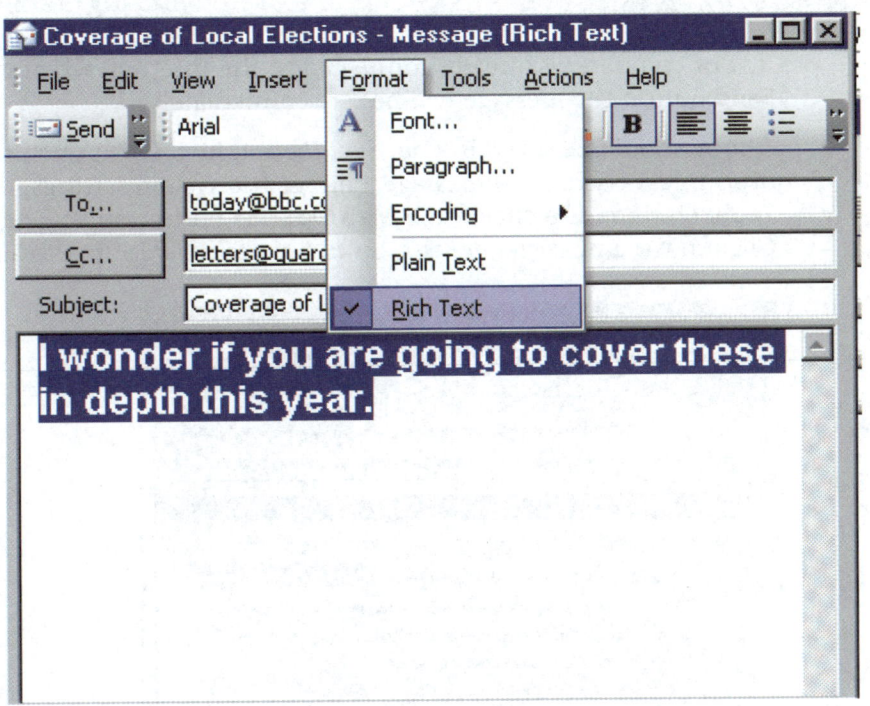

FAILURE TO ENTER AN E-MAIL ADDRESS ACCURATELY IS A CRITICAL ERROR.

Copying an e-mail

It is easy to send a copy of a message to another recipient – simply type their full e-mail address in the *Cc:* box.

To send a copy of your message to someone without showing their details to the other recipients, open the *Bcc:* box by selecting this option on the **View** menu and type their address here. This is called a *blind copy*.

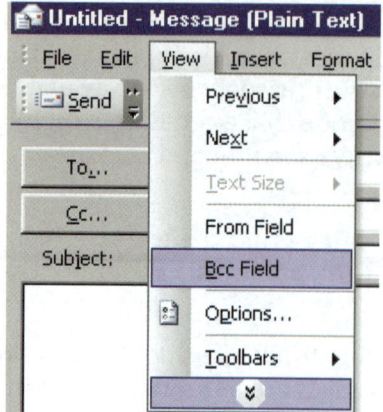

Sending an e-mail

If your computer is already connected to the Internet, when you click the **Send** button the message will be sent immediately.

A copy should be saved in your *Sent Items* folder. If, on opening the *Sent Items* folder there is no message, change the system settings. Go to **Tools/Options** and click the **E-Mail Options** button on the *Preferences* tab. Click in the *Save copies of messages in Sent Items folder* box to add a tick.

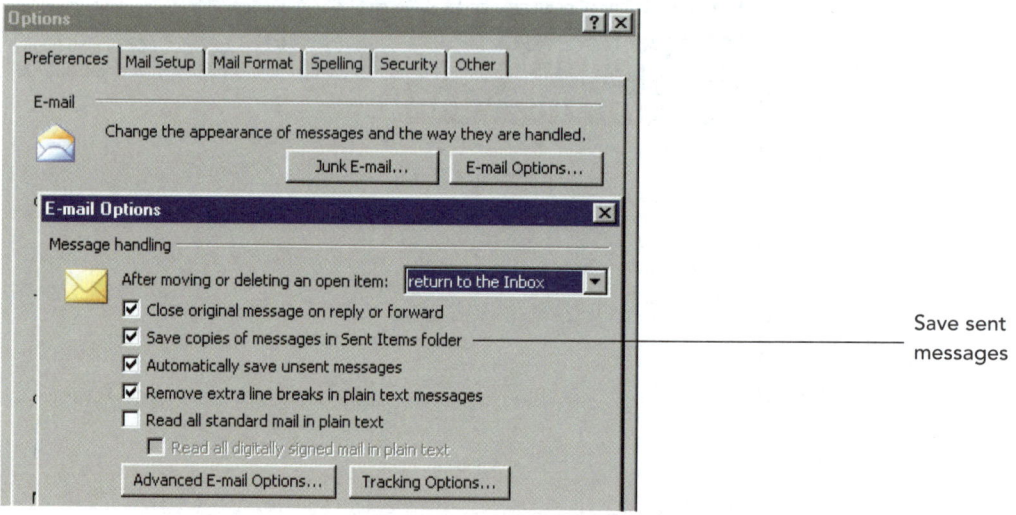

Save sent messages

If you are offline (unconnected), you may be informed that the e-mail will be stored in your *Outbox*, or your e-mail will close automatically and you will return to the main window. You will see a green (1) next to the *Outbox* showing that it now contains a message ready to send.

At this stage, you could click the **Send/Receive** button on the main toolbar and send the message, or wait until you have created several messages. When you eventually click the button, you will be able to connect and send all the messages at the same time.

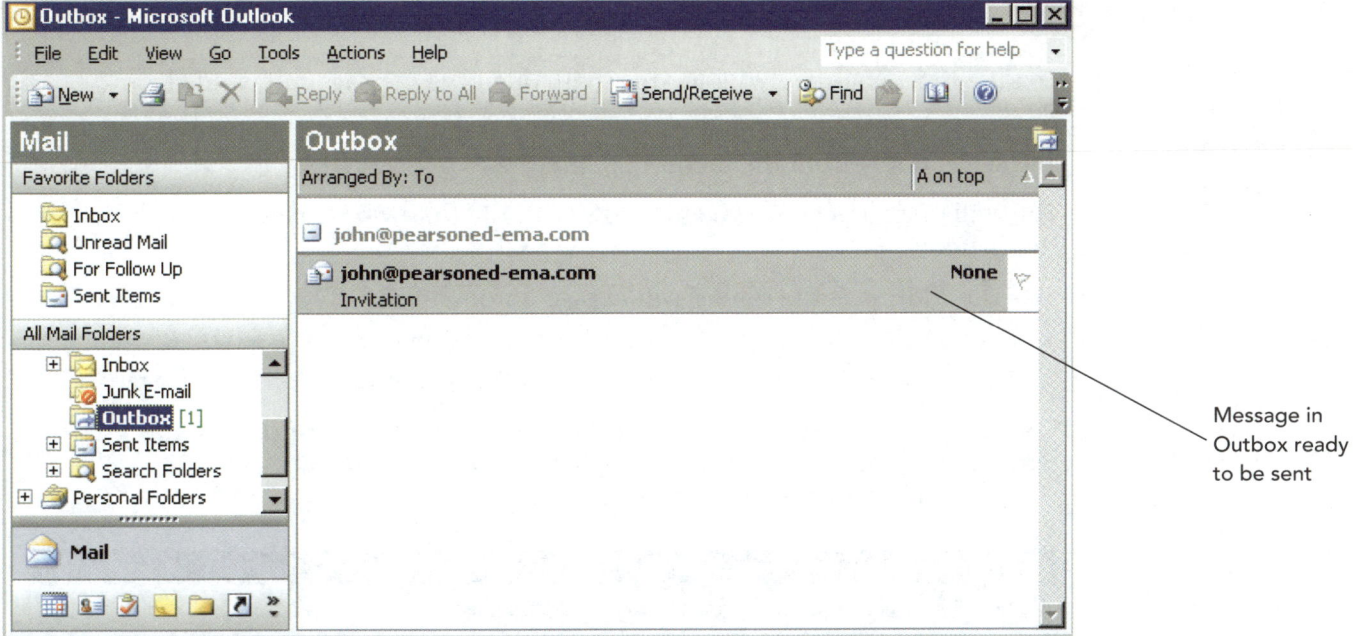

Message in Outbox ready to be sent

Receiving an e-mail

When you click the **Send/Receive** button to send any messages you have created, you will also receive messages waiting for you. Even if you have no messages to send, click this button to see whether anyone has written to you since you last checked your *Inbox*.

Exercise 2

1. Create an e-mail message to send to John at Pearson (a dummy address), with a copy to yourself. It should have the following entries:

    To: john@pearsoned-ema.com

    Cc: Your own full e-mail address (e.g. me@myISP.co.uk)

    Subject: Sending messages

    Message: I am practising sending messages and look forward to receiving one to open and read.

2. Add your name at the end of the message and check for spelling and other errors.

3. Click the **Send** button and, if necessary, click **Send/Receive** and connect to the Internet to send the message.

4. Wait a short while and then check for new mail. You should find that a copy of the e-mail has arrived.

5. Make sure you can fully open and read the message.

6. Close the message and return to the *Inbox*.

Replying to an e-mail

Reply

Reply to All

Forward

To save time when replying to an e-mail, open the message fully and click the **Reply** button on the toolbar  Reply , or right-click a closed message and select **Reply** from the menu that appears.

This will open a new message window with the following boxes already completed:

- *To* – the address of the sender will appear automatically
- *Subject* – this will be the same as on the original message, preceded by *Re*:
- *Message window* – this will normally contain the text of the original message.

You can either delete the previous message text or leave all or part of it as a reminder of what has been written. Click at the top of the message and write your reply before sending as normal.

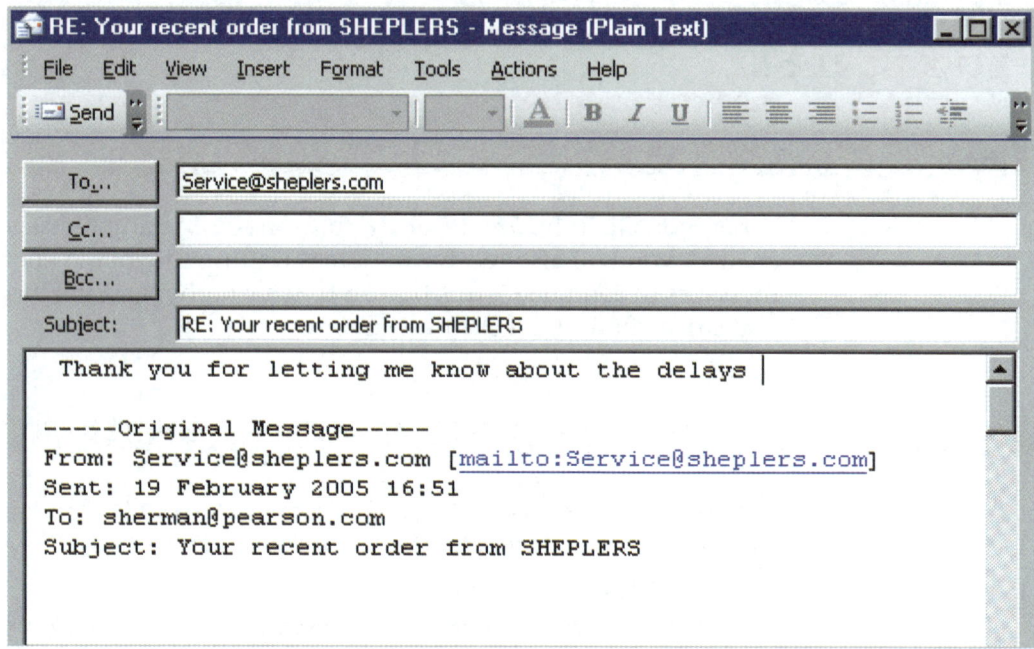

Reply to All

If there are several names in the *To:* or *Cc:* box, you can copy your reply to everyone by clicking **Reply to All** Reply to All . Clicking **Reply** will only send your reply to the original author of the message.

Forwarding an e-mail

If you receive a message that you want another person to read, forward it by clicking the **Forward** button Forward .

A new window will open containing the message text. The *Subject*: box will display the original subject text preceded by *Fw*:

Complete the *To*: box with the e-mail address of the new recipient and send the message as normal. If you are forwarding a message that had a file attached to it, this will be forwarded at the same time.

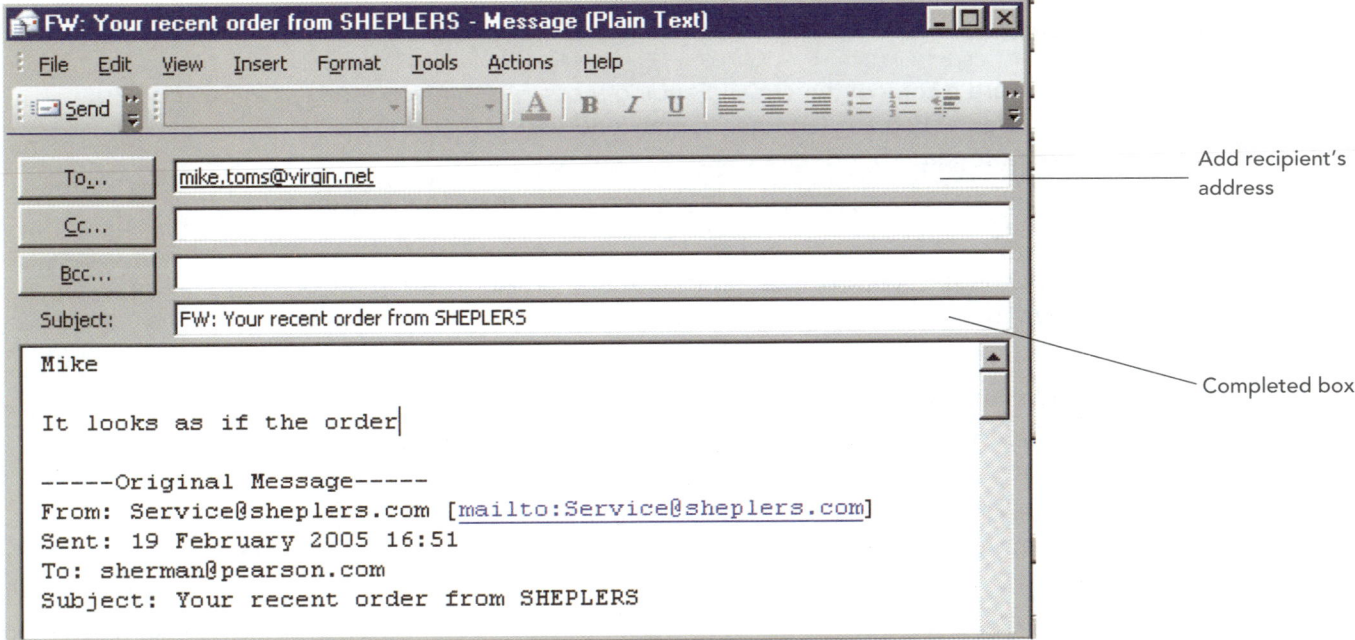

Add recipient's address

Completed box

Deleting an e-mail

To delete a closed message, click it when it is displayed in the *Inbox* and press the **Delete** key, or right-click and select **Delete**. The message will be moved to the *Deleted Items* folder. To remove it completely, right-click the folder or open the **Tools** menu and select **Empty "Deleted Items" Folder**.

Printing e-mails

To print a copy of an e-mail, including header details such as the subject,

date and who it is from, open the message and click the **Print** 🖨 button on the toolbar. Before printing, go to **File/Print Preview** to check that all the details are visible.

Common mistake

Using a computer that does not print parts of the e-mail that need to be displayed for New CLAIT assessment purposes – e.g. headers or attachments. If this is the case, you can use the *Print Screen* facility to provide evidence of what the e-mail looks like (explained in Unit 1).

1. Forward a copy of the e-mail *Sending messages* that you received in Exercise 2 to Sarah at Pearson (another dummy address). Her address is sarah@pearsoned-ema.com

2. Leave the message text but, at the top of the message, add the following:

   Sarah

   I thought you would want to see that I am practising using Outlook.

   (Your name)

3. Send the message.

4. Open your *Inbox* and print one copy of the message you received showing all header details.

5. Now delete this message and check that it has appeared in your *Deleted Items* folder.

Answer

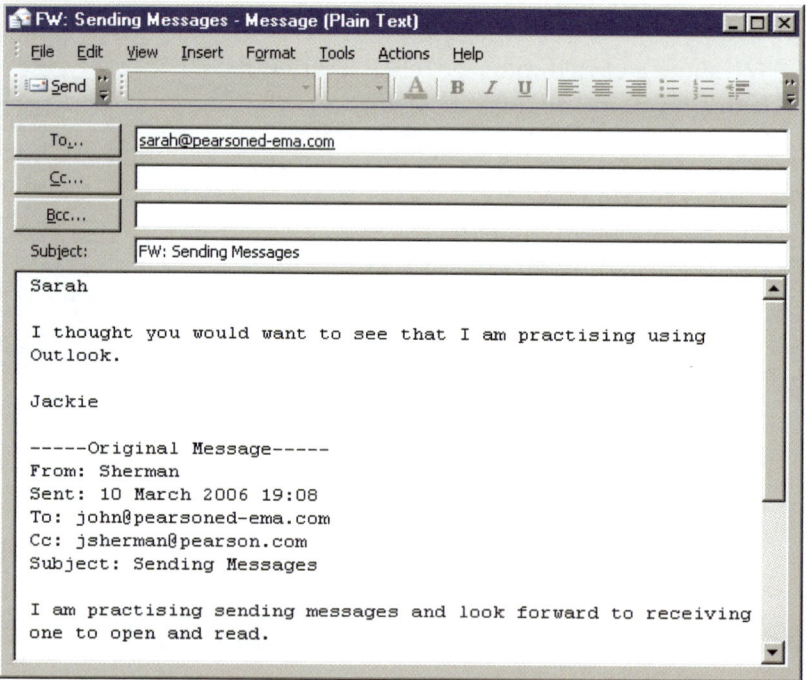

Attaching files to e-mails

A common reason for sending e-mails is to use the system to send photos, maps, reports etc. electronically. Any file saved on your computer or a disk can be attached and sent with an e-mail.

To attach a file, open a new message window and create a message. At any stage, click the **Attach** button or open the **Insert** menu and click **File**. This will open the *Insert File* window. Browse through your folders until you find the file you wish to attach and select it. Then click the **Insert** button or press **Enter**.

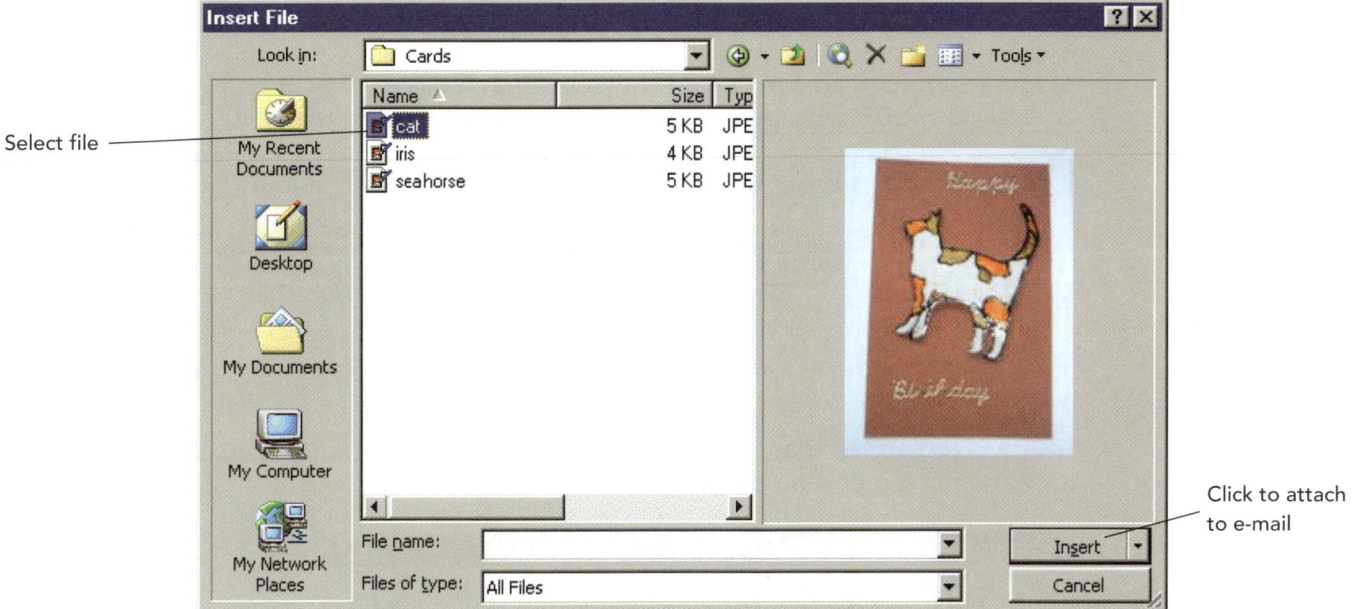

Select file

Click to attach to e-mail

Back in your message, the attached file will either be visible at the end of the message or displayed in a new window at the top of the message. Complete the message and send it as normal.

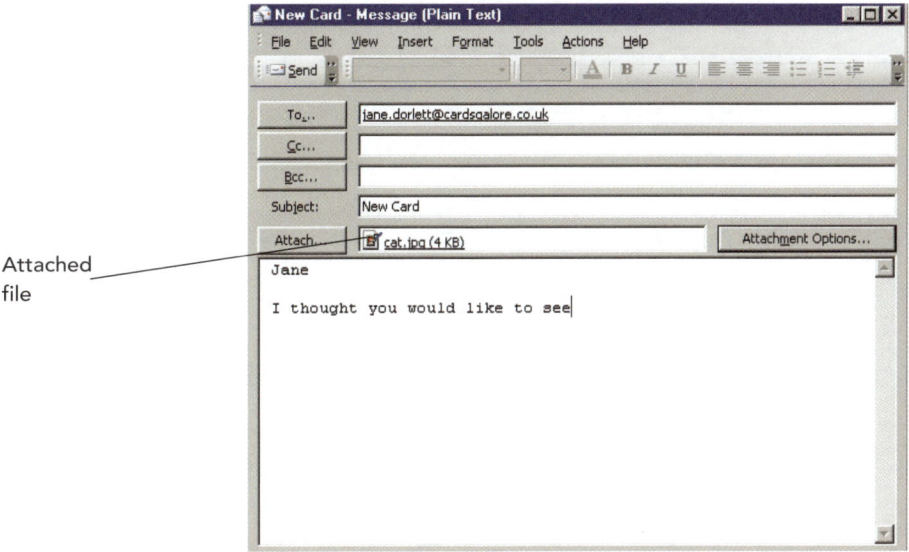

Attached file

FAILURE TO ATTACH A SPECIFIED FILE, OR ATTACHING THE WRONG FILE, IS A CRITICAL ERROR.

Exercise 4

1. Start a new message to be addressed to John at Pearson (`john@pearsoned-ema.com`), and copy it to yourself.
2. The subject of the message is `Attachments`.
3. Type the following message: `I am sending you a copy of one of the exercises I carried out for Unit 1.`
4. Add your name.
5. Now attach one of the files you have saved onto your computer.
6. Send the message with its attachment.

Opening attachments

When you receive an e-mail, you will know that it has an attachment because a *paperclip* symbol will appear next to the message details in the *Inbox*.

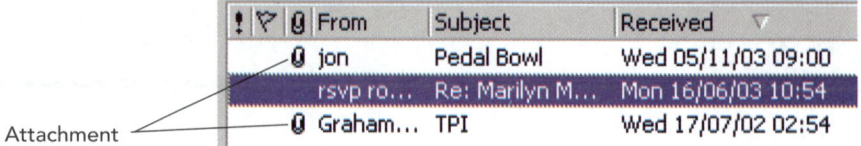

Attachment

Fully open the message and double-click the attachment file name if you want to view it.

You will be warned that attachments can contain viruses, and be advised to save the file rather than open it directly.

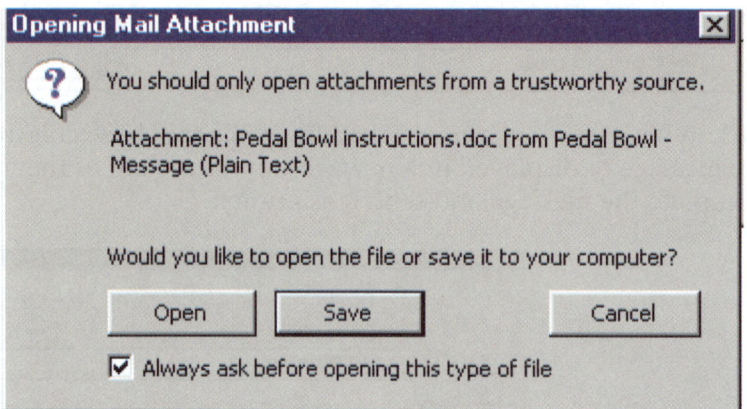

Saving attachments

Attachments are automatically saved into a temporary folder on your computer, but you may want to save them to a more accessible location.

There are two ways to save an attachment.

- *An attachment that you have opened on screen* – go to **File/Save As** and save the file with a suitable file name into a folder on your computer.

- *Messages with attachments that you have not opened* – select the message and go to **File/Save Attachments**.

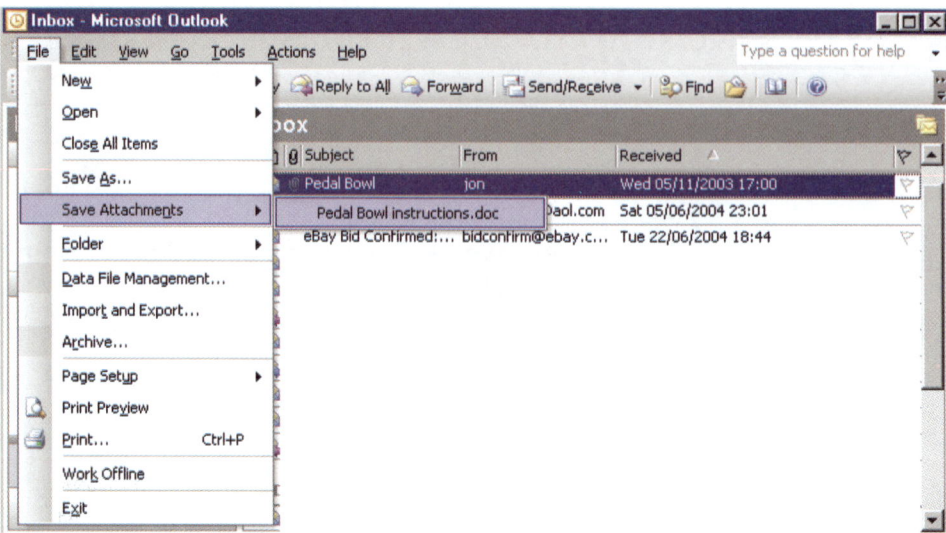

All the attached files will be listed. Click a file to open a *Save Attachments* box. Complete the location and file name boxes and click **OK**.

If there are several attachments, select **All Attachments** and click **OK** to save them all into the same folder, which you will need to select in the process that follows.

Printing attachments

You can open any attachment by double-clicking and then printing in the normal way by clicking the **Print** button.

Exercise 5

1. Check your *Inbox*.
2. When the message *Attachments* arrives, confirm that you can open and read the attachment and then close the file and the e-mail message.
3. Save the attachment to a new location, e.g. a floppy disk. If you try to save it to the original location, you may receive an error message saying there is already a file with the same name there. An alternative is to save it with a different name.
4. Delete the e-mail message.
5. Open the attachment you saved and print a copy.

Saving a draft e-mail

If you close your message instead of clicking **Send**, you will be asked whether you want to save it. If you click **Yes** it will be placed in the *Drafts* folder. Open the folder at any time to retrieve the message.

You can also save a message you are working on by going to **File/Save**.

Contacts (addresses)

It is a good idea to start saving details of all the people you write to in an electronic address book. In Outlook the address book is known as the *Contacts* folder.

To add a new e-mail address, click **Contacts** in the folder list and then click the **New** button to open a *New Contact* window.

Complete as many boxes as you want to, but you must include the full
name and e-mail address. Click **Save and Close** to save the entries.

Save changes

Complete
details

Complete
details

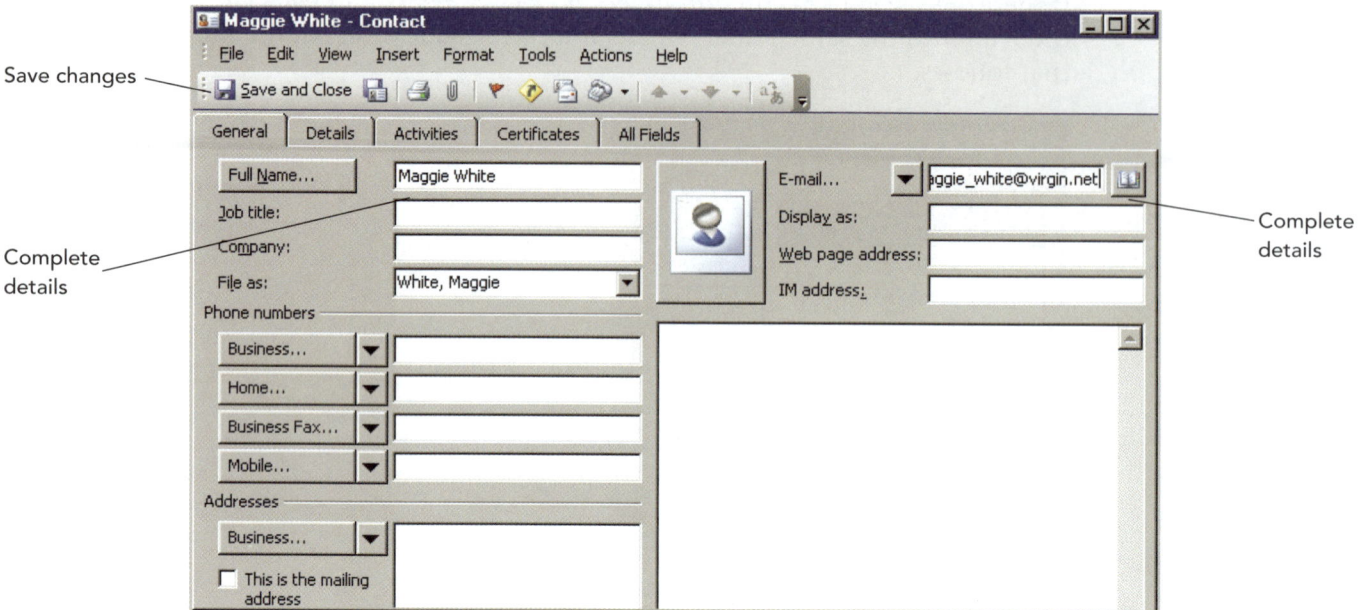

You can view your *Contacts* list by opening the folder. Select different ways
to view the details by opening the **View/Arrange By** menu and clicking
Current View. Select a view by clicking its name.

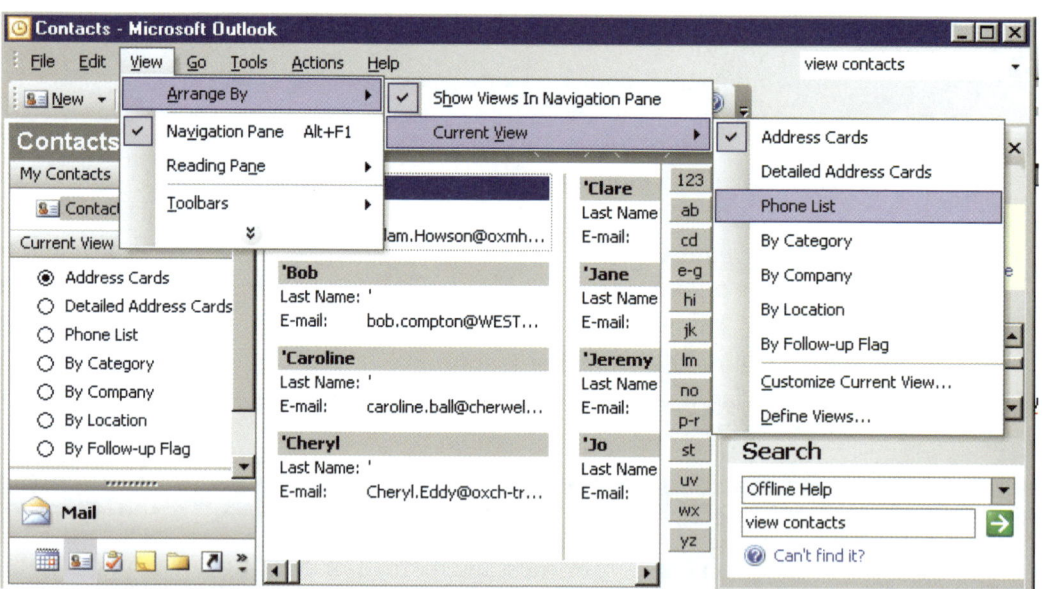

When viewed as a phone list, you
can add an address at the top of
the list directly on screen, or
double-click the entry box to
open the *New Contact* window.

Type here or
double-click for
the *New Contact*
window

For New CLAIT, you will be asked
to print out a copy of entries in
your *Contacts* folder. Either take a screen print (see Unit 1) or open an entry
fully and go to **File/Page Setup** and select a style. Click the **Header/Footer**
tab to add your personal information to the top or bottom of the printout

and then click **Print Preview**. Check that all details are visible before printing a copy.

Adding addresses automatically

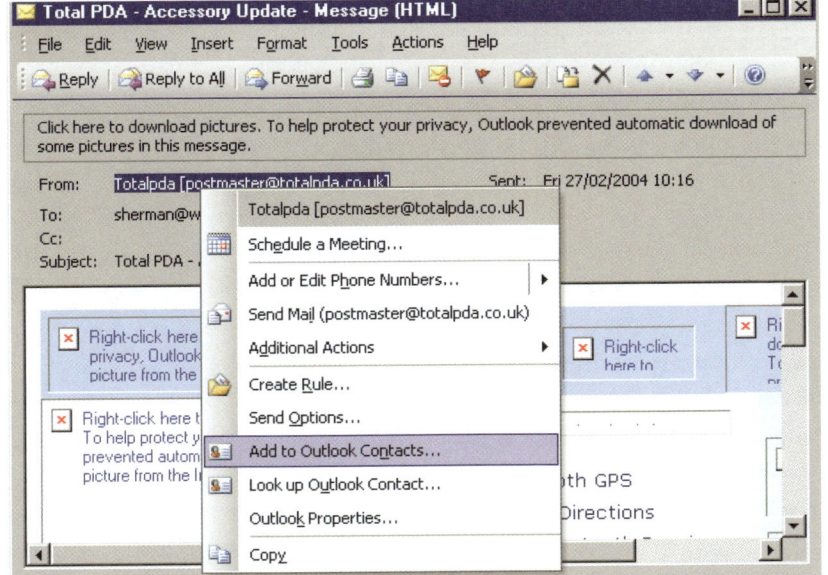

When you receive a message, you can add the sender's address to your list of contacts automatically. Right-click the address in the *From:* box and select **Add to Outlook Contacts**.

If you later want to add other details such as the postal address or telephone number, open *Contacts* and double-click the name of your new contact.

Retrieving a contact automatically

Once you have addresses in your *Contacts* folder, you can bring them into your messages by clicking the **To:** or **Cc:** box in your new message window.

This will open the *Contacts* list. Here you can select the name of any recipient and add it to the correct box by clicking the appropriate button. When all the names you want have been selected, click **OK** to return to your message.

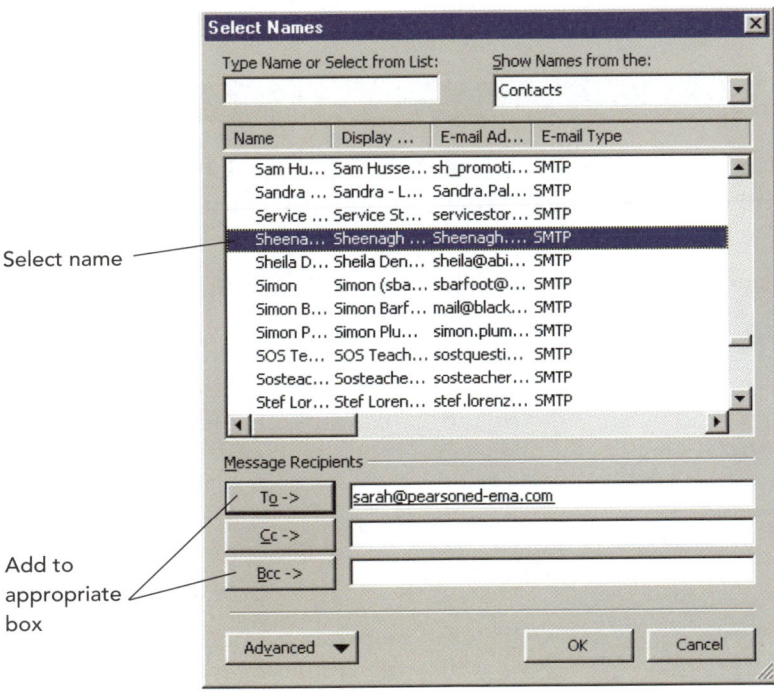

Select name

Add to appropriate box

Help

As with most MS Office applications, you can use the *Help* menu to find information or type a question into the *Ask a Question* box showing in the top right-hand corner of the screen. Press **Enter** to display shortcuts to help topics.

Exiting Outlook

Close Outlook by clicking the **Close** button in the top right-hand corner. If you have messages in your *Outbox*, you will be reminded that they have not been sent.

Exercise 6

1. Open your *Inbox* and find the welcome message from Microsoft or any message you have received (except responses from *pearsoned-ema*).
2. Add the address on the e-mail to your address book.
3. Now add John at Pearson's e-mail address to your address book. His full name is `John Murray` and his address is `john@pearsoned-ema.com`.
4. Create a new message to be sent to Microsoft, or the contact you have added to your address book. Copy this message to John. Add their e-mail addresses automatically to the *To*: and *Cc*: boxes from your *Contacts* folder.
5. Give the message the subject: `Thanks`
6. Type the following message: `I am sure I will enjoy using Outlook and will contact you if I have any problems.`
7. Add your name at the end of the message.
8. Select the option to save the message, so that it is moved to your *Drafts* folder.
9. Close Outlook.
10. Reopen Outlook, locate the saved message and delete it.
11. Check that it appears in your *Deleted items* folder.
12. Close Outlook.

The World Wide Web

The Internet is the name given to the networks of computers that are linked together and enable computer users to send and receive information electronically across the world.

One of the most important roles for the Internet is to allow you to view multimedia pages of text, images, sound and video. These pages are known as web pages and the millions of pages currently available make up the Word Wide Web (referred to as 'the Web'). Interrelated pages published on the Web by an individual organization are referred to as a *website*.

Opening a browser

To view a web page, you need some software known as a *browser*. Many different browsers are available, but one of the most common is Internet Explorer, provided by Microsoft. Windows machines that you buy often have this software pre-installed and so you may see a blue icon shortcut to Explorer on your desktop or the taskbar. You may also see an icon representing your ISP which, when double-clicked, will open into the browser window.

As soon as the browser opens, you will be offered a **dial-up** button to click if you are not already connected to the Internet, as you cannot browse through web pages without being online.

Browser window

The web page that is displayed each time you open your browser and connect is called your *homepage*. This may be the welcome page of your ISP's website or it may have been changed to a preferred starting point for a Web session. For pages to appear in your browser window you must be connected to the Internet – the pages are then downloaded onto your machine.

Toolbar buttons

Address (URL) accessed

Web page

Source: From the Pearson Education website, www.pearsoned.co.uk. Reproduced with permission.

There are seven toolbar buttons showing in the browser window that you will need to be able to use for New CLAIT.

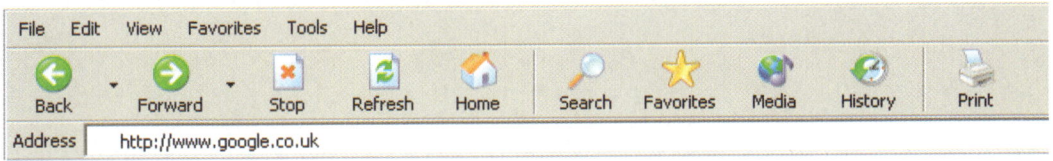

- *Back* – after you have visited a number of web pages, click this button to step back through the pages and return to one visited earlier.
- *Forward* – go forward to a page you have returned from.
- *Stop* – cancel the downloading of a page if it is taking too long.
- *Refresh* – reload the page – e.g. if the images are distorted.
- *Home* – return to your opening web page.
- *Favorites* – a list of shortcuts to pages that you have saved because you may want to revisit them.
- *Print* – print a copy of the web page shown on the screen.

Also note the *Address* box underneath the toolbar buttons as this is where you type the address (URL) of any web page you want to visit.

Hyperlinks

Web pages display a mixture of text and images. Good websites will also provide an index. To visit another page on the same website, or a page on a different site that covers relevant information, move the mouse pointer

over any element. Whenever it changes from an arrow to a hand 🖐 clicking the hand will open a related page.

This is because the hand appears when you are over an embedded link – a *hyperlink* – to a new page. This link is written into the page in HTML code and is recognized by the browser software. Hyperlinks may be images, labelled buttons or text, which is often underlined and/or a different colour. Sometimes, a small pop-up window will appear showing what the linked page will offer.

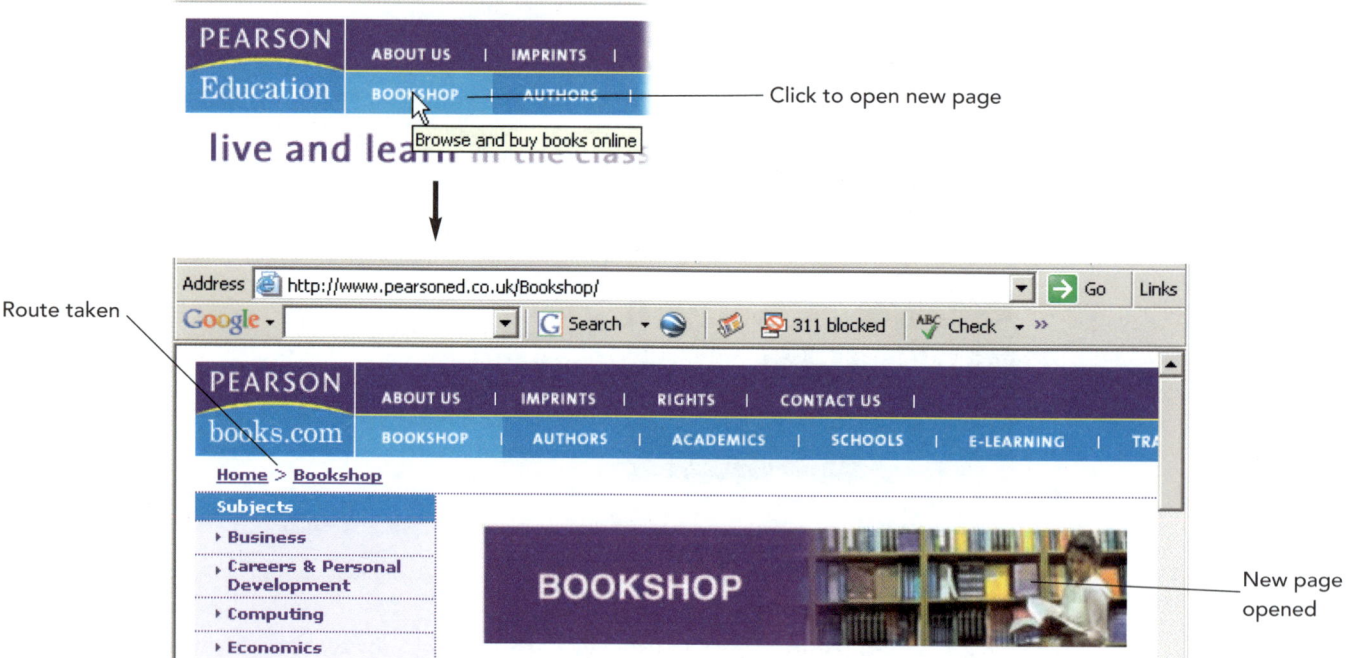

Source: From the Pearson Education website, www.pearsoned.co.uk. Reproduced with permission.

Every page on the Web has its own unique address or URL (Uniform Resource Locator). To visit a website quite unrelated to that of your home page, you will need to type the address in the *Address* box and then press **Enter** or click the button labelled **Go**.

Each address has a standardized format and you *must* be accurate with spelling and punctuation:

- www. – pages on the Web
- name – [e.g. pearsoned, microsoft, bristol, rspb, derbyshire]
- type of organization – these will usually follow the convention:
  - .co.uk for a British company
  - .com for an international company
  - .org.uk for a charity or public body
  - .gov.uk for a local or national government
  - .ac.uk for an academic institution.

Full Internet addresses might therefore be:

- www.pearsoned.co.uk (Pearson Education)
- www.microsoft.com (Microsoft)
- www.bristol.ac.uk (Bristol University)
- www.rspb.org.uk (Royal Society for the Protection of Birds)
- www.derbyshire.gov.uk (Derbyshire local authority).

When typing an address into the *Address* box, you won't need to enter `http://` but this will appear automatically to show that the page follows the hypertext protocol or convention used for most web pages. You can type an address in either upper or lower case.

Sometimes the URL will display entries separated by a forward slash /. This shows the subfolders and final page details of any individual web page stored on the website at any one time – for example www.bbc.co.uk/lifestyle/newyear/calendar.shtml is the URL for a desktop calendar provided by the BBC on lifestyle programmes in the new year.

Exercise 7

1. Open your browser and, if necessary, connect to the Internet.
2. You need to find out the Latin name for a common garden bird.
3. Visit the website for the Royal Society for the Protection of Birds. Their URL is `www.rspb.org.uk`.
4. On the site, click the button labelled **Birds**.
5. Now click **A to Z of UK Birds**. Use the alphabet to select **R**, scroll down and open the page on the **robin**.
6. Make a note of its Latin name.
7. Close your browser.

Erithacus rubecula

Searching web pages

Index

Information on a particular topic is often available only from a specific website. For example, the opening hours of the British Museum would clearly be found most easily by visiting the museum's own website and using the index of links provided.

Click Visit in the index to link to the page offering details of the opening hours

Search engines

However, information on a vast range of subjects – from growing cacti to the names of all of Shakespeare's plays – could be almost anywhere. To find the answers, you need to visit a website aimed specifically at helping people to locate information on the Web. Such sites are known as *search engines*.

Many search engines are available, and people have their own favourites, but some of the most popular include:

- www.google.co.uk
- www.yahoo.co.uk
- www.altavista.com
- www.lycos.com

These sites provide a box – the *search* or *query* box – in which you enter brief details about the information you are seeking. Some sites will also offer a directory search, through categories of grouped websites.

Keywords

It is important to take care when entering words or phrases into the search box. These words, known as *keywords*, will be used by the search engine to locate any web pages containing the same text. The more specific the keywords, the fewer and more relevant the results are likely to be.

Methods for limiting the length of the search list include:

- clicking the UK checkbox or adding UK to the list of keywords to restrict the results to British sites
- putting "quote marks" round words to search for a specific phrase
- using AND or + to display web pages that must include particular words or phrases, or NOT or − to exclude web pages that contain particular words or phrases.

Source: Google (www.google.com).

Start the search by clicking the **Search** button or pressing **Enter**.

When the results of the search are displayed, scroll down through the list and open any pages that look as if they will provide the information you are seeking. To open a page, click the blue underlined title. You can now scroll through the page or use any on-screen search boxes or index to find the information.

Return to the list by clicking the **Back** toolbar button.

Keywords

Google™

Web | Images | Groups | News | Froogle | Scholar | **more »**

Candle making kits | Search | Advanced Search
Preferences

Search: ○ the web ○ pages from the UK

Number of relevant sites found

Web

Results **1 - 10** of about **176,000 English** pages

Candle Making Supplies
www.RusticEscentuals.com   Molds, Wax, Fragrance Oil & More! Wholesale Prices

Sponsored Link

Candle Kits
Candle Making Kits are the very best way to learn. All our **kits** contain everything you need to get started and **make** your first **candle**.
www.**candle**makers.co.uk/cmproduct/**candlekits**.html - 22k - Cached - Similar pages

Click title to visit a site

Candle Making Supplies
Candle Waxes. **Candle Kits**. Wax Additives. **Candle** Dyes. **Candle** Wicks. **Candle** Lacquers and paints. Applique Wax Sheets. **Candlemaking** Sundries. **Candle** Perfumes ...
www.**candle**makers.co.uk/cmproduct/cmsframe.html - 5k - Cached - Similar pages

Craft Fair Suppliers of **Candle Making**
Trade supplies: plaque craft, silk painting, **candle making**, glass painting and frame decorating **kits**. *, Poth Hille, London, 020 8534 7091 ...
www.craft-fair.co.uk/suppliers.cfm?SubCatno=144 - 22k - Cached - Similar pages

The Essential Survival Guide to **Candlemaking** ~ LINKS PAGE!!
Rocky Mountain **Candle** - **Candlemaking** supplies Loveland, Colorado ... Amazing Gel **Candle** Embeds CA - Glass embeds, **kits**, scents and wicks ...
www.**candlemaking**.org.uk/greatpages.html - 36k - Cached - Similar pages

Source: Google (www.google.com).

FAILURE TO LOCATE THE CORRECT PAGE IS A CRITICAL ERROR.

Common mistake

Not finding the requested information. This is either because you used a poor keyword search or you did not take enough care when reading the instructions.

Printing web pages

Common mistake

Printing the search list rather than the correct web page.

To print a web page that is open on screen, click the **Print** button. If the *Print* dialogue box opens, check that you are printing the correct pages and then click **OK**.

FAILURE TO PRINT THE CORRECT PAGE IS A CRITICAL ERROR.

Exercise 8

1. You need to find out whether any colleges in Sussex offer electronics A level courses.

2. Go to a search engine, such as `www.google.co.uk`, and type an appropriate phrase into the search box.

3. Open the page for any college that offers the course.

4. Find a page on the website that provides a description of the course and print a copy of the page.

5. Close the browser window and, if necessary, disconnect from the Internet.

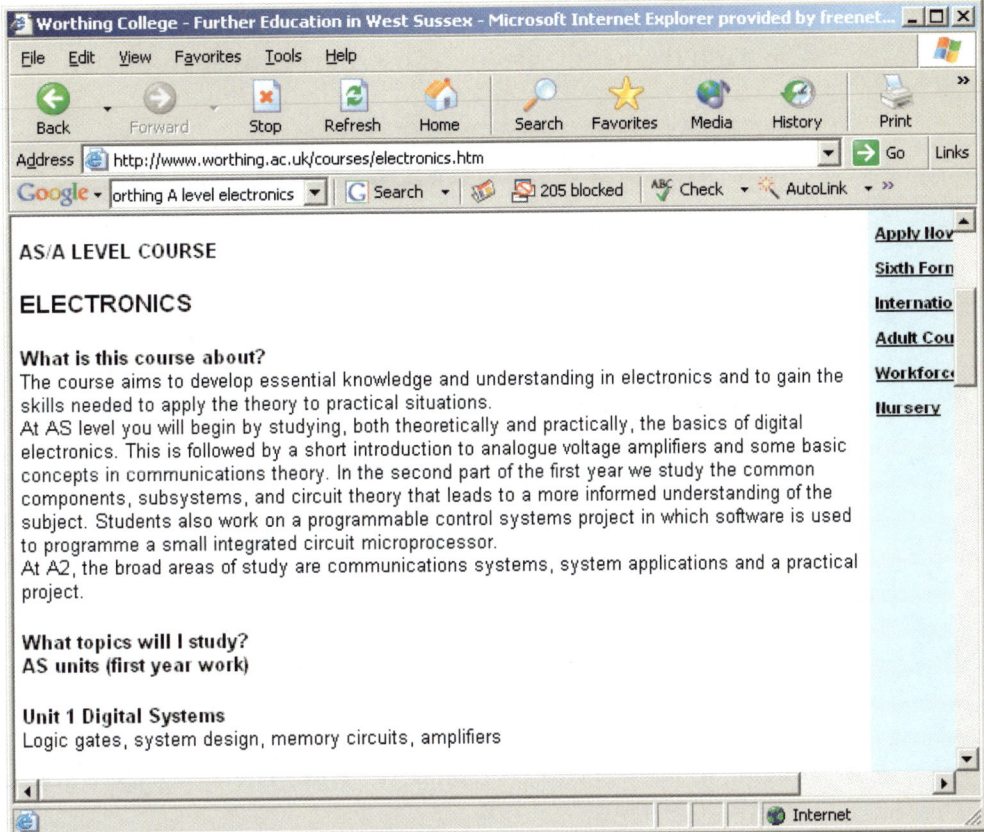

Source: From the Worthing College website (www.worthing.ac.uk).

Bookmarking web pages

Having discovered a web page that you might like to revisit during a future Internet session, you can save a link to the page in a special folder referred to as *Favorites*. The process is known as *bookmarking*.

For New CLAIT, you need only add the page URL to the bottom of a list of favourite pages, but you could create subfolders within the *Favorites* folder to group links that have a common theme.

1. With the web page open on screen, click the **Favorites** toolbar button or open the **Favorites** menu and click **Add**.

Click to add URL

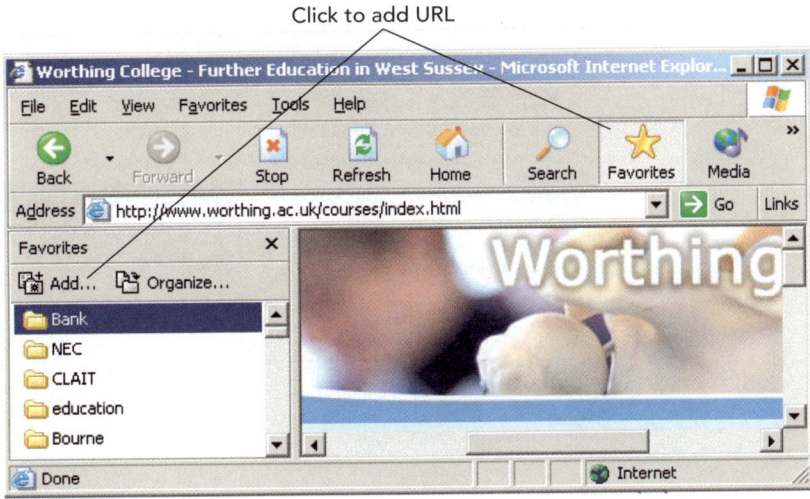

Source: From the Worthing College website (www.worthing.ac.uk). Reproduced by permission.

2. You will be offered a box in which to amend the page name if it is too long, and to select an appropriate folder in which to store the link. If the folders are not visible, click the button labelled **Create in <<**, and create a new folder if there isn't one in the list that seems appropriate.

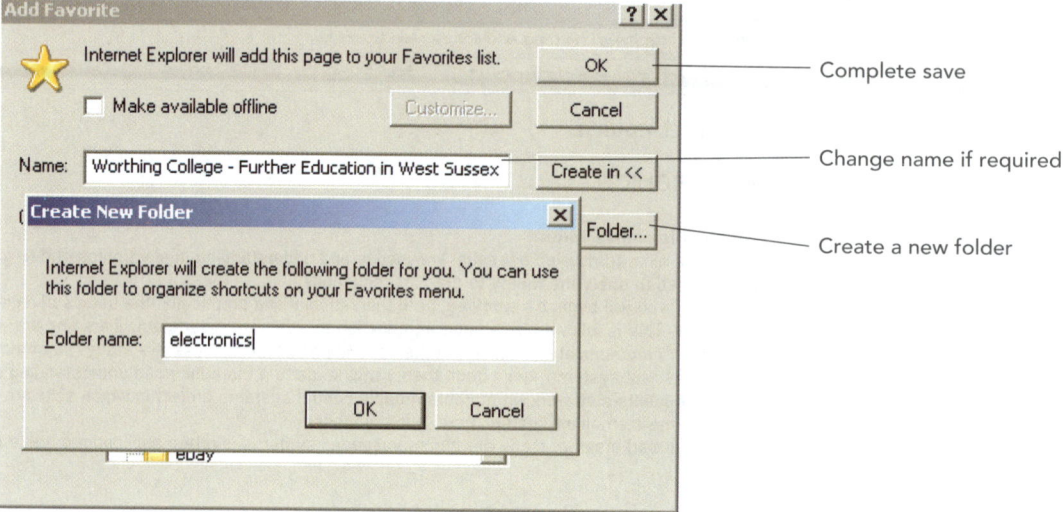

3. With the correct folder selected, click **OK**.

4. Next time you want to open the page, open **Favorites**, click the folder name to open it and then click the URL. The web page will immediately open on screen.

5. If you want a quick method for bookmarking a page, hold **Ctrl** and press the letter **D**. This will add the URL of the current page to the bottom of the folders list.

6. To tidy up your favourites, open the **Favorites** menu, click the **Organize** button and use the options to move, delete or rename URLs.

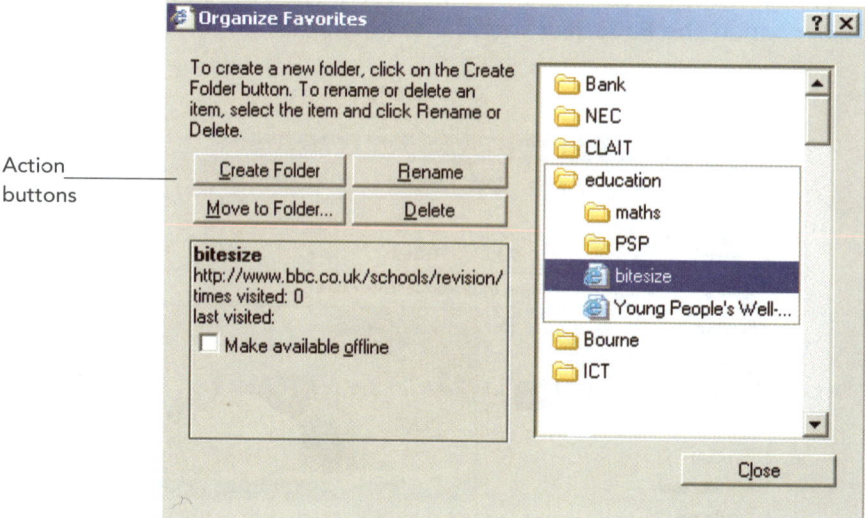

Saving from the Web

Web pages

To save a web page, click the **Save** button and follow the normal save procedures. The text and images will be saved together in web page format unless you choose, for example, to save the text content only.

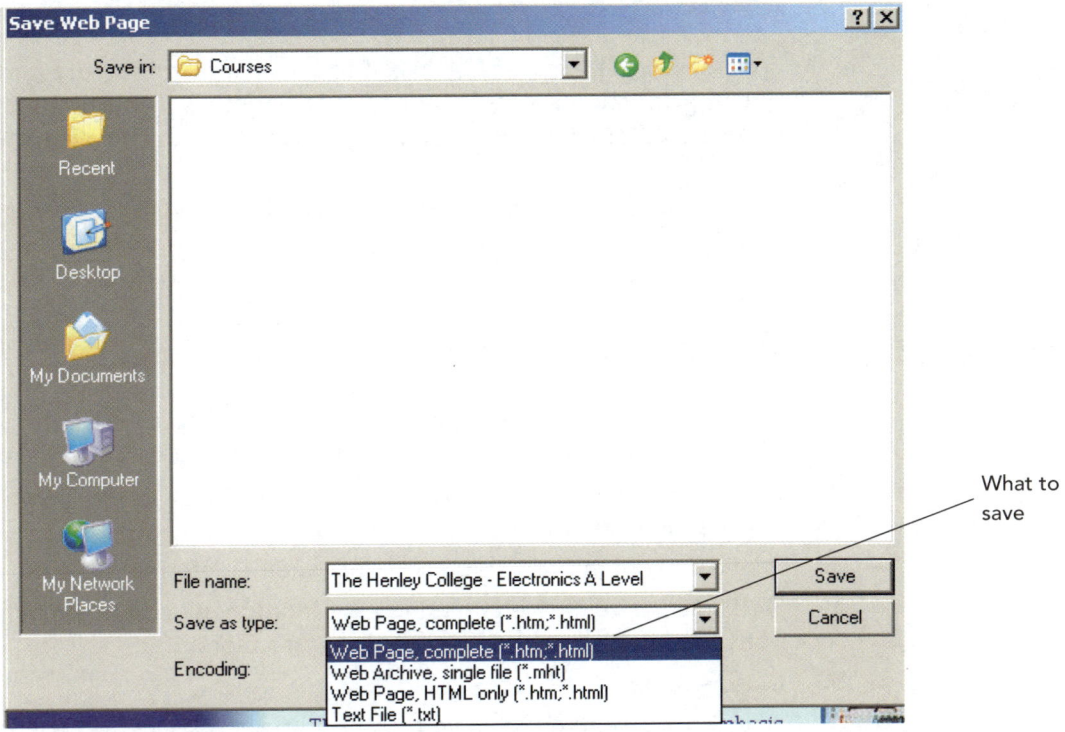

What to save

Images

Images on the Web are files in their own right, and so they can be saved separately. Do this by right-clicking any picture and selecting **Save Picture As**. You may also be offered a short toolbar that includes a *Save* option.

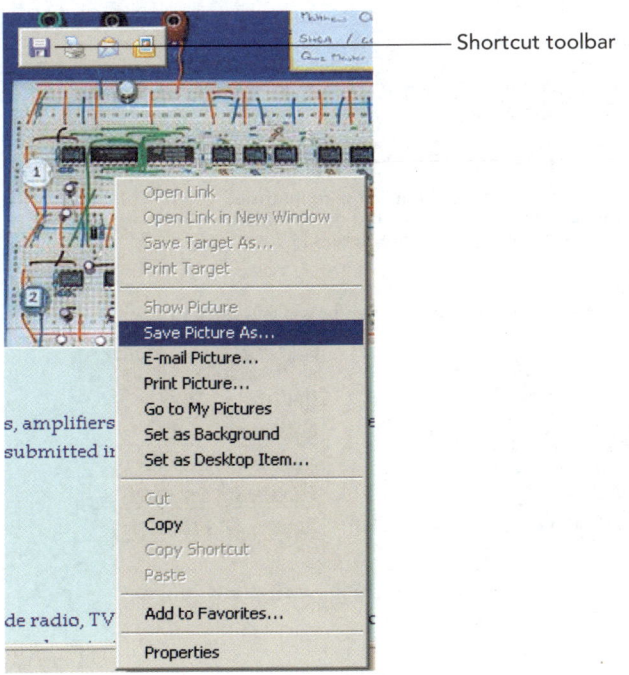

Shortcut toolbar

When the *Save Picture* dialogue box opens, find an appropriate location for the file, change the file name if it is not clear and click **Save**. Web images are usually in either *jpeg* or *gif* format, which keeps them compressed but visible on a web page, so leave the file type as it appears.

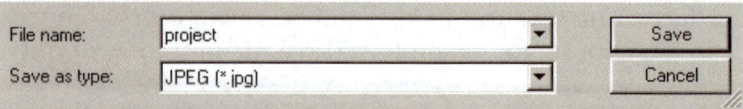

For New CLAIT, you will be asked to locate a saved picture and take a screen print showing its location and file details. For guidance on how to do this see Unit 1. If necessary, select **Details** from the *View* menu.

FAILURE TO SAVE THE SPECIFIED IMAGE FROM A WEB PAGE IN THE FORMAT REQUIRED IS A CRITICAL ERROR.

Exercise 9

1. Open your browser and use a search engine to find a web page that provides UK weather information. The page must contain at least one image.

2. Bookmark the page. If you want to, store the URL in a new *Favorites* folder labelled `Weather`.

3. Print a copy of the web page showing weather information.

4. Find any picture on the page and save it onto your computer with the file name `weatherpic`. It must be in either *jpeg* or *gif* format.

5. Close your browser.

6. Find the file *weatherpic* on your computer and take a screen print showing its location and file type.

7. Add your name to the screen print as a header and print a copy.

Answer Step 3

Met office homepage

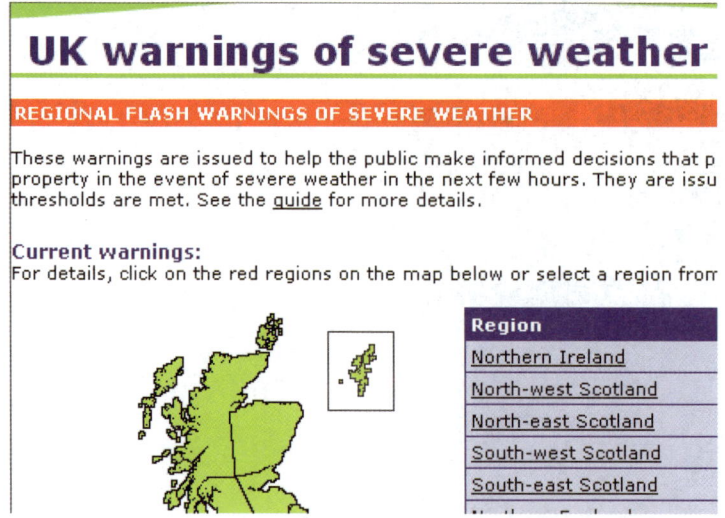

Source: From the Met Office website (www.metoffice.gov.uk). © Crown copyright 2006. Published by the Met Office. Reproduced with permission.

Image file

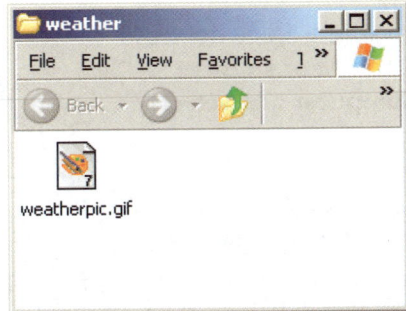

weatherpic.gif

Reading pages offline

In some organizations, or at home if you do not have broadband, you may prefer to work offline as much as possible to cut down on connection charges. However, if you close the browser window, you will lose the page that was on screen.

To keep the page open offline, look for a flashing computer icon in the bottom right-hand corner of the screen ![icon]. Double-click this and then click the **Disconnect** button in the dialogue box. The page will remain open for you to read until you close the browser.

Netiquette

This is the name used to describe your behaviour when working online and communicating with others electronically. These rules are taken from the book *Netiquette* by Virginia Shea but many websites will provide their own advice.

- Rule 1: Remember the human
- Rule 2: Adhere to the same standards of behaviour online that you follow in real life
- Rule 3: Know where you are in cyberspace
- Rule 4: Respect other people's time and bandwidth
- Rule 5: Make yourself look good online
- Rule 6: Share expert knowledge
- Rule 7: Help keep flame wars (i.e. emotional outbursts) under control
- Rule 8: Respect other people's privacy
- Rule 9: Don't abuse your power
- Rule 10: Be forgiving of other people's mistakes.

Viruses

It will probably not be possible to virus check your whole machine if you are at work or study in a college, but you need to be aware that software provided by companies such as Sophos, McAfee, Norton and Grisoft is available to install on your computer. It will check Internet files, floppy disks and e-mails for malicious programs. Where you are responsible for the antivirus software, you should go online every few days and download the latest version as viruses are being written continuously.

If you can, hover over the icon for your virus checker displayed on the taskbar, or double-click it to view more details.

You could also check any removable storage devices your computer has. Right-click the **A:** or **D:** drive showing when you open **My Computer** and select **Scan for viruses**.

Device to be checked

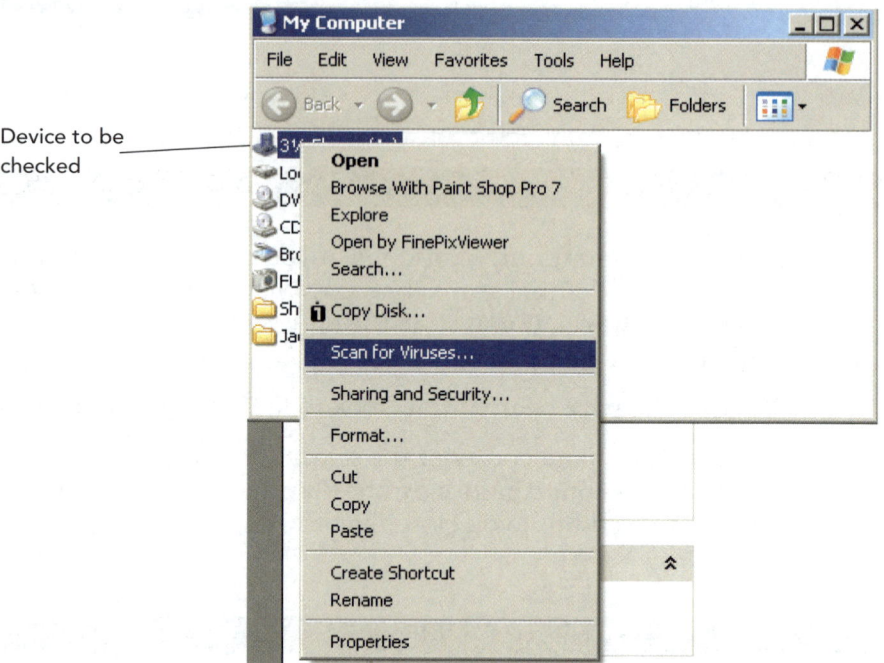

Exercise 10 – a full assignment

1. Log on to your e-mail system and open your *Inbox*.

2. Before carrying out the main tasks, create a message to go to Sarah at Pearson (sarah@pearsoned-ema.com).

3. Make sure you send a copy of the message to yourself.

4. The subject of the message is Kitchens.

5. Add the following message text:

   Sarah

   I have been searching for useful web pages that will tell me how to design my new kitchen. I have found several ideas and thought you might like to see a picture of one I like.

   (Your name)

6. Attach the image file *kitchen.gif* from the CD. If you can, attach it directly from the CD so that it is not saved on your computer.

7. Send the message.

Task 1

1. When the copy of the e-mail arrives in your *Inbox*, open the message.

2. Make a note of the name of the virus scanning software on your computer, which should be set to scan e-mail attachments.

3. Save the e-mail attachment *kitchen.gif* outside your mailbox in your working area.

4. Use the *Reply* facility to reply to the sender of the message *Kitchens*.

5. Enter the following message text:

   ```
   Thank you for sending the picture which I will keep for
   information.
   ```

6. Add your name under this sentence.

7. Check your message for errors.

8. Check that your e-mail system will save your *Sent* message(s).

9. Send the reply.

10. Close the reply message if it does not close automatically.

Task 2

1. Use the *Forward* facility to forward the original message *Kitchens* and its attachment to: john@pearsoned-ema.com

2. Do not change anything in the original message *Kitchens*.

3. Add the following message text:

   ```
   Sarah sent this and I thought you might like to see it too.
   ```

4. Add your name under this sentence.

5. Check that the attachment *kitchen.gif* is correctly attached to the message.

6. Check your message and correct any errors.

7. Check that your e-mail system will save your *Sent* message(s).

8. Send the message and its attachment.

9. Delete the message titled *Kitchens* from your *Inbox*.

10. Take a screen print of your *Inbox*. Add your name as a header and print one copy.

Task 3

1. Store the following details in your e-mail address book:

   Name/Title: Sarah Smith

   E-mail address: sarah@pearsoned-ema.com

2. Produce a printout of this entry from your address book.

3. Make sure your name is clearly displayed on this printout.

4. Create a new e-mail message to *Sarah* using the stored address from your address book.

5. Use the *Copy (cc:)* facility to make sure a copy of this message will be sent to: yasmin@pearsoned-ema.com

6. Enter the message subject Bathrooms

7. Enter the following message text:

   ```
   Attached is the file you requested.
   ```

8. Add your name under this sentence.

9. Attach the file *bath.jpg* from the CD.

10. Check your message and correct any errors.

11. Check that your e-mail system will save your *Sent* message(s).

12. Send the message and its attachment.

13. Locate the e-mail messages you have sent and print a copy of each. Make sure that header details (*To, From, Date* and *Subject*) and all the message text is clearly printed.

14. On the prints of the forwarded message and the new message, make sure there is clear evidence of the correct attachments.

15. Log out of your mailbox and exit the software securely.

1. Open your browser.

2. You are going to visit the *BBC Homes* pages to find a picture of bathrooms.

3. Go to **www.bbc.co.uk** and use the *A–Z Index* to locate the *Homes* and then *Design* pages. Alternatively you could search for *bathrooms* on the BBC website.

4. Look at some of the pages on bathrooms and find one with a picture of a bathroom.

5. Save a picture of a bathroom onto your computer in *jpeg* or *gif* format.

6. Name the picture `bathroom1`.

7. Save the web page in your Favorites folder.

8. Print the entire page.

9. Now use a web-based search engine to locate web pages other than those on the BBC website that provide information on bathroom design.

10. Bookmark one page.

11. Print just the first page.

12. Exit the web browser securely.

13. Access your working area.

14. Take a screen print of your working area, making sure that file details for the saved image files *kitchen* and *bathroom1* are clearly visible.

15. On your screen print enter your name and the name of your virus scanning software.

16. Print the screen print.

17. Check all your printouts for accuracy.

Answers

Task 3 Step 2

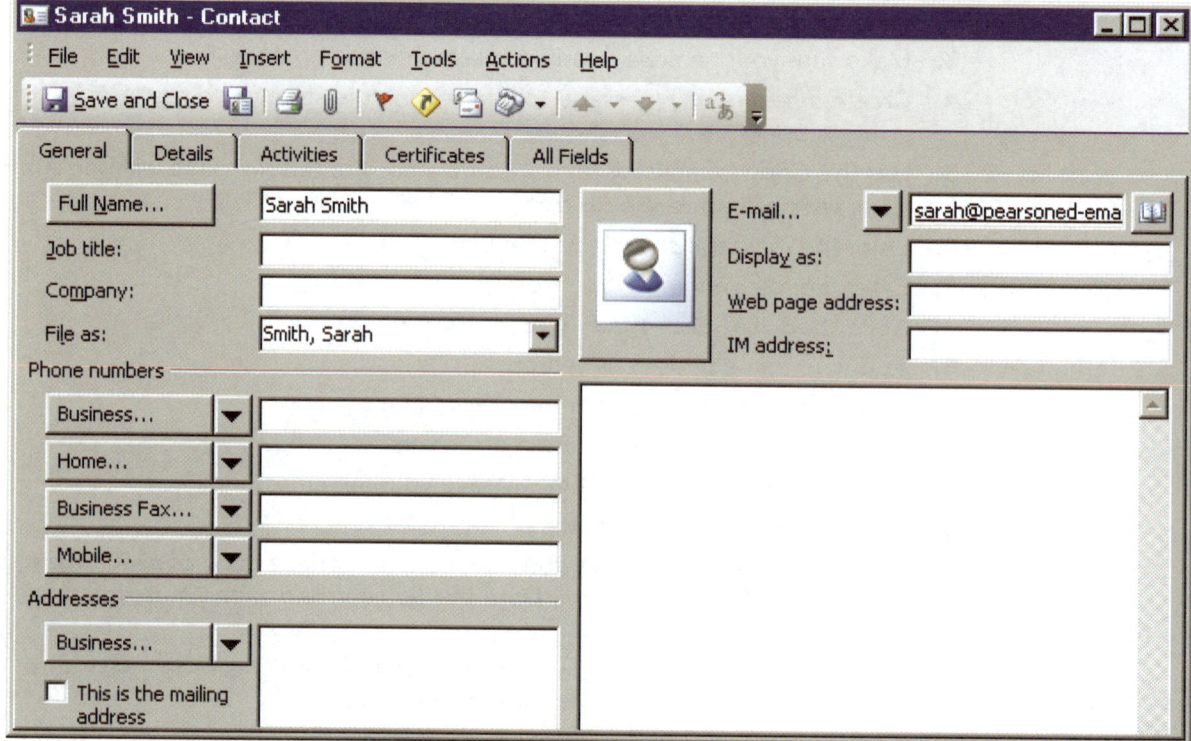

Task 3 Step 13 Sample printout

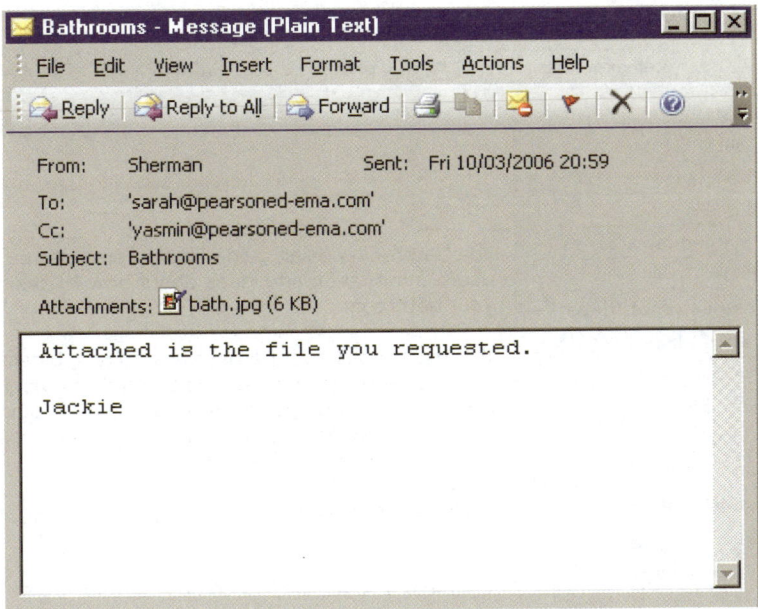

Task 4 Step 7

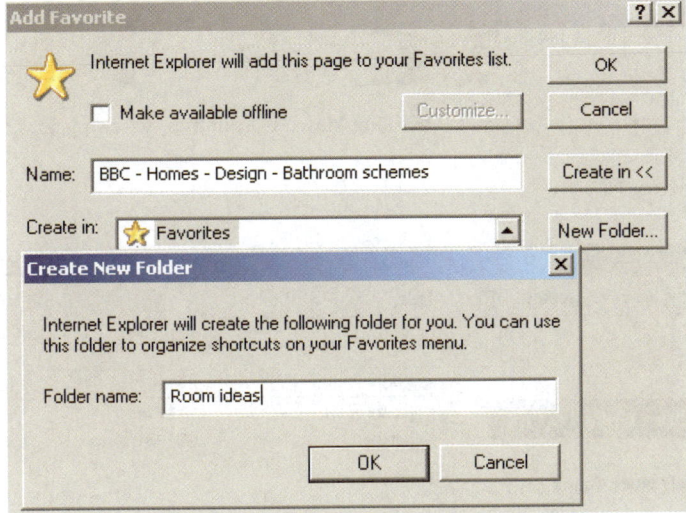

Task 4 Step 11 Sample printout

Source: *The Bathroom Design Guide.* Thanking Masco Corporation (www.masco.com) for its contribution.

Task 4 Step 14

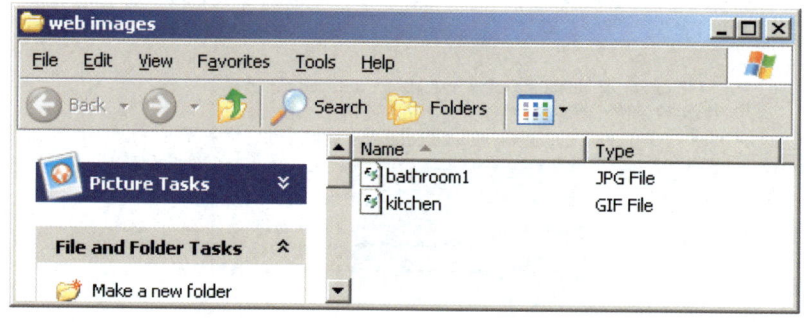

Self-assessment checklist

I feel confident that I can now: ✓

Open an e-mail system

Open and read messages

Send an e-mail

Copy an e-mail

Forward an e-mail

Print an e-mail displaying header details

Delete an e-mail

Open an attachment

Save an attachment to my computer

Attach a file to an e-mail

Add an address to an address book/contacts list

Retrieve an e-mail address from an address book

Open a browser

Go directly to a web page using its URL

Use a search engine

Bookmark a web page

Use a local search facility on a web page

Save a web image

Exit e-mail and browser applications

Summary of critical errors

- An incorrect, inaccurate or omitted e-mail address
- A missing or incorrect attachment
- Failure to locate and print web page(s) containing the required information
- Failure to save an image from a web page in the specified format

access Find and open a web page

active cell The cell showing a black border in which any data will appear as you type

active window When more than one window is open at the same time, this shows a blue title bar and is the one in which you can work

alignment The position of image, text or numbers on the horizontal (usually) or vertical axis on a page or within a cell

application (software) A computer program that is designed to help you carry out specific tasks – e.g. word processing or desktop publishing

AutoShape A toolbar button that can be activated to draw a specific shape on the page

bitmap image A graphic (picture) created when using software such as Microsoft Paint – made up of hundreds of coloured dots known as pixels

bookmark A link to a specific web page on your computer in a folder known as *Favorites* in Internet Explorer

browse The act of searching through files on the computer or pages on the Web

browser Software that allows you to view web pages on the Internet

cell An individual square on a spreadsheet or in a table

chart A visual display of numerical information – common chart types include column, pie and line

click Press down the left mouse button when the pointer is over a menu, toolbar button or page entry to give instructions

clipboard Part of the computer memory used to store text or images temporarily before they are copied or moved

composite copy A printout where all the colours in a desktop publication print on the same page

criteria The basis for searching a database

crop Cut off unwanted parts of an image

cursor Black flashing bar showing the position for text or number insertion

database An organized body of related information that can be sorted and searched

data type A standard form of data, e.g. text, currency or number – data typing provides a way to define the behaviour of data

default Settings for your work or equipment – e.g. page margins or the number of copies to be printed – that are selected automatically but which can be changed if preferred

demote text Move text on a presentation slide down to a lower level

desktop The opening screen viewed after loading a computer's operating system

desktop publishing Using a computer to assemble type and graphics and design page layouts before printing – abbreviated to DTP

dialogue box A small window that opens via a menu offering choices from drop-down lists, buttons or checkboxes

domain name Part of a web address displaying an organization's registered name, location and type of business – e.g. *pearsoned.co.uk*

download Access and view a web page on your computer

e-mail Messages sent electronically from one computer to another

expression A group of symbols that make a mathematical statement – e.g. *>10* means *greater than 10*

fields Searchable items in a database – field names are the headings under which fields are stored, e.g. colour, price, size etc.

file The combination of text and images created when working at your computer that can be named and saved – files created using different applications have common names, e.g. word processed *documents* or spreadsheet *workbooks*

file extension The code used to indicate which type of file has been saved

floppy disk Removable file storage disk that can hold around 1.4 Mb data and is referred to within the computer as $3\frac{1}{2}$" Floppy A:

folder A named area on a disk that can be used to group related files

font A specific style of type – e.g. Arial, `Courier` or Times New Roman

footer Information that appears at the bottom of every page in the margin area – e.g. page number or date

format Change the appearance of text, numbers or whole documents

formula Instructions typed into a cell that will result in a calculation being performed

function Predefined formula that performs calculations by using specific values, called arguments – e.g. the *SUM* function will total entries in a column or range of figures

function key A key at the top of the keyboard that does not correspond to any character but carries out a particular task – e.g. *F1* opens the *Help* menu

gif file Compressed image files containing up to 256 colours – a common file type for drawings on the Web

hard disk Main storage area for programs and files in a computer

header information that appears at the top of every page in the margin area – e.g. page number or date

HTML HyperText Markup Language – the code used to write web pages

hyperlink Code embedded in a web page that, when clicked with the mouse, opens a new page or e-mail message window

icon Pictures representing programs or files, or that help identify the function of toolbar buttons

indent Move text in from the margin

integer Whole number

Internet Networks linking millions of computers around the world

ISP Internet Service Provider – an organization that provides the facilities enabling you to use the Internet to find information, and to send and receive e-mails

jpeg file Image file that is compressed in size but displays in full colour – a common file type for photos on the Web

justify Align text and add spaces so that left and right margins are straight

keyword Word(s) used to search a database or the Internet – keyword searches locate results by exactly matching the search word(s)

landscape Paper orientation where the longest sides are top and bottom

legend The key on a chart that identifies the data series

log in (or log on) To perform a sequence of actions at a computer that establishes a user's identity and sets up default characteristics for the session

maximize Expand a window so that it fills the screen

menu Choice of options related to one activity – e.g. an *Insert* menu offers the option to insert dates, page numbers, symbols or pictures

minimize Keeping a file or program open, but out of the way, as a button on the task bar

netiquette Expected behaviour when communicating online

overtyping Pressing the *Insert* key causes typing to replace text on the page rather than insert it between entries – return to insert mode by pressing the key again

password A unique string of characters that a user types as an identification code to restrict access to computers and sensitive files

placeholder Shortcut on a presentation slide to text entry or programs offering the opportunity to create charts, images or other objects

portrait Paper orientation where the shortest sides are top and bottom

preview View a page before printing or check an image or template before use

primary key A column or columns that uniquely identifies a row in a table

program Computer instructions – often used to denote a particular application

promote text Move text on a presentation slide up to a higher level

query Object within a database that is designed to search for specific records

raster image Image made up of dots of colour known as pixels

record All the fields for any one item in a database

resolution The spacing of pixels in an image – it is measured in pixels per inch, ppi (or dots per inch, dpi) and, as the number is fixed, increasing the size of an image decreases its resolution and the image sharpness

restore down Reduce the size of a window to one that allows the desktop or other open windows to be viewed at the same time – in this mode, a window can be moved or resized

right-click Clicking the right mouse button over a screen item to display a relevant menu of options

scale The range from minimum to maximum values for the *y*-axis of a chart

scroll Move up or down a page by clicking the appropriate arrow in the scrollbar or dragging the grey box up or down

search engine A website holding a vast database of web pages that you can search using keywords

select (highlight) Identify those specific items on the screen that will be amended when actions such as formatting or deleting are carried out – selected items usually take on a different colour or are highlighted

server A computer on a network that is dedicated to a particular purpose and which stores all the information and performs the critical functions for that purpose – examples include mail, file and Web servers

shut down procedure The steps followed to shut down a computer correctly

sizing handles Boxes round the edge of selected objects – when the pointer is positioned on a sizing handle, it changes shape to indicate the direction in which the object will be resized

software Instructions in the form of programs – may control the computer (systems software) or carry out specific tasks (applications software)

sort Reorder records or lists – e.g. alphabetically or in descending order of size

spreadsheet The collection of text and numerical data providing information on one topic – e.g. an annual budget, class exam results or local house prices – created using software that can perform calculations

taskbar The bar across the bottom of the screen housing the *Start* button and any open windows

template A file that is used to create similar files based on its content and style but which is left unaltered

toolbar Rows of buttons that carry out related tasks – e.g. drawing or chart toolbars

update Save recent changes to a file

URL Uniform Resource Locator – the Internet address of a web page

username The name that identifies a user to a computer network; generally used in conjunction with a password to establish the user's right of access – it may also be called the account name or user ID

vector image An image made up of individual, scalable objects defined by mathematical equations rather than pixels

virus Rogue program written to cause damage to computer systems

web page A multimedia document – usually created using HTML code – that is published on the Internet and viewed through a browser

website A collection of web pages found at the same address published by a single organization

wizard A series of interrelated help screens that guide you through the creation of items such as charts or letters

word wrap When text is typed using a text editor or word processor, words are moved automatically onto the following line whenever the right-hand margin is reached

World Wide Web The collection of millions of web pages that can be viewed after connecting to the Internet

Index

Note: Page numbers in **bold** indicate glossary entries.

access **289**
Access
   exiting 122
   opening 97
   see also databases
active cell 57, **289**
active window 6, 7, **289**
addresses
   e-mail 255
      contacts *see* contacts
   URLs 272, 273, **292**
alignment 29, 62, 136, 163, **289**
apostrophe 17
application (software) **289**
   see also under individual applications
artwork canvas 212
attachments 264–7
   creating 264–5
   opening 266
   printing 267
   saving 266–7
AutoReport 117–18
AutoShapes 189–91, 192–6, **289**
   see also e-images
averages 68–9
awkward symbols 17
axis titles 76, 79
axis values 76, 89

back toolbar button 272
backgrounds 212
   colour background for web pages 239–40
   e-presentations 181–2
bitmap images 198, 219, **289**
black and white charts 85
black and white printing 207
blind copy 259
bold 27
bookmarking web pages 277–8, **289**
borders 40–1, 66, 142
   e-images 192–3
browser window 271–2
browsers 230, 231, **289**
   opening 271–3
   printing from 243
   viewing web pages in 242–3, 271–2
browsing 15, **289**
bullets 42, 166–7

capitals 16
category labels 76, 79–80
cell addresses 57, 67

cells 57, **289**
   alignment 62
   borders 66
centring text 29
character spacing 135
chart area 76
Chart Wizard 77–80
charts and graphs 55, 75–90, **289**
   adding titles 80
   black and white 85
   changing chart type 80
   closing 81
   comparative 86
   creating 77–80
   deleting 82
   elements of 76
   formatting 82–5
   legends 79, 85
   line graphs 86–7
   moving 82
   opening a data file 77
   opening an existing chart 82
   print preview 86–7
   printing 85–6
   resizing 82
   scaling 89
   selected charts 82
   selecting data 77
   titles 83–4
   types of 75–6
   using the keyboard 80
circles 191
clicking the mouse 7, **289**
clip art 145–6, 168–9
clipboard **289**
closing
   artwork 191
   charts and graphs 81
   databases 102
   documents 19
   e-presentations 161
   e-publications 134
   spreadsheets 59
   web pages 235
   windows 6
clustered comparative charts 86
Code view 231
colour, printing in 207
colours
   backgrounds to e-presentations 181–2
   backgrounds to web pages 239–40

colours (continued)
  and borders in e-images 192–3
  working with in e-images 218
column charts 76
  see also charts and graphs
columns 57
  deleting 72
  inserting 71
  inserting a text file in e-publications 139–40
  widening 40, 61–2, 104
commas 17, 61
comparative charts 86
composite copy 138, **289**
computer art 188
  see also e-images
contacts (e-mail) 256, 267–9
  adding addresses automatically 269
  retrieving automatically 269
copying
  AutoShapes 194–5
  e-mails 259–60
  files 14
  formulae 70
  vector objects 223
criteria, search 113–14, **289**
cropping 148, 202, 213–14, **289**
currency 61, 99
cursor 16, **289**
  positioning 18–19
cut and paste 13, 36

data labels 76, 79–80
data series 76
data types 99, **289**
databases 95–126, **289**
  adding personal details 117
  amending records 105
  closing 102
  creating a database file 97
  deleting records 107
  entering records 103–4
  finding and replacing 107–8
  opening 103
  primary key 101–2
  queries 111–17, **291**
    expressions 113–14
    printing 116
    running 114
    saving 114
    selecting field names 111–12
    showing and hiding fields 116
    sorting records in queries 115
  reports 117–22
    creating an AutoReport 117–18
    displaying data in full 120
    headers and footers 121
    naming 120

  orientation of 119
  saving 121
  using Report Wizard 118–19
  sorting records 109
  starting a new database 102
  tables 96, 98–102
    data types 99
    field properties 99–100
    fields 98–9
    opening 98
    printing 105–6
    renaming 101
    saving 100–1
  widening columns 104
datasheet view 100
dates 61, 99–100
decimals 61, 99
default 9, 105, **289**
deleted items 256
deleting
  AutoShapes 196
  charts 82
  columns/rows 72
  e-mails 263
  files or folders 12
  legends 85
  records in database files 107
  text 20, 133, 163, 166
demoting text 165–6, **289**
Design view 120
  web pages 231
desktop 6–8, **290**
desktop publishing (DTP) 128, **290**
  see also e-publications
dial-up button 271
dialogue box 101, **290**
digital camera images 224–6
  image resolution 225
  printing 226
  text on 226
displaying data in full 40, 61–2, 104, 120
documents 8, 16–46
  alignment of text 29
  bullets and numbering 42
  closing 19
  deleting text 20
  edit and replace text 37–8
  entering text in 16–18
    awkward symbols 17
    new lines 17
    word wrap 18
  formatting text 26–8
  headers and footers 41
  indents 43
  inserting new text 18–19
  line spacing 32–3
  moving text 35–6

opening a saved document 25
overtyping 20
page orientation 35
paragraphs 20–1
print preview 33–4
printing 24
proofreading 31
saving 21–3
    saving a new version 23
selecting text 26
setting margins 32
spelling and grammar checker 30
starting a new document 16
tables 39–41
undoing mistakes 20
updating 22
using Help 45–6
word count 43–4
domain name **290**
double-click 7
double line spacing 32
download **290**
drag and drop 36
draft e-mails 256
    saving 267
drawing
    objects in e-publications 143
    shapes in e-presentations 173–4
drawing canvas 190

edit and replace 37–8, 107–8, 176–7
e-images 187–227
    AutoShapes 189–91, 192–6, **289**
        adding text 194
        colours and borders 192–3
        copying 194–5
        deleting 196
        layers 193
        rotating 195
        squares and circles 191
        straight lines 190
        transparency 194
        working with 192–6
        working with multiple shapes 196
    closing artwork 191
    computer art 188
    digital camera images 224–6
    Paint Shop Pro 210–24
        artwork size 211–12
        creating a new file 211–12
        launching 210
        measurement units 211
        pictures in 213–16
        saving 216–17
        Selection tool 212
        toolbars 210–11
    picture files in 198–203

cropping 202
file types 198
flip or rotate 199
importing an image 198
moving an image 199–201
resizing 202–3
printing 224
    camera images 226
    in colour or black and white 207
saving artwork 196, 216–17
selecting appropriate software 189
setting the size of artwork 196–7
text 203–6
    rotating 205–6
    stretching 204
vector objects 219–23, **292**
working with colours 218
e-mail 254, 255–70, **290**
    attachments 264–7
    contacts 256, 267–9
    copying messages 259–60
    creating messages 258–9
    deleting messages 263
    folders 255–6
    forwarding messages 262–3
    Help menu 270
    printing messages 263
    reading messages 257
    receiving messages 261
    replying to 262
        reply to all 262
    saving a draft 267
    saving sent e-mails 260
    sending messages 260–1
e-mail addresses 255
    contacts *see* contacts
e-mail links 238
e-presentations 157–86
    alignment of text 163
    backgrounds 181–2
    bullets 166–7
    closing 161
    creating new presentations 160
    deleting text 163, 166
    drawing shapes 173–4
    edit and replace text 176–7
    formatting text 162–3
    headers and footers 177–8
    inserting lines of text 166
    opening an earlier saved version 167
    page orientation 175
    pictures in 168–70, 175
    printing 178–9
    promoting and demoting text 165–6
    saving 163
        saving a new version 164

e-presentations (continued)
  slide master 175–6
  slides *see* slides
  spell check 173
  views 160
  working with text 160–1
e-publications 127–55
  adding text 133
  alignment of text 136
  borders 142
  closing 134
  deleting text 133
  drawing objects 143
  formatting text 135–6
  headers and footers 150
  indents and spacing 137
  inserting a text file 138–40
    columns 139–40
  margins 131
  moving a text box 133
  opening an existing publication 129, 132
  page orientation 130–1
  pictures in 145–9
    inserting 145–7
    manipulating 147–9
  printing 138
  resizing a text box 133
  saving 132
    as a different version 132
  spell check 142–3
  starting point 129–30
    new 129
    new from a design 129
    publication saved previously 129
  viewing a publication 132
Excel
  exiting 90
  opening 56–7
  see also spreadsheets
exiting applications
  Access 122
  Excel 90
  FrontPage 247
  Outlook 270
  PowerPoint 162
  Publisher 150
  Word 46
expressions 113–14, **290**
external links, in web pages 237

Favorites folder 272, 277–8
field names 98–9, 106
  selecting 111–12
fields 98–9, **290**
  properties of 99–100
  showing and hiding 116
file extensions 8, **290**

files 8–9, **290**
  attachments *see* attachments
  copying 14
  creating a database file 97
  deleting 12
  moving 12–13
  names and extensions 8
  opening 9, 77
  renaming 11
  searching for 14–15
  storing in folders 8–9
  types of 8
fill handle 70
find and replace 37–8, 107–8, 176–7
flip or rotate 148–9, 195, 199, 214
  see also rotating
flood fill 220
floppy disks 8, **290**
folders 9–12, **290**
  creating and naming 9–11
  deleting 12
  renaming 11
  searching for 14–15
  storing e-mails 255–6
  storing files in 8–9
folders list 10, 13
fonts 27, **290**
  font size 28, 135, 162–3
  font types 27, 136
footers 41, 73–4, 121, 150, 177–8, **290**
formatting **290**
  charts 82–5
  numbers 60–1
  pictures 147–9, 170
  text 26–8, 60, 135–6, 162–3, 175–6, 232–3
  vector objects 221
formula bar 57
formulae 67, **290**
  copying (replicating) 70
  printing 73
forward toolbar button 272
forwarding e-mail messages 262–3
FrontPage
  exiting 247
  opening 231
  see also web pages
full justification 29, 136
function keys **290**
functions 68–9, **290**
  averages 68–9
  totals 68

gif files 198, 280, **290**
grammar check 30
  see also spelling check
graphs *see* charts and graphs
gridlines 66

handouts 178
hard disk **290**
headers 41, 73–4, 121, 150, 177–8, **290**
headings
   printing tables 106
   spreadsheets 66
   styles for web pages 233
health and safety 4
Help menu 45–6, 270
highlighting *see* selecting (highlighting)
home toolbar button 272
homepage 271
HTML 230, 231, **290**
hyperlinks 235–9, 272, **290**
   e-mail 238
   external 237
   internal 235–6
   testing 243
hyphen 17

icons 6–7, **290**
images *see* e-images; pictures
inbox 256
indents 43, 137, **290**
index 274
integers 61, **291**
internal links, in web pages 235–6
Internet 254, 270, **291**
   see also e-mail; World Wide Web
Internet Service Provider (ISP) 255, **291**
italics 27

joining up paragraphs 21
jpeg files 198, 280, **291**
justifying text 29, 136, **291**

kerning 135
keyboard 80
keywords 275–6, **291**

landscape orientation 35, 105, 130–1, **291**
launching programs 7–8
layers 193, 214–15
left-aligned text 29
legends 76, 79, **291**
   formatting 85
letter spacing 135
line graphs 76, 86–7
   see also charts and graphs
line spacing 32–3, 137, 166
lines, drawing 190, 220
links *see* hyperlinks
log in (or log on) 5–6, **291**
logging off 47

magnification 132
margins 32, 65, 131

marquee 212
maximizing 16–17, **291**
menu **291**
minimizing **291**
mistakes, undoing 20
mouse, clicking 7
moving
   charts 82
   files 12–13
   images 199–201, 216
   text 35–6
   text boxes 133, 161
multiple shapes 196

Name box 57
naming
   folders 9–11
   reports 120
netiquette 281, **291**
new lines 17
new versions, saving 23, 59, 132, 164
Normal view 160, 171
notes page 178
numbering 42
numbers 99
   entering in spreadsheets 58
   formatting 60–1

online communication 254
   see also e-mail; World Wide Web
opening
   applications
      Access 97
      Excel 56–7
      FrontPage 231
      Outlook 255
      PowerPoint 159
      Publisher 129
      Word 16
   browsers 271–3
   database files 103
   e-mail attachments 266
   files 9, 77
   saved charts 82
   saved documents 25
   saved e-presentations 167
   saved e-publications 129, 132
   saved spreadsheets 63–4
   tables 98
   web pages 235
order of slides 173
orientation
   pages 35, 105, 130–1, 175
   reports 119
   spreadsheets 65
outbox 256
Outline tab 160, 171

Outlook
  exiting 270
  opening 255
  see also e-mail
overtyping 20, **291**

Paint Shop Pro *see* e-images
page orientation 35, 105, 130–1, 175
paragraph breaks 20
paragraphs 20–1
  creating new paragraphs 20
  joining up 21
passwords 5–6, **291**
percent style 61
personal details, adding 117
pictures
  clip art 145–6, 168–9
  cropping 148, 202, 213–14, **289**
  in e-presentations 168–70, 175
  in e-publications 145–9
  from file 146–7, 169
  flip and rotate 148–9, 195, 199, 214
  formatting 147–9, 170
  importing images into artwork 198–203
  importing and positioning in web pages 245–6
  moving an image 199–201, 216
  Paint Shop Pro 213–16
  resizing 147, 202–3, 215–16
  saving from the Web 279–80
  types of picture files 198
  see also e-images; slides
pie charts 76
pixels 198, 219
placeholders 159, **291**
plot area 76
portrait orientation 35, 105, **291**
PowerPoint
  exiting 162
  opening 159
  see also e-presentations
presentations *see* e-presentations
preset shapes 220–1
Preview 231, **291**
primary key 101–2, **291**
print preview 33–4, 64, 86–7, 105
printing
  charts 85
  database tables 105–6
    headings 106
  documents 24
  e-images 224
    in colour or black and white 207
    digital camera images 226
  e-mail attachments 267
  e-mail messages 263
  e-presentations 178–9

e-publications 138
formulae 73
queries 116
screen print 25–6
spreadsheets 64–6
tables 105–6
web pages 240–1, 276
  from a browser 243
  showing the source code 240–1
programs **291**
  launching 7–8
promoting text 165–6, **291**
proofreading 31, 104, 143
Publisher
  exiting 150
  opening 129
  see also e-publications

queries 111–17, **291**
  see also databases
quote marks 17

raster images 198, 219, **291**
reading e-mail messages 257
reading web pages offline 281
receiving e-mail messages 261
records 96, 98, **291**
  amending 105
  deleting 107
  entering 103–4
  sorting 109
    in a query 115
  see also databases
refresh toolbar button 272
relational databases 102
renaming
  files or folders 11
  tables in a database 101
replacing *see* edit and replace
replying to e-mail messages 262
  reply to all 262
Report Wizard 118–19
reports *see* databases
resizing
  charts 82
  images 147, 202–3, 215–16
  text boxes 133, 161
resolution, image 225, **291**
restore down 16–17, **291**
right-aligned text 29
right-click 7, **291**
rotating
  pictures 148–9, 195, 199, 214
  text 205–6, 223
rows 57
  deleting 72
  inserting 71

rulers 211
running a query 114

sans serif fonts 136
save as 23, 59, 132, 164
saved documents, opening 25
saved spreadsheets, opening 63–4
saving
  artwork 196, 216–17
  documents 21–3
    new versions of 23
  e-mail attachments 266–7
  e-mail drafts 267
  e-presentations 163
    new versions of 164
  e-publications 132
    different versions 132
  images from web pages 279–80
  queries 114
  reports 121
  sent e-mails 260
  spreadsheets 58–9
  tables in a database 100–1
  web pages 233, 279
scale **292**
  scaling charts or graphs 89
screen print 25–6, 263
screen tip 6
scrolling 17, **292**
search criteria 113–14, **289**
search engines 274–5, **292**
searching
  for files or folders 14–15
  web pages 274–6
selecting (highlighting) **292**
  charts 82
  data for a chart or graph 77
  objects in Paint Shop Pro 212
  text 26
selection handles 133
sending e-mail messages 260–1
sent items 256
serif fonts 136
server **292**
shading 40–1, 66
showing or hiding fields 116
shut down procedure 47, **292**
single-click 7
single line spacing 32
size
  resizing *see* resizing
  setting for artwork 196–7, 211–12
sizing handles 82, 120, 161, 170, 190, 202–3, **292**
Slide Master 175–6
Slide Show 160
Slide Sorter 160

slides
  changing slide order 173
  layout 159
  new slides 171
  Normal view 171
  orientation 175
  Outline or *Slides* tab 171
  printing individual slides 178
  see also e-presentations
Slides tab 160, 171
software **292**
sorting **292**
  records 109
    in a query 115
source code 240–1
spacing
  character spacing 135
  line spacing 32–3, 137, 166
spelling check 30, 104, 142–3, 173
Split view 231
spreadsheets 53–75, **292**
  cell addresses 57, 67
  cell alignment 62
  cells 57, **289**
  closing 59
  creating a new file 58
  deleting columns/rows 72
  entering and amending text 57–8
  entering numbers 58
  formatting
    numbers 60–1
    text 60
  formulae 67
    copying (replicating) 70
    printing 73
  functions 68–9
  headers and footers 73–4
  inserting columns/rows 71
  opening a saved spreadsheet 63–4
  printing 64–6
    borders and shading 66
    gridlines and headings 66
    orientation and margins 65
  saving 58–9
  widening columns 61–2
squares 191
Start menu 7–8
starting up the computer 5
stop toolbar button 272
straight lines 191
stretching text 204
subtract symbol 17

Table of Contents link 46
tables 39–41
  borders 40–1
  databases *see* databases

tables (continued)
    displaying all data 40
    opening 98
taskbar 6–7, **292**
template 16, **292**
testing links, in web pages 243
text
    adding 133, 175, 194
    alignment 29, 62, 136, 163
    deleting 20, 133, 163
    on a digital camera image 226
    documents
        entering text 16–18
        inserting new text 18–19
    on e-images 203–6
    entering and amending in spreadsheets 57–8
    entering on a web page 232
    e-presentations 160–1, 175–6
        inserting and deleting lines of text 166
        promoting and demoting text 165–6
    formatting 26–8, 60, 135–6, 162–3, 175–6, 232–3
    inserting text files into e-publications 138–40
    inserting text files on a web page 244
    moving to a new position 35–6
    rotating 205–6, 223
    selecting 26
    stretching 204
    vector objects 222–3
text boxes
    adding to e-presentations 160–1, 175
    adding to e-publications 133
    in e-images 203–6
    moving 133, 161
    resizing 133, 161
text wrapping 148, 199–200
titles
    charts 76, 79
        adding 80
        formatting 83–4
    report titles 120
toolbar 16, **292**
    Paint Shop Pro 210–11
totals 68
transparency 194

underlining 27
underscore 17
undoing mistakes 20
updating 22, 59, **292**
URLs (Uniform Resource Locators) 272, 273, **292**
username 5, **292**

vector objects/images 219–23, **292**
    copying shapes 223
    flood fill 220
    formatting 221
    lines 220
    preset shapes 220–1

text 222–3
    see also e-images
viewing/views
    e-presentations 160
    e-publications 132
    web pages 231–2
viruses 281–2, **292**

web authoring software 231
web browsers see browsers
web page addresses see URLs
web pages 229–51, 270, **292**
    applying a background colour 239–40
    appropriate software 231
    bookmarking 277–8, **289**
    closing 235
    entering text 232
    formatting text 232–3
        heading styles 233
    hyperlinks 235–9, 272, **290**
    importing and positioning images 245–6
    inserting a text file 244–5
    opening 235
    printing 240–1, 276
        from a browser 243
        showing source code 240–1
    reading offline 281
    saving 233, 279
    searching 274–6
    testing links 243
    URLs 272, 273, **292**
    viewing in a browser 242–3, 271–2
    views 231–2
websites 270, **292**
widening columns 40, 61–2, 104
windows 6–7
wizards **292**
    Chart Wizard 77–80
    Report Wizard 118–19
Word 189
    exiting 46
    opening 16
    see also documents
word count 43–4
word processing 3–4
word wrap 18, **292**
workbooks 58
World Wide Web 270–82, **292**
    bookmarking web pages 277–8
    netiquette 281
    opening a browser 271–3
    printing web pages 276–7
    reading pages offline 281
    saving from 279–80
    searching web pages 274–6
    viruses 281–2
    see also web pages